Harold E. Stassen

Harold E. Stassen

*The Life and Perennial
Candidacy of the
Progressive Republican*

ALEC KIRBY, DAVID G. DALIN *and*
JOHN F. ROTHMANN

Foreword by Lewis L. Gould

McFarland & Company, Inc., Publishers
Jefferson, North Carolina, and London

LIBRARY OF CONGRESS CATALOGUING-IN-PUBLICATION DATA

Kirby, Alec, b. 1962–
Harold E. Stassen : the life and perennial candidacy of
the progressive Republican / Alec Kirby, David G. Dalin and
John F. Rothmann ; foreword by Lewis L. Gould.
p.   cm.
Includes bibliographical references and index.

ISBN 978-0-7864-6554-5

softcover : acid free paper ∞

1. Stassen, Harold Edward, 1907–2001.
2. Presidential candidates — United States — Biography.
3. United States — Politics and government —1945–1989.
4. Republican Party (U.S.: 1854–) — History — 20th century.
5. Conservatism — United States — History — 20th century.
6. Governors — Minnesota — Biography.
7. Minnesota — Politics and government — 20th century.
I. Dalin, David G.   II. Rothmann, John F.   III. Title.
E748.S784K67 2013   977.6'052092—dc23   [B]   2012041672

BRITISH LIBRARY CATALOGUING DATA ARE AVAILABLE

On the cover: Harold E. Stassen, photographer
Harris & Ewing, ca. 1940 (Library of Congress)

Manufactured in the United States of America

*McFarland & Company, Inc., Publishers
Box 611, Jefferson, North Carolina 28640
www.mcfarlandpub.com*

Acknowledgments

Like an engaging novel, the Stassen plot is often complex. In seeking to unravel it we have accumulated many debts. Staff members of the Manuscript Division of the Library of Congress, the Bentley Historical Library at the University of Michigan in Ann Arbor, and the Dwight D. Eisenhower Library all went out of their way to help us find information relevant to Stassen's career. To the Minnesota Historical Society we owe a particular debt. Sandra Markham of the University Archives and Records Center at the University of Pennsylvania assisted me in researching Stassen's tenure as president of that university. Harold Stassen, Glen Stassen, Kathleen Stassen, Joseph Ball, Bernhard LeVander, Ed Larson, Tom Swafford, Walter Judd, Bradley Nash, George MacKinnon and Robert Matteson were all generous with their memories. Special thanks to Professor Leo Ribuffo for his criticism and suggestion of an early draft of this book. Karl Toepel deserves appreciation for providing information and advice. We appreciate the encouragement from Jim Worthen. Finally, extra special thanks to Mary Ellen Kirby, for all her assistance in the preparation of this manuscript.

Inevitably, the individuals who have come to our aid in this project will find within these pages some interpretation or conclusion which will leave them aghast. Needless to say, for any misinterpretation, error of fact, or any other shortcoming, the authors bear sole responsibility.

Yet oft-times in his maddest
Mirthful mood
Strange pangs would flash along
Childe Harold's brow,
As if the memory of some deadly feud
Or disappointed passion lurk'd below....
— Lord Byron, *Childe Harold's Pilgrimage*

Political experts interested in long-term trends say Stassen's success at the polls may have revolutionized long-established methods for seeking presidential nomination. Stassen's forthright quest for votes may end much of the traditional coyness of aspirants. In the future, it is thought that more candidates will frankly announce their intentions well in advance of election year and work openly for delegates to the conventions, as Stassen has done for the past eighteen months.—*Newsweek*, May 3, 1948

... [I]n this modern atomic age with all of its uncertainties and dangers and confusions, I believe that faith in God and in the value and worth of a human being is the solid rock upon which to build a happy and well-spent life.

I hold that every man has within him a regard for the well-being and the dignity of his fellow men. At times this might be pretty well covered over. At times it might be encased in a hard shell built up by bitter experiences or by evil objectives. But I believe it is always there, deep down inside.

This is the Reverence for life of which Albert Schweitzer writes from Africa. It is a sentiment inborn in man which even the most ruthless dictators cannot completely wipe out.

Thus I believe that man was meant to be free. Throughout history most of mankind has been ruled and dominated by other men. There have been many cruel and oppressive governments. Even at this time, halfway through the twentieth century, one third of the peoples of the world are living under dictatorships. But history also shows that even when people have been dominated for centuries, they continue to have an intense personal desire to be free. I believe this, too, is an inborn part of man himself.

Above all I believe there is a God. There is a power beyond all mankind and all of this earth. This faith and this belief are the foundation for America. It is the foundation for a worthwhile life. This I believe.— Harold Stassen, *This I Believe* (1954), pages 140–141, written for Edward R. Murrow

Table of Contents

Foreword by Lewis L. Gould

In the 1970s and 1980s, Harold Stassen became the equivalent of a political punch line. His perennial and unsuccessful candidacies for the Republican presidential nomination provided pundits and insiders with a touch of amusement amid the serious business of picking the G.O.P. standard bearer. Sometimes a kind commentator might mention that Stassen had once been a major figure in the party, but most often condescending dismissal was the fate of a man who had moved into self-parody.

In the second half of the twentieth century, Republicans began a race away from their own complex history that has persisted to the present time. As the regional variety and ideological diversity of the party was forgotten, a figure such as Harold Stassen was first dismissed, soon ignored, and then airbrushed out of G.O.P. history. As this first, perceptive biography of the man reveals, however, there was more to Harold Stassen than a long, sad twilight. Alec Kirby, David G. Dalin and John F. Rothmann make a vigorous and convincing argument that Stassen was an interesting and consequential figure. His blend of internationalism and relative liberalism on social issues represented a road not taken for his party. Had Stassen prevailed in an Oregon debate with Thomas E. Dewey and obtained the nomination in 1948, he would have had a reasonable chance against Harry S Truman in the general election. Of such near misses are national careers made and lost.

The authors are friendly to Stassen and impressed with his achievements as governor of Minnesota, presidential candidate, and advocate of arms control in the administration of Dwight D. Eisenhower. They have much new information on Dewey, Richard Nixon, and Eisenhower himself. They demonstrate how Stassen extended a tradition of midwestern progressive reform that had been born at the turn of the twentieth century and nurtured in the work of Robert M. La Follette, Sr., Jonathan P. Dolliver, and Albert J. Beveridge. At the same time, they delve with insight into the areas where Stassen's political slips ended the bright promise of his early years in public life.

The Republican party of Harold Stassen is gone now. A man of his talents and frailties would have no place in the era of ideological conformity, "no new taxes," and ever smaller government that are the ruling tenets of the G.O.P. As the authors show, that is a sad result because the modern political system could use the energy and humane sensibility that Stassen brought to his conservatism. Harold Stassen had long needed a good, incisive biography, and in Kirby, Dalin and Rothmann he has found three writers who have done him the justice that his life in politics merited.

Lewis L. Gould is the Eugene C. Barker Centennial Professor Emeritus in American history at the University of Texas at Austin. One of the country's leading scholars of the American presidency, he is the author of many books and articles, including *The Presidency of Theordore Roosevelt* and *Grand Old Party: A History of the Republicans.*

Preface

It is a curious fact that although Harold Stassen's name appears regularly in the events of American politics and foreign affairs in the 1930s, 1940s and 1950s, no full-length study of his career has ever been published. This is due, no doubt, to the fact that his name has for more than a generation been synonymous with political buffoonery, the dubious legacy of his many quixotic political campaigns. Apparently, no one has taken him seriously as a subject for historical study.

This is regrettable. Harold Stassen's career was a pioneering one with long-term consequences for American political and diplomatic history. In 1948 he assembled a remarkably creative and nearly unstoppable presidential campaign organization at the grassroots level. Preceding the later strategies of George McGovern and Jimmy Carter, this organization attempted to utilize the power of primaries as a method of building momentum for a presidential nomination. His strategy caught his opponents off guard and forced Thomas Dewey into a desperate and dramatic confrontation in the Oregon primary. While a series of errors cost Stassen both the primary and the nomination, the method of seeking a party's presidential nomination would never be the same. Moreover, Stassen's failure to capture the nomination signaled the last serious effort by liberals to control the Republican Party; no liberal Republican since then has amassed such an enormous grass roots following as Stassen in 1948.

In 1952 Stassen lumbered back onto the presidential stage in characteristically controversial fashion, launching an attack on Robert Taft in order to assure the GOP nomination either for (according to Stassen) Dwight Eisenhower or for (according to his critics) himself. During the Eisenhower administration he held a variety of foreign policy posts, culminating in his dramatic effort to achieve a nuclear test ban treaty with the Soviet Union in 1957. His failure to achieve that treaty did not tarnish a significant accomplishment: Stassen had managed to shift the basic U.S. arms control strategy from disarmament to the more realistic goal of arms limitation, a strategy which was to guide American foreign policy for the next twenty-five years.

As a central figure in American politics for fully two decades, Stassen often found himself at the center of the controversies of his time. For the most part, his role was that of a constructive advocate of liberal change, often leading him into hopeless causes: the defeat of Joe McCarthy at the peak of his power; opposition to Taft-Hartley; civil rights; respect for nonaligned nations; and U.S.–Soviet rapprochement.

An often brilliant man when the subject was politics or public policy, Stassen suffered from a fatal weakness. His dramatic early success against long odds convinced him that he was somehow destined for greatness. That his early career was so remarkably free of reversals and defeats meant that he never had to question his methods and abilities or even his ultimate destiny. Never pushed into a period of reflection after a crushing personal or professional defeat, Stassen by middle age, for all his native intelligence, was fundamentally a shallow man when the subject was Harold Stassen. Never doubting his ultimate success, his reach tended more and more to exceed his grasp, ultimately bringing his career and reputation to ruin. Yet, from 1938 to 1958 Stassen's accomplishments were genuinely breathtaking and often of lasting impact in American political and diplomatic history.

The three authors of this volume came separately to the conclusion that Harold Stassen's absence from the historical literature of the mid-twentieth century was a severe omission.

Alec Kirby

As a seventeen-year-old activist in the 1980 presidential campaign I first came across Harold Stassen and, like my fellow volunteers, chortled at an old toupee-topped man seeking the Republican nomination. One day during the Republican National Convention that year, at which I served as a "Youth Delegate," I happened to meet him, alone and unrecognized, in a hallway. I stopped and introduced myself and was struck with his sober and thoughtful remarks about challenges facing U.S. foreign and domestic policy. The next year, as a college freshman, I began a long fascination with Harold Stassen, picking up tantalizing tidbits of his odyssey from professors, books and magazines. By the time I began a PhD program at George Washington University in Washington, D.C., I was determined to write a doctoral dissertation about his career. That dissertation, directed by Professor Leo Ribuffo, formed the nucleus of this book.

David G. Dalin

As early as my high school years, when I precociously wrote a twenty-page paper entitled "A Short History of the Republican Party, 1946–1952," I have been intrigued with the history of twentieth century Republican Party politics generally, and with the all-too-little-known political career of Harold E. Stassen particularly. As an undergraduate at the University of California at Berkeley, and a PhD student at Brandeis University, I had the opportunity to read James T. Patterson's excellent *Mr. Republican: A Biography of Robert A. Taft*, Donald R. McCoy's *Landon of Kansas*, and Leo Katcher's *Earl Warren: A Political Biography*. Over the years, as my interest in American political biography increased, after reading Richard Norton Smith's *Thomas E. Dewey and His Times* and Gayle B. Montgomery and James W. Johnson's *One Step from the White House: The Rise and Fall of Senator William F. Knowland*, as well as biographies of Richard Nixon, Henry Cabot Lodge, Jr., and Barry Goldwater, I became intrigued, and surprised, by the fact that while almost every other Republican politician and presidential candidate of the mid-twentieth century has been the subject of one or more book-length biographies, Stassen alone has been ignored by scholars of twentieth century American politics and Republican Party history. Stassen alone had yet to find his biographer.

Over many years also, my good friend and coauthor John F. Rothmann has encouraged my interest in the possibility of researching and writing a political biography of Harold Stassen. Alec Kirby's excellent PhD dissertation on Stassen, which John Rothmann first brought to my attention, reinforced our dream of writing Stassen's definitive political biography. More recently, the publication of James Worthen's excellent work *The Young Nixon and His Rivals: Four California Republicans Eye the White House, 1946–1958*, encouraged us to pursue publication of a Stassen biography. This collaborative effort to publish the long-overdue political biography of Harold E. Stassen is the fulfillment of our shared dream.

John F. Rothmann

Each one of us has an explanation for our interest in Harold Stassen. Mine began with my general interest in defeated candidates for president of the United States. On February 29, 1964, I read in the *San Francisco Examiner* that Governor Stassen would be staying at the San Francisco Airport Hilton to attend a meeting of the California Republican Assembly. At the age of fifteen, already active in the Teenage Republicans, I picked up the phone, called the Hilton and asked to be connected to Governor Stassen's room. Stassen answered the phone, we had a brief conversation and he invited me to join him that day at the Hilton, and subsequently at the Republican National Convention held that year in San Francisco. That was the beginning of my relationship with Harold Stassen.

I was to see Governor Stassen often through the years. We met in Wisconsin in 1968 when I was working for Richard Nixon in Wisconsin and he was campaigning for president. Despite his clear concerns about Nixon, he thought that it was wonderful that I was involved in a national presidential campaign. We met again in San Francisco on June 26, 1985, at the Charter Day Luncheon at the Fairmont Hotel. It was the celebration of the fortieth anniversary of the signing of the United Nations Charter in San Francisco. I had a lovely visit with Stassen and his wife, Esther.

When Stassen died in 2001, I interviewed his son, Glen, for my radio program on KGO Newstalk 810 AM in San Francisco. During the course of the interview we discussed Stassen's life and work. At the end of the interview, I quoted Stassen from his interview with David Frost in 1968. Frost asked Stassen, "And how would you like to be remembered? What would you like the first sentence of your obituary to say?" Stassen replied, "He laid the foundation for a lasting peace." Glen asked me to send him a copy of that interview. The words chosen to appear on Stassen's gravestone read, "He laid the foundation for a lasting peace."

Harold Stassen's nephew, Bob Stassen, sent me a copy of the videotape of Stassen's ninetieth birthday party. He also sent me the tape of Stassen's funeral. As I listened to Alec Kirby's eloquent eulogy, I realized that Stassen must be given his due. Almost ten years later, we three authors have banded together to chronicle the life and times of Harold E. Stassen.

1. Formative Years

When the Great Depression mercilessly devastated the world economy in the 1930s, farm prices in Minnesota followed obediently. As the amount paid for milk to Dakota County producers plunged to sixty-eight cents per 100 lbs., farmers felt their temperatures rise in the opposite direction. This heated group was ready for action, and they grimly called for a meeting in the town of Farmington.

The agenda included something more than group therapy for the heretofore independent and proud farmers of Dakota County, who could now no longer support their families. One speaker leaped up and, to an approving roar, shouted that they should dump their milk and block the highways to force a price increase. At least one farmer present, though, voiced reservations. "Suppose the sheriff or county attorney try to stop you?" "Then we'll run them down or club them out of the way," came the fierce reply, followed by a wave of cheers. In the midst of the commotion one red-headed, ruddy, two-hundred-pound man walked slowly to the front of the audience. The clamor stopped; the farmers knew Harold E. Stassen, the county attorney.

One farmer present was Edward Thye, destined to become governor of Minnesota and, later, a United States senator. According to Thye, Stassen faced the crowd and said, "Men, I appreciate your situation and want to help you. But I must tell you as county attorney that if you violate the law I will prosecute you. But, I think there is a better way to meet the situation." He went on to suggest that a committee be appointed to seek higher prices through negotiation. As a lawyer, he would represent them in litigation for no fee. In true happily-ever-after fashion the committee was established, prices increased by 25 percent, and farmers became the devoted core of Stassen's political constituency.[1]

This incident revealed early on the level-headed courage which marked the conduct of Harold Stassen as county attorney, governor, naval officer, presidential candidate, president of the University of Pennsylvania, cabinet officer in the Eisenhower administration, and private attorney. Farmers present at the meeting must have marveled at the cool, detached resolve of their county attorney, who was still in his twenties.

Stassen knew what life was like on a farm; at fifteen, he ran his parents' forty-acre concern in South St. Paul when his father was seriously ill. His paternal grandfather had immigrated to the United States in 1871 from Austria; his mother had arrived in America early in life from Germany and boasted Norwegian ancestry.[2] Later, in the crucial Oregon primary in 1948, Stassen's lineage would help him win the support of the state's considerable Scandinavian population.[3] Stassen was born on April 13, 1907. From the beginning he acted like the proverbial young-man-in-a-hurry. He graduated from high school at age fifteen, then, after working for his parents, received a bachelor's degree at age twenty from the University of Minnesota. Returning to his alma mater for law school, he became an attorney in 1929.[4]

The years Stassen spent at the University of Minnesota are noteworthy, for they are suggestive of the energy and ambition which would mark his later adventures. All the while, he supported himself with jobs ranging from bakery "grease-boy" to Pullman conductor. The journalist John Gunther reflected in *Harper's Magazine* in 1946 that Stassen's "record in undergraduate activities — he practically ran the campus — is unmatched to this day."[5] Indeed, an accounting of his activities reads like the university's telephone book. He was president of Silver Spur, the junior honorary society; president of Grey Friar, the senior honorary society; a member of Scabbard and Blade, an honorary ROTC fraternity; captain of the University Rifle Team; a member of the debating squad; a participant in the Northern Oratorical Contest; and a State Day Convocation Student Orator. While in law school, moreover, he was a member of the Law Review.[6]

Harold Stassen was a man of deep religious faith. He was a member of the American Baptist Convention and later in life was unanimously elected as its president. His life-long active involvement later led to his becoming president of the International Sunday School Convention and he was a founder of both the National Council of Churches and the World Council of Churches.

Harold Stassen as a boy, 1922 (Minnesota Historical Society).

Of special note is Stassen's exacting skill as a marksman. In 1925 he established a perfect score of four hundred points at the Camp Perry National Intercity Rifle Matches. As a member of the University Rifle Team, he was selected by his teammates to represent the United States in worldwide competition; the American team scored a convincing triumph.[7] His reputation and skill were solid enough for him to be placed in an ROTC circus act, where he shot off Christmas tree ornaments he had attached to the brass buttons of a fellow soldier's uniform.[8] "That was the first night of the circus," Stassen recalled years later. "When that act was completed, President Kaufman of the University of Minnesota caught us behind stage and he was trembling and he said, 'Don't you *ever* do that again.'"[9] Little wonder then that as county attorney Stassen felt comfortable in grabbing a rifle and leading a posse in a successful hunt for two convicted murderers who had escaped from jail.[10]

When it came to the critical decision of marriage, Stassen hit a bull's-eye. In 1929 he married Esther Glewwe, with whom he would share a loving, warm relationship until her death in 2000. Esther, like Harold, was born in humble circumstances, the seventh of twelve children of German immigrants who lived above a grocery store they owned in South St. Paul. Stassen recalled seeing Esther for the first time at a Sunday school picnic. The young couple's relationship bloomed and they were married on November 14. It was the beginning of a loving collaboration and resulted in two children, Glen and Kathleen.

Such a gregarious and energetic figure as Stassen inevitably became the center of a

Harold Stassen's parents, William and Elsie Stassen (left), with Harold and his wife, Esther, ca. 1940 (Minnesota Historical Society).

large network of friends and acquaintances who later formed key positions in the 1948 presidential campaign. Underclassman Cyrus Olson became a member of Stassen's law firm and took charge of the "Paul Revere Riders," the innovative Stassen get-out-the-vote squad. Alfred Lindley, whom Stassen had met as an opponent in a mock railroad case in law school, became treasurer of the Minnesota Fund, which financed Stassen's activities before and during his White House bid. George MacKinnon met Stassen during their first year of law school and went on to serve one term in Congress before working as a special assistant for Stassen in 1952. Another law school classmate, Elmer Ryan, a Democrat, became Stassen's partner in a South St. Paul law office the two young men opened after graduation.[11] Their law office had been operating for only a matter of months before Stassen declared himself a candidate for Dakota County attorney. His vigorous campaign under-mined his health and on election day he was in a hospital, suffering from tuberculosis. His victory at the polls was due largely to the efforts of Ryan, who relentlessly campaigned for his stricken colleague. In 1934 Stassen returned the favor by taking to the stump for Ryan in his partner's successful quest for election as a Democrat to the United States House of Representatives.[12]

Despite his youth, Stassen as county attorney closed his share of gambling houses, took a hand in labor disputes, and broke up a communist group in a meat-packing union.[13] He began to be widely regarded as effective and professional. By 1936 he had become pres-

Harold Stassen with his wife, Esther, daughter, Kathleen, and son, Glen, ca. 1945 (Minnesota Historical Society).

ident of the County Attorney's Association; held a key position in the state bar association;
been elected as a delegate to the Republican National Convention; and organized the Young
Republican League.[14] The latter was an effort to reignite the stagnant Minnesota GOP, dor-
mant since Floyd Olson's election as governor in 1930 as a Farmer-Laborite. For six years
the popular governor maintained a well-disciplined and tight political organization. In 1936,
however, cancer claimed his life. His successor, Elmer Benson, lacked Olson's political fire
and authority, and the Olson political machine began to disintegrate. By unhappy coincidence, for Benson, the state was hit by the recession of 1937–1938 and consequently by a
wave of strikes. As public discontent mounted, Republicans sniffed victory.[15]

On November 18, 1937, Stassen formally began his campaign for governor at a testimonial dinner in Hastings.[16] Ostensibly the affair was arranged by friends and supporters;
yet it strains credulity to imagine that the event was not engineered by Stassen himself.
According to John Gunther, Stassen acted as his own campaign manager, directing and
planning events according to his political instincts. Stassen's initial quest for state office was
nothing more, or less, than a demonstration of raw political talent, mercifully unaided by
old guard GOP regulars, who futilely supported Martin A. Nelson, the gubernatorial nominee of 1934 and 1936, or Minneapolis Mayor George Leach for the Republican nomination
for governor.[17] It would not be the last time Stassen would triumph over entrenched party
professionals.

Harold Stassen (left) with his father, William, ca. 1939 (Minnesota Historical Society).

Harold E. Stassen as the newly elected governor of Minnesota, ca. 1939 (Minnesota Historical Society).

Stassen's potential for popular appeal impressed Minnesota business leaders, who pined for a Republican victory after eight years of Farmer-Laborite rule. Minnesota taxed the ore produced from the rich Mesabi iron range in the north, and steel companies had endured an increase in their taxes under the Olson and Benson administrations. Their enthusiasm for a Republican governor was matched by milling, banking and manufacturing concerns that resented the growth in unionism. These companies, according to Dale Kramer of the *New Republic*, provided considerable backing to the Stassen campaign.[18]

Despite this corporate support, the electoral steel of the young candidate was an alloy of young people new to politics combined with average voters with an infrequent history of participation in primary elections, forged to strength in the heat inevitable in a frenzied, volunteer crusade. The Young Republican League which Stassen had organized served as a font of eager volunteers, augmented by a "rowdy, pistol-shooting, horse-riding organization from the South St. Paul stockyards, called the 'Hook-em cows,'" which distributed literature and urged voters to the polls in a fashion replicated by the Stassen "Paul Revere Riders" in the 1948 campaign.[19] Having swept to a convincing primary victory, Stassen set out after Elmer Benson, blasting the incumbent as the head of a "corrupt city-slicker machine." The young Republican pledged a state labor relations act and spoke vaguely about doing something for "Minnesota's forgotten men," the farmers.[20] Benson helplessly flailed about the state, calling Stassen a "drugstore cowboy," and was buried under the largest landslide recorded in a Minnesota gubernatorial election to that point. At age thirty-one, Stassen was the youngest individual ever to be elected governor of any state in the history of the nation.[21]

Stassen's years as governor were successful and accomplished. He quickly became known as efficient, honest and moderately liberal. Indeed, the first three months of his administration brought him national attention, as he demonstrated skill and finesse in the development of a labor relations bill. His skill was required. The rural-dominated legislature, now under

Harold E. Stassen (left) being sworn in as governor of Minnesota for his second term, 1941 (Minnesota Historical Society).

Republican control, had been elected largely because of the perception that the Farmer-Labor party had openly encouraged strikes; and freshmen legislators hungered for a punitive labor bill. Their plans were ultimately dropped after an all-night meeting with the governor, and the legislature passed instead the Stassen-crafted Labor Relations Act.[22] This act, popularly known as the "count-ten law," provided for a thirty-day waiting period before a strike which involved the public interest (as defined by the governor). During this period, business and labor were to meet with a three-member board appointed by the governor representing the state, business and labor, respectively. If the board and the parties failed to agree on a settlement, a strike still existed as an option after the thirty days ended.[23] Enacted into law, the formula seemed to work; the number of strikes was reduced. Significantly, organized labor, aware that Stassen had successfully fought off a more stringent measure, was generally supportive of the governor.[24]

Another well-recognized achievement was the passage of a new plan of control over state finances. The plan placed responsibility in a commissioner of administration, or business manager, for all state purchasing, budgeting, and financial management. Further, in an interesting preview of the 1980s federal Gramm-Rudman-Hollings Act, the business manager was directed by law to reduce spending if tax receipts dropped. Stassen would later claim that this feature alone saved two million dollars over two years.[25] Regardless of the precise sum that can be attributed to the business manager, the overall fiscal health of the state indisputably improved before Stassen left office: A thirty-nine million dollar deficit was turned into a three million dollar surplus; yearly expenditures dropped from one hundred six million to ninety-two million in 1943, while the state property tax was cut almost in half. Meanwhile, the state payroll was slashed from seventeen million to ten million, and a pioneering civil service system was instituted.[26]

2. Early Career

As Stassen was proving by his accomplishments to be a "boy wonder" with substance, national acknowledgment of the young governor was quickly forthcoming. The news media found "sudden Stassen" irresistible. "Every move he made," one journalist recalled, "every speech, was news. He was the youngest state Governor in United States history, he was bold and unpredictable and courageous and marvelous newspaper copy."[1] To the national Republican party, invigorated by a renaissance in the 1938 elections, the young governor was a symbol of new-found life, a political phoenix arising from the ashes of 1932. In his first year in office Stassen was elected chairman of the National Governors' Conference, an honor repeated in 1940.[2] Shrewdly, the GOP selected the young and exciting governor to deliver the keynote address at the Republican National Convention that year, with Wendell Willkie being the dark-horse favorite for the nomination.[3]

At first glance Stassen and Willkie seemed to be a perfect match. Both were progressive in their politics. Both wanted the Republican Party to be the liberal party, both were internationalist in outlook, both fought isolationism and both were young, dynamic and ambitious. Later, the problems that evolved in the Stassen-Willkie relationship stemmed from their mutual ambition to be president of the United States.

Stassen's designation as the temporary chairman and keynoter of the Republican National Convention was viewed as a triumph for a man who at thirty-three was too young to be nominated but seemed to be destined for national political leadership. Stassen's keynote speech was delivered on June 24, 1940. Although an unexceptional speech with no truly memorable lines, it established Stassen as a voice and a force within the Republican Party. What happened was critical for Stassen and his political future.

It was the initiative of John and Gardner Cowles, Jr., that first brought Stassen and Willkie together face to face. The Cowles' roots in Minnesota were deep. Best known as the publishers of *Look* magazine, they were also the publishers of the *Minneapolis Star* and *Tribune*. Mike Cowles described their efforts and how they connected to Stassen:

> Willkie's only hope, we all agreed, was to gain exposure to as many delegates as possible in the little time remaining before the convention.... "Come out to Minneapolis and St. Paul," John said. "I will see to it that you will be the main speaker at a Republican dinner scheduled in St. Paul next week." I promised to deliver the Iowa delegates if he would come down to Des Moines after the St. Paul meeting.
>
> John flew back home and went directly to see Harold Stassen, then the boy-wonder governor of Minnesota. Stassen reluctantly agreed to accept Willkie as the main speaker at the Republican gathering. John then bought time on six radio stations in Minnesota. As with many brilliant extemporaneous speakers Willkie's delivery of a written address was flat and unimpressive. Obviously underwhelmed, the delegates responded to Willkie's thirty-minute speech with a little polite applause. But then Willkie the natural showman took over. The night was hot and he removed

Governor Harold E. Stassen speaking to the Minnesota legislature, ca. 1940 (Minnesota Historical Society).

his coat. He tossed his speech up toward the ceiling and the pages fluttered down over the audience.

"Now that we're off the air," he said, "I'm going to tell you how I really feel about the Roosevelt Administration." Twenty minutes later he had those staid Republicans standing on their chairs, applauding, whistling and yelling their heads off. The Willkie magic had worked, and to insure its staying power John invited the Minnesota delegates to his house for drinks and to talk to Willkie personally.[4]

The Willkie magic deeply impressed Stassen. Stassen had declared himself to be neutral in the race for the nomination. Willkie's great success in his speech caused Stassen and Republicans across the nation to sit up and take note of Willkie's seemingly improbable quest for the Republican nomination. At the same time, Willkie took note of Stassen. He even went so far as to remark that "he had more respect for Stassen than for any other man in American political life."[5]

What happened next was to be very important for Willkie, Stassen and the Republican Party. At around midnight on the night of June 23–24 Arthur Krock, the Washington correspondent of the *New York Times*, joined by his colleague Turner Catledge, set the wheels in motion for the Stassen-Willkie relationship at the convention. In his memoirs, Krock recalled what happened that night in Philadelphia:

"Catledge and I set off from the Bellevue-Stratford Hotel to the Benjamin Franklin to see Alf M. Landon [the Republican Presidential nominee in 1936]. We wanted to discover how he would eventually line up his support. As we reached the Benjamin Franklin corner we saw Willkie standing by a taxicab with Mrs. Willkie. He greeted us jovially, said he was going to another hotel to get some sleep (there was no room in his small headquarters, he had discovered), and asked us to come along so that we might talk things over.

We went to Chancellor Hall ... where a sleepy night clerk told a sleepy bellboy (the only one) to show the party upstairs. Arrived there, Mrs. Willkie went into the bedroom to lie down. We knew she took off her shoes; we could see her small stockinged feet through an angle of the corridor between the living room and the bedroom.

I asked Willkie how things were going, a usual banality. He said he thought surprisingly well; he had many unexpected offers of support; it was a tough row to hoe; but now that he was in it he would see it through with everything he had.

I asked him if he had a floor leader. He didn't seem to know what I meant, and asked in turn if one was needed. Catledge and I, restraining our astonishment (already lively because of the smallness and amateur character of the headquarters, the stuffy little hotel, and the absence of any companions when the Willkies set out for their sleeping quarters), then explained the duties of a floor leader, and the necessity for one plus a strategy committee. We explained that since it was secondary support Willkie was seeking and his task was to get more votes on each ballot — taken from his reserve strength after [Thomas E.] Dewey and Senator [Robert] Taft had had their "runs" — he must have a group that would manage the accessions, the rate of these accessions, etc. We described how it was necessary for him to have well-known politicians, being known (unlike himself) to the state leaders, to roam the floor to say to this delegation that the other was about to "plump for Willkie," and regulate the pace of his bid when the time came to make it.

Willkie seemed surprised that so much organization was necessary, interested in the description of its workings and quick to understand them, though he gave the impression the plan was wholly new to him.

"Who would be a good floor leader?" he asked. I suggested Governor Baldwin of Connecticut, not dreaming the capture could be made. "He's very friendly with me," said Willkie. "I'll try to get him." Then he asked about Governor Stassen of Minnesota. I said that as Keynoter the Governor probably could not drop his neutrality. Catledge corrected me and said of course he could, as soon as his keynote was delivered; that keynoters always did. So Willkie said he'd "try" for Stassen, that he was very hopeful he could get him.[6]

The next question was how to get Stassen to commit to Willkie. Joseph Barnes, a Willkie biographer and confidant, described the events that followed as Stassen made his decision to back Willkie: "The two Cowles brothers, Willkie, and Stassen finally got together at one o'clock in the morning of June 25. For an hour, they went over a state-by-state review of Willkie's chances, in great detail and with great frankness. Then Stassen announced that he would support Willkie, but only on condition that he could be his floor manager. He felt he had to be sure that no mistakes were made. There was no other deal, not even discussion of how it should be announced."

There was more at stake than 1940. Both Willkie and Stassen were aware that the other had ambitions to occupy the White House. After Stassen committed to Willkie the discussion continued with the Cowles brothers present. Joe Barnes described what happened next:

A relaxed mood followed; all four men had been tense until the decision had been made. "Well, Wendell," Stassen said, "the time may come when I'll ask you to return the favor." He would be glad to, Willkie answered he had a feeling that for himself it was now or never. There was some more talk about what might happen in four years' time, Stassen repeating his warning that he might be around asking for help and Willkie assuring him that he would certainly be welcome. At least two of the men present agree that no bargain was struck and that there was no firm commitment which extended beyond the next day's session, but twisted memories of the conversation by both Willkie and Stassen helped to spoil their relationship by 1944.[7]

The next day, June 26, at 10:55 A.M., a mere five minutes before the meeting of the Minnesota delegation, Stassen broke the news to Roy Dunn, the national committeeman from Minnesota, that he would support Willkie and be his floor leader at the convention. When the decision was reported, Stassen was viewed by some as a hero. The Dewey and Taft forces, however, and many in the Republican establishment viewed Stassen as a villain. Their fury knew no bounds. Stassen had permanently damaged his reputation. After all, as keynoter and temporary chairman of the convention he was supposed to stay neutral. It was a blow to his reputation that would come back to haunt him in the years ahead.[8]

Still, following Willkie's triumph at the convention Stassen was one of two individuals seriously considered for the position of Republican National Chairman. The other contender was Representative Joseph W. Martin, Jr. In the end, Willkie chose Martin. Stassen was then named chairman of the Campaign Advisory Committee.[9] The position was more title than substance. During the rest of the campaign Stassen traveled on the Willkie campaign train and spoke out for Willkie and his cause. With Willkie's defeat in November Stassen began to consider his options.

In 1941 the Republican Party found itself ripped apart over what to do in a world torn by war. The isolationist wing of the party was led by Senator Robert A. Taft and Senator Arthur H. Vandenberg. They believed that the United States should stay out of the war in Europe. Equally vocal in opposition to isolationism were Wendell L. Willkie and Harold E. Stassen. On December 6, 1941, the *Nation* published an article by Arthur M. Schlesinger, Jr., entitled "Can Willkie Save His Party?" Schlesinger leveled a blast at the Republican Party: "The Republican Party has failed to measure up to the obligation of the crisis. Though individuals have rejected the official line, the party, as a political group, has steadfastly opposed almost every measure before Congress to carry out a vigorous foreign policy and

Wendell Willkie, Republican presidential candidate (center), on whistle-stop campaign with his wife, Edith (left), and Harold Stassen (right), 1940 (Minnesota Historical Society).

generally by decisive majorities. It has systematically harassed, sabotaged, and obstructed the attempts of the [Roosevelt] Administration to work for the destruction of Nazism."[10] Schlesinger went on to commend Willkie, who "comes on the stage in his gallant but lonely attempt to tell the Republican Party the facts of life.... He is trying to point out to them that the future of liberty in America, not just the future of Franklin Roosevelt, is dependent on the defeat of Hitler."[11]

One week later, in the December 13 edition of *The Nation,* responses were offered under the title "The Future of the Republican Party," with a note by the editors that these responses "were written before the outbreak of Japanese-American hostilities."[12] Four leading Republicans with starkly contrasting views offered their opinions. The four were Wendell Willkie, Arthur Vandenberg, Harold Stassen and Robert Taft. The editors of *The Nation* pointed out that "both Senator Taft and Senator Vandenberg, representing the isolationist point of view in the discussion, have since announced their complete support of the country's war effort."[13] Stassen boldly proclaimed himself "as one of the Republicans who have been early, consistent and outspoken in opposition to isolationism and in support of the foreign policy of the present federal Administration."[14]

The Japanese attack on Pearl Harbor on December 7, 1941, ended the debate, and the Republican Party united behind the battle to win what was now known as World War II. The distrust of Stassen by the isolationist wing of the Republican Party remained. Stassen may have been right in the end, but they would never forget or forgive his opposition to their position.

Running for reelection in 1942, Stassen announced that he would resign as governor in the spring of 1943 to enter the United States Navy. As he prepared for his departure, Stassen was asked to write a review for the *New York Times* of Willkie's book *One World.* In 1942 Willkie, accompanied by Mike Cowles and Joe Barnes, at the behest of President Roosevelt departed on a trip that would take him around the world. His efforts were rewarded with wide bipartisan acclaim. Stassen was asked to write the review because he and Willkie were both internationalists and friends. Much to the shock of many, Stassen wrote a critical review of the book. The review appeared on April 11, 1943, under the headline "Report on a Wakening World." Stassen opened his review on a conciliatory note: "The strength of the book is its keen narration of observations made on the trip. In this respect picturesque reporting of territories and of men share equally. It is a good bird's eye view, literally as well as figuratively." Towards the end of the review Stassen became highly critical of Willkie's book: "There is some weakness in a tendency to be dogmatic and belligerent in the statement of them. Forgivable exaggerations are noted. The concrete suggestions of the manner in which the nations of the world will become free and work together are limited. There would seem to be an overemphasis on the wrongs of British colonial administration and an under-statement of the evils of communism." Stassen concluded his review with the observation that "both those who agree and those who disagree will find this a book they will want to read."[15]

Willkie was stunned by the Stassen review. Lem Jones, Willkie's 1940 campaign press secretary and close confidant stated that "this review was one of the deepest hurts Willkie received because he regarded Stassen as a dear friend."[16] Willkie was quoted as saying, "If Harold felt that way, why did he have to write it?"[17] Arthur Hayes Sulzberger, the publisher of the *New York Times* and a friend and supporter of Willkie in the 1940 presidential campaign, offered to let Willkie respond to the Stassen review. Willkie declined the offer.[18]

Political observers concluded that Stassen's critical review may have stemmed from what was becoming increasingly clear — Stassen and Willkie both wanted to lead the liberal wing of the Republican party. Both men intended to run for president in 1944. Once friends and allies, Stassen and Willkie were now political rivals.

The leading candidates for the Republican nomination in 1944 were Wendell Willkie, Thomas Dewey, Harold Stassen and Douglas McArthur. Stassen, like McArthur, was on active military duty. He did not formally declare that he would be a candidate but he did not discourage his friends and supporters from advancing his possible candidacy and said that if nominated he would run. For the Republicans the decisive moment in the quest for the nomination would come in Wisconsin on April 4.

Stassen's decision to allow his name to be entered in the Wisconsin primary was a real blow to Willkie's candidacy. Willkie needed a united block of liberal Republicans to win the primary; Stassen's non-candidacy divided that all-important group of voters. Willkie's dislike of Stassen grew. It was reported that he disliked Stassen "more than he did Dewey." As Willkie appeared to be fading in his quest for the nomination, Henry Luce of *Time* and *Life* and the Cowles brothers, in *Look,* began promoting Stassen as the progressive, liberal voice and face of the Republican party. Willkie's bitterness boiled over when, while campaigning in Appleton, Wisconsin, Willkie was told about Stassen's statement that he would accept the nomination if offered. It was reported that Willkie "exploded in unprintable words."[19] Lem Jones told the press to "forget the comments." He told them "a more printable statement" would be forthcoming. The statement that was released showed clearly

Thomas Dewey's presidential campaign in Minneapolis, Minnesota, 1944 (*Minneapolis Tribune,* Minnesota Historical Society).

Willkie's anger at Stassen and his recognition that Stassen's covert efforts were hurting his candidacy:

> It is difficult to know from his announcement whether Governor Stassen is a candidate or not. As I have emphasized in the campaign in Wisconsin, the only way our system can function is through public discussion. The primary in Wisconsin is for the purpose of providing the people of Wisconsin with a method of making a choice after they have heard discussion of the issues.
>
> Obviously those who seek the preference of the voters should discuss the issues with them or if they have rendered themselves unable to do so, then it occurs to me they should decisively, not ambiguously, withdraw from the contest.
>
> All the men for whom delegates in Wisconsin can say in very simple and unambiguous language that they do or do not desire the voters of Wisconsin to vote for the delegates pledged to their respective candidacies.[20]

When Stassen's friend Senator Joe Ball of Minnesota came to Wisconsin to further the Stassen campaign Willkie bitterly observed that he demanded a United Nations declaration against any dismemberment of Germany or violation of her territorial rights: "I do not happen to be wise enough to know just what should be done about Germany, but I am smart enough to know the effect on German-American voters in Wisconsin and Nebraska of such chatter."[21]

The results of the Wisconsin primary were a disaster for Willkie. The final count brought about the end of the Willkie candidacy. Dewey won seventeen delegates, Stassen came in second with four delegates, followed by McArthur with three and Willkie with none. Dewey was nominated on the first ballot by the Republicans at their 1944 convention. Willkie did not attend and was not mentioned during the proceedings. Stassen was absent due to his continuing military duty. Willkie died on October 8, 1944, without making any endorsement of either Dewey or Roosevelt in the November election.[22]

On December 1, 1945, Willkie's close friend and confidant Bartley C. Crum wrote an article for the *Christian Science Monitor* entitled "Proposal for a Liberal Republican Party," citing his friend Willkie. Crum called for the Willkie vision to be fulfilled. The void left by Willkie's death had to be filled by what he termed "progressive and liberal leaders." Citing Willkie as "the great liberal of our generation," Crum turned his eye to others who might pick up the mantle of leadership. He cited Senator Leverett Saltonstall, observing that he "has continued the realistic course he began as Governor of Massachusetts." He continued that "although hampered by their past records, Senator Vandenberg and Governor Dewey are advancing toward a more practical approach to the atomic age." Crum reserved his most positive comments for Stassen: "Captain Stassen has never flinched at party displeasure in his efforts to bring today's problems before the people."[23]

As Stassen prepared to run for president in 1948 he was clearly the heir of the Willkie legacy. He was the hope of the liberal progressive wing of the Republican Party. Stassen believed that with that support he could win the nomination and the election in 1948.

The keynote speech in 1940 gave Stassen a national, even international, platform to articulate his worldview, which was only yet coming into focus. The first outline of his speech generally embraced the conventional Republican perspective that the United States should avoid entangling alliances and wars. He even planned to agree with Minnesota's isolationist stalwarts, Senator Henrik Shipstead and Congressman Harold Knutson, in calling for a repeal of the Reciprocal Trade Agreements Act of 1934, under the theory that low tariffs hurt the farmers of the Midwest. The final draft, however, was purged of isolationist rhetoric, largely at the importuning of Wendell Willkie.[24] Moderate in outlook, hopeful in its view of the future, the address was rather tedious in delivery. Though the keynoter drew sustained applause with his plea that America "keep burning the light of liberty," his nearly hour-long address had delegates squirming. One observer, H.L. Mencken, wryly commented that Stassen's age appeared to be somewhere between seventeen and thirty-three.[25] After the convention Stassen was selected to become chairman of the Willkie campaign advisory committee.[26]

Meanwhile, Stassen handily won reelection as governor in Minnesota's last peacetime elections. Yet, with the war the central issue in American life after Pearl Harbor, it was inevitable that the young governor would not be content to sit on the sidelines. With a continuing impressive record through his second term, Stassen announced, eight months before facing reelection in 1942, that he would indeed seek a third term as governor. He also calmly stated, "The drive for victory against the totalitarian forces that threaten the future of free men will be conducted in the main by the young men of my generation. I want to be with them." He said that he would resign after the first legislative session of his third term was complete.[27] In the meantime, he busily occupied himself with the study of international affairs. In June 1942 he joined a rising chorus of leaders, which included, among others, Wendell Willkie, Henry Wallace and Sumner Welles, calling for some kind of postwar organization, which he called a "world association of free peoples." Standards for membership would be strict. Nations were to guarantee to their citizens religious freedom, elective government, and "fair internal justice." The organization would include a world police force to keep the peace.[28]

If Stassen's ideas on foreign policy were somewhat rough-hewn in June of 1942, he had refined them considerably by January 1943. At a meeting of the Foreign Policy Association of Minneapolis the governor delineated "the most specific program yet laid down for world cooperation," according to *Time*. Stassen declared, "It is my proposal that we should contemplate, and begin to plan now, for a definite continuing organization of the United Nations of the world." His proposal included plans for a one-house parliament out of which would arise a world council, its chairman selected by the parliament and its seven members then chosen by the chairman with approval of the parliament. The duties of the organization would include disarmament of Axis nations; a United Nations court and military force; administration of international airports and sea lanes; and programs to increase world literacy and trade.[29] The specific and comprehensive proposal was highly regarded, and undoubtedly was a factor in the State Department's later recommendation to President Roosevelt that Stassen be appointed to the San Francisco conference which drafted the United Nations Charter.

A choice assignment awaited Stassen when, true to his word, he resigned his governorship on April 27, 1943, in favor of his hand-picked successor, Edward Thye. Commissioned as a lieutenant commander, thirty-six-year-old former governor Stassen was selected to be flag secretary — or administrative assistant — to Admiral William "Bull" Halsey in the Pacific. Stassen recalled that it was only after the war that he learned how he had been ordered to this important post. "Secretary Knox and the Joint Chiefs," he recalled, "had decided, not telling me about it, that the real need was administration of the fleet, so that's why they sent me out there right away." The battle-hardened Halsey was initially skeptical about the bright-eyed boy wonder from Minnesota. "I reported for duty," Stassen reflected, "and the Admiral looked up at me and said, 'Are you here to work?' I replied, 'Yes, Admiral.' And he said, 'Go to it.' That was my first interview." The skepticism did not last. Halsey began calling him "Harold" and demonstrated great respect for the lieutenant commander, who said that the two "developed a tremendous relationship."[30]

William F. Halsey (right) having coffee with Harold Stassen, 1945 (*St. Paul Dispatch*, Minnesota Historical Society).

While Stassen was in the Pacific, his supporters in Minnesota were boosting the former governor for the presidency in the 1944 Republican primaries. The Minnesota GOP, in its annual convention in November 1943, passed a resolution urging the nomination and election of Harold Stassen as president.[31] Leading the effort was state party chairman Dr. R.C. Radabaugh and George Crosby, a former Willkie supporter and member of a wealthy Minneapolis milling family. The two men entered Stassen's name in the Nebraska primary, where he won, being the only candidate on the ballot — a write-in effort by supporters of Thomas Dewey fell short — and in the Wisconsin primary, where he finished a respectable second to Dewey.[32] Although the campaign demonstrated impressive regional strength, it did not catch fire nationally. Stassen's place in the military precluded any political activity on his part, and in the absence of a candidate the campaign inevitably faltered, as did the effort on behalf of the similarly situated General Douglas MacArthur. It appears that not even the former governor's supporters expected to win the nomination that year; Stassen later spoke of the efforts of Radabaugh and Crosby as resulting from an idea they had "to keep my name alive," suggesting that the two men were really looking more toward 1948 than 1944.[33]

Stassen was enjoying considerably more success in the Pacific than in the presidential race. He shed thirty pounds, reducing his weight to a mere one hundred ninety-five, and was elevated to the rank of commander. He did not escape free of injury; when the guns of his ship reared upwards and blasted incoming Japanese fighters, the resulting shock rever-

Naval officer Harold Stassen (center) with Mrs. Rose Spencer (left), Harold's wife, Esther, and an unidentified gentleman, ca. 1945 (Minnesota Historical Society).

berated underneath to the deck where the hapless officer was standing and crunched his teeth.[34] Yet the commander had no time to mourn the loss; in February of 1944 came word that President Roosevelt had appointed Stassen to serve on the United States delegation to the San Francisco Conference to draft the charter of the United Nations.[35] The high point of Harold Stassen's life was his participation in the founding of the United Nations in San Francisco.[36]

The journey began with a speech to the Gridiron Club on December 9, 1939. Stassen was asked to represent the Republican Party at the annual gathering of what has been termed a historic evening with "America's leaders, the press, and other men of power at Washington's exclusive Gridiron Club."[37] The individual selected to speak for the Democratic party was the president of the United States, Franklin D. Roosevelt. Everyone at the dinner knew FDR. He was in his ninth year as president and was a familiar figure to all of those gathered that night. Stassen, on the other hand, was new to most of those assembled. The thirty-two-year-old Stassen was in his first year as governor of Minnesota. He was untested on the national stage and this was his debut.

Gridiron Club speeches are all off the record. In 1976 Harold Brayman, a noted political journalist who covered the presidential campaigns of Alfred E. Smith, Franklin D. Roosevelt, Alfred M. Landon and Wendell L. Willkie, compiled the definitive account of these remarkable evenings, including all of the events surrounding the Gridiron antics. His recounting of the events of December 9, 1939, captures the triumph that night as Stassen faced Washington's power elite[38]:

A really notable speech was made that night by a young man of thirty-two who had burst over the Republican political scene like a star shell on the Fourth of July, Harold Stassen, the Republican governor of Minnesota. He had stood up successfully to the labor unions in his state and despite Minnesota's long liberal and Democratic tendencies, he was so popular that the polls showed 80 percent of the people of Minnesota thinking he had done a good job.

He himself was not eligible for the Presidency in 1940 because he was too young, but just a few months after this dinner he joined the meteoric campaign of Wendell Willkie, was Willkie's convention floor manager in Philadelphia and by astute leadership was a big factor in bringing the Republican nomination to Willkie. He was introduced by [Raymond] Clapper as "a man whose majority went up after his election instead of down."

"This sizzling Gridiron of our nation's Capitol," Stassen began, "bears at least one resemblance to the football gridiron with which we in Minnesota are more familiar. It is plenty rough. As a mere sophomore in the school of government, now that the ball has been snapped to me, I am frankly uncertain whether to pass, punt, or run with the ball. However, I recognize that I have one distinct advantage tonight. I am perhaps the only man at this head table who is willing to say unequivocally, 'I will not run for President in 1940.'"

Paying his respects to the Washington press gallery, he remarked that it was "through their eyes that we in the Middle West observe national affairs. In addition to their reporting of events, we have also found that they always predict correctly what is going to happen. That is, among them they always predict every possibility and all we readers a thousand miles away have to do is discover which one is right.

Then shifting quickly to President Roosevelt, he continued:

[I]f the reports that you bring us are in any respect lacking ... we can always obtain a crystal clear picture of our national government presented objectively, dispassionately and impartially by tuning in on a fireside chat. The metaphors used by the President have been very helpful. His reference to the quarterback technique in his administration gave us a better understanding of those headlines we read so frequently — "New Deal Shifts to Right," and "New Deal Shifts to Left."

We could sympathize with the quarterback when Ray Moley came out of the huddle and headed for the wrong goal, then again, when Henry Wallace turned out of bounds in California. There have been times when the fumbles of the team have been alarming, and they've been slow on the "recovery." Sometimes it seemed to us that the quarterback was the only member of the team who knew all the signals. We did get right up on the edge of our seats when every man in the backfield bobbed up with the ball, and we rose right up for a good look at the razzle dazzle when Garner and Farley galloped around right end; Ickes skirted the left; Wallace bucked the line; and the quarterback threw a delayed pass to McNutt, all of the same play.

Out in Minnesota, he noted they had been among the first to make many of the real advances in social welfare. But, he said, "we have learned by the hard and expensive way that the royal economists of the New Deal can be just as mistaken as the economic royalists.... Happily, we have been among the first to correct these mistakes, and generously, we hope the nation will not be too far behind."

Then Stassen set forth a Republican program which was largely to be adopted as the basis of the Willkie campaign the following year: "Labor relations should be improved — not by cracking down on business and not by crushing labor, but by extending a helping hand to both." Elaborating, he called for mandatory cooling-off periods before either a strike or a lockout, labor conciliators and labor courts, and a moderate code of unfair practices as to both capital and labor.

He urged parity subsidies for the farmers, aggressive marketing of surpluses at home and abroad, and an agricultural program "controlled more by workers in the field and less by field workers from Washington." He called for research and invention and discovery as a means of developing new industrial enterprises to "bring work to men standing idle in the streets, and to capital lying idle in the banks. It must be encouraged by relieving it of many of the burdens that established industry can and must bear.... Courageous capital willing to venture out into new fields can be let out of the doghouse without being led into the White House."

He called for a sounder financial base for the government, simplification of administration, and government employees who "are servants of the people instead of corporals in a political army." "I am convinced," he said "that this revolution would be worth the price even if it involved abandoning the Jackson Day dinners."

He sounded a call against the domination of government by business and also the domination of business by government. "In the separation of the two," he said, "we see the safeguarding of individual rights and a defense against special privilege, either economic or political. Government, in our view, must supply a cushion against the harsher features of a free economic system, but it cannot successfully furnish a bed on which society can go to sleep." He advocated "more missionary work for democracy with a breadbasket than with a bayonet."

"History has shown that the rights of the individual citizen have been wrested from rulers," he said, "by the people within a country and not by those from without. Dictators

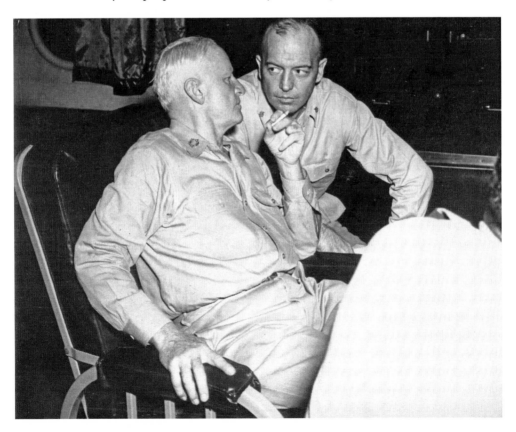

Harold E. Stassen (right) with Admiral Chester W. Nimitz, 1945 (Minnesota Historical Society).

and totalitarian states and the loss of liberties have occurred when economic difficulties either formed the background for the iron hand to fall or caused the people to voluntarily exchange their liberties and a known lack of food for a hope of better nourishment. It is rather our destiny to demonstrate the success of free individual enterprise under a democratic government on this continent, and to so utilize the great productive capacities of this country, that we help to bring about a world environment of abundance in which dictators cannot thrive." These Stassen described as the landmarks which "we of the Midwest seek to establish." He continued:

> We note that Noah seems to have been the inspiration for one persistent practice of successive national administrations. They present their blessings, two by two. We vividly recall — "Two blades of grass where one grew before." And this administration has given us two unions in every shop, two secretaries in the Department of war, two days of Thanksgiving, two secretaries of state, the one that works late at his office and the one that is early at the White House. Some say two cabinets the one with Murphy and Farley, and the one with Cohen and Corcoran. There are times when we are inclined to advocate the extension of this principle so that we have two Presidents, one to take care of domestic affairs and one to watch for and report submarines off the Coast.
>
> Gentlemen of the Gridiron — May I express to you my appreciation for this invitation. I salute you on your great traditions. Mr. President, may I say to you that I realize the heavy burdens and extreme responsibilities of your position. Even though I disagree with the sum total of the New Deal, I respect your judgment and the integrity of your motives. May I assure you that my remarks tonight have been given in the "spirit of the evening."

This speech was in the top Gridiron tradition: partly serious, partly witty, with the wit directed both at his Gridiron hosts and at the opposite party and its leadership, and all delivered in a gracious, friendly spirit. It did much to make Stassen a figure of national stature.

Immediately after he finished, the Gridiron Club put on a skit. Ulric Bell walked out on the stage in an apparent interruption of the program. "Who are the gentlemen with you?" President Clapper asked. "I do not recognize them as members of the Gridiron Club."

"They are not," answered James L. Wright. And then they were announced: Former governor Alf M. Landon of Kansas, Colonel Frank Knox of Chicago, John Hamilton, chairman of the Republican National Committee, Charles D. Hilles and Henry P. Fletcher. All were on the stage in person. Bell announced to Clapper that "after hearing that brilliant oration these Republican Kingmakers decided to simplify party strategy. They have concluded not merely to delay their 1940 convention, but to dispense with it altogether and draft Governor Stassen at once as the party nominee."

"This is very embarrassing to me," Clapper replied. "In introducing Governor Stassen I omitted to say that a few little items like the Constitution of the United States and the calendar stand in his way. He will be only thirty-three years old and therefore ineligible to be elected President in 1940."

There was consultation on the stage. The participants held a brief whispered conference, shook their heads and closed the skit with Bell announcing, "I have just consulted Governor Landon and he makes this suggestion: If the President of the United States feels now as he did about Thanksgiving Day, maybe he will oblige the Republicans by changing the date of Governor Stassen's birth." (That year President Roosevelt had proclaimed Thanksgiving Day as the third Thursday in November instead of the fourth.)[39]

Roosevelt was very impressed by Stassen and this view was reinforced by Stassen's battle against isolationism and support for the liberal internationalist Wendell Willkie at the Republican Convention and subsequently in the campaign of 1940. Roosevelt had been an advocate of Woodrow Wilson's plan for the League of Nations. The failure of that organization led Roosevelt to believe that it was essential that a new organization emerge from the ashes of World War II. To that end, twenty-six nations gathered in Washington, D.C., on January 1, 1942, to embrace the Atlantic Charter. They called themselves the United Nations and issued a declaration pledging to win the war and ultimately the peace. On January 7 Governor Stassen spoke out at a joint meeting of the St. Paul and Minneapolis Foreign Policy Association at the University of Minnesota for a United Nations that would help to build a secure peace at the end of the war.

On April 29, 1943, Stassen was ordered to active naval duty in the Pacific. Prior to his resignation and departure as governor, he completed an article for the *Saturday Evening Post*. Published on May 22, 1943, "A United Nations Government" received wide attention. One of those who read the article and was impressed was Franklin D. Roosevelt. He was delighted that the Republican Stassen, whom many talked of as a future leader of the Republican Party if not a future president of the United States, would speak out in such a bold, forthright fashion.

Said Stassen, "The nations of the world must not merely agree that they wish to live together in peace; they must establish a mechanism of government to achieve that end. I do not propose that, as Americans, we should place all our eggs in the international basket. But the time certainly has come for us to place some of them there. There they may hatch something better than frequent and constantly more devastating wars."

As the war moved toward its conclusion Roosevelt turned his attention to what would come next. He remembered the lesson of Wilson's failure to include Republican leaders in the process of putting forward the proposition of United States participation in the League of Nations. Roosevelt was determined not to make that same mistake.

Consulting with Secretary of State Edward Stettinius during the Yalta Conference in February of 1945 Roosevelt made his final decisions on who would be the delegates. He selected two members of the United States Senate: Democrat Tom Connally of Texas and Republican Arthur Vandenberg of Michigan, both leading figures in their respective political parties. From the House of Representatives he selected Sol Bloom, a Democrat from New York, and Charles Eaton, a Republican from New Jersey. Roosevelt selected the dean of Barnard College, Virginia Gildersleeve, a highly respected academic and woman, to join the delegation. Roosevelt wanted someone who had served in the war, represented the younger generation, and was a recognized figure. Who better, thought Roosevelt, than the progressive, internationalist former Republican governor of Minnesota and lieutenant commander in the Navy, Harold Stassen.

Only thirty-seven years old when asked to serve, Stassen was the perfect choice to insure a bipartisan delegation to the San Francisco conference. To lead the delegation, Roosevelt named his secretary of state, Edward Stettinius. In a masterstroke of political genius, Roosevelt named John Foster Dulles, the man who would have been Dewey's secretary of state had Dewey won the election of 1944, as an adviser and active participant in the delegation. Roosevelt had learned his lessons from Woodrow Wilson's mistakes in 1919. He had named a balanced, nonpartisan delegation to participate in the founding conference of the United Nations.

Stassen recalled the circumstances surrounding his selection, remembering "President Roosevelt sent a cable to Admiral Halsey — I was serving then as his Assistant Chief of Staff for Administration in the Pacific war — stating that he would like me to be on the delegation. I think President Roosevelt was then on his way back from the Yalta Conference.... Roosevelt had decided, apparently, that he wanted me to be the third of the Republicans on the delegation. So he sent this cable to Admiral Halsey and Admiral Halsey called me in and threw the cable across the desk and said, 'Here, do you want to do this?' It was a complete surprise to me and, of course, I very much wanted to do it, because this was a basic objective, practically, in my life, and I thought I had kind of left this behind when I went on active duty in World War II, and I told the Admiral 'I'd like very much to do it.'"[40] Stassen met Roosevelt briefly in the Oval Office on the morning of February 21 and the deal was done.

Roosevelt died suddenly in Warm Springs, Georgia, on April 12, 1945. Stassen was already in San Francisco. When he heard the news, he was, he recalled, "in the offices of the *San Francisco Chronicle* talking to Paul Smith."[41] Stassen recalled that "President Truman made a rather prompt decision that he wanted the same delegation to carry it forward. So in effect then he re-appointed us all."[42] On April 25, 1945, just thirteen days after President Roosevelt's death and twelve days before Germany's surrender, fifty nations assembled in San Francisco for the beginning of their historic deliberations.

Stassen's efforts at the conference were truly impressive. Thirty-seven reporters covering the conference voted Stassen and Australian foreign minister Herbert V. Evan as the two most effective delegates in San Francisco. The signing of the charter on June 26, 1945, was a moment of celebration. Stassen had played a critical role in the crafting of the final document.

Stassen's leadership was acclaimed by many participants. Eliahu Elath, a representative of the Jewish Agency for Palestine recorded in his diary that "our people who saw Stassen

Harold E. Stassen signing the United Nations Charter, 1945 (Minnesota Historical Society).

were impressed by his firm stand in preventing any damage to our interests and by his determination not to give in to any pressure to reach a compromise with the Arabs at our expense."[43] Elath went on to observe that "his attitude to Jewish problems has been very warm, and he has already shown his friendship in many concrete ways at the Trusteeship Committee meetings."[44] The appreciation for Stassen was nearly universal.

An essay by Barbara Stuhler summed up the view of Stassen at the San Francisco Conference:

> He put together the working paper and initiated a procedure of informal negotiations outside the regular meetings of the consultative group which greatly facilitated the proceedings. He proved useful in other ways. In her autobiography, Dean Gildersleeve described an occasion when Stettinius "failed to grasp the rather complicated question which was being raised. Mr. Stassen ... got up from his chair at the end of the room, walked quietly along and sat down beside our Chairman to help straighten out the tangle." Senator Vandenberg alluded to this same ability in a diary entry in which he called Stassen "one of the ablest young men I have ever known, with not only a tremendous capacity for hard work but also with an equal facility for going to the heart of difficult and complex problems; with a fine personality and a superb earnestness in pursuing the highly important assignment which he has carried here; and with the greatest tenacity in his fidelity to his ideals."[45]

One of the most significant events for Stassen was meeting Amos J. Peaslee. Born in 1887 in Clarksboro, New Jersey, Peaslee was to make his mark and his fortune as a lawyer. Peaslee was a Republican and an internationalist. In 1942 he wrote a book entitled *A Permanent United Nations*.[46] Peaslee's pro–United Nations position was strong and determined. He wrote with a clear vision:

> The International Community should be organized, as recommended recently by the Inter-American Juridical Committee of the Pan American Union, with "no nation privileged to remain aloof from the organization."
> It should adopt a written Constitution which will reserve to nations entitled to national status, their inviolate sovereign rights, and which will delegate to a permanent United Nations powers of government which lie outside the national spheres, and the power to administer temporarily or permanently those areas whose inhabitants cannot safely be entrusted with sovereignty.[47]

Peaslee became a key supporter of Stassen in his effort to become president in 1948 and again in 1952. He served as editor and arranged for publication of *Man Was Meant to Be Free*, a collection of Stassen's speeches and statements published in 1951 in anticipation of the 1952 campaign.

Peaslee had come to admire Stassen when they met in San Francisco. They shared a common vision of the world's future. Peaslee was to reflect, "The man in public life in America who impresses me most is Harold Stassen.... I had admired the cut of his jaw since 1940.... Positions which he took fearlessly at critical moments have repeatedly proved his wisdom."[48] He was to manage Stassen's 1948 East Coast campaign, was a delegate to the Republican National Conventions of 1948, 1952 and 1956 and then served on Stassen's White House staff in 1957 and 1958. Peaslee was a key partner of Harold Stassen's through the 1940s and 1950s.

Stassen's belief in the United Nations never wavered. Reflecting on the importance of the United Nations on its fortieth anniversary Stassen observed, "The organization has many problems, but it's important to remember that it has done what we most hoped it would do. Here we are forty years later and there was no third world war." Stassen believed that "preventing such a world war was our number one objective forty years ago."[49]

The celebration of the fortieth anniversary of the signing of the United Nations Charter in San Francisco took place in the summer of 1985 amidst great fanfare. Only three of the original participants who signed the charter in 1945 were present: Charles H. Malik, member of the Delegation of Lebanon, General Carlos P. Romulo, who had served as chairman of the Delegation of the Philippine Commonwealth and Harold E. Stassen, member of the Delegation of the United States of America. Each participated in the Charter Day Luncheon, held on Wednesday, June 26, in the grand ballroom of the Fairmont Hotel. Stassen was joined at the event by his wife, Esther.[50] Within a very short time only Stassen would still be alive.

Stassen was deeply concerned about the future of the United Nations. In 1994 he wrote *United Nations: A Working Paper for Restructuring* and in it said that "the United Nations must

Harold E. Stassen's signature on the United Nations Charter, 1945 (Collection of John F. Rothmann).

become more effective in peacemaking, more effective in peacekeeping, the children, women and men of the world. A rising tide of worldwide public opinion holds that the United Nations urgently needs to be restructured to accomplish these goals. I suggest that a restructuring be accomplished in the year 1995, the fiftieth year of the United Nations." To that end Stassen reviewed the existing charter on one page and did a detailed rewrite on the opposite page. He boiled his suggestions down to ten key points[51]:

1. A regular annual conference at the United Nations of representative leaders of the religions of the world. The goal would be to find nonviolent and just solutions for future interrelationships of the peoples of the world (chapter 24, *A Working Paper*).

2. A small, elite multilingual United Nations Legion of volunteers, with not too many from any one state or race or religion. The legion should be well equipped and well trained to respond promptly to Security Council decisions regarding potential trouble spots (chapter 8, *A Working Paper*).

3. A super peacemaking corps of experienced negotiators, mediators, and arbitrators to take long-term, continuing assignments to the most difficult international problems (chapters 13 and 14, *A Working Paper*).

4. A Research Institute on People and Governance to study, suggest, and report on forms, methods, and revisions of national, regional, and international organizations, with special attention to future, worldwide conditions for health, economic opportunities, and human rights (chapter 25, *A Working Paper*).

5. A continuation of a general assembly of the United Nations, with every sovereign state member having a voice and a vote, but with voting power to be proportionate so that a more realistic, democratic and sensible scale of voting rights can be achieved (chapter 4, *A Working Paper*).

6. An administrative council in the General Assembly to act continuously with the secretary-general. The council would have regional representation and be of functional size (such as twenty-five members). It would foster regional cooperation, help defuse local conflicts, and improve world forums and administrative functioning (chapter 6, *A Working Paper*).

7. A new method of regular financial support, such as a small, one-half of 1 percent charge on all international trade of goods, materials, oil, and minerals (chapter 23, *A Working Paper*).

8. A Universe Environmental Institute to focus worldwide attention and scientific expertise on the quality of the water, air, and land of the globe (chapter 7, *A Working Paper*).

9. An effective inspection system and corps to monitor the continuing reduction of the offensive armaments of the world (chapter 9, *A Working Paper*).

10. A continuation of the Security Council, but with the addition of Japan and Germany as permanent members (and perhaps one or two others), and with a revision of the single-member veto power (chapter 5, *A Working Paper*).[52]

Although no action was taken on Stassen's recommendations, the future structure of the United Nations is being actively discussed by world leaders today. Stassen's active proposals are among those that remain on the table as a future restructuring of the United Nations is considered. Throughout the remainder of his life Stassen continued to speak out and to speak for the United Nations. He never lost faith in the vision that he so clearly articulated at the founding of the United Nations in 1945. On July 5, 1945, Stassen gave a speech entitled "The United Nations Charter." He urged the Charter be read by "every citizen of our country and to every boy and girl." Stassen conceded that "taken as a whole, the Charter is a human document. It is not perfect. It has its weaknesses.... May the cynics of today who scoff at the United Nations be as wrong as [the] cynic of yesterday who scoffed at the United States."[53]

Walter Lippmann called Stassen "a recognized American national leader"; columnist Thomas L. Stokes labeled him the "most interesting new figure on the American political scene." James Reston was perhaps the most impressed, believing that the former governor was outstanding and "an able negotiator on complex and often unfamiliar subjects, patient but firm."[54] Stassen urged a twelve-point U.S. foreign policy, including proposals as conventional as "complete, decisive victory over Japan" and as debate-engendering as "use of U.S. economic strength to advance living standards of other peoples."[55]

Time for editorializing was short, though; Commander Stassen's leave was up and he hurried back to the Pacific, where he stood with Admiral Halsey when the U.S. fleet steamed into Tokyo Bay. The carnage over, Stassen was ordered to see to the freeing of prisoners of war. He began the task at Omari Prison Camp Number 8, near Tokyo, where he was cheered by American prisoners of war. Less impressed was a stubborn Japanese colonel, who protested, "I have no authority to release these prisoners to you." Retorted Stassen, "Colonel, you have no authority, period." He proceeded to go sleepless for seventy hours while he tended to the release of thirteen thousand men and their transport to waiting hospital ships. Mission accomplished, Stassen was discharged as a captain in November 1945 to a large homecoming celebration, where Halsey called him "a great naval officer, a great governor, fit for any job you want to give him." To inquiring reporters Stassen praised General MacArthur's occupation policy in Japan, came out for universal military training; and said he would not support Minnesota senator Henrik Shipstead's reelection bid.[56] Returning to his home state, Stassen resumed his political career.

3. Political Pioneering

The New York theater community, an arena with perhaps more competition than in the meanest political precinct, beamed with approval after the Broadway debut of *State of the Union* in the fall of 1945. This comedy, written by Howard Lindsey and Russel Crouse and later made into a film featuring Katharine Hepburn and Spencer Tracy, portrayed the experiences of a visionary and honest airplane manufacturer who would very much like to be president of the United States. Republican Party bosses, quick to appreciate the political attractiveness of the industrialist, embrace him as one of their own and remind him to be careful about what he says. Eventually the would-be president's self-respect rules and he walks out on the party bosses. Before that, however, he receives sage advice from a veteran politico: "Stay out of Minneapolis. That's Stassen territory."[1]

Better, though, to have referred to *all* Minnesota as the political domain of the GOP boy wonder. Three years before *State of the Union* hit Broadway, the liberal Stassen hit the state's old-guard Republicans with a stunning 1-2-3 knockout, sweeping the offices of United States senator and lieutenant governor with candidates touting Stassen's brand of liberal internationalism while he himself cruised to reelection.[2] In 1946 he scored a convincing replay as his allies captured the remaining senate seat and, again, the governor and lieutenant governor post. Stassen himself had declined to seek state office.[3]

Still, the forceful Stassen sirocco which blasted through Minnesota had not, in the fall of 1945, caused much of a disturbance in the national political atmosphere, although in the spring of 1946 the former governor privately calculated that a fourth to a third of all GOP district organizations were supporting him for the 1948 nomination.[4] Yet the conservative *Tulsa Tribune* only modestly exaggerated the facts in September 1946 when it claimed that "he hasn't got a Chinaman's chance."[5] It is all the more remarkable, then, that less than two years later a large plurality of Republican voters in states with presidential primaries selected Stassen over New York governor Thomas Dewey, as the Minnesotan collected 806,906 primary votes to second-place Dewey's 354,440.[6]

The seemingly unstoppable steamroller which flattened Dewey and conservative Ohio senator Robert Taft in Republican presidential primaries is worthy of attention both as a human odyssey and as a watershed in American political history. The human odyssey is a tale which evokes respect, for there is a Lincolnesque quality to the emergence of Harold Stassen as a presidential candidate in 1948, the distinctly American epic of a rural boy fighting for education and elevation above provincial surroundings, all the while holding fast to fundamental principles and values. Three aspects of this human adventure command attention and wonder.

First, Stassen would run for president as an internationalist, supportive of the United Nations and foreign aid. Yet the soil in which the Stassen political seed was planted was not a promising place for a liberal internationalist to take root. With two prominent Republican senators, Ernest Lundeen and Henrik Shipstead, Minnesota and its GOP remained in the late 1930s a sturdy bulwark of isolationism, impervious to the national trend toward the brand of internationalism promoted by the Council on Foreign Relations and the Foreign Policy Association.

In the 1970s Barbara Stuhler of the World Affairs Center at the University of Minnesota credited the ultimate shift in the state's politics toward internationalism to Harold Stassen, Senator Joseph Ball, and Congressman Walter Judd.[7] Stassen, as the first of this triumvirate to assume office,[8] spoke for a policy whose time had not arrived — until *he* did. When asked how he had found the courage to speak for such an unorthodox view of world affairs, the former governor revealed his considerable political acumen. "I looked at the enlistment rates in the navy," he recalled. "I found that Minnesota had the highest enlistment rate per hundred in the country ... I looked at that and said, 'isolationism, hell!'"[9] Stassen forged his own opportunities in Minnesota.

Second, the Stassen presidential star reached its zenith literally on his forty-first birthday, April 13, 1948, the date of the Nebraska presidential primary. By 1948 Stassen had engineered a meteoric rise to fame.

Third, as a liberal, Stassen was bitterly opposed in the presidential race by Republican Party regulars, those officials who had successfully fought off Wendell Willkie in 1944. As early as June 1946 Milburn Akers, chief political writer for the *Chicago Sun*, noticed an organized "Stop Stassen" movement within the GOP.[10] Undaunted, Stassen leaped to shake hands at rural barbecues, church socials and local town meetings. When political experts scratched their heads and wondered how the Stassen boom had happened, one campaign aide replied, quite simply, "Why I guess Harold Stassen started it."[11] In the face of palpable hostility, the former governor relentlessly worked toward his national ambitions.

Note the flavor of a Greek tragedy in the Stassen tale: The opposition which was destined to doom his career came invariably and inevitably from the same quarter. As a young politician and as a presidential candidate, and later as a cabinet officer in the Eisenhower administration, Stassen encountered resistance from conservative GOP leaders. Just as inevitably, Stassen refused to accommodate his opponents by moderating his views.

The other element which compels the study of Stassen's political adventures is the fact that his 1948 campaign represented a watershed in American political history. In two respects, this watershed marked a change in direction in how White House aspirants sought the nomination of their party.

First, Stassen was the first to exploit the power, then latent, of presidential primaries. In common wisdom, George McGovern and Jimmy Carter were the first "outsiders" to do an end run around party chieftains and move to the forefront of their party by vigorously campaigning and doing well in political primaries, thereby demonstrating strength and building enough momentum to make their candidacies virtually unstoppable. Yet this campaign strategy was pioneered by Harold Stassen in 1948. This is a point forgotten today; yet the new approach was quite obvious to contemporary observers. "Whether or not he finally realizes his ambition to be president..." the *Arkansas Gazette* editorialized in April 1948, "Harold Stassen has already earned a place in American political history. It is even possible that he has brought into being a new type of political campaign as precedent-setting in its way as William Henry Harrison's portable log cabin and free-flowing cider barrel."[12] The *Milwaukee Journal* marveled that "the Stassen candidacy is beginning to assume the aspects of a true grassroots movement, the first this nation has seen for a long time."[13]

Nationally syndicated columnist Thomas Stokes noted that "the test by ballot ... has unveiled a new and formidable figure in Harold Stassen ... [who] has forced a change in primary campaign technique."[14]

There was, perhaps, some precedent for the Stassen campaign in the 1940 effort of Wendell Willkie. Oren Root, twenty-eight-year-old grand-nephew of former secretary of state Eliehu Root, gathered a numerically impressive army of volunteers by borrowing a hundred fifty dollars, placing ads in newspaper personal columns promoting the idea of "Willkie Clubs," and setting up shop in his mother's apartment.[15] So impressed was James David Barber that he has credited the 1940 Willkie campaign with signaling a change in presidential nominating contests. "Willkie's story," Barber wrote, "can be seen in retrospect as marking a key transition in American politics: The decline of the parties as nominators."[16]

While the Willkie campaign may have been a feint toward the decline, Barber, in his eagerness to spot key transitions, overlooks exactly *what* was being transferred to *where*. The point is not that Willkie had a large army of devoted followers beyond, even excluding, party leaders; popularity, after all, was not novel. The key to the decline of parties is the rise of political primaries, which were by the 1970s to be the locus of presidential nominations. Yet Wendell Willkie in 1940 entered not one primary; his sole effort to compete in a primary contest did not occur until 1944, when he went down to a crushing defeat in Wisconsin.[17]

In an eclipse which was not unreasonably taken for a permanent demise, presidential primaries seemed in early 1948 to be little more than a quaint artifact of the progressive movement of the early twentieth century. According to progressive cosmology, the American political universe featured big business interests as the metaphysical "first mover," yanking on strings which directed the absurdly named party "bosses" who in turn produced suitably obedient candidates. It was a sordid affair, progressives believed, with the stench of smoke-filled rooms lacing candidates from both parties at all levels and branches of government. Progressives were convinced that the key to a healthy change of political air was to transfer the power of nominations from party leaders to voters, thus establishing in the political universe a new center of gravity in "the people" rather than in business interests.[18]

Florida enacted the first presidential primary law in 1901. Party officials, under the law, held the option of holding a party primary to choose a candidate as well as delegates to the national convention. Three years later Governor Robert M. LaFollette of Wisconsin, following the 1904 Republican National Convention at which the credentials of his progressive delegation were rejected, began agitating for a presidential primary in his state. The following year the legislature provided for mandatory direct election of convention delegates. As the reform impulse gathered strength nationwide in the ensuing years, the number of presidential primaries across the United States proliferated. By the dawn of the New Freedom era, twelve states had enacted primary laws that provided for the direct election of delegates, a preferential vote (indicating candidate popularity) or both. Under Woodrow Wilson the number of primaries exploded to twenty-six.[19]

Yet the reform impulse was subsequently abandoned in the more pressing battle to make the world safe for democracy in World War I, and in the ensuing 1920s crusade to make the peace safe for normalcy. The number of primaries declined, never having noticeably achieved their purifying promise. Party bosses who had never entirely lost their grip on power once again ruled virtually unchallenged.[20] Reports of the death of presidential primaries, however, proved to be greatly exaggerated; in 1948 they were still powerful enough to propel a candidate to the front of national popularity polls, if only a White House aspirant utilized them.

Stassen, not beloved by conservative party bosses, built a campaign strategy around the presidential primaries, using them as a fulcrum to hoist himself to the political fore by building momentum and demonstrating his electoral mettle. By the time of the convention, he and his supporters hoped, his primary victories would have created a public demand for his nomination at a time when his more timid Republican opponents were reeling from his primary election punches. Had it not been for a fatal error late in the primary season, this scenario very probably would have been played out at the Republican National Convention in Philadelphia in June of 1948.

A second and related aspect of Stassen's campaign which makes it an American political watershed is the early and open method in which the candidate made his White House ambitions known. Frankly admitting his goal, Stassen announced for the presidency almost two years before the November 1948 presidential election and relentlessly traveled some one hundred eighty thousand miles across the nation seeking support. Not for Stassen was the front porch "campaign" of Benjamin Harrison or William McKinley. While today it is taken for granted that a presidential aspirant must announce early and campaign vigorously, Stassen was the first major candidate to do so. He caught Thomas Dewey napping and delivered a rude awakening to the New Yorker in April 1948.

4. Preparing for the Pilgrimage

According to a Confucian proverb, a great journey begins with a single step. After Harold Stassen's discharge from the Navy, he began in earnest his journey in quest of the Republican nomination for president — an odyssey which would take him literally across the planet and include over one hundred eighty thousand miles of travel within the United States. Like the pilgrimage of Byron's Childe Harold, the journey was an epic of challenge and new experience.

When the retiring naval officer told reporters at his homecoming celebration in November of 1945 that he would not support Minnesota's Republican senator Henrik Shipstead for reelection in the senatorial primary, the press, in an understandable leap of faith, assumed that the ambitious Stassen would run himself. Yet in March of 1946 he announced that he would not be a senatorial candidate, yielding to Governor Ed Thye, who had, in fact, urged Stassen to take the office himself. Rather, the former governor declared that he would spend the next two years visiting the Soviet Union, Europe and South America, and talking about international and domestic issues in all forty-eight of the United States. It was, he insisted, his hope to build and reshape the Republican party, leading it to support the United Nations and work to develop harmony between American organized labor and management.[1] The ever-skeptical fourth estate raised its eyebrows, noting that the Minnesotan could much more easily accomplish his goals as a GOP senator.

Ed Thye himself later remarked that Stassen's decision to forego the Senate seat led to talk about the presidential hopeful's lack of good judgment. Particularly disappointed was Walter Judd, a member of Congress from Minnesota. In Washington, D.C., Stassen called on Judd in the congressman's office. "I tried to talk him out of it and didn't succeed," Judd recalled ruefully. "Stassen said, 'Oh, I'm not interested in the Senate. I want to go out and talk about national affairs and debate the issues.' I said, 'Do you want to have some influence or don't you?'" Judd, who decades later maintained that Stassen had "one of the best minds I've ever dealt with in public life," called the decision not to run for the Senate the first serious mistake of the Stassen presidential quest.[2]

Stassen, though, never admitted regret, recalling that he sincerely did not want to serve in the legislature, feeling that his skills centered more on administration.[3] Criticism aside, the decision allowed Stassen to begin planting, through vigorous personal cultivation, his presidential campaign structure at the grassroots level. By definition, a grassroots campaign requires a cadre of eager, enthusiastic volunteers from the most populous cities to the most humble hamlets. The formative steps in assembling the Stassen army were taken a little over a week after he disclaimed any interest in the U.S. Senate, when he announced the creation of "Republican Open Forums" to encourage discussion groups among voters. The organization would pick topics (the first two would be "What shall our policy toward Russia be?" and "What shall our labor policy be?"), prepare discussion questions and relevant research, and hold meetings where citizens could debate options and select policies. The opinions of each group would be polled monthly.[4]

The advisory committee of the Open Forums included such congressional luminaries as Senator Wayne Morse and Representatives Walter Judd and Christian Herter. The executive director of the Open Forums was Henry T. McKnight, an indefatigable Minnesotan who promptly informed the press that he would have twenty thousand forums in operation by the time of the 1948 Republican National Convention. Not quite reaching this ambitious number, the organization quickly spread throughout the nation, as Open Forums were established in thirty-seven states barely one month after the announcement of their creation.[5]

The Open Forums were likened in the media to the Willkie Clubs of 1940. Stassen expressed dismay at the comparison. "They were just campaign organizations," the former governor said of the Willkie groups with palpable disdain in his voice. Stassen insisted that his organization was designed not so much to promote a specific candidate as to stimulate debate and to liberalize the Republican party.[6] An examination of the research material and discussion outlines sent to each forum reveals that, whatever the motivation in their creation, the clubs tangled with tough issues in a thoughtful and probing manner, quite ignoring the polemics of ideology, a remarkable achievement in an era of increasing national conservatism.

Yet Stassen could not invariably buck the conservative tide which would in a matter of months sweep into office the Republican eightieth Congress. In the summer of 1946 the Minnesotan stumbled into a wrong turn on the road to the Republican nomination. In the Republican primary in Nebraska, three-time Governor Dwight Griswold was seeking to wrest the GOP senatorial nomination from the stolid conservative incumbent, Hugh Butler. It must have appeared to Stassen that the contest represented the final battle at Armageddon, with Griswold, whose internationalism surely caused Stassen's globally minded heart to leap, representing the Good at its liberal best. The Minnesotan hurried to the Great Plains state to stand with Griswold.

An indignant Butler and his supporters reacted like quarantine officers responding to an immigrant virus. Nebraskans had voted for Stassen in their 1944 presidential primary, but resented his role as a meddler in their affairs. Like Franklin Roosevelt in 1938, Stassen received for his involvement a stinging rebuke in Butler's 2 to 1 landslide victory. Griswold subsequently was appointed by President Truman to serve as the American aid administrator in Greece; a chastened Stassen limped home. The conservative *Chicago Tribune* gleefully chirped that "there was nothing left of Harold, his presumptions or his platform... Stassen is eliminated.... He is as dead politically as Willkie after the Wisconsin primary in 1944."[7] *The Nation* more charitably mused, "On July 8 he will have a second chance, this time supporting Gov. Edward Thye in his battle to retire Senator Henrik Shipstead.... He would be hard put to survive a second defeat."[8]

The comparison with Nebraska was not particularly apt. Thye won the primary and the general election with little effort, while committed Stassenite Luther Youngdahl won the governor's chair. Despite the relative ease of the victories, the Minnesota successes were important for two reasons. First, Stassen regained national political respect; he had, after all, backed two winners. Second, both Thye and Youngdahl were to become active supporters of the Stassen presidential campaign.

Their involvement stemmed from a meeting with Stassen in early December 1946. Stassen, who had not yet announced publicly that he would seek the presidential nomination, spoke with the two men in Minneapolis. On December 5 Bernhard LeVander, chairman of the Minnesota Republican Party, wrote to an associate that Stassen, "after talking with Ed and Luther, has asked that we form the 'Stassen for President Volunteers' ... with Ed and Luther as Honorary Chairmen, Rose [Spencer, state GOP co-chair] and myself heading it up.... Our first job will be an extensive mail solicitation," he added, "setting as our goal $500,000."[9] The Stassen presidential campaign was born.

Yet Stassen supporters had been organized in a manner of sorts at least since May. It was on May 4 that the first copy of the *Minnesota Letter* was issued from Suite 1215 of the Pioneer Building in Minneapolis, which also happened to be the headquarters of the state GOP. Edited by Leif Gilstad, who was also an employee of the state GOP, the *Letter* was addressed to "friends of Harold Stassen" and labeled "personal and confidential." The first issue said that the purpose of the *Letter*, which would be issued periodically, was to keep supporters of Harold Stassen briefed on "developments." It promised that it would be authoritative and not propaganda: "It will report the bad news with the good."[10]

The formation of the Stassen for President Volunteers was a signal development, for it marked the maturation of Stassen's plans. The public "coming out" took place on December 17, 1946, at the Mayflower Hotel in Washington, D.C. Announcing that he was opening an office in the nation's capitol, Stassen told reporters, "I do intend to be a candidate for the Republican nomination in 1948. I intend to develop and present a definite, constructive and progressive program to our Republican party. And on that basis, I intend to let my supporters present my name in the primaries and to the Convention in 1948."[11]

Although they were fully aware of Stassen's presidential ambitions, the early and open admission of candidacy must have caught reporters by surprise, as political etiquette required the candidate to pretend the office was seeking him, not the other way around. Asked why he put the matter in the future tense, the Minnesotan laughed, "All right. I am a candidate if you want to put it that way. I want to be frank and open about it."[12]

The "frank and open" approach of December 17 stood in sharp relief to the more conventional strategy of Senator Robert Taft, who a mere twenty-four hours earlier, in reply to an Associated Press query in Atlanta, insisted, "No, I do not consider myself to be an active candidate for president." More truthfully, Senator Arthur Vandenberg announced, also on December 17, that he was not a candidate.[13] The uniqueness of the Stassen approach was obvious.

The liberal Stassen appeared to be facing a mighty battle against overwhelming odds. The November elections seemed to have ushered in a conservative era, and a Gallup poll noted that the Minnesotan had slipped while Dewey shot up twelve points. At the annual Gridiron meeting three days before he announced his candidacy, Stassen's woes were noted and, in true Gridiron fashion, mocked. A baritone, playing the part of Stassen in a political skit, sang a parody on "The Curse of the Aching Heart" and blamed it all on the Republican Old Guard.[14] Undaunted, the former governor continued to piece together his campaign organization. It included the best and brightest Minnesota had to offer. Bernhard LeVander, as chairman of both the campaign and the state GOP, already had a lengthy relationship with Stassen.

LeVander was introduced to Stassen by LeVander's brother, who had joined Stassen's South St. Paul law office after graduating from law school in 1935. In the summer of 1938 Stassen — then running for governor — called on the twenty-two-year-old future party chairman and asked him to drive his campaign car. LeVander quickly agreed, and the two went on the road together for the first time on July 4, 1938. After making perhaps six appearances throughout the day, the two young men returned home exhausted at two in the morning. Seeking to utilize his time wisely, Stassen kept a Dictaphone in the car, working through stacks of correspondence between speeches. After a month of chauffeuring, the candidate asked LeVander to try his hand at answering correspondence during a speech. As LeVander performed the job well, Stassen put him in his campaign office as a scheduling and correspondent assistant. By 1948 LeVander, now an attorney, had acquired considerable political skill and national contacts through his duties as state party chairman.[15]

In charge of the financial details of the campaign was Alfred Lindley, a Minneapolis attorney of the Pillsbury family, who took charge of the Minnesota Fund, which financed Stassen's travels from the time he was discharged from the Navy. Described in the media as "a dour, bristle-haired lawyer," Lindley was in fact a warm and generous man whose death years later in a skiing accident caused Stassen deep sorrow. Associated with Stassen since their days as law school classmates, Lindley was charged with soliciting funds from large contributors, a task he performed with considerable success, and keeping track of expenditures.[16]

Hailing from Wisconsin, Vic Johnston managed the Stassen campaign in the crucial primary in his native state before assuming management of Stassen's Washington, D.C., office in April 1948 and organizing the Stassen "spontaneous demonstration" at the Republican National Convention in June. Regarded as a savvy tactician and publicist, Johnston had served as publicity director throughout Stassen's tenure as governor before directing the Minnesotan's forces in the 1944 Wisconsin primary. In 1946 he assisted Joseph McCarthy in his successful bid for the U.S. Senate and served briefly as McCarthy's administrative assistant in Washington, D.C., thus establishing a link between Stassen and the senator, who would vigorously back the Minnesotan throughout the 1948 campaign. After 1948 Johnston served as executive director of the GOP Senate Campaign Committee before managing the Washington, D.C., office of Robert Taft in 1952.[17]

Working to promote Stassen in eastern financial circles was Amos Peaslee, who had made a fortune as a patent lawyer in New Jersey. Later an ambassador in the Eisenhower administration, Peaslee took charge of the Stassen eastern headquarters in New York's Sheraton Hotel.[18]

Initially holding court in the Washington, D.C., office was Earl Hart, destined to play a fateful role in Stassen's presidential fortunes. Hart, an Ohio native, plunged into politics when he assisted Harold Burton, later a Supreme Court justice, in a successful race for mayor of Cleveland in 1935. Hart also worked for Burton's reelection campaigns in 1937 and 1939 and aided in his election to the U.S. Senate in 1940, after which he became Burton's Washington, D.C., administrative assistant. In that capacity Hart demonstrated considerable political skill, and was elected president of the Senate Secretaries Association. "I was the only Republican to hold the job in nobody knows how long," Hart recalled contentedly. "They couldn't remember who was the last Republican."

The Washington, D.C., Stassen campaign office in Hart's charge was located in the LeSalle Building at 1028 Connecticut Avenue, NW. The office suite was bounded on the south by a creaky elevator and on the north by an air shaft. The previous occupant, a freight company, had gone bankrupt and departed, leaving behind desks, lamps and furniture, which comprised the décor of the Stassen office. No doubt Hart was delighted to return to Ohio in the spring of 1948 to take charge of the Minnesotan's ill-fated campaign against Robert Taft, a campaign he had strenuously urged be undertaken.[19]

The Stassen staff member destined to become most prominent, Warren Burger, became chief justice of the Supreme Court in 1969. The same age as Stassen, Burger was a St. Paul lawyer who had been active in Stassen's gubernatorial campaigns. He joined the presidential effort in January of 1948 officially as chief of staff in charge of the campaign office housed in the Minneapolis Pillsbury Building. Later he was also responsible for recruiting delegates at the various state conventions and caucuses before leading the effort to enlist new delegates at the national convention while keeping current Stassen supporters within the fold.[20]

Burger apparently assumed a great deal of the responsibility for the management of the campaign; Bernhard LeVander, officially the chairman of the organization, referred to Burger as "kind of the overall chairman" and spoke well of his performance. Still, the records in the Minnesota Historical Society hint that Burger's skills in business management left something to be desired. These records include several memos, respectful but chiding in tone, from LeVander to the future chief justice, reminding him of needed tasks. For example, in a February 1948 memo, LeVander wrote to Burger: "Just a reminder about posters of Stassen. They will do us no good sitting in the store room and should be allocated for use in the primary states." Another February memo reported: "In checking up I find that some of our state managers have not as yet gotten the list of managers in other states.... I thought we had it understood two weeks ago that such a list would be sent to all men in the field." A letter from one campaign official, Robert Herberger, to another, Daniel Gainey, grumbled that "several people here in Chicago gave me the same story I have heard frequently in Minnesota — namely, that it was next to impossible to get an answer to any letters sent to Harold's office.... It makes it difficult for enthusiastic Stassen workers to be constantly reminded of the fact that letters to Stassen go unanswered."[21] Memos notwithstanding, LeVander, while conceding that perhaps Burger "may have needed to be reminded sometimes," stressed that the future chief justice was principally concerned with delegate recruitment and faced an enormously hectic schedule.[22]

While these men formed the core of the Stassen campaign, their efforts were augmented by many prominent, and wealthy, individuals. In Philadelphia, Jay Cooke, great-grandson of the Civil War financier and also a one-time Republican candidate for the U.S. Senate, led the successful Stassen write-in campaign in the Pennsylvania primary. In Chicago, active Stassen supporters included former under secretary of the Navy Ralph Bard, United Airlines president William Patterson, and Walter Paepeke, chairman of the board of Container Corporation of America.[23]

Yet a fortuitous pedigree or employment was not required of the Stassen forces. While the directors were often well-known, the actors were an amalgam of American society, befitting a drama played out at the grassroots, although volunteers in the Minnesota office were drawn from a pool of seven hundred individuals of whom a substantial number were debutantes and society women. The very name of the central campaign organization, Stassen for President Volunteers, emphasized that, for Stassen, participatory democracy was no empty shibboleth.[24]

Stassen for President Volunteers stood at the apex of the presidential effort. Featuring Senator Ed Thye and Governor Luther Youngdahl as honorary chairmen and Bernhard LeVander and Rose Spencer as cochairs, the Volunteers planned strategy and directed the movement. The largest component of the organization was the mighty Neighbors for Stassen, chaired by Daniel Gainey of Owatonna, Minnesota. As a self-made business executive, Gainey had a great deal of wealth and a huge fund of energy to devote to the Stassen cause.[25]

The principal task of the Neighbors was promotional: reaching the friends, relatives and acquaintances of Stassen supporters by letter and personal contact. The organization was a pioneering concept, for it was a campaign structure created not to round up delegates and official party backing, but instead to create a blaze of grassroots support, with the hope that the resulting heat would warm party leaders to Stassen.

Bernhard LeVander noted at the time that the Neighbors "has no direct relationship to the political operation of seeking delegates [handled by the Stassen for President Volunteers], but can have a substantial bearing on that subject by influencing public support.[26]

Neighbors charged no dues, raised no money and sought no endorsements. Financed by the Volunteers, the organization operated like a chain letter. Each Neighbor was to locate persons anxious to volunteer, keep them informed of Stassen's activities, and convince them to make their own contacts. The names of all individuals contacted were sent to the Neighbors' Minneapolis office where a central file of names was collected. The office supplied kits to Neighbors containing information about Stassen and even a model letter Neighbors could use when writing to acquaintances about Stassen.[27]

Thus, Neighbors sent letters to their friends about the former governor. If the friends were interested, the Neighbors' office took over. The effort grew rapidly and by June of 1947, according to an internal memo, there were four thousand one hundred Minnesota and nine thousand out-of-state Neighbors, representing every one of the forty-seven other states, this at a time when the 1948 presidential campaign had not even registered with most Americans. The memo noted, moreover, that these were recorded, minimum figures.[28] By January 1948 the Neighbors enrollment list had mushroomed to nearly thirty thousand, twice the number of GOP workers on the national Republican mailing list,[29] before peaking at forty-nine thousand in April 1948.[30]

Having helped to launch this avalanche of support, the executive director of Neighbors for Stassen, Mark Forgette, was by the summer of 1947 restlessly casting about for new outlets. He found them in the idea of voter-specific subsidiaries of the Neighbors group, such as Secretaries for Stassen, Students for Stassen, and so forth. Forgette took it upon himself to organize these groups and charged them with promoting Stassen among their colleagues. He herded members of the Minnesota bar into a "Minnesota Lawyers for Stassen Committee," with the task of urging lawyers within the state to contact attorneys in other states and send them literature about Stassen, which would be provided by the Neighbors.[31] In 1947 and into 1948 Forgette dashed around the United States, leaving in his wake teachers, insurance salesmen, veterans and others organized into pro–Stassen groups. It was Bernhard LeVander, though, who apparently can take credit for a particularly prestigious "catch" as he oversaw the creation of Doctors for Stassen under the chairmanship of Dr. C.W. Mayo of the Mayo Clinic in Rochester, Minnesota.[32]

The specialized grouping of voters was sometimes taken to unusual extremes. A "Former F.B.I. Agents for Stassen" club was organized by a former agent from Popestone, Minnesota, which eventually sent literature to over one hundred former F.B.I. agents.[33]

If, as H.G. Wells believed, democracy dies five miles from the parish pump, it was necessary for the Stassen campaign to find a way to preserve its grassroots character even as it grew into a national movement. The Neighbors organization, by its very success, had by the spring of 1948 become obsolete. The Minneapolis office could no longer effectively coordinate the local contacts burgeoning across the country.

In March, Neighbors for Stassen was replaced with a new organization, Citizens for Stassen. The new campaign structure still served as a branch of the Stassen for President Volunteers and still faithfully executed its letter-writing duties; yet now the coordination of Stassen forces was decentralized throughout the nation through a network of volunteer groups chartered by the Minneapolis headquarters. Seeking to preserve its local flavor and maintaining prominent roles for individuals, each group was to have no more than twenty-five members. Chapters were advised to undertake activities they could most effectively carry out among several choices. They could, for example, sponsor the formation of at least four other chapters; promote special groups such as Nurses for Stassen; concentrate on fundraising for the national campaign; or form a contact committee to visit local Republican leaders and urge them to support Harold Stassen.[34] Citizens for Stassen represented an evolution in the campaign, as it embraced increasing numbers of supporters. Yet the grassroots, outside-party-channels philosophy remained its core feature. "By showing great popular support for Harold Stassen, delegates will be influenced to support him at the convention," a Citizens leaflet noted.[35]

Of course, no presidential campaign since Andrew Jackson has survived without revelry. In December 1947 Stassen fired off a memo to Mark Forgette, proposing a campaign song called "We Want Stassen" sung to the tune of "I've Got a Sixpence." The ever-conscientious Forgette solemnly formed a committee to study the matter and, in a return memo, assured his boss that "considerable thought was given not only to the song in question" but to other musical options as well.

His first concern was with the line in "We Want Stassen" that proclaimed, "We want Stassen to serve us all his life." Too morbid, Forgette and his committee observed; they changed this to "We want Stassen the man we represent." What about the tune? It wouldn't do. It was originally a British composition and, anyway, it had never made the hit parade. Servicemen were generally acquainted with it, though. Still, better try another. Forgette and his associates then rewrote "Minnesota, Hats Off to Thee":

> *Harold Stassen*
> *We're all for you.*
> *Merchant, miner, veteran*
> *and farmer, too!*

Perhaps the tune sounds too immature because of its college connotation. Better forget it. Besides, it's too regional.

At this point of despair, it occurred to someone to rewrite "Anchors Aweigh." Such a rewrite may leave the campaign open to criticism of capitalizing on Stassen's service record. "But," one 'Anchors' booster protested, "it's well-known, marching and stirring, suggestive of the service, but there would be no mention of service in it." The committee composed the words:

> *Stassen for President*
> *Stassen for me!*
> *Stassen for everyman*
> *Who loved liberty-y!*
>
> *Stassen — 'tis freedom's voice*
> *Hark to her call.*
> *"Stassen for President"*
> *Means liberty and happiness for ALL!*

In his memo to Stassen, Forgette noted: "Liberty, freedom, happiness are general words, but are traditional and powerful and meaningful.... Recommend this song for your consideration."[36]

The professional direction of the Stassen strategy and the political competence with which it was carried out raises intriguing questions about the campaign's genesis and institutional structure. By early summer 1948, Stassen had risen from long shot to popular favorite for the nomination. Was the effort entirely a grassroots movement? Clearly Stassen's support was based outside regular party channels, yet the seed of this local support was planted and cultivated, perhaps controversially, by the state GOP organization in Minnesota, which after 1938 was quite controlled by Harold Stassen. A renegade effort nationally, the movement sprang from the party officialdom in Minnesota.

The symbiosis between the Stassen for President campaign and the Minnesota Republican Party was explicit, as the state GOP became an arm of the former governor's White House bid. The Republican State Central Committee, housed in the Minneapolis Pioneer Building, provided Stassen with office space upon his discharge from the Navy until the presidential campaign opened its own office in the Pillsbury Building. Bernhard LeVander served simultaneously as chair of both the state party and the Stassen campaign. He insisted at the time that all state party activities for Stassen were undertaken on the authority of the annual state Republican conventions, which instructed that all necessary steps be taken to assure the nomination and election of Harold Stassen as president.[37]

Nonetheless, these state conventions arrived at their expressions of support through the careful choreography of party leaders, including LeVander. On February 26, 1946, for example, LeVander wrote Warren Burger about an upcoming state GOP convention. He reported that he and his associates had drafted a resolution commending the state's congressional delegation and the two members to the U.S. Senate. He then nonchalantly asked, "Shall we have a good strong resolution endorsing Harold referring to recent gains in the support of the people, etc.? It seems to me that this is desirable. Who shall we assign to draft such a resolution...? Do you think we should save it for the state convention, or should we begin some crude forms of it out in the district conventions?"[38]

In early 1947 LeVander, perhaps feeling a bit sensitive about the state GOP/Stassen connection, noted that only one item of literature promoting Stassen for president had been issued by the Republican State Committee, and it had been "financed by state contributions."[39] Yet the literature to which he referred, *The Man America Needs*, an elaborate booklet replete with photos of Stassen with everyone from Admiral Halsey to Stassen's parents, does not contain any disclaimer about financing. Nor does LeVander mention who provided the contributions.[40]

Irrespective of how *The Man America Needs* was financed, the state GOP clearly spent a great deal of money indirectly to promote Harold Stassen. The party brochure *Minnesota Marches On*, which was issued as Stassen entered the Navy, was ostensibly material boosting Ed Thye, the newly seated governor; yet the pamphlet prominently featured Stassen, including a section entitled "Looking Ahead to Making the Peace," which discussed the erstwhile governor's foreign policy.[41]

When the presidential campaign began in earnest, LeVander and state party co-chair Rose Spencer sent to state GOP leaders nationwide letters, not directly promoting Stassen but obviously intended to have that effect. One letter, dated February 19, 1947, noted Stassen's rise in the Gallup polls, and asked innocently, "We would be glad to get your reaction to political trends in your state."[42] Some letters, written by others, were a cruder pitch for support. Margaret Andrews, secretary of the state party, sent a letter on official stationery to Republican women in Oregon six days prior to the crucial primary in that state. The letter listed "reasons why I believe Harold Stassen is the man who can be elected President of the United States."[43]

Such a symbiotic relationship between the Stassen campaign and the state GOP, which controlled the Minnesota government, carried with it obvious dangers that accusations, whether well founded or not, of conflict of interest would be raised. Given the precarious situation, the campaign and state party conducted itself with a high degree of probity and was remarkably free of controversy.

Curious developments did occur on at least one, and perhaps two, occasions. On July 25, 1947, Clear Dethmers, director of Rough Fish Removal in Minnesota, was dismissed from state employment by the state conservation commissioner at the request of Luther Youngdahl, who by then had been elected governor and was serving as honorary cochair of the Stassen for President Volunteers. Dethmers, Youngdahl said, had acted illegally as a state employee under the civil service in soliciting and receiving political funds. According to Youngdahl, "The funds sought were for use of the Minnesota Stassen-for-President Committee." LeVander told reporters that day that the checks received by the campaign had been returned.[44] Indeed, LeVander had in fact taken action to return the money, although the checks were not actually returned at that point. Rather, LeVander had written to the contributors asking whether they wished to have their checks returned to them. As of July 30, five days later, none of the four contributors had responded, and LeVander sent them another note: "We regret that we have received no reply to our letter to you of July 25.... Accordingly, we feel constrained at this time to return your contribution."[45]

The matter was quickly forgotten by the press. The illegality of a state employee soliciting political funds was made more serious by the fact that it was for a candidate supported by the party in control of the state government; yet the prompt action of Youngdahl and LeVander clearly places them above suspicion, and the incident appears to have been nothing more than a misunderstanding inevitable in such a volatile situation.

A second development in the case which was not reported in the press arouses interest. At the time of his dismissal, Dethmers was said to have accepted the decision with equanimity, praising Youngdahl for his competence and integrity. Yet on August 27 Cliff Benson, an Ortonvill attorney, wrote LeVander: "At your convenience I would appreciate it if you would write me just what the situation is in reference to the dismissal of Clear Dethmers. Some friends of his have recently contacted me and other people out here, and have felt that something should be done for him. From the outside appearance it looks to me like he got a pretty raw deal. Anything you tell me will be kept in strict confidence." On September 2 LeVander responded: "This matter is long and involved, so I would prefer to discuss it orally with you rather than attempt to set it down in a letter." On October 4, LeVander received a telegram from a Harry Kluntz, whose relationship to the campaign is unclear. "I sure wish," the telegram stated succinctly, "you would take care of Clear Dethmers and right soon."[46]

It would be irresponsible to suggest improper behavior by anyone involved at a high level in the Stassen campaign, for there is no evidence to support the accusation and a great deal to suggest deep personal integrity on the part of the Stassen team. The contributions involved in the Dethmers case were ridiculously small, three for one hundred dollars and one for fifty dollars, and, in any case, as successful as the campaign was in soliciting funds the leadership must have known they could never match the financial muscle of Robert Taft and Thomas Dewey. Further, there is no hint of any other scandal throughout the campaign, despite hysterical and undocumented charges during the Ohio campaign by supporters of Taft, who accused Stassen of trying to "buy" the nomination — a curious accusation, given the fact that Stassen's expenditures in the state primaries were far below those of both Taft and Dewey. Yet it is quite possible that the press could have tormented the Minnesotan with distracting questions about his finances. Despite honorable conduct by the Stassen army, its closeness with the state party in Minnesota, and thus its government, was a potentially dangerous relationship.

Funds for the campaign came from one of two channels, either the mail solicitation of the Stassen for President Volunteers, or the Minnesota Fund, headed by Alfred Lindley. The Volunteers' effort was aimed at small contributors, with a limit on contributions set at one thousand dollars, while Lindley concentrated on larger sums. Lindley's success is clear in a revealing letter by Daniel Gainey to a friend and Stassen supporter in Philadelphia, "The leaders and top executives," he wrote, "of such notable firms as the following are all out for Stassen and his cause. The General Mills crowd, M & O Paper Company, Minnesota Mining and Manufacturing, Minneapolis Honeywell, all of the big banks, all of the owners of the big newspapers; such big stores as Daytons and Donaldsons, the owners and operators of all the big insurance companies here ... and so on down the line."[47]

Despite this support the massive campaign never had the resources that it felt it needed. For example, LeVander noted that an important effort in rounding up delegates involved sending "field men" to the various states which chose delegates by convention rather than primary election, which included a vast majority of states. These field men attempted to build bridges to delegates in an attempt to make them favorable to the Stassen camp. "We never had the personnel to go to all the states," LeVander recalled. "Since they were volunteers, we weren't paying them anything."[48]

Though the Stassen strategy centered on building up a clamor for the former governor at the local level, his support was by no means limited to the grassroots. An unusual Gallup poll conducted in the summer of 1946 asked individuals listed in *Who's Who* how they ranked possible presidential aspirants. A careful cross section of men and women in the publication was taken to cover the professions, labor and business. The results showed Stassen the runaway favorite of these prominent individuals with 48 percent and Thomas Dewey a distant second with 15 percent.[49]

Yet the Minnesotan's support would always center on Main Street. Largely this was due to the creative strategy of generating a popular demand for Stassen; but more important was the vigorous action of the indefatigable candidate himself. As a prelude to what was to follow after the presidential season formally opened with the New Hampshire primary, two spurts of activity on Stassen's part in 1946 and 1947 demonstrated his tireless penchant for campaigning.

The first burst began with his announcement of candidacy on December 17, 1946. Days later he held a widely covered press conference criticizing the president's budget proposal. He received more national attention on January 23 when he participated in *Town Hall Meeting of the Air* from High Point, North Carolina, after which he met with Republican leaders from all over the state at a luncheon.

Next was an address at the annual Kansas Day Celebration sponsored by the Republican Party of Kansas at Topeka on January 29, where Stassen was introduced by the already venerable Alfred Landon, the 1936 nominee. February 5 found him in Dayton, Ohio, where he spoke twice at National Cash Register; once before an audience of NCR executives and guests of the president of the company, and then before an assembly of 2,600 of NCR's employees. That evening he addressed the Annual Community Fund Dinner of Dayton, which typically had a turnout of two hundred fifty but on that night had a sellout crowd of eight hundred.

Two days later, he was in Washington, D.C., testifying before the Senate Committee on Labor and Public Welfare on what was to become the Taft-Hartley law; Stassen's opinions on the law were to be of signal importance in the Ohio primary.[50] From the nation's political center he hurried to its financial center, and Dewey stronghold, to give the Lincoln Day address before the National Republican Club at the Waldorf-Astoria Hotel in New York City, which was carried nationwide on radio, newsreel and television. He then flew to Arizona, Montana and California to meet with Republicans and scout out political alliances.[51]

While the campaign swing demonstrated the endurance of Stassen and his linebacker's build — his weight was now a sturdy two hundred thirty pounds — the trip was not gaffe free. Lief Gilstad, editor of the *Minnesota Letter*, published a quotation found in a Phoenix newspaper attributed to Arizona Republican National committeeman Clarence Budington Kelland: "If the Republicans should choose Harold Stassen to be our standard-bearer, I will be a very happy man." Unhappily, Gilstad had not checked the quotation's accuracy, and Kelland fired off a sizzling letter of his own to the editor. "My experience in Arizona," he snarled, "with Stassen's friends is that if he ever hopes to become a presidential nominee, his first step must be to muffle, stifle or exterminate them. They are inept, inexperienced, and politically smashing Stassen's china with club feet." Gilstad probably did not greatly assuage Kelland when he wrote to him proposing to retract the quote, but offering no apology.[52]

Still, the candidate's peripatetic efforts were rewarded in a subsequent Gallup poll showing his presidential stock rising while Dewey's slumped.[53]

On February 22 Stassen embarked on a nine-week world tour culminating in a chat with Joseph Stalin, thus establishing what would become a sine qua non of presidential candidates — that they show their worldliness by mingling with the Communists they denounced on the hustings. It was an exhausting eighteen-country tour.

In Paris he met with foreign minister Georges Bidault, Premier Paul Ramadier, President Vincent Aurial, and Communist labor boss Benoit Frachon before touring a Renault factory and a textile plant. He then investigated the black market in Italy, spoke with Jan Masaryk in Czechoslovakia, and Prime Minister Clement Attlee in England prior to traveling to the Soviet Union.[54] Stassen's interview with Stalin gave the candidate the opportunity to demonstrate the "toughness" dear to American hardliners, while his very presence in the Kremlin hinted a willingness to negotiate beloved by liberals.

As Matteson pointed out, the high point of the trip was meeting with Stalin. Historian and Soviet studies scholar Gaurrel D. Ra'anan described the Stassen-Stalin meeting: "Perhaps the most significant among Stalin's public pronouncements during this period ... was the interview he granted to the Republican presidential aspirant Harold Stassen, on April 9, 1947."[55] Stassen was to meet Stalin at 11:00 P.M. He was joined by Cooke and Matteson. Stassen wrote:

> Stalin moved out from behind his desk and came across the room to meet us. He is chunkier than I had expected, and his hair is thinner and grayer than his pictures indicate. His plain khaki uniform with a single decoration — the Medal of the Hero of Socialist Labor, a small gold star hung on a red ribbon — fitted him loosely across his chest, as if he had recently lost weight. But his step was quick, his eyes alert, his handshake firm. Molotov was immediately behind him, and he introduced us.
>   The place looked like any other board room — about 35 by 20 feet, carpeted floors, modern furniture, and indirect lighting; pictures of Lenin at a desk and of Lenin speaking, and of Marx

and Engels and—curiously enough—oils of Field Marshals Suvorov and Kutuzov, heroes of war against Napoleon and the Turks. A long conference table stood at the left, with leader chairs for the fourteen members of the Politburo.[56]

Joseph Stalin's chief question to me, during our meeting, concerned our American economy. Other members of the all-powerful Politburo with whom I talked in Russia inquired also as to its postwar health and its prospects for the future.

Stalin leaned across the table, looked at me between somewhat narrowed eyelids, and spoke his question in Russian. His pale, slight, nervous interpreter, Pavlov, sitting between us, quickly relayed the question in English.

"Do you expect an economic crisis in America?" Stalin had asked.[57]

Stalin wanted to talk economics. Their discussion did not signify a major shift in the relations between the United States and the Soviet Union. It did provide Stassen with the opportunity to buttress his foreign policy credentials by meeting and engaging in conversation with Stalin. (On May 8, 1947, a "Protocol of the Interview" was published in *Pravda*. For Stassen it truly was the most important moment of his European journey.) Anxious to prove his mettle, the former governor confronted Stalin with his past comments that capitalism and communism could not exist in harmony, and Stalin denied making the statements. The two went on to discuss methods of avoiding world depression.[58]

As it happened, Stassen's interview coincided with the Moscow Conference, and thirty-five special correspondents from the United States were then in Moscow. The *New York Herald Tribune*, however, had not been allowed to send a correspondent to the Soviet capital and Stassen innocently asked Stalin why this was so. After a brief conference with Molotov, Stalin reportedly responded, "A part of the American correspondents have an ill mood toward us. But this *Herald Tribune* case is an accident. It is an outstanding newspaper." The reporter's accreditation came two days later. A reporter from a rival U.S. paper wryly asked the Minnesotan, "Are you on the *Herald Tribune* payroll?" Stassen explained that he had happened to run into Geoffrey Parson, Jr., editor of the Paris edition of the paper, who had told him of the *Tribune*'s problem.[59] Stassen would not be the last presidential candidate to curry favor with the media.

Returning to the United States, Stassen kept up a steady schedule of public appearances through November 11, when he began a second burst of activity, that continued virtually without respite until after the Republican National Convention in June 1948. The occasion was the publication of his book *Where I Stand*, in which he discussed his views on foreign and domestic issues. In a chartered plane replete with correspondents, he made campaign appearances in Colorado, Arkansas, Louisiana, Florida, and finally Chicago before November 22. Two days later he was in Milwaukee for a rally intended to mark the official opening of his campaign.[60]

The close of 1947 saw the Stassen for President campaign in full swing at the grassroots long before any of the other White House aspirants had bestirred themselves from their smoke-filled rooms. The other candidates were concerned principally with winning over party leaders who controlled state delegations; the Stassen strategy, in contrast, envisioned a public demand for a Stassen nomination that would-be kingmakers would be unable to resist. The centerpiece of the strategy was a dynamic, winning performance in the state primaries. His campaign structure in place, Stassen left for New Hampshire.

5. The Ascendancy: New Hampshire

Having completed the required homework, Stassen launched his campaign for the presidential nomination. Impervious to the rightward political tilt of the postwar era, Stassen charged, uphill, to the left, gathering in his wake a movement of rank-and-file Republicans blithely dismissing the national Zeitgeist and seeking to yank their party into modern-day nationalism.

Coming as it did in a period of political conservatism, there is an air of the mysterious in the movement, like a river flowing from an unseen source. The political waters in January 1948 were, as yet, unstirred; within three months they would reach a veritable flood tide of support for the Minnesotan before quickly ebbing. To force into focus this brief parting of the political sea, we begin where Stassen did, with the New Hampshire primary of March 9, 1948.

Stassen's strategy in New Hampshire was not markedly different from his efforts in the following primaries in Wisconsin, Nebraska, and Oregon. As in those later contests, he waged a highly personal campaign at the local level, largely bypassing party leaders; yet he never developed in the Granite State the large devoted following that would appear for him elsewhere in the country.

As a midwesterner, Stassen was too unknown and his opponent, Thomas E. Dewey, from New York, too well-recognized for Stassen's tactics to fully succeed. Absent a core of enthusiastic volunteers, there was no way for Stassen to overcome the opposition of state party leaders. Still, New Hampshire must be counted as a victory for Stassen, for despite the disadvantages of being unknown by the rank-and-file and opposed by the GOP leadership, he nevertheless managed a credible showing in the state's primary. It was, in the tiny New England state, a well-performed prelude to the thunderous symphony the campaign would perform in the Midwest.

On January 7, as Stassen opened his eastern office under the charge of future ambassador Amos Peaslee, he presented an optimistic face to the press about his chances for the Republican nomination. "We have moved into first place in several polls in the Middle West where we are known best," he beamed. Perhaps, but the tiny eastern seaboard state of New Hampshire had little truck with the Midwest. On that same day, the Republican Party leader in New Hampshire, state senator Joseph H. Geisel, announced to the press that within three days he would lead a group of prominent state Republicans in issuing a call to draft Dwight Eisenhower for president.[1]

Under the state's arcane presidential primary system, men and women who wished to cast votes at the national convention of their party ran for delegate, plunking down a ten-dollar filing fee, declaring whom they would support at the convention (they could also run as "uncommitted" or "favorable to"), and campaigning for election. If victorious, on the first ballot the delegate was required to vote for the candidate, if any, to whom he was pledged. Each presidential candidate hoped that his delegates would defeat the delegates pledged to other White House aspirants. The presidential candidate who emerged from the most primaries with the most delegates would inevitably be declared the "winner" by the press and pundits.

In a highly unusual move, Stassen announced that he would release his delegates from their obligation to vote for him at the convention, so that they would be free to consider supporting another candidate should they see fit. Indeed, he did not even wish his delegate candidates to run "pledged" to him, preferring that they run as "favorable to." This was a policy the former governor would maintain throughout the primary season. Stassen later insisted that it was a matter of principle to him that delegates be given a choice, "It's part of my philosophy of an open Republican party," he explained.[2]

The sum total of Republican delegates from New Hampshire was exactly eight. Minuscule though the state's delegation was, an "at least respectable showing" for any candidate participating in the primary was deemed imperative. Then, as now, the state was perceived as a bellwether proclaiming who was hot long before any perceptible change in the political climate was noticeable nationwide. Accordingly, Harold Stassen went to New Hampshire seeking a ringing endorsement of his prospects.

As the filing period for delegate candidates opened on January 9, Stassen's campaign did not sound particularly healthy. When secretary of state Enoch Fuller opened his office door to filing delegate hopefuls, he was almost flattened by a surge of Eisenhower supporters. By the end of the day, Fuller had filed seven delegates for the general and two for Thomas Dewey. Stassen had one delegate candidate pledged to him, state senator Earl S. Hewitt, who was also a well-known newspaper publisher, of Hanover, and one candidate who listed himself as "favorable to Stassen."[3]

The next day still another delegate-aspirant filed as pledged to Eisenhower, causing Republican U.S. senator Charles Tobey to reflect happily that nobody could stop a campaign to line up all eight of New Hampshire's delegation for Ike, "not even the general himself."[4]

Nevertheless, the hearts of Dewey and Stassen supporters must have leaped when they beheld the January 12 issue of the *Concord Daily Monitor,* which reported that Eisenhower would soon make a statement on his intentions, perhaps withdrawing from the race. Taft made no effort in New Hampshire as he concentrated on winning over party leaders. The next day Ike issued a statement through Gen. Floyd L. Parks, head of the public information division of the Army, saying that he would "make no statement with regard to the New Hampshire primary," which was good enough for his supporters. Charles W. Tobey, Jr., son of the U.S. senator, chirped that the announcement "is gratifying to those of us who are most anxious to give the people an opportunity to express their preference at the polls."[5]

Undaunted, the *Hanover Gazette,* published by Stassen delegate candidate Earl Hewitt, went ahead and announced that "reports from Washington are that General Eisenhower is pretty peeved over the situation in New Hampshire.... [He] is said to really feel that a man who has been occupied with military affairs as long as he has, and out of civilian life, has no place in the White House."[6]

Stassen of course agreed, and announced that he would tell where he stood on national issues in a January 27 speech in Concord before the New Hampshire Federation of Young Republicans. It would be his second recent appearance in the state, having addressed a meeting of the New Hampshire and Massachusetts Weekly Publishers at Hampton Beach the previous September. He also declared that he expected to have a full slate of delegates running in the election, despite the fact that at the moment he only had one pledged and one favorable to his credit.[7]

His urgency may have been brought on by the fact that Thomas E. Dewey had just formally declared his candidacy for the presidency and promised a vigorous campaign in New Hampshire.[8] The announcement took most political observers by surprise; it had been expected that Dewey would more closely follow the tradition of appearing to be sought after for the office. The shift in strategy was viewed as a reflection of the power of the Eisenhower movement and the feeling of the New York governor's advisors that he would have to become an avowed candidate in order to have a prayer against the popular general.[9]

It would be the third presidential effort by the forty-six year old New York politician and the second time he would openly and vigorously, but this time, not too vigorously, seek the Republican nomination. In 1940 Dewey had embarked on a whirlwind tour of Wisconsin, while Senator Arthur Vandenburg of Michigan, his chief competitor for the Republican presidential nomination, remained in Washington, solemnly citing his senatorial duties. Dewey thus decisively did to Vandenburg in Wisconsin what Stassen would do to Dewey in 1948, blow away the competition with a personal hands-on campaign before the state's primary voters. At the 1940 convention, Dewey led on the first ballot before being overtaken on subsequent ballots by Wendell Willkie.[10]

Like Stassen, Dewey's career sprouted early, yet never reached full blossom. Born on March 24, 1902, in Owosso, Michigan, he graduated from the University of Michigan in 1923 and Columbia University Law School in 1925. His meteoric career began after an inauspicious debut — he was fired from his first job as a researcher for a New York law firm. Quickly hired by lawyer George Medalie, Dewey became Medalie's chief assistant when Medalie was appointed U.S. attorney for the Southern District of New York. Shortly before the trial of a prominent mobster and bootlegger, Waxey Gordon, Medalie resigned. Dewey had been so active in the preparation of the trial that there was no alternative but to appoint him acting U.S. attorney. The fame Dewey earned in the subsequent victory over the mobster led to his appointment as a special prosecutor in New York City.

In 1937, after a brief stint in a law firm associated with John Foster Dulles, Dewey was elected New York City district attorney. He lost his first gubernatorial bid in 1938, but came close enough to win the respect of national Republicans, and he was on his way.[11]

The New Yorker was not the only candidate unnerved by Eisenhower; the Stassen campaign in mid–January 1948 was busily trying to induce the Dewey for President forces to join with them in convincing New Hampshire U.S. senator Styles Bridges to become a favorite-son candidate for president, with the obvious hope that a Bridges slate, empowered by New Hampshire native pride, would defer any show of strength by the Eisenhower forces until the campaign moved to Wisconsin. There, in the Midwest, Stassen could fight on familiar terrain and with better odds. Operating on the same logistical logic, Dewey refused, preferring to make his stand in the East.[12]

Resignedly circling the wagons, Stassen announced on January 19 that John W. Guider, former Washington lawyer, had been named chairman of the New Hampshire Stassen for President Committee. Guider was a graduate of the U.S. Naval Academy and had served, like Stassen, in the Navy during World War II. Exuding confidence, he told reporters that James P. Lynch, editor of the weekly *Exeter News Letter* would handle publicity.[13]

The three-cornered contest between Dewey, Eisenhower and Stassen split state Republicans. Although Eisenhower remained the clear front runner — by late January he was still the only contestant with a full slate of delegate candidates — it began to appear that even Ike would not carry an unambiguous stamp of approval from the primary.

Frank Sulloway, the Republican national committeeman, mused that "there is much indecision and conjecture ... and no apparent unity in the Republican high command as to what ... should be done."[14] Eisenhower did, however, and on January 23 bluntly stated, "I am not available for and would not accept nomination to high political office."[15] General Sherman himself would have been pressed to be more specific.

In a letter to Leonard V. Finder, publisher of the *Manchester Union-Leader*, Eisenhower gave two reasons he had previously "refrained from making the bald expression: it would smack of effrontery and," the second and deeper reason, there was a "persistent doubt that I could phrase a refusal without appearing to violate that concept of duty to country which calls upon every good citizen to place no limitations upon his readiness to serve in any designated capacity." Ike resolved this dilemma by reasoning that "unless an individual feels some inner compulsion and special qualifications to enter the political arena — which I do not — a refusal to do so involved no violation of the highest standards of devotion to duty."[16]

The stunned New Hampshire Eisenhower supporters generally refused immediate comment to the press on the decision, although Senator Tobey revealed the linguistic sensitivity of a contract lawyer by noting that though Ike had stated he "would" not accept the nomination, he did not say he "could" not. Stassen, in Washington, D.C., also refused comment, although Senator Joseph McCarthy, a Stassen supporter, called the statement "grand" and Senator Ed Thye claimed to have expected it all along.[17]

The general's withdrawal caused shock waves that reverberated far beyond the small eastern seaboard state. Eisenhower, according to a Roper poll published by *Fortune* magazine, had been the leading contender for the nomination, and *the only Republican candidate who would be favored over President Truman if the race were held immediately*. Roper later changed his mind and favored Dewey over Truman; 1948 was not a good year for pollsters.

National Republican leaders began to envision a convention hopelessly deadlocked between Dewey and Taft. Significantly, for his political philosophy was a close replica of Stassen's, the presidential stock of Senator Arthur Vandenberg skyrocketed. Vandenberg had stated repeatedly that he was not a candidate; but his observation that he would have no choice but to serve if drafted made some party leaders salivate. Nonsense, Vandenberg snorted, nobody ever gets nominated unless he connives for it, and in 1948 Vandenberg was not in a conniving mood.[18]

Nine of the eleven candidates pledged to Eisenhower announced that they would withdraw, while the remaining two stubbornly clung to their candidate. With this competition out of the way, hundreds of potential or actual Stassen supporters converged in Concord on January 26 to hear and see the former Minnesota governor in person; indeed his schedule seemed designed to insure that he would be able to meet every resident of the state.

Stassen addressed the Exchange Club in Manchester before hurrying to Concord for a 4:00 P.M. courtesy call on the governor. After an hour's meeting with the state's chief executive, he held a reception for the general public before going to the home of Republican National committeeman Frank Sulloway, where he and Governor Dale were dinner guests.

The next day Stassen held a reception in Exeter, followed by a luncheon with the town's Lions and Kiwanis clubs and its chamber of commerce as sponsors. That afternoon he toured the Exeter Manufacturing Company and held yet another reception at the University of New Hampshire in Durham before addressing the student body that night in a speech sponsored by the New Hampshire Federation of Young Republicans.[19]

The timing of the Stassen tour could not have been more propitious, coming as it did at a time when erstwhile Eisenhower activists were searching for a new champion. The Minnesotan "will probably get the bulk of the Eisenhower supporters," publisher Leonard V. Finder of the *Manchester Evening Leader* predicted.[20]

Actually, Eisenhower supporters appear to have simply vanished, although Stassen was greeted in his campaign swing with new pledges of support, among them a former governor, Huntley N. Spaulding. Spaulding explained that after voting for Dewey as a delegate at the 1944 Republican National Convention, he quickly lost confidence in the New York governor during the ensuing campaign. Dewey "did not come out for a single principle of government," Spaulding complained. "Instead, he dealt in generalities and tried to out-do the Democrats in making promises to the voters."[21]

The Minnesotan's performance at the municipal auditorium in Concord was vintage Stassen. In what was to become typical of his appearances, he limited his speaking to only twenty minutes before submitting to nearly an hour of give-and-take from the audience. Not altering his stump speech in the conservative state, he called for broad new government-sponsored programs for construction of at least one million homes a year and a new system of "economic insurance for workers to meet unexpected debts arising from sickness, accidents, etc., of more than $250 a year per family."[22]

After the question and answer period ended, Stassen dashed to the exit to shake hands and thank members of the audience for their attendance. When the crowd had filed out, he was approached by two of his candidates for delegate, state senator Earl Hewitt and Concord executive councilor Donald G. Matson, who had recently announced his support for the Minnesotan. Stassen posed for a picture with Matson, but to the surprise of onlookers, he refused to pose with Senator Hewitt.

Soon afterward, at a press conference at the Eagle Hotel in Concord, Stassen reiterated his previous announcement that he would not support any pledged-to-Stassen candidates, and that his state campaign chairman, John Guider, would announce the names of the unpledged candidates the presidential aspirant wanted to represent him in the primary.[23]

Hewitt, running as a pledged-to-Stassen delegate and present at the press conference, looked horrified and quickly asked where he stood. "Well," Stassen replied, "I'd like to talk with you." It is unknown what transpired during the conversation, but an hour later Hewitt told reporters that he would stick to his guns and continue to run as a "pledged." "I honestly feel that Mr. Stassen is making a mistake," Senator Hewitt explained, "but I cannot make him see it. I have felt all along that the time has come when New Hampshire voters want a chance to directly register their choice for president. My pledged candidacy provides that opportunity. I consider it a duty to the voters to continue my pledged position." Guider, for his part, observed that Stassen since the previous November had made clear his preference for unpledged candidates, reminding primary voters and candidates that "legal commitments under the New Hampshire statute will not be requested, so that the delegation will in fact be free to use their own judgment in the national convention and will not be irrevocably committed." Stassen added that he desired to keep his support centered on his "official" slate of eight delegates in order to avoid a dilution of strength, and for that reason found it necessary to repudiate some candidates.[24] If there was any political fallout from the delegate controversy, it was not noted by the press, and Stassen seemed untroubled when he departed the next day for a political tour in Maine.

His last action in New Hampshire was to issue the first of what was destined to become many futile challenges to Dewey to a debate on foreign and domestic issues. With the swagger of a western cowboy, Stassen told reporters he would meet with the New York governor at any time and any place, the only condition being that the debate be under "impartial sponsorship." Noting that Dewey had recently entered the Oregon primary, Stassen speculated that the New Yorker might now "change his tactics" and discuss issues.[25]

Dewey's tactics were markedly different from Stassen's and would remain so through the campaign, at least until the Oregon primary in May. In New Hampshire, Dewey, unlike Stassen, made no effort to repudiate any supporter; neither, however, did he endorse or campaign for any delegate-hopeful.[26] Thus, with Eisenhower out of the race, Dewey remained an active candidate almost in name only; until the end of the primary season he never approached Stassen's level of involvement. Indeed, after the nomination he would become almost indifferent to the campaign.

While Stassen — and, in the general election, Truman — would constantly strive to make themselves the center of attention, Dewey seemed to be content to be, as James David Barber later wrote, "the blandest news source since Millard Fillmore."[27] Bland or not, the Dewey forces were on the move. On February 4, they received a fresh impetus as it was announced that Governor Charles Dale of New Hampshire, a candidate for delegate-at-large, would support the New York governor.

This was grave news for Stassen supporters, since their opposition could now boast of four high profile delegate candidates. The others included Republican state committeeman Robert W. Upton, ex-governor Robert O. Blood, and Congressman Charles Holden. The Stassen campaign was not without good news. Former congressman Foster Stearns of Hancock announced that he would file for delegate-at-large unpledged but favorable to the Minnesota former governor: "Eight years of personal acquaintance with Harold Stassen have convinced me that he offers ... leadership."[28]

Yet New Hampshire voters were demonstrating increasing skepticism about Stassen, as momentum appeared to be building steadily for Thomas Dewey. Herbert Brownell, a Dewey supporter and former chairman of the Republican National Committee, stumped the state for the governor, declaring that "there is every indication that Mr. Dewey will carry New Hampshire by an overwhelming majority."

Certainly if the contest centered on who could corral the most prominent Republicans of the state, there would have been little contest. Political experts noted that the turnout at a dinner at which Brownell spoke for Dewey looked hauntingly like an official convention of New Hampshire's Republican Party. Among those at the dinner who gave testimonials of their faith in the New Yorker were state representative Joseph Geisel, the erstwhile president of the state's ill-fated "Draft Eisenhower" club, and house speaker J. Walker Wiggin of Manchester, who took the occasion to announce that he would file as an unpledged Dewey delegate-at-large. State luminaries in the Dewey camp thus included the governor, the vice chairman and one member of the state GOP committee, the speaker of the state house of representatives, and more than forty county, city and town Republican Party committee officials.[29]

On February 10, the filing deadline for delegate candidates arrived, and the Dewey campaign took the opportunity to streamline their forces. Four Dewey candidates withdrew entirely, reducing to one the number of races that would pit members of the New Yorker's political family against each other, thus guarding against a split in his support. This maneuvering was not required of the Stassen forces, which met the deadline with exactly eight candidates for the eight seats, this including Republican National Committee member Frank Sulloway, who did not make any public declaration of loyalty to Stassen or anyone else, but who was still "claimed" by the Minnesotan's campaign.[30]

For two reasons it still appeared that Stassen had jockeyed himself into a surprisingly good starting position in the delegate race, especially considering the support among GOP leaders for Dewey. First, Stassen succeeded in preventing any competition from arising within the ranks of his supporters. With last minute corrections, the Dewey forces reduced much of their division, but not all, as in the first congressional district three Dewey candidates would compete for two available seats. Second, the Stassen campaign did a remarkably good job of "spin control" after the repeated snub to Earl Hewitt. Hewitt refused to criticize Stassen, and the issue immediately disappeared from the press. As the primary campaign entered the home stretch, Stassen seemed to be in good form.[31]

The final month of the New Hampshire campaign brought into sharp relief differences in strategy between the two camps which would remain for much of the primary season. Dewey ran as if he were the nominee already, expressing dismay at the Truman administration for a vague foreign policy and an inflationary domestic policy. Stassen, meanwhile, ran as if he were running for state representative, greeting voters and speaking to local issues. On February 26, announcing to the press Stassen's plan to return to the state for a three-day tour beginning March 2, campaign chairman John Guider asserted that "this whirlwind tour will wind up the most intensive bid for voters ever made in New Hampshire by a presidential candidate."[32]

While self-serving, Guider's comment would not have been rejected by political experts in the Granite State. Leon Anderson, a reporter for the *Concord Daily Monitor*, called it "the most unusual presidential primary campaign in New Hampshire history." Its uniqueness stemmed from the intense campaign being waged by both candidates. "Supporters of Governor Dewey ... prepared an avalanche of ten thousand pieces of mailed literature to be descended upon the New Hampshire populace early next week," he wrote. Meanwhile, the "whirlwind Stassen tour, which will include both day and night speeches and public receptions in seven cities and larger towns, is frankly a 'do-or-die' daring last-minute attempt to win at least some of the eight seats."[33]

A sharper dichotomy was noticed by the *Portsmouth Herald*, which supported the candidate from Minnesota: "Mr. Stassen approaches the presidency with no sign of old-line party affiliation.... He was frank in his opinions, engaging in his manner, and he made no abject bows to the powerful state Republican machine.... Dewey, on the other hand, rode into our state on a well-oiled machine created to grind out votes and pass out political appointments."[34] Accurate or not, this was precisely the image the Stassen campaign sought to convey. With one week to go, the Minnesotan began his final swing in New Hampshire.

The tour suffered an inauspicious start: poor weather and his daughter's cold forced a one-day delay in his travel plans. When he arrived he was greeted by an editorial in the *Manchester Morning Union* pointing to recent Gallup polls which showed the likelihood of a Republican victory in November. "This placed a grave responsibility on American voters in the Republican primaries," it said as it promptly endorsed Dewey.[35]

In New York the governor, clearly enjoying himself, hinted to reporters that his campaign would in April, the month of the crucial Wisconsin and Nebraska primaries, shift from the current "passive" stage to one of aggressive action. The governor added that adjournment of the New York legislature, scheduled for mid–March, would permit him to take advantage of "some of the many requests for personal appearances outside the state."[36] In other words, Dewey was too busy to go to New Hampshire and campaign.

Not having that problem, Stassen arrived in Littleton, New Hampshire, at 2:00 P.M. on March 3, in a thick snowstorm. There he met with four of his delegate candidates and with John Guider before hurrying off to a much delayed luncheon at the local Rotary Club. Next he held a press conference, then went to the town of Berlin for a major address.

Before a packed auditorium, he said that while asking New Hampshire voters to cast their ballots for delegates who had been given the blessing of the Stassen for President state committee, he would make no attempt to "control" the delegates if they were elected. "These candidates are not a group of pledged delegates. I do not have, and I will not seek or accept any control over them," he said. "They will be free to exercise their own good judgment at the Republican national convention ... as to candidates, as to platform and as to party leadership."[37]

The next morning Stassen spoke to an overflow crowd (loudspeakers were set up outside) at Dartmouth College, where he called for establishing a United Nations force in the Middle East to keep the peace. "It would be definitely wrong," he said, "if this country did anything alone."[38] While he spoke, Henry A. Atwood, president of the First National Bank of Minneapolis in Minnesota, was writing several thousand letters to Dartmouth College alumni, urging them to support Stassen. The letter contained a statement by Ernest M. Hopkins, president-emeritus of Dartmouth: "Governor Stassen's candidacy carries a greater appeal to me and more persuasion that I find in any of the others being prominently mentioned for the nomination.... His record of accomplishment is a satisfying one. He has youth, character, personality, and proved capability.... I hope he may be nominated."[39] After the speech the incumbent Dartmouth president, John Sloan Dickey, invited Stassen and five of his delegate candidates to lunch, after which the Minnesotan dashed to Keene, New Hampshire, to give an address in a local high school auditorium. Following an appearance in Nashua late in the evening, he reached Lowell, Massachusetts, at midnight, where he caught a train for New York. By the next afternoon he was in Milwaukee, Wisconsin, addressing a luncheon group.[40]

As he departed for Lowell, Stassen expressed satisfaction with his campaign swing, confident of "success" in the delegate race, but refusing to predict how many of his supporters would be elected. He also said he regarded the New Hampshire vote an important test but believed the Wisconsin primary to be a better measure of candidate strength.[41]

Cynics might have regarded the comment as an effort by Stassen to hedge his bets, and surely that was a motive; yet the candidate's comment struck at an essential dilemma for the Stassen campaign in New Hampshire, a perplexity born of the state's presidential primary system. For it became increasingly apparent that the struggle centered not wholly, or even mostly, on the strength of the White House aspirant, but on the popularity of his delegate candidates. Later contests in Wisconsin, Nebraska, and Oregon would revolve around the vote-getting potential of the presidential hopeful, state personalities and political "machines" playing a peripheral role.

One on one, Stassen could compete successfully against the cool and detached New York governor, at least until Dewey became more like Stassen and less like a "man on a wedding cake," as Alice Roosevelt Longworth described him. On the East Coast in March, Stassen found himself in the ring not against a stuffy New York politician but against a whole constellation of popular New Hampshire politicos. On election day voters would be asked to vote for these prominent and respected local VIPs, or for lesser known Stassen candidates. The verdict about the popularity of Stassen and Dewey themselves was thus considerably muddled.

Stassen himself recognized the problem of "overcoming politically familiar names," but he perhaps underestimated the difficulty of the task. In retrospect, a rally held for Dewey on March 6 can be seen as symbolic of the political situation in the Granite State. In attendance were some of the leading political figures in the state, including the New Hampshire governor. Yet Thomas Dewey was not there, and nobody could shake his hand or challenge him with a difficult question and Dewey could not say anything controversial. It fell to Governor Dale to present an autographed photograph of Dewey to the oldest Springfield, New Hampshire, registered Republican, and to speak in general terms about Dewey and his record.[42] Dewey did not have to risk or bother with personal campaigning because of the high name recognition of his candidates for delegate.

Despite the prominence of the Dewey slate, the New Yorker's strategists were aware of the effect that personal campaigning could have. Robert Upton, vice-chairman of the Republican State Committee and Dewey delegate-hopeful, observed, "The situation is complicated by the personal appeals of the various candidates for delegates, but in spite of this I expect that Governor Dewey will win a decisive victory...." Conversely, strategists for Stassen were quite aware of the effect that a well-known slate of delegates could have. While Stassen state chairman John Guider predicted that up to five delegates would go to the Minnesotan, Stassen publicity man James Lynch delivered himself of a seven-to-one, for Dewey, prognostication.[43]

Less partisan political observers believed Stassen's three trips to New Hampshire and aggressive campaigning had put Dewey in a defensive position, and the New York governor needed to win at least six of the eight delegates in order to be able to claim victory; anything short of six would severely injure the campaign as it headed for the important Wisconsin primary. Ironically, in one respect the prominence of Dewey's slate hurt him, for it raised expectations and the feeling that if the New Yorker could not win with so prominent a backing, how could he expect to win the White House?[44]

The endorsement race turned bizarre twenty-four hours before the polls opened when Sherman Adams, unopposed candidate for the Republican gubernatorial nomination, endorsed John P. Carlton, a Stassen delegate, and Viola Adams, a candidate for alternate delegate for Dewey. "These two people are going to head up my election campaign next fall," he explained, "and I thought it would be nice if they could start off by winning tomorrow."[45]

Meanwhile, the Dewey forces were adopting the same tactic used by their candidate in Wisconsin in 1940, exaggerating the strength of their opponent and predicting impending doom for their man. In Wisconsin eight years earlier Dewey had predicted that he would finish second to Arthur Vandenberg, even though he had a private poll showing him with a significant lead. When Dewey won by a two-to-one margin, the surprise and publicity had given his candidacy a significant lift.[46] Now Dewey supporters were publicly saying that the best they could hope for would be four of the eight delegates and that anything more would be a "landslide."[47]

Of course, such a claim was preposterous, as unwittingly revealed the day before the election by Governor Dale in an interview with Roscoe Drummond, chief of the *Christian Science Monitor*'s Washington bureau, and a host of other reporters. In the interview, Dale predicted a victory margin of seven-to-one, with Republican National committeeman Frank Sulloway the only Stassen candidate to win.[48]

On election day a near record of over forty-seven thousand Republicans dutifully went to the polls. Almost immediately bad news for Stassen began to pour in; early returns threatened to make Governor Dale's prediction of a seven-to-one Dewey victory come true. In late reporting one of Stassen's delegates, William Saltonstall of Exeter, squeaked out a narrow victory over the Dewey delegate by a three hundred eighty-four vote margin out of almost fifteen thousand votes cast in that district. The only other Stassen victor was Foster Stearns, who edged out Frank Sulloway for one of the four at-large seats.[49]

Perhaps because of the pre-primary posturing, sentiment on the implications of the vote was mixed. In Wisconsin, where the crucial primary was less than a month away, the *Wisconsin State Journal*, which supported Stassen, called New Hampshire a "setback."[50] The national press was more charitable. According to the Associated Press Stassen "...kept himself in the thick of the race for the Republican nomination." The AP observed, "Politicians thus regarded the New England result as pretty much of a standoff. They turned their eyes westward for the next battle — Wisconsin's primary on April 4."[51]

New Englanders regarded the result, as the *Manchester Morning Union* stated, as "hardly encouraging to the former flag secretary to Admiral William 'Bull' Halsey," after his strenuous personal campaigning. Yet the paper also noted that few presidential aspirants had bothered to wage such a personal effort, and Stassen had to overcome the high name recognition of his opponent's delegates; thus, two delegates might now be regarded as a draw.[52]

For his part, Stassen seems to have accepted the outcome with equanimity. He made no overblown claims of victory, saying only that his showing was strong, and that the defeat had not affected his national campaign. His supporters were more enthusiastic. Senator Joseph McCarthy went so far as to predict that Dewey would withdraw from the rest of the primaries after the "squeaker in his own backyard."[53] For the moment, Stassen had to concentrate on avoiding a squeaker in his backyard of Wisconsin. For while the Stassen campaign was forgiven for receiving only two out of three delegates in the East, a decisive victory was needed in the Midwest.

Stassen's campaign in New Hampshire was in retrospect a grassroots campaign without the grassroots. Stassen had gone to the Granite State to cultivate broad contacts, but ultimately was too new a face on the East Coast to reap much of a political harvest. The political ground was rocky and the loyal following he attracted in other states never grew very impressively. The fertile plains of the Midwest were to be very different political territory, though.

Even as New Hampshire Republicans were going to the polls, bands of young people, farmers, veterans and others were coming together under the aegis of Citizens for Stassen. Their efforts, augmented by powerful political leaders in Wisconsin, presented Thomas Dewey with a bitter harvest on April 6.

6. The Ascendancy: Wisconsin

Like the universe in eastern philosophy, the political cosmos in Wisconsin seemed by 1948 to have a will of its own, dispensing victory and defeat while oblivious to the flailing of mortal politicians.

In 1940 Wisconsin had rewarded vigorous personal campaigning by a thirty-eight-year-old district attorney from New York with a dramatic victory over a prominent U.S. senator. Yet if Wendell Willkie saw in Thomas Dewey's victory over Arthur Vandenberg the message that all it took was intensive, personal campaigning, he was sorely mistaken. In 1944 Willkie staked all on an exhausting tour through the state, and was cruelly rejected, receiving not so much as a single delegate, while Dewey coasted to victory not even bestirring himself from the governor's chair in New York to which he had been elected in 1942. Impressed, in 1948 Dewey would use the same tactic.

Harold Stassen, however, was no ersatz Willkie. Avoiding the 1940 nominee's mistakes, Stassen built up a loyal and enthusiastic following at the grassroots level while not alienating the state party leadership. The candor with which Stassen spoke and the passion of his rigorous, hand-to-hand electoral fight made Dewey's absence glaring. Four years earlier Willkie had crisscrossed Wisconsin alienating party loyalists, Dewey, safe in the governor's mansion, appeared statesman-like. In 1948, however, he looked like he was hiding from combat.

Except for a brief moment in the spring when it appeared that a boom was developing for Dwight Eisenhower, Dewey in 1948 seems to have initially viewed presidential primaries as a nuisance and Harold Stassen as a pest buzzing around the primary states, to be swatted at the New Yorker's leisure. Less confident, however, were his advisers. Edwin F. Jaeckle, New York state GOP chairman and Dewey confidant, warned the governor that Douglas MacArthur and Stassen posed a major threat. Unmoved, Dewey voiced no objections as delegate candidates filed for election pledged to him.[1] The Wisconsin presidential primary of April 6, 1948, was, like the New Hampshire contest, an opportunity for voters to directly select delegates to the national convention of their party. At stake were two delegate seats in each congressional district and four at-large seats, for a total of twenty-seven.

Candidates for delegate secured petition signatures from registered voters, then filed with the secretary of state to appear on the ballot. Along with their names, a slogan of up to five words could appear, identifying the White House aspirant the delegate-hopeful supported, such as "Stassen for President," or "Dewey in '48." Unlike New Hampshire, there was no legal requirement in Wisconsin that delegates actually vote at the convention for the candidate they supported in the primary, thus relieving Stassen of the need to explain that he would not require delegate loyalty, although by custom delegates virtually always supported their candidate on at least the first few ballots.[2]

In New Hampshire Stassen had been plagued by the fact that his candidates for delegate were lesser known than the Dewey slate. Ironically, Stassen's Wisconsin delegates were more politically prominent; yet the importance of delegate name recognition was, in the opinion of Stassen's Wisconsin campaign manager, Vic Johnston, less crucial.

In a memo written one year before the primary laying out proposed strategy to national campaign chairman Bernhard LeVander, Johnston wrote, "It is a matter of debate who carries the ball, the Presidential candidate or the delegate candidates. Generally speaking, I believe that the actual candidate for President is the one being voted on.... [F]or example, in 1944 [Fred] Zimmerman as a delegate candidate outran the field tremendously — later misled by what he thought was his popularity, he ran for Supreme Court Justice and took a terrible beating."[3]

Another difference between New Hampshire and Wisconsin was that in the Dairy State Stassen had the support of prominent leaders in the Republican Party. Most important, this included former state GOP chairman, Tom Coleman, who still served on the state party committee and reputedly controlled a vast political machine in the state. Through Coleman Stassen secured the support of freshman U.S. senator Joe McCarthy, for whom Vic Johnston had served as a campaign aide in 1946 and later as administrative assistant in Washington, D.C.[4]

Perhaps because of his background Johnston was careful to avoid bruising the feelings and pride of veteran Wisconsin politicos, a mistake he attributed to the ill-fated Willkie campaign of 1944: "In setting up Wisconsin, care should be taken not to ... antagonize the regular Republican organization" by endorsing delegate candidates not acceptable to the party leadership. "This does not mean," Johnston continued, "that hide-bound reactionaries should be selected but it must be remembered at all times that these delegates are running as Republicans."[5]

Johnston also stressed that the leadership in the Wisconsin effort should be located in a committee drawn from native stock, and he recommended Joseph McCarthy to chair the group. "Naturally," Johnston observed diplomatically, "the candidate for President controls the strategy and makes the plans." But Johnston urged that these decisions be transmitted directly to McCarthy, who should be charged with carrying them out. The memo envisioned an active role for the committee:

> The committee should do everything possible to promote Stassen in various districts. They should suggest public appearances for him and other speakers in his behalf. Women's activities, Young Republican activities and all efforts should be handled by this committee. Methods developed in Minneapolis and other states should be turned over to this committee for execution.... The accent of the campaign must be Republican.[6]

Johnston's memo reveals the extent to which he and Stassen supporters in Minneapolis valued grassroots contacts. Also, by emphasizing Republican themes Johnston was avoiding the blunder made by Willkie in 1944, who in his unsuccessful grassroots effort angered party loyalists into working against him. While Stassen would "go to the people," he would not turn his back on party officials in Wisconsin. Indeed, the Stassen campaign tried initially to court them.

In the summer of 1947 this effort reached its zenith with the Wisconsin Republican State Convention. A straw poll was to be taken among delegates to determine which of the presidential aspirants was preferred. Mindful of the value in appearing to be the choice of state GOP leaders, the Minnesota Neighbors for Stassen came to life. In the ten days prior to the straw poll, the Neighbors sent eight hundred postcards to supporters in Minnesota, urging them to contact Wisconsin Republicans; called or wrote every Minnesotan who had reported specific Wisconsin contacts, reminding them of their contact and asking that the Wisconsin individual be reached about the GOP convention; contacted the chairmen of the various Stassen voter groups (e.g., insurance groups, sales groups, students for Stassen, and so forth) and asked them to contact Wisconsin delegates; and sent letters directly to Wisconsinites who had written to Stassen.

The effort was not particularly successful, with Dewey winning the straw poll with three hundred twenty-one votes to Stassen's two hundred eighty-six; yet by his effort, the Minnesotan had sent a message that he was, within limits, a team player.[7]

Still, Stassen was at his best on the hustings, and it was there that he built his success. In December of 1947, still the only candidate openly seeking the nomination one year after his announcement, Stassen began what was to become a major theme in his campaign: The power to decide the nomination should belong to the voters, who should base their decision on the candidate's record and knowledge of the issues. By openly campaigning, Stassen was not only telling the voters where he stood on matters of public policy, but he felt he was also encouraging the public discussion of issues vital to democracy.

Speaking in Milwaukee, Stassen inveighed against the "presidential pickers." It was, he said, "their view that the correct thing to do is to go through very elaborate operations of looking the other way; that the difficult, hard controversial issues of the day should be avoided and the people should not be told our view upon them.... These riders of regal reaction hold that a position of photogenic availability should be maintained until such time as a key group of their own men, with delegates in their pockets, make ... secret deals for a nomination."[8]

Beginning what would be Stassen's standard mode of travel in the states with primaries after New Hampshire, a chartered bus was used to take the candidate and attending reporters to wherever a crowd might be gathered. The bus was actually an innovative idea. In 1944 Willkie had used a caravan of thirteen cars, which proved awkward, while trains and airplanes had obvious difficulties in a rural state. With the rear seats removed, reporters on the bus, of which there were usually four or five — although in the final week this number jumped to more than a dozen — were provided with a work table for their typewriters, and a mimeograph machine operated by Stassen's secretary, Ed Larson. Between towns Stassen typically held impromptu press conferences with the reporters; when the bus arrived at its destination, it would be met by a messenger from Western Union, who would collect and file the news stories recorded on the road.[9]

Reporters could count on news from Stassen, who seemed to thrive on venturing into untested political waters. Beginning a two-day campaign swing on March 6, Stassen charged directly into the so-called isolationist belt along the state's southern boundary. In speeches at Milwaukee, Ft. Atkinson, Milton and Beloit he declared, "In the Republican Party we must develop the dynamic determination to get a program that will not look to the past." He praised Arthur Vandenberg for helping move the Republican Party in an international direction, and claimed that the Michigan senator was "one of the greatest statesmen of our time."[10] Stassen's audience had to pay attention as, literally as he spoke on March 6, one candidate the conservative crowd might have voted for removed himself from the Wisconsin competition.

Senator Robert Taft wired Perry J. Stearns, a Milwaukee attorney who was attempting to organize a slate of Taft delegates, saying, "I should much prefer that you do not file. After thorough consideration, I feel that it would not be to my interest to have anyone in Wisconsin running for delegate pledged to me." Stearns, for reasons not clear, interpreted the wire to mean that Taft wanted to defer to Douglas MacArthur. Yet it would seem more logical to conclude that Taft realized he could not possibly hope to beat two candidates with strong regional ties to the Dairy State: MacArthur, who was born in Wisconsin and thus claimed favorite son status, and Stassen, who lived next door in Minnesota. What is certain is that Taft was still vigorously pursuing the nomination and would make a distinctly Stassen-like stand in Nebraska.[11]

On March 7 Stassen completed his two-day tour, remarking only that he was "pretty well" satisfied with the result. The tour was significant for two reasons. First, he concentrated his appearances in "hostile" territory: conservative districts that would be expected to vote for MacArthur delegates. In these districts he attracted respectable crowds. The second reason, perhaps more significant when the election was still one month away, was that in the hostile territories he had apparently earned the respect of party leaders. According to Rex Karney of the *Wisconsin State Journal*, "In each town in which he speaks, most politically important citizens either are definitely on his side or at least drop around for a look-see."[12] While winning many friends, Stassen was making few enemies.

While Stassen was returning to Minnesota, the MacArthur campaign continued to build steam. Lansing Hoyt, national chairman of the MacArthur for President Club and head of the Wisconsin MacArthur for President Club, announced in Milwaukee the opening of a national headquarters in Washington, D.C., to coordinate all phases of the MacArthur for President movement. Located at 1333 Connecticut Avenue, NW, the office was located next door to the Republican National Committee and was headed by Warren E. Wright, former Illinois state treasurer.[13]

Meanwhile, two prominent labor leaders were announced as delegate candidates for MacArthur. At a joint announcement, Ernest A. Nelson, state secretary of the American Federation of Labor (AFL) Typographical Union, and F. Lee DeChant, secretary of Local 715 of the AFL International Brotherhood of Electrical Workers, said "the first step toward shaping a government policy to permit management and labor to work in harmony" would be the election of the general as president.[14]

The general apparently thought so, too. In an announcement from Tokyo, MacArthur said he would accept the 1948 Republican presidential nomination if it were offered to him, although he would not campaign for the honor himself. He did, however, seem to encourage his Wisconsin supporters. "I have been informed," he said, "that petitions have been filed at Madison and signed by many of my fellow citizens of Wisconsin, presenting my name to the electorate for consideration at the primary April 6. I am deeply grateful for this spontaneous display of friendly confidence. No man could fail to be profoundly stirred by such a public movement in this hour of momentous import."[15]

Profoundly stirred, too, were Dewey and Stassen. The *Wisconsin State Journal*, miffed because their offer to sponsor a debate between Dewey and Stassen had been rejected by the New Yorker (Stassen accepted) speculated that the decision would force Dewey to campaign in the state. Stassen stoically commended the general for his "forthright statement,"[16] but his campaign staff broke into a collective sweat. Vic Johnston told the *New York Times* that the Minnesotan's prospects had looked good. "Now," he lamented, "the whole picture is fouled up." The Macarthur sentiment, he noted, is "probably pretty considerable. If it were a straight Dewey-Stassen fight, I think we'd get a good majority of the delegates. But we can't be sure whether MacArthur is going to drain strength away."[17]

If the Wisconsin political veteran Johnston expressed uncertainty about the velocity of the MacArthur movement, he could easily be forgiven, for the general's support consisted of an odd amalgamation of ideological groups. At its head was none other than the progressive former governor Phil LaFollette, running as a MacArthur delegate. Also backing the general was the hard-core isolationist crowd and erstwhile America First members. Finally, MacArthur received the support that would surely have gone to Robert Taft had the senator not taken himself out of the Wisconsin contest. This group included the Republican right wing along with influential industrialists and bankers who advocated a tough labor policy.

The alliance of these forces led to obvious questions. Would progressive followers of LaFollette follow him in his support of MacArthur? Would Republican regulars be able to reconcile themselves to working with the former Progressive leader LaFollette? Was the isolationist vote large enough to make a difference? Would voters who opposed putting a military man with no other experience in the White House hopelessly split their support between Stassen and Dewey?[18]

While the general's opponents fretted over these questions, MacArthur began to show strength among the rank-and-file. A straw poll conducted by a radio station in Green Bay in mid–March showed the general was a clear favorite, with two hundred twenty-seven votes to Dewey's one hundred forty-one. Stassen garnered a dismal forty-two votes — behind the reluctant Eisenhower, who received fifty-four votes, and Harry Truman, who received forty-five.[19] Even in Japan MacArthur received support, as thirty-five Tokyo residents signed a petition praising their occupier and recommending him for the presidency.[20]

Stassen replied by stepping up his campaign. On March 10 he invited four Wisconsin newspaper editors to participate in a radio interview to be held five days later. The half-hour broadcast was to be the first of a series of four such interviews before the election.[21]

Dewey, meanwhile, dispatched Harold Talbot, a New York stockbroker and campaign fundraiser, to the Dairy State to solicit funds and to investigate whether a personal campaign appearance would pay electoral dividends. Talbot received a barrage of pleas from Wisconsin supporters that Dewey come to the state or face annihilation at the polls. A reportedly impressed Talbot reported the news to Dewey over the phone.[22] In New York Dewey met with Raymond Moley in the governor's city apartment to discuss a possible campaign appearance. Moley later wrote of it:

> [Dewey] said this was the most difficult decision he ever had to make. He knew he was going to lose the primary, although he thought General MacArthur and not Harold Stassen would beat him. I felt that he should go. So did his able secretary, Paul Lockwood, who participated in the conversation. Lockwood and I were subjected to a beating that lasted three hours. We turned our brains inside out, but Dewey brushed off every argument.
> That night Dewey met with Herbert Brownell and Russell Sprague, who at one in the morning finally convinced him to go.[23]

Dewey did not actually leave his state to head for Wisconsin until March 31, and the move smelled of a desperate, eleventh hour bid. The *Wisconsin State Journal*, learning of Dewey's decision, scoffed in an editorial that the New York governor, "long allergic to the Wisconsin air," had "reluctantly decided to show his face to the presidential primary countryside, after all. It is high — if not past — time."[24]

On March 15 Stassen began another tour of Wisconsin, beginning with his broadcast interview with the four newspaper editors that his campaign staff had arranged earlier. The editors questions centered on agricultural policy, which enabled Stassen to present his liberal commitment to using government programs to bolster farm income. "This means," the candidate declared, "that our export policies, utilization of farm products for new industrial uses, school lunches, better diets, economic storage, and favorable financing would be directed to maintaining full parity and a complete fair share of the national income." If farm income fell below its "fair share" he urged additional support payments to farmers. "Farm groups in Minnesota have always been more than friendly to me," he added. In response to a question of civil rights, Stassen pointed to his record as governor and noted, "I was in favor of civil liberties ... long before Mr. Truman was."[25]

Republicans at the national level would have done well to read copies of the broadcast. For the rest of his life Dewey himself believed that he lost the November election against President Truman because he, Dewey, could not hold the farm vote[26]; Stassen, from the Midwest and advocating liberal government programs to maintain basic levels of parity, would surely have been more successful with that voter block.

Moreover, Stassen would have out-flanked the president on the left when Truman solicited the votes of urban blacks with his appeal for civil rights. As Governor of Minnesota, Stassen had a well-earned reputation as a liberal on issues concerning minorities. "I was the first governor in the United States," Stassen recalled, "to appoint a black officer on the staff of the National Guard.... His name was Samuel Ransom, and it was said to be against the rules at that time, to have an integrated staff, and I said, 'It's the wrong rule,' and I appointed him.... That was a pioneer appointment."[27]

Ransom, who later went on to become a decorated major in the U.S. Army, took an interest in the Stassen presidential campaign, which, characteristically, did not fail to promote Stassen's civil rights record. In April of 1948 Ransom and Milton Williams of the *Twin City Observer* met with Bernhard LeVander and recommended that a black be sent "on a little swing down East" contacting the editors of leading newspapers and informing them of Stassen's record. LeVander promptly wrote a memo to Warren Burger endorsing the idea and speculating that a "couple hundred dollars spent on this would not be amiss."[28] It seems clear that Stassen would have effectively competed with Truman for black votes.

During Stassen's mid–March Wisconsin tour, the now almost Dickensian apparition of Dwight Eisenhower once again surfaced. Although it was too late for the former general, now president of Columbia University, to be entered into the Wisconsin contest, a New York advertising executive, Torrey Stearns, on March 15 announced the creation of "People for Eisenhower." This came despite Eisenhower's adamant statement that he would not accept the nomination. Nevertheless, Stearns planned to have voters throughout the United States send postcards to the campaign office, where he optimistically said they would be "loaded on trucks" and sent to the Republican National Convention.[29]

Like performers when their audience begins to wander away, the announced candidates were under pressure to draw attention back to their particular stage. After his radio address, Stassen was approached by farmers from the Wisconsin Association of Cooperatives, who were investigating the agricultural policies of each of the candidates. Accepting their invitation to appear before the organization, the Minnesotan boldly challenged Dewey to appear with him before the group. He did not use the word "debate," though few doubted his intention. Dewey, still not ready to make his appearance in Wisconsin, mischievously ducked the challenge by inviting a three-person delegation from the association to visit him at — of all places — his Dutchess County, New York, farm.[30]

Stassen kept plugging away in Wisconsin. Before leaving Milwaukee the former governor, who had worked as a Pullman conductor to pay his way through school, visited the shop of the Chicago-Milwaukee Railroad. The shop superintendent promptly offered Stassen a job, with a leave of absence, "so he can absent himself from work here for the duration of his term as president of the United States."

The next day, March 16, Stassen spoke at a Manitowoc breakfast and to a joint meeting of the Neenah-Menasha Service Clubs.[31] He then hurried off to Fond du Lac to meet with the Farmer's Association. This politically important meeting took place in a closed-door session in Room 340 at the Retlaw Hotel and involved ten of Wisconsin's most influential farm leaders, who listened as Stassen outlined his ideas on agriculture and submitted to questions. As this group included prominent farmers, Stassen was aware that if they swung their collective weight behind one candidate, they would have significant influence. After the session, Stassen would say merely that "the discussion was very thorough."

The farm leaders agreed, and days later announced their support for Dewey.[32] Yet Dewey had not mingled with the average farmer and had not visited local communities. He had garnered an endorsement from prominent individuals, but had not, however, won the respect of the small farmer. This was made clear in polls conducted by the magazine *Wisconsin Agriculturist and Farmer*. Since October 1947 Stassen had been the first choice of the magazine's monthly surveys. The last poll before the primary, taken about the same time Stassen attended his ill-fated meeting with the "prominent" farmers, showed the former governor to be the first choice of 41 percent of Wisconsin's farmers, with Dewey a distant third, after MacArthur, with 25 percent.[33]

The result of the *Wisconsin Agriculturist and Farmer* polls was one example of how the Stassen campaign was catching fire. In the summer of 1947, Neighbors for Stassen had made a vigorous, though futile, effort to win the support of delegates to the Wisconsin Republican Convention. Yet on March 21, 1948, it was reported that a new poll taken of Republican county chairmen revealed Stassen as the favorite for the presidential nomination. According to the *Milwaukee Journal*, Stassen's "margin was surprising, especially since it reversed the position of last June's vote at the Republican state convention." In the new poll, Stassen was the first choice by a two-to-one margin.[34]

On March 20 the former governor returned to his home for the state convention of the Minnesota Republican Party. Speaking before the convention, Stassen attacked the Truman administration for backing away from the creation of an independent Palestinian state. "A confused change is proposed to the Security Council for the amazing reason that lawless Arab resistance to the United Nations persists," he said, calling the policy, "an invitation to international anarchy." After his speech, the convention unanimously pledged Minnesota's twenty-five delegates to work "to make certain" Stassen's nomination.[35]

The next day the peripatetic candidate was back in Wisconsin to launch another campaign swing with a tour through Wausau, Wisconsin Rapids, and Marshfield. With the election little more than two weeks away, the growing attendance at Stassen's appearances were a clear indication that momentum was building for his candidacy.

Before a capacity crowd of three hundred fifty citizens in Marshfield, Stassen was introduced by a former Republican county chairman, David Bogue, who told the cheering crowd, "I can't see why a delegation of farmers from Wisconsin has to go to New York to see if a candidate out there knows which end of a cow is the production end." Perhaps sensing that the threat to his performance in the primary was now from MacArthur rather than Dewey, Stassen made a point of directing his fire at the general. "From what I can tell from the papers who support him," Stassen remarked, "I think he puts too much emphasis on pouring American funds into Asia."[36]

The papers Stassen referred to were probably those of the Hearst chain, most notably the *Milwaukee Sentinel*, which in the weeks before the primary became less a source of news than of campaign propaganda for MacArthur. Literally every day from March 1 through April 6, the *Sentinel* managed to print a front-page "news" story on the general. The paper also printed ad hominem attacks on, and random innuendo about, MacArthur's rivals. One of the *Sentinel*'s columnists managed within the space of one article to imply that Arthur Vandenberg was an ill cardiac patient who could not be trusted, and that Stassen was receiving "plenty of money" from an individual who was known to be morally debauched and politically corrupt. No evidence was provided.[37]

On March 23 Stassen continued his Wisconsin tour, swinging through Portage, Jefferson and Milwaukee, where he "respectfully" suggested that MacArthur sit down at a radio microphone in Tokyo and engage in a MacArthur-Stassen discussion of American foreign policy. Expressing a "high regard" for the general, the Minnesotan nevertheless charged that MacArthur's proposed foreign policies "would sink America too deep into Japan, China and Asia and would cost billions of American dollars and require a large American Asiatic army at a time when our greatest danger is from the Communist menace in Europe."

Exactly what those foreign policies were and how Stassen learned about them — MacArthur had made no comments about what his views were — he did not say. Still, the request was transmitted via wire to Phil LaFollette at the MacArthur campaign headquarters in Milwaukee. LaFollette refused to forward the request; "partisan politics," he sniffed.[38]

Stassen angrily fired a second telegram to LaFollette in which he owned to being "surprised that you take upon yourself the authority to speak for Gen. MacArthur on foreign policy and to hold my telegram without forwarding it to him." He went on to repeat his accusation that MacArthur's policies would bog the United States down in Asia while leaving Europe vulnerable.[39] LaFollette did not respond. But the *Milwaukee Journal*, neutral in the primary, noted bitterly, "It becomes increasingly obvious that Gen. MacArthur is not going to tell the people of Wisconsin where he stands on the major issues of the day."[40]

With MacArthur in Tokyo and Dewey in Albany, Stassen attracted increasing attention as he mingled with voters, who watched as he benignly patted a dog that wandered up on the stage where he was speaking or as he drank coffee and ate doughnuts with hundreds of men and women in the basement of the Washington Park Presbyterian Church in Milwaukee after an auditorium speech.[41] "Here is Mr. Stassen," observed one editorial echoing an increasingly typical sentiment, "touring the hamlets of the state, volunteering his view on the most explosive issues.... Contrast that formula with those of Gov. Dewey out in Albany. He hasn't said six words on a national or international problem. And he gives no one a chance to ask him. Gen. MacArthur is busy in Japan."[42] His supporters, though, were busy in Wisconsin. Fred Zimmerman, the secretary of state and MacArthur delegate candidate, used his government office as a veritable campaign headquarters, sending out literature, apparently at state expense, for the general. The *Wisconsin State Journal*, noting this fact and supporting Stassen, sputtered with outrage.[43]

Yet the Minnesotan was not without his backers. Senator Joseph McCarthy, six days prior to the election, sent out a pro–Stassen "Dear Folks" letter to his constituents on stationery with the title "United States Senate." The stationery held a disclaimer: "Not furnished at Government expense," although it was not specifically stated that none of the cost of the mailing was borne by McCarthy's senatorial office. The letter ignored Dewey while aggressively attacking MacArthur, making passing reference to the general's divorce and questioning his claim to be a Wisconsin native.[44]

Finally, on March 27, definitive plans for Dewey's visit to Wisconsin were announced. From Albany, the New Yorker said that on the evening of Wednesday, March 31, he would leave for a midwestern campaign swing, with the first stop the next day in Racine for a luncheon with Republican state leaders. After appearances throughout the state on April 1 and 2, he would leave on Saturday, April 3, for Nebraska. "The time has come," Dewey said in an announcement that must have struck Wisconsinites as rather belated, "for a frank and blunt statement of the complex and serious problems confronting our nation and the world."

Learning of the New Yorker's itinerary, the Stassen campaign promptly announced that the Minnesotan would also be in Milwaukee on April 1, and was renewing his challenge to Dewey to debate with him.[45] Dewey did not respond to the invitation. Still being the national front runner for the nomination, he saw little advantage in providing Stassen with further publicity. According to a Gallup poll released on March 28, 34 percent of Republicans nationwide selected Dewey as their first choice for president, although this was down two percentage points from a similar poll taken two weeks earlier. MacArthur placed second with nineteen points while Stassen trailed with fifteen.[46]

Yet, as Raymond Moley pointed out in a later book, Dewey knew by the beginning of March that he would not win Wisconsin but expected a second-place finish behind MacArthur. As the month drew to a close, word of this began to leak to the press, which reported the governor as feeling compelled only to get more delegates than Stassen. Joseph McCarthy could barely contain his delight. "I am glad to know that Gov. Dewey finally has publicly admitted that Harold Stassen is the man he must defeat if he is to secure the nomination," he exclaimed, calling the Dewey campaign swing "a last desperate effort to salvage delegates."[47]

Exactly how desperate the New Yorker was is unknown, but literally as he announced his plans to visit Wisconsin, his campaign received a setback from the Wisconsin Association of Cooperatives, which repudiated the endorsement that Dewey had received from the leadership of the organization. Moreover, it was revealed that one of the three-person delegation that went to visit Dewey at his Dutchess County, New York, farm to "investigate" the governor's agricultural policies was in fact a 1940 Dewey delegate still eagerly promoting the New Yorker. In the association's newsletter issued on March 27, the farmers' group bitterly stated, "We are anxious that our people know that the farm leaders who are playing politics in this election are not speaking for all the farm people.... These men purported to have studied the farm programs of all three candidates and made up their minds in favor of one of them. There is a suspicion abroad that the decision was made long before any of the candidates were consulted."[48] Meanwhile, Stassen, taking the offensive, told interviewers during a radio press conference that if he were elected, he would appoint as secretary of agriculture someone from the Midwest.[49]

In the last two weeks the Dewey campaign floundered around Wisconsin, sinking noticeably under the Stassen and MacArthur tides. Three of the governor's aides from New York, Hamilton Gaddis, Hickman Powell, and Thomas Stephens, rushed to the Badger State and desperately patched together an intensive publicity drive.

In the days before the election thousands of letters to Wisconsin voters were mailed, special rural and urban editions of a Dewey tabloid, *Republican Good News*, were distributed, and a huge advertising campaign was launched, featuring rebroadcasts of the candidate's radio speeches.[50] According to preliminary campaign spending reports filed with the Wisconsin secretary of state, Fred Zimmerman, a MacArthur delegate hopeful, on March 30 the New York governor had spent $23,854 in the contest up to that point, a considerable sum, though less than the $29,671 spent by MacArthur. Stassen's grassroots campaign had spent a mere $14,861. These sums were spent both to promote delegate candidates and to enhance the White House aspirant's name throughout the state.[51]

Stassen began his final week of campaigning by blasting the Truman administration for what he called its "half-way measures" in handling the Soviet Union, which probably was an attempt to preempt MacArthur's anticommunist stand. Speaking before a thousand people jammed into the gymnasium at Carroll College in Waukesha, Wisconsin, Stassen said he thought war between the superpowers could be avoided, but not by the Truman administration. In his speech the increasingly confident Minnesotan did not directly attack or even seriously mention his two Republican opponents, but blasted the Truman administration for failing to stop shipments of machine tools and other vital equipment to the Soviet Union. Stassen reminded the audience that he had been calling for a halt in the shipments since November, and had sent Truman a telegram about the matter on March 16. He then read to the audience Truman's "evasive" reply, and charged the president with believing that Russia was a "friendly nation." That, the candidate declared, "is diplomatic thinking of the past."[52]

Fate was to provide an ironic twist to Stassen's charge that the United States was sending vital equipment to the Soviet Union. In 1954, while Stassen was serving as director of foreign operations for President Eisenhower, Joseph McCarthy, on the floor of the Senate, launched a scalding attack on the administration for allowing the allied nations to ship "the sinews of economic and military strength," meaning machine tools and equipment, to the Peoples' Republic of China. Stassen, who had already fought his erstwhile supporter in a tangle over McCarthy's private negotiations with Greek shipowners, once again leaped to the defense of the administration by denying the senator's charge and adding that McCarthy was "frantically reaching for headlines."[53]

The political partnership of Stassen and McCarthy ended bitterly. Years later Stassen would express sorrow over the course that his former supporter had taken. "He became so extreme," Stassen reflected. "I tried to pull him back, but he was very adamant."[54]

Continuing his foreign policy thrust, Stassen the next night not only repeated his criticism of the Truman administration as insufficiently anticommunist, but also delighted conservatives with a scathing assault on the Soviet Union, which followed, he said, "destructive and obnoxious foreign policies." In a reflection of the mounting excitement his candidacy was causing, Stassen's remarks were wildly cheered by a crowd of twenty-two hundred, jammed into the fifteen-hundred capacity Memorial Chapel at Lawrence College in Appleton.

Large crowds continued to follow the candidate the next day as he visited the Ripon schoolhouse where the Republican Party had been founded, then attended a luncheon at Waupun, and an afternoon meeting with farm leaders at the Sun Prairie farm of Wilbur Renk, who was one of the Stassen delegate candidates. Later he discussed his views on federal aid for education at a speech in Madison before delivering yet another speech, this time over CBS radio.[55]

Whenever Stassen sought to undercut his Republican opponents, he was increasingly aiming his fire at MacArthur, who unlike Dewey seemed to be emerging late in the campaign as a candidate with at least some widespread support, although not nearly as much as Stassen's.

At the Minnesotan's Appleton speech, crowds filing into Memorial Chapel passed through lines of small boys carrying "Vote for MacArthur" sandwich boards. The boys told reporters they had been hired by a stranger who promised them fifty cents an hour to carry the signs around the chapel. Stassen volunteers provided the young boys with Stassen campaign buttons, and in a short time the children carrying "Vote for MacArthur" signs were covered from head to toe with Stassen advertisements. Inside, the former governor told the audience, "You pass on MacArthur."[56]

The hapless Thomas Dewey arrived in Racine, Wisconsin, on April 1, April Fool's Day. Attention, however, remained with Stassen. Columnist Marquis Childs attended one of the Minnesotan's appearances, and reflected, "This is a meeting in the oldest tradition of our political life. Here on the hustings is a candidate for the highest office, meeting the voters face-to-face, giving ready answers to questions." He noted that the audience listened with "something of the speaker's earnestness."[57] The *Wisconsin State Journal* editorialized that Stassen must have "lifted the thousands of hearts in his audience" with his message of world peace.[58]

Only after the election, however, was it clear exactly how much of an impression Stassen had made with his grassroots, meet-the-people campaign. In the days before the balloting experts believed the race too close to call, although there was a consensus that Dewey would not finish in first place. Laurence Kelund of the *Milwaukee Journal* quoted anonymous party leaders who predicted that MacArthur would receive half the delegates, while the state's congressional delegation, he wrote, were privately predicting that the general would get anywhere from thirteen to nineteen of the state's twenty-seven delegate seats.[59]

Stassen himself felt obliged to tell a press conference that he would continue his campaign even if he were dealt a defeat in the Wisconsin race. He also tacitly agreed with a reporter's comment that the primary had turned into a "popularity contest." "How can there be sharp issues," Stassen complained, "when one candidate has not expressed himself on many of the issues and another candidate, because of the position he holds, hasn't expressed himself on any of the issues?"[60]

The weekend before the election, the Stassen campaign received good news from outside the state. A majority of delegates supporting Harold Stassen were selected by state party conventions in both Iowa and Maine. In Iowa, twelve delegates who backed Stassen were elected to be delegates, while Dewey could manage only six and Robert Taft one, with the remaining two delegates uncommitted. On the same day in Maine, considered Dewey's backyard, seven of thirteen delegates sent to the national convention were for Stassen, with the remainder being divided among Dewey with two, Vandenberg with one and three uncommitted.[61] The results were a promising omen.

On Saturday afternoon, April 3, one hundred fifty University of Wisconsin students who called themselves the "Stassen Minutemen" went door-to-door in Madison, dispensing campaign literature and urging voters to go to the polls. Already at work were the Stassen "Paul Revere Riders," a caravan of young people who drove around leafleting doorways and parking lots. In the week prior to the election three hundred forty carloads of the "Riders" blanketed one thousand towns and villages.[62]

Meanwhile, Stassen supporters were celebrating mud. Recent rains had muddied farmland, which Wilbur Renk, a farmer and Stassen delegate hopeful, saw as a good sign. "Farm-

Young supporters campaigning for Harold Stassen, 1947 (Philip C. Dittes, Minnesota Historical Society).

ers won't be in their fields by election day.... And that's good for Stassen, who is strong on the farm." The weather forecast for election day called for partly cloudy skies with scattered showers.[63] The hoped-for rain did not happen, but it hardly mattered for Stassen. The results were not even close. Nineteen of Stassen's delegate candidates were elected. Douglas MacArthur finished second with eight. Dewey received none.[64]

The impact of the election was best put by the *Wisconsin State Journal*, which stated, "Wisconsin has given the nation — and the world — something startling — and refreshing — to think about. By lifting Harold E. Stassen to a tremendous, phenomenal victory, it has given notice that the people demand the voice in making their president this time. It tells the anxious kingmakers that the Republican nominee is not to be picked from a smoke-filled room..."[65]

Another editorial noted "Harold Stassen traveled the highways and byways, he talked to the people, he stated his views frankly...."[66] This did not impress everyone. Robert Taft dismissed Stassen's victory as "merely" due to personal campaigning. Also downplaying the victory was Dewey, who managed to say that April 6 had been a "pretty good day" for him. He noted that his New York delegation gave him ninety convention seats, which alone gave him a hefty lead in the delegate count.[67]

Yet both Taft and Dewey missed the point. Stassen, by virtue of a grassroots campaign in a state primary, had grabbed center spotlight on the Republican stage. Unlike any GOP candidate in the history of the party, Stassen had bypassed the party leaders and propelled himself to the front of the pack in the race for the nomination. He was now, as Marquis Childs put it, a "formidable contender for the nomination" in what Childs thought was a "minor revolution."[68]

After his triumph in Nebraska, the Minnesotan's regional success would have national implications, as he replaced Dewey in the polls as being the favorite for the nomination. In the later primaries, his opponents, with varying success, would try to mimic his campaign techniques. For the moment, however, as the candidates traveled to Nebraska for the next primary, the political landscape was suddenly very different.

7. The Ascendancy: Nebraska

On Wednesday morning, April 14, 1948, Robert Taft stood in the senate cloakroom glumly watching the returns from the Nebraska primary come through a news ticker. A colleague asked, "Is Stassen still winning?" "Yes," Taft replied, adding hopefully, "but Dewey and I together have more votes than he has." The Senator was correct, but just barely; in the final returns Stassen received 43 percent of the votes, while Dewey followed with 35 percent and Taft placed third with 11 percent.[1]

Six days before the election, Stassen, ebullient from his stunning Wisconsin triumph, embarked for Nebraska exclaiming, "The prairies are on fire and getting hotter for Stassen all the time."[2] They would never be hotter than they were in the aftermath of the 1948 Nebraska primary. Stassen and his supporters had been stoking the political coals in the state for some time, not without getting burned. The ensuing heat had driven the Republican nomination from the smoke-filled room and onto the Great Plains, where the flames consumed Robert Taft, who would yet take his revenge, and critically burned the candidacy of Thomas Dewey, who in Oregon would arise like a phoenix from the Nebraska ashes.

The Great Plains state was an unlikely place for such dramatic events; of the candidates for the Republican nomination, only Harold Stassen had made definite plans to enter the primary as late as January. Thomas Dewey, who had cruised to victory in the state in 1940 in the wake of his Wisconsin breakthrough, had ignored Nebraska in 1944, although his supporters launched a last-minute write-in effort after Wendell Willkie withdrew from the race. The primary was still a yawn, with Stassen, as the only candidate on the ballot, winning easily. Since Stassen was in the Pacific with Admiral Halsey, and Dewey was pretending not to be a candidate, no prospective nominee had made a personal effort in the state. The contest was, in a word, boring.

Nebraska was not the only state with a dull presidential primary; in many states across the nation the only widely perceptible effect of the elections was to drive voters into the arms of Morpheus. The problem was that smart presidential hopefuls were traditionally careful to enter only those primaries where they were confident they could win, and where there was no "favorite son." Instead, candidates concentrated on meeting with party leaders who controlled state delegates, and presidential primaries languished. Of the 1,057 delegates to the 1948 Republican National Convention, only one hundred fifteen would be chosen in primary contests.[3]

Musing that the democratic process would be supercharged by a public contest over the presidential nominations of both parties, a thirty-two-year-old editor of the *Journal* newspapers in Lincoln, Nebraska, came upon a mischievous scheme to force a lively contest — in his state, at least. Raymond McConnell, Jr., a deceptively soft-spoken graduate of Williams College, noticed that Nebraska's 1911 primary law neither required a candidate's permission to put his name on the ballot nor permitted any nominee to withdraw his name. To put a name on the ballot, all that was required were one hundred signatures from each of the state's four congressional districts. McConnell formed the Nebraska Bi-Partisan Committee to do just that, assuming, correctly, that no candidate could afford a humiliating loss and if one aspirant came to the state to campaign, all serious candidates would have to come too. The committee filed President Truman's name in the Democratic primary, and dropped plans to add Henry Wallace when the former secretary of commerce announced his third-party candidacy. On the Republican side, the committee filed the names of Gov. Thomas Dewey, Gen. Douglas MacArthur, Rep. Joe Martin, Harold Stassen, Sen. Robert Taft, and Gov. Earl Warren. Delegates to the national conventions, elected in their own district contests, would be under pressure to support the candidate who won the statewide primary.[4]

Your Friend and Neighbor
HAROLD E. STASSEN
For President

Campaign postcard, 1948 (Collection of John F. Rothmann).

The committee had also gathered signatures for Sen. Arthur Vandenberg of Michigan. However, with the exception of Eisenhower, no one since Sherman had done more than Vandenberg to plead that he was not interested in a presidential nomination. His reluctance dismayed Republican internationalists, among them Harold Stassen, who in February 1948 called the senator "the statesman who best applies to world problems the concepts of Lincoln."[5] "I had a great regard for Senator Vandenberg," Stassen recalled, and noted that at the Republican convention he, Stassen, and his supporters had tried to convince Vandenberg to allow them to attempt to secure the nomination for the Michigan senator. "He never really wanted to get in there and tackle it," Stassen reflected.[6]

The cigar-chewing, formally mannered Arthur Vandenberg had the appearance of a senator sent straight from Hollywood central casting. Earlier in life he had written Horatio Alger-type stories for national magazines, a song about silent movie queen Bebe Daniels ("Bebe, Be Mine") that became a popular hit, and two worshipful books about Alexander Hamilton. He had also edited a Grand Rapids, Michigan, newspaper, in which he denounced Sinclair Lewis for mocking small midwestern towns and the Babbitts who lived in them.[7] Ironically, he and Lewis, who were born in Minnesota, became friends. In May of 1948 Lewis wrote Vandenberg, chiding the senator for privately expressing doubts about Stassen's consistency on issues, and adding, "I think that the next President of the United States is going to be Arthur Vandenberg.... I have a great idea for helping him during the first three terms of his presidency: Stay to hell out of Washington."[8]

McConnell was about to file the signatures with the secretary of state when he received a telegram from Vandenberg on March 1. Vandenberg told the young editor, "Since I am not a candidate for the nomination and since I have asked my own Michigan friends neither to present nor support my name in the Republican convention, I should not be included in the referendum. I therefore very earnestly request that you shall not file any petitions for me in Nebraska.... I deeply hope that you will respect my wishes in this matter."[9]

Although McConnell could not have known it at the time, the Michigan senator was not being coy, but rather speaking directly from his heart. Three months earlier Vandenberg had drafted a letter to Arthur Summerfield, a Republican national committeeman from Michigan, proposing a complex scheme in order to release Michigan delegates to the GOP convention to support other candidates. According to the Vandenberg scenario, there would be an exchange of letters between Summerfield and Vandenberg, which the senator would send to Governor Kim Sigler before making them public. The first letter would be from Summerfield, pledging the delegation's support for Vandenberg, but requesting clarification of the senator's wishes. Vandenberg would then write back emphasizing that he was not a candidate and urging that delegates be released from any obligation to a Vandenberg candidacy.[10]

This Summerfield letter was only a draft, and there is no record that it was ever sent. Vandenberg definitely did send the GOP committeeman a one-paragraph letter on January 1 in which he requested that "my name shall *not* be presented or supported either in the Michigan State Convention or in the National Convention at Philadelphia." Moreover, to one supporter who had written to him pledging financial support for a Vandenberg presidential campaign, the senator responded, "I would prefer that you use your 'spare dollars' to organize for my protection *against* any such ... unwelcome eventuality" as a presidential nomination.[11] Arthur Vandenberg did not have Potomac fever.

McConnell, though, believed he saw the symptoms. Hours after receiving Vandenberg's telegram of March 1, the Nebraskan sent a return wire innocently protesting that his committee was "interested only in giving the Nebraska voters a real and full choice among all the seriously mentioned presidential possibilities." Still, he added, "in view of your telegram of this morning, we are withholding the petitions for you while awaiting this question: "If you were nominated ... would you accept the nomination?" McConnell, like a sheriff who had his suspect surrounded, warned Vandenberg to come out with an answer by 3:00 P.M. the next day or else. With contempt dripping from every word, Vandenberg sent his reply: "I decline to speculate with utterly improbable contingencies. Your question defies intelligent answer. I have heretofore made my position clear. I shall not discuss it further."[12]

With Vandenberg on the ticket, Stassen, who only one month before had compared the Michigan senator to Abraham Lincoln, now found himself awkwardly opposing the modern-day equivalent of the Great Emancipator. Moreover, could the house of Republican internationalism stand in Nebraska when it was divided against itself? At a press conference on March 4, two days after Vandenberg's final reply to McConnell, the Minnesotan stated, "I am pleased to see the favorable attention being given Senator Vandenberg in the Republican Party. He is a great statesman." "But," one reporter persisted, "do you consider him a threat to your own candidacy for the presidential nomination?" Stassen replied, "No, I don't consider him in that way."[13]

Although skepticism would be understandable, it is logical and compelling that Stassen was sincere in his remarks. Though a political David, Stassen had clearly demonstrated in his career a willingness to engage any Goliath whom he considered a threat, if not to himself, then to his brand of internationalism. And that included giants no smaller than Vandenberg.

Wendell Willkie, Thomas Dewey and Robert Taft had all seen Stassen's teeth. No shrinking violet, the Minnesotan felt deeply that Vandenberg would have been a good choice for the nomination, and was ready to support him. Stassen remembered later, "I have always had a philosophy of thinking in terms of the future well-being of the country rather than my individual status, and that kind of puzzles a lot of the media and so on, that's why they can't figure out why I do a lot of the things I do.... I felt very strongly that the policies of Dewey and Taft were not adequate for the future of the country. I had a lot of ideas about what those policies ought to be, but I was perfectly willing, and in fact desirous of getting Vandenberg to come forward."[14]

But would the Republican internationalist vote be split by the presence of both Vandenberg and Stassen on the Nebraska ballot? Stassen's campaign staff craftily took the potentially vote-splitting situation and used it to advance their candidate. Since Vandenberg was well-known (more so than Stassen before the primary), and had publicly disclaimed any interest in the nomination, the Stassen campaign on March 5 issued a statement urging Nebraskans "friendly to U.S. Senator Arthur Vandenberg and his realistic foreign policies" to support and vote for Stassen, thus linking the dark horse with the prominent senator. "Vandenberg specifically requested," the statement went on, "that his name not be filed in the Nebraska presidential primary. The Michigan senator also asked that if his name was entered that his Nebraska friends should vote for another candidate." The Stassen campaign was confident that the unspecified contender would turn out to be Stassen.[15]

What was surely on the minds of the Minnesotan's supporters was the 1946 Republican senatorial primary in Nebraska, when Stassen had backed Dwight Griswold in his unsuccessful bid to oust the isolationist Hugh Butler. Griswold's electoral burial under the Butler landslide had two implications for the fortunes of Harold Stassen. First, in the short run, Stassen's political prestige received a serious blow, and he plummeted six points to 34 percent in a nationwide Gallup poll, while Dewey rose three points to 38 percent.[16] Second, Stassen now had to contend with a senator in control of a powerful statewide machine and hankering for retribution. As the state, and the nation, began to focus on the Nebraska primary, it was thought that Senator Butler would support his like-minded colleague Robert Taft in order to exact his revenge on Harold Stassen. However, the collection of Taft papers now deposited in the Library of Congress suggest that, actually, Butler's support of Taft was payment for support that Taft had given Butler two years earlier. Taft had always been suspicious of the liberal Minnesotan, and kept an extensive file on Stassen which now fills five large folders in Taft's papers. During the senatorial primary campaign a Taft staffer prepared a memo on Stassen, analyzing his writings and public comments. The Taft office forwarded a copy of this memo to the Butler office, suggesting that Taft sought to aid his friend while discrediting the political prestige of his young enemy.[17]

Not easily intimidated, Stassen began to lay plans for a Nebraska campaign long before Raymond McConnell began gathering signatures. By late 1947 the Minnesotan had won the support of State Senator Fred Seaton, who agreed to serve as his Nebraska campaign manager. On January 11, 1948, at Stassen's request, Bernhard LeVander flew to Omaha to meet with Seaton, who explained the contours of politics in the Great Plains State, taking care to point out rough terrain where Stassen might stumble. In a memo to Warren Burger about the meeting, LeVander recalled that Seaton had called attention to the "utter lack of any Stassen organization in Nebraska."

Meanwhile, the state GOP "organization is predominantly Taft at this time, with Stassen having some strong friends in it." Seaton went on to recommend that Stassen publicly support the efforts of McConnell to secure an "all–Star" primary. Also, Seaton said he would need twenty thousand dollars to establish a campaign office, and he wanted a poll taken in the state within thirty days.[18]

Seaton's haste was not without cause. Taft, unhappy with, but resigned to, having his name on the ballot, began his Nebraska campaign early. On February 14 he traveled to Omaha, where he claimed for himself the title of "true liberal." In a speech at a dinner for Nebraska party leaders, he charged the Democrats with attempting to solve "every" national problem by creating a new government bureau, which increased the power of the federal establishment over the lives of individuals. Wrapping himself thus in the liberalism of Jefferson, Taft argued that "no party which pursues that program can claim the term 'liberal,'" which he felt was properly an effort to "avoid all detailed regulation by the government."[19] At a press conference the next day, the Ohioan said he found the political situation in the Great Plains State encouraging, then took off for Washington, D.C., to battle Truman's request for foreign aid.[20]

Later, Taft would partially adopt the Stassen strategy of grassroots campaigning. For the moment, though, his fledgling effort was a textbook example of old-style Republican politics. His strategy revolved around the regular Republican organizations and business and financial interests. His chain of command ran through his senate colleagues down to state organizations in which the senators had influence.

In Nebraska, Hugh Butler controlled, or was reputed to control, a tight state GOP organization. Taft's campaign manager, Representative Clarence Brown of Ohio, told reporters in January 1948 that Butler would "look after" Taft's interests in Nebraska. Brown went on to explain that Taft would not have the time to do much in the state personally, but would depend on Butler and his associates.[21] After Stassen began to look like a significant threat, however, Taft found more time in his schedule.

On March 11 Stassen flew to Alliance, Nebraska, to begin a three-day campaign swing, calling the primary, now commonly referred to as the "All-Star" primary, the "most significant" in the nation. He was met at the airport by Fred Seaton and a delegation of western Nebraska businessmen cochaired by J.L. Saylor, who was also chairman of the Box Butte County Republican Party.[22]

After a brief meeting the group hurried off to an auditorium where a capacity crowd of one thousand had gathered. Stassen told them of his meeting with Jan Masaryk in 1947. He spoke of the Czech patriot's "tragic death" and criticized the communist coup in Czechoslovakia as "showing that you cannot depend upon the word of the communist leaders to keep the people's freedom." Asked during his question-answer session whether he felt the United States was drifting toward a war with the Soviet Union, Stassen replied that he had the "sober optimism" that if American policy remained strong and consistent, "We can win without the tragedy of a third world war."[23]

After his speech in Alliance, Stassen traveled to Scottsbluff, where he outlined his program for federal support to maintain the income of farmers that was winning over rural voters in Wisconsin. The next day, after a breakfast talk in North Platte, the campaign proceeded to McCook. This stop turned out to be more than routine. In the heart of the Nebraska southwest, the city was thought to be a Butler stronghold; for that reason both Stassen and reporters took great interest when a delegate candidate from the area told Stassen that he resented being pushed around by the senator. "The Butler machine," Carl Marsh complained, "is backing Taft in this state and I very much resent it. Butler, as senator from this state, should not be handling the campaign for Mr. Taft, nor should he attempt to use his machine for that purpose." He added, "Butler is trying to hand the Nebraska national convention delegates to Mr. Taft, and I don't like it." Fred Seaton, surveying the reaction to Stassen in McCook, declared the Minnesotan's reception to be "beyond expectations."[24] On Saturday, March 13, Stassen closed his tour with appearances in Kearney, Grand Island and Beatrice before leaving for Wisconsin in the late evening.

Although Stassen had made appearances in Nebraska many times before, the tour that ended March 13 was important and an omen of his future visits. He had spoken to more than seven thousand persons in the eight cities he visited; he had answered questions and drunk coffee and chatted with patrons at a Lincoln drugstore. By the time he left, Burt James, political writer for the *Nebraska State Journal*, observed that "the general feeling was that the former Minnesota governor's chances of winning the April 13 Republican presidential primary had been considerably improved...." Stassen himself saw a grassroots movement budding in the Plains State. "[T]he days of campaigning in Nebraska have been successful beyond anticipation," he told reporters. "Indications of support from members of the regular Republican organizations, down to younger men and women who never have taken part in a campaign reminds me of my first campaign in Minnesota in 1938."[25]

As if to confirm Stassen's confidence in the support he was receiving from young people, a mock Republican convention at Wayne State Teachers College, in Wayne, Nebraska, a few days later "nominated" Stassen by a hefty margin over Thomas Dewey.[26]

The success of Stassen's grassroots campaign, as the *Omaha World Herald* noted, led to speculation that further activity could be expected from the other "All-Stars." This speculation was confirmed four days after the Minnesotan departed, as Max Miller, general chairman of the Nebraska Taft for President Committee, announced that Taft would return to Nebraska on April 5 and 6, on a tour that sounded suspiciously like Stassen's. Not at all, Miller protested, stressing that Taft felt a tour was necessary to discuss foreign policy. "Our office had been besieged by phone calls asking for Taft's reaction to the President's proposals.... Taft's supporters feel they should have his views."[27] Not to be outdone, the Stassen campaign announced on March 20 that Bernhard LeVander would travel to Lincoln on March 23 to speak before a chapter meeting of the YMCA.[28]

The next day, the Taft senate office announced a distinctly Stassen-like campaign itinerary. Taft would bring his wife, who would take a campaign swing of her own through eleven cities, while the senator would appear in twelve cities before the two met in Fremont on the night of April 7, as the tour was extended one day. The itinerary of both Tafts could have been taken from Stassen's appointment book, including small breakfasts, lunches and dinners and meetings with community organizations.[29] But before the Tafts could get to Nebraska, Stassen had already been there once again, this time arriving in Omaha on March 24 to tell a receptive audience that he favored strengthening the Pick-Sloan Plan (the federal program to develop the Missouri Valley) and the creation of a ten-state regional authority to administer the completed development projects.[30]

Meanwhile, Thomas Dewey, having watched first Stassen and then Robert Taft take to the hustings, abandoned his Governor's Mansion campaign and sallied into Wisconsin before traveling to Nebraska. His decision to actively campaign was given great notice in the Great Plains State, and Taft supporters promptly delivered themselves of the opinion that Dewey was afraid of Taft. No response by Stassen was reported, although by that point in late March, it hardly needed to be said that the Minnesotan was giving chills to the New Yorker in Wisconsin. Nebraskan political pundits traced the announced Nebraska tours of Dewey and Taft to the fear that Stassen's grassroots tours might be working.[31]

And they were working. Simply, voters liked it when presidential candidates spoke in their municipal auditoriums, drank coffee in their local drugstores, answered their questions, and otherwise demonstrated their respect. That is why the cerebral Robert Taft changed strategies and took his wife to Nebraska. With the stubbornness of a New Yorker, Dewey did not learn this lesson until it was — almost — too late; after the nomination, he forgot it for good.

When Dewey's Nebraska schedule was announced, the Stassen campaign promptly repeated a trick they had played when the New Yorker announced his Wisconsin schedule. They announced that, coincidentally, Stassen would be in the same city on the same day as Dewey and was renewing his call for a debate. The Dewey campaign haughtily refused.[32]

Meanwhile, the Tafts arrived in Nebraska on Monday, April 5, to try their hand at grassroots campaigning. At a Scottsbluff breakfast meeting the senator spoke to three hundred fifty persons before traveling to a street corner in Ogallala where two hundred persons waited to greet him. He spoke for a half hour before giving a speech in a North Platte theater with an attendance of about three hundred. That evening Taft, in a speech in Grand Island, attempted to wrestle in on the respect that farmers were paying to Stassen and, to a lesser degree, Dewey, by announcing an agricultural policy which sought to give the farmer "the freedom to run his own farm," meaning no production controls or rationing in peacetime. Mrs. Taft spent her first day traveling three hundred miles from Sand Hills to Alliance, giving four speeches to over five hundred people.[33] Unfortunately, the day was marred for the Tafts when the senator, asked his opinion on the concept of an "All-Star" primary, said, "I think it is foolish." He complained that there were too many factors in such an election and that it proved or disproved nothing. Offended Nebraskans had to be content with Mrs. Taft's comment that the primary was "a pretty good idea, I think." She added that "of course, if every state did it, it would be terribly expensive and some candidates wouldn't be able to cover the whole country."[34]

The Tafts left the state on Wednesday night, April 7, as Thomas Dewey was arriving. The trip was billed a success, but clearly the senator's trip lacked the punch of Harold Stassen's campaign swings, as the crowds were generally smaller and less engaged in the speakers' remarks. Adopting the Minnesotan's trademark, Taft at the end of his speeches asked the audience for questions, but he was rarely presented with many. Moreover, his answers were detailed and lengthy. Not surprisingly, as one newspaper account written on Monday evening observed, "The Taft crowds ... have not shown the enthusiasm they displayed for Stassen."[35]

Also on the same day Dewey arrived in the state, evidence of the fierce loyalty Minnesotans felt for Stassen was evident in the arrival in Nebraska of three Minnesota women who came to work for their former governor. In a statement, they said that they wanted "to remind Nebraskans of the qualities of Mr. Stassen for the Presidency. Our greatest argument is that both Gallup and Roper polls show that he is the only one who can best Mr. Truman." All three expressed enthusiasm for the "All-Star" primary, noting that it was in keeping with Stassen's idea that the people should have every opportunity to know the views of the candidates.[36]

That night Dewey arrived in Grand Island to begin his two-day tour, arriving only hours before Stassen returned to the state. He was met at the airport by his Nebraska campaign manager, J. Lee Rankin, and a crowd of two hundred who waited for the one hour and twenty-five-minute late airplane in the chilly air. The New Yorker apologized for being late. "I ran into a head wind," he said. "But I am used to that because I ran into one Tuesday in Wisconsin." Asked what he thought of the "All-Star" idea, he replied, in a devious dig at Stassen, "It's a fine idea. The only trouble is that those with jobs can't get away to campaign as much as they'd like to." He added that the New York legislature had passed "one thousand bills which required my study and that is the real reason for my delay in visiting Nebraska." Told that Hamilton Fish, an isolationist former congressman from New York, had suggested that Dewey withdraw from the presidential race because of his poor showing in Wisconsin, the governor replied, "I was the one chiefly responsible for retiring Mr. Fish to private life," referring to Fish's defeat in 1944.[37]

A major target of the New Yorker in his hunt for votes were farmers, and the next day he traveled to rural Nebraska with his proposal to produce surplus food for storage as a method of ensuring farm income. Yet he also sought to demonstrate his worldliness, with a major address on foreign policy that night at the University of Nebraska Coliseum in Lincoln. He said the United States should direct its foreign policy, including the Marshall Plan, toward building a "United States of Europe," although he took care to note that "just cash and gifts can't avert war." Significantly, the speech was attended by a huge and enthusiastic crowd, estimated at seventy-five hundred.[38] This was the first indication that the New Yorker had bypassed Taft, Hugh Butler notwithstanding, in Nebraska support, and had now only to contend with Harold Stassen.

While Dewey was speaking at the Coliseum, five miles away Stassen was speaking at Huskerville, a housing project for student veterans located at the former Lincoln Army Air Base, where he was asked, "How would you cope with John L. Lewis?" The former governor replied, "By using the Taft-Hartley Law and using it promptly," which delighted the audience. Earlier that day Stassen had spoken before cheering crowds at the University of Nebraska, Nebraska Wesleyan University and Union College, all in Lincoln.[39] Coincidentally, Luther Youngdahl, who had in 1946 succeeded Ed Thye as governor of Minnesota and who had traveled to Nebraska to stump for Stassen, was in the city of Minden that night promoting Stassen's labor record before a group of businessmen.

Despite the receptive audiences that came to Stassen appearances, the campaign was still nervous about the clout wielded by the Butler machine. At a press conference, the Minnesotan surely understated his concern by indicating that he did not discount the strength of the Butler group. "It is quite a strong organization," he admitted. But reporters noted that his campaign staff were constantly asking of Nebraskans how many votes Butler could deliver.[40]

Stassen, who had publicly predicted before the Wisconsin primary that he would win a majority of delegates in that state, refused to predict the outcome of the Nebraska contest, ducking reporters' queries by saying, "We've followed the policy of discussing the issues and letting the voters decide." Reminded that in an earlier visit to Nebraska he had said that "if the trend of support continues" he would carry the state, he said merely "indications are that we are gaining support."[41]

On April 9, Senator Ed Thye, Stassen's hand-picked successor as governor of Minnesota, arrived in Nebraska for a two-day campaign swing for his mentor. Concentrating on the eastern corner of the state, Thye recited Stassen's qualifications as governor, San Francisco United Nations delegate and naval officer. Governor Youngdahl, meanwhile, continued his Plains State appearances, targeting Swedish voters, going so far as to sing a song in Swedish he had learned on a recent trip to Europe.[42]

In the final days of the campaign, the intensity and suspense in the state were palpable. Thomas Dewey took to directly asking his audiences for their support, something he had not done before, and extended his Nebraska tour by an extra day. Increasingly he focused on politics, arguing that he, not Stassen or Taft, could best compete against Truman, whom he attacked in increasingly vociferous language. "It's about time," he said in Omaha, "that we ... insist that our government stop listening to the left-wingers, the communist propaganda and its own fears and doubts and start believing whole-heartedly in our system."[43]

From Omaha, Dewey traveled to Fremont, where, coincidentally, Stassen was headed also. Learning that the two might both be embarrassed by an unexpected meeting, Stassen told the driver of his chartered bus to stop at a café in Scribner, a town with a population of about nine hundred fifty. As Stassen, his staff and ten reporters strolled into Addie's and Carrier's Café, they were mistaken by Addie Legband, the coproprietor, for the Polka Orchestra, the band scheduled to play that night. When the candidate admitted that he was not a musician but only a presidential candidate, word leaked out and the humble café was besieged by autograph seekers, one of whom handed a blank check for the Minnesotan to sign. He politely declined.[44]

Finally arriving in Fremont, the former governor ignored Dewey in his remarks and repeated his support for federal development of the Missouri Valley. While in Fremont, Stassen, in standard American political form, posed for pictures with two elephants at a circus at the municipal auditorium.[45]

On April 9 Stassen departed from Omaha for Washington, D.C., to attend the National Press Club's annual Gridiron Dinner. As he left, the press reported that the "general attitude of the Stassen camp may be summarized as confident, but not cocky."

Dewey remained in Omaha, attacking the Truman administration for "ineptness" in foreign affairs. Stassen supporters might have felt distinctly less confident had they seen the crowds that turned out for the 1944 nominee — Dewey was surrounded by excited Nebraskans.[46] Still, Dewey's opponents could take heart that even the evidently popular governor had his bad moments. In Alliance, Dewey and his entire party got lost in the City Auditorium building. They took the wrong door and ended up pounding on a door leading to the fire department, where bemused firemen pointed the candidate in the right direction. When he finally reached the podium, a bull terrier trotted around the audience for several minutes before clambering up on the stage, where Dewey, according to press accounts the next day, growled, "Go away," to the dog.[47]

On April 10, the former New York prosecutor rested his case with Nebraskans and departed for Albany the next morning. His tour had been extremely impressive, and considered in retrospect, probably was largely responsible for the fourteen-point margin that separated him from third-place Taft in the balloting. In three days he had visited eleven towns by bus and three by air and talked to some twenty-three thousand persons. Yet, neither he nor anybody else would make specific predictions about the outcome of the primary, although Dewey implied that he felt he was ahead. His campaign staff said that Stassen was the man to beat.[48]

Meanwhile, in San Francisco, J. Howard McGrath, the Democratic National committee chairman, told reporters that Dewey and Taft had reached an agreement to work together to stop Stassen. Without citing his source, McGrath said that the contenders would throw their delegate to the strongest of the two at the GOP convention. "That's absurd," sputtered Hugh Butler, who insisted, "There isn't any deal. Bob Taft is in this fight to win and I am very confident that he's going to do just that next Tuesday," in the Nebraska primary. Dewey spokesmen also vehemently denied the rumor.[49]

On Saturday, April 10, the Stassen campaign played its final ace, as the "Paul Revere Riders" took to the streets. Across Nebraska, roughly one thousand Stassen supporters piled into some two hundred fifty cars, driving to nearby towns to greet people on the streets and distribute Stassen campaign literature. They were directed in Nebraska by Phil Mullin of Friend, who emphasized that all who took part were Nebraskans who were volunteers and paid their own expenses. At the end of the day, Mullin boasted that more than four hundred towns and cities in all ninety-three counties of the state had been covered. The Riders had concentrated on areas with a population of more than five hundred within thirty miles of their hometowns. Wearing huge "Stassen Paul Revere Riders" badges, they distributed one hundred twenty-five thousand pieces of literature.[50]

With the polls due to open in less than twelve hours, Stassen stepped off a plane in Omaha for a final speech, billed "the most important of the campaign" by Fred Seaton, before twelve hundred supporters; it was broadcast live across the state. His speech concentrated on foreign affairs, and Stassen took a bitterly hard line against communism. "It is my view," he said, "that events of these brief years since the war make clear that an aggressive communist infiltration, using communist party organizations, who take their orders from Moscow, is a principal component of Russian foreign policy. I hold that the communist party organization should be promptly outlawed in all freedom loving countries in the world."[51] The outlawing of the communist party was an area of sharp contention between Stassen and Dewey, who opposed the policy. Unfortunately for Dewey, neither candidate had made it a prominent issue during the Nebraska campaign; unfortunately for Stassen, it would become one during the Oregon contest.

In a final pitch for support, Stassen in effect, invited Nebraska to get on his bandwagon: "I pledge to you tonight, that it will be my constant endeavor to so conduct myself in Republican leadership in the years ahead that the people of Nebraska may never have cause to regret this early and strong support.[52]

On the morning of April 13, as Nebraskans were going to the polls, Stassen, accompanied by his wife, attended a breakfast thrown by the Nebraska campaign staff in honor of the Minnesotan's forty-first birthday. After the breakfast, the Stassens departed for St. Paul, where they soon started receiving calls from excited supporters.

The race was not even close. From the moment returns began to be reported from the various precincts, Stassen never lost the lead. Dewey could muster victories in only seven of the ninety-three counties. In the largest turnout for a primary in Nebraska history, Stassen polled 80,522 votes, an amazing 43 percent of the total in a seven-candidate field. Dewey trailed with 63,885 votes, 35 percent, while Taft garnered a dismal 21,288 votes, or 11 percent. Far behind, with less than 5 percent each, finished Vandenberg, MacArthur, Earl Warren, and Joseph Martin, in that order. Although the vote was officially only a "popularity contest," nine of the delegates to the Republican national convention, also elected that day, pledged to abide by the state's decision and support Stassen. Three others said that they would "probably" support Stassen, one stubbornly announced his allegiance to Dewey, and one remained uncommitted.[53]

Stassen's victory was widely attributed to his grassroots effort, or as the *Omaha World Herald* put it, "the efficient organization that worked for him and the tremendous amount of personal campaigning he did.... Mr. Stassen won the election ... by hard hand-shaking and campaigning over a long period of time."[54]

Yet there were clouds looming on the horizon. Before the primary Stassen had predicted, accurately, that he would win the farm vote. He did, and in a big way, but he lost major cities like Omaha, just as he had lost large population areas in Wisconsin and New Hampshire. The premise, though, of the Stassen challenge to Robert Taft in the Ohio primary was that unionized workers in industrial areas, angered by the Taft-Hartley law, would vent their hostility by voting against its principal sponsor. Yet Stassen had no record of carrying industrial areas; even in Minnesota his support had been rural-based. Nevertheless, on April 14, Stassen left for Ohio.

8. The Decline: Ohio

Presidential aspirants rarely entered primary contests in the home state of any possible opponent. Ostensibly, this was done out of respect for the home turf of the rival; yet two realities belied this gentlemanly veneer. First, an "outlander" was not likely to win against a hometown hero, and nobody wanted to be tinged with a crushing defeat. Second, opposing a candidate on his home ground would turn a potential ally into a bitter enemy at the national convention. Thus, Harold Stassen's decision to enter into the Ohio primary raised the eyebrows as well as the temperatures of Ohio conservatives who might otherwise have supported Stassen at the national convention in Philadelphia.

Officially, the reason for entering the Ohio primary was Stassen's belief in "letting the people decide" the Republican nominee. The Minnesotan argued that he really did not have a choice in the matter. Given his professed belief in giving voters a choice, it would have been hypocritical to ignore the Buckeye State contest. Also, Stassen was committed to moving the Republican Party toward more liberal policies, and what better way to stimulate debate than by competing against "Mr. Republican" himself?

Regardless of the importance that the former governor attached to his ideals, hardheaded politicians on his staff, notably Earl Hart, the manager of his Washington, D.C., office, looked at the political odds in Ohio and saw a possible victory. Stassen's name on the ticket would be a magnet, it was thought, to liberals and union workers in industrial areas of the state enraged by the Taft-Hartley Act. With an impressive showing in Ohio, Stassen would simultaneously knock Taft out of the race while consolidating his claim to the leadership of the liberal, international wing of the party, which he hoped was large enough, or could be made large enough, to carry him to the nomination.

The decision to enter the Ohio contest was not made without considerable study. The principal "point man" for the investigation was Hart, a veteran of politics in the Buckeye State. In the summer of 1947, Stassen went to Columbus to deliver an address. Accompanying him on the trip was Bernhard LeVander, who described the trip in a memo to Fred Hughes, a St. Cloud, Minnesota, attorney and Stassen supporter. Hughes, reading over the memo, responded with a forceful letter arguing against challenging Taft. Hughes noted that from LeVander's letter, it appeared that Stassen's reception in Ohio "lacked the spontaneity and drive which characterizes our affairs." As a result, Hughes argued, "I think we should stay out of Ohio. The small numerical gain, as well as the larger psychological, which would come from a few delegates garnered in Ohio, would not justify our risking the loss of our friendly disposition."[1] LeVander hardly needed this advice, since he was to become a principal opponent of an Ohio challenge. "I felt that we shouldn't spread ourselves too thin," the campaign chairman recalled. "We had limited resources. We had certain key primaries that we felt were strategically important to win, like Wisconsin, Nebraska, Oregon, and that Ohio was one that ... we had a poor chance" of winning.[2]

Hart disagreed. In November of 1947, Stassen sent him on a tour of Ohio to "make a survey of the situation." From November 17 to 21 Hart visited Dayton, Cleveland, Youngstown, Toledo, and Akron and came back enthusiastic. "I have told the governor," Hart later wrote to LeVander, "that there are Stassen delegates in Ohio if he wanted to go in there and get them." In addition, the eager Hart asserted his conviction that if Stassen entered the Ohio primary he would have, also, to challenge Thomas Dewey in New York, reasoning that Stassen could not justify "home turf" competition with one rival and not the other.[3] Yet Hart from the beginning had been excited about entering the Ohio primary and it is a reasonable suspicion that he saw little in the Buckeye State that he did not want to see.

Senator Robert Taft, ca. 1952 (Ohio Historical Society).

Indeed, as LeVander read Hart's report to Stassen on the Ohio expedition, he must have wondered whether he and Hart were talking about the same Ohio. LeVander promptly wrote his own memo to Stassen, in which he objected that Hart's "conclusions do not seem entirely warranted by what he reports the feeling is at the meetings [in Ohio, with state Republican leaders]. If these men advise us to stay out of Ohio giving Taft the right of way, it is hard for me to conceive how they would be willing to carry on the campaign on your behalf in the event you decide to run." The cautious LeVander also objected to Hart's logic in declaring that it was necessary to challenge Dewey in New York if Stassen challenged Taft in Ohio. "I do not follow the theory that it would be necessary for you to go into New York," he said. "You could, I think, explain the differences in operation in the two states since in Ohio you have an open primary, whereas in New York you have mixed primary and convention laws. Another reason might be that Ohio is considered a Midwestern state where your natural support and strength is stronger and the demand for your entrance had been greater." But the chairman was careful to add, "Let me make myself clear: On the basis of Hart's report, I do not advise going into Ohio."[4]

Aside from his concern about spreading the Stassen campaign too thin and suffering a potentially irreparable setback, LeVander opposed challenging Taft because the chairman saw in "Mr. Republican" and his delegation potential allies at the national convention.

Despite the ideological chasm that separated the conservative Ohioan and the liberal Minnesotan, LeVander as a state GOP leader was sensitive to the implications of the bitter personal feelings that existed between Taft and Thomas Dewey.

"It was my feeling," LeVander recalled, "that because of the tremendous animosity that existed between Taft and Dewey, that we might be able to benefit eventually — if we handled things right — and get Taft's votes at the convention. By going into Ohio, where we had a very slim chance of winning, where we would have to spend a great deal of time ... we would unnecessarily antagonize" the Ohio senator. Serving simultaneously as chairman of the Minnesota Republican Party and of the Stassen campaign, LeVander was not without insight into politics in the Buckeye State, and was likely a more dispassionate observer than the native Hart.

In the summer of 1947 LeVander was invited by the Ohio GOP, controlled by Robert Taft, to Columbus for a large conference of Republican leaders. "I got the feeling," LeVander reflected, "that there was not as much real animosity or friction between the Stassen and Taft crowd as you might expect ... based on the philosophical differences. And given what you might call a political hatred between Taft and Dewey, I thought we might pick up support at the right time."[5]

Despite LeVander's misgivings the brash Hart appeared determined to lead a charge into Ohio. In January of 1948, when Stassen had yet to make a final decision, he went off to his home state to organize a slate of delegate candidates should the decision be made to challenge Taft. The primary in Ohio, as in New Hampshire and Wisconsin, was in actuality a contest between delegate candidates, each competing in his own district for the honor of going to the convention. Each candidate could run either "pledged" to a White House aspirant, in which case the delegate was required to vote for him at the convention on at least the first ballot, or as "uncommitted." Hart's decision to go to Ohio in January reflected his determination to have a slate of "pledged" delegates at the ready should he receive his longed-for order to go ahead with the challenge. It appears that Hart, by mid–January, was attempting to build momentum behind a decision to contest Taft, so that it would have been difficult to call a halt to it and stay out of Ohio. In an extraordinary memo to LeVander written on January 14, Hart noted that Stassen would not make a decision about Ohio until the end of the month, then continued the memo as if the matter was quite settled. "This was a hard decision for the governor to make," he wrote in a tone like a victor uses to console his defeated opponent, "and of course it is a big gamble. However ... I feel we can win some delegates."[6]

Only days after Stassen made his final decision to contest Taft, a Gallup poll reported that voters were becoming less, not more, sympathetic to organized labor's effort to repeal or revise the Taft-Hartley Act. By February 1948, 40 percent of voters who had heard or read about Taft-Hartley favored its revision or outright repeal. This compared with 53 percent just after Congress had overridden Truman's veto in the summer of 1947.[7] The Taft-Hartley Act was the Republicans' effort to turn the tables on organized labor. In 1935 the Democratic party, in control of the executive and legislative branches and invigorated by a renewed mandate in the 1934 elections, passed the Wagner Act.

The federal government now, for the first time, was firmly granted the authority to vigorously help labor in its unequal struggle to organize and bargain collectively for fair and equitable conditions. In November 1946, however, the Republicans captured the legislative branch and passed, over Harry Truman's veto, the Taft-Hartley Act, which listed "unfair" labor practices: The closed shop, any coercion of nonunion workers; secondary boycotts and jurisdictional strikes; refusal to bargain in good faith; political contributions by labor unions. Labor leaders were required to sign a pledge that they were not communists. Employers could now sue for breach of contract. Where a strike threatened the national health or safety, the president could secure a court injunction that would provide an eighty-day "cooling off" period before the strike could begin. Also, all unions were required to register with the secretary of labor and provide regular financial reports.[8]

Stringent though the law was, Harold Stassen could claim at least some part of the credit for moderating the bill when it appeared before the Senate Labor Committee. In February 1947, while the committee was wrestling with the bill, Stassen was asked to testify about labor policy. When the bill finally passed, the *Minnesota Letter* celebrated that "it is well worth noting how much the final verdict resembles the proposals made by Stassen." Nine of ten recommendations made by Stassen were accepted; of the ten "don'ts" Stassen warned the committee to avoid, all were left out.[9] The Minnesotan supported the provisions allowing for courts of inquiry, the eighty-day clause, the injunctive power in the government; provisions seeking to prevent strikes in essential industry; provisions against jurisdictional strikes; and provisions against the secondary boycott.[10]

Yet the former governor nonetheless had sharp differences with Taft-Hartley, and these objections formed the core of his appeal to Ohio voters. Stassen called for the repeal of the law's provision which was "interpreted to mean that a union newspaper cannot print articles about political campaigns," arguing that this violated the concept of a free press. The Stassen campaign was to receive favorable coverage from union newspapers during the Ohio primary, Taft-Hartley notwithstanding.[11] Also, the Minnesotan opposed "those provisions restricting the union shop which go so far that it makes it impossible to renew contracts which both employers and men wish to renew." Finally, Stassen opposed the portion of the law that required all union officers to sign affidavits that they were not communists. "It is against the American grain," the former governor complained. "The provision should be that only if accused of being a communist should the requirement of signing an affidavit be required, and if not signed, the persons who did not sign might have the proof presented against them, and if duly proven they should be barred from union leadership." Exactly who was to decide whether the charges were "proven" or not, Stassen did not say.[12]

Stassen obviously felt that these objections were significant, calling them "examples of our more liberal approach to this problem." Yet in the same speech where he laid out the objections noted above, he also declared, "I hold as an essential addition to American world policy that the Communist party organization should be promptly outlawed in America and in every freedom-loving country in the world."[13]

The Taft campaign pounced on what they saw as an inconsistency in objecting to the anticommunist provisions of Taft-Hartley and the call for outlawing the Communist Party, quite overlooking the fact that Stassen would brook no communist affiliation even in union members. In an unsigned memo to the senator, a Taft staff member called attention to the "major inconsistency between his positions" and charged, "to say the least, his thinking is fuzzy, for he doesn't approve the one and approves the other." The staff member also made the more reasonable point that Stassen did not recommend that the Communist Party be outlawed when he discussed the party at length in his book *Where I Stand*. In fact, the former governor "seemed" to lean in quite the other direction, indicating that this would make martyrs of communists.[14]

To the exasperation of Robert Taft, the accusation of inconsistency never "stuck." Aside from the dubious merits of the charge, perhaps the reason is that despite Taft's ultimate, or perceived, success in the primary, he remained clearly on the defensive throughout the campaign and was too busy defending himself and his political base to spend much time taking the offensive, although he would from time to time make the attempt. Yet, of the two, Stassen was obviously the antagonist.

He first threw down the gauntlet in a speech in Cleveland in March 1948, where he told two thousand persons jammed into a public music hall that he would enter the Ohio primary because "it is my view that our Republican party should present to the American people this year a dynamic, forward looking, humanitarian program." He added that Robert Taft was not "realistic and imaginative in foreign policy." Specifically, Stassen charged that Taft had "stated in New England that he had 'no knowledge' of any Russian intention for military aggression. This," the former governor went on, "undoubtedly accounts for his opposition to preparedness."[15] By this Stassen surely meant Taft's opposition to universal military training, which the Minnesotan supported and the Ohioan opposed.

Also in Cleveland was Earl Hart, who had moved to Ohio to take charge of the campaign. Hart rounded up delegate candidates in eleven of the twenty-two districts, each of which would elect two delegates, and one candidate at large. These districts had been carefully selected as areas where union membership was high and, it was hoped, disaffection with Taft considerable. Stassen explained that he had entered delegates in only eleven districts because he "wanted to test the issues" rather than, he assured Ohioans, "take over the state Republican organization."[16]

In March, Hart was busily establishing headquarters in principal cities throughout the state. He reported to Warren Burger and treasurer Alfred Lindley that he had secured considerable financial support from Ohio, hopefully enough to make the Buckeye State effort self-sufficient. Among the major contributors was the president of the National Cash Register Company, who agreed to underwrite or raise funds to keep the Dayton headquarters solvent, and the president of the Ferro Enamel Corporation, who undertook the same mission for the office in Cleveland. Hart did request five hundred dollars from Lindley to help set up an office in Akron, but assured the treasurer that the person in charge of the office, Raymond Finley, of a major Akron bank, hoped to receive enough support to keep it going on his own. Finley had hinted that Harvey Firestone, Jr., would be a principal contributor, but as yet no commitments had been made.[17]

Meanwhile, Robert Taft and his staff and supporters were girding for battle. A staff member of the senator sent a memo to his boss suggesting that "some friendly Ohio newspaper" should wire Stassen, sending him a list of ten votes taken in the U.S. Senate during the 80th Congress. The paper would then challenge Stassen to say whether he would have voted for or against each measure. Apparently, Taft never acted on the suggestion.[18]

Late in March, Ohio congressman and Taft campaign chairman Clarence Brown asked his staff to investigate a report in the *New Ulm Minnesota Journal* that Stassen, while governor of Minnesota, received help from state Democratic "boss" Ed Flynn during the 1942 elections in exchange for later unspecified favors. The staff member, undoubtedly to Brown's chagrin, found the report to be without foundation[19]; yet the investigation reveals the seriousness with which the Taft forces viewed the Minnesotan's challenge and signaled that LeVander's prediction of animosity between Stassen and Taft had come to pass. Aside from the bitterness that would naturally flow from a home-state challenge by an outsider, resentment was also caused by a fundamental difference of political orientation between the two candidates.

Stassen took pride in the grassroots nature of his effort, while Taft and his supporters came from a more traditional perspective that party leaders should choose the presidential nominee. This is starkly revealed in a memo prepared for Taft analyzing Stassen's campaign techniques. "The modus operandi of Harold E. Stassen," the memo read, "and his cohorts is by this time pretty well known in political circles: the thorough tactics of infiltration into a contested area, of bringing in outside workers, of the 'Paul Revere Riders,' etc." The memo clearly had no use for such renegade behavior.[20]

Plotting their strategy, the Taft forces received help from William J. Campbell from Oshkosh, Wisconsin. Campbell had been a delegate candidate for Stassen in the 1944 Wisconsin primary; but by 1948 he had switched his allegiance to Douglas MacArthur, for whom he ran as a delegate candidate while serving as vice-chairman of MacArthur's Wisconsin Campaign Committee. After losing both elections, Campbell began sending letters to Taft and Rep. Brown, informing them of Stassen's campaign tactics in Wisconsin and proffering advice on how best to meet them.

Campbell's letters were strident in tone as he charged that Stassen received illegal help from Senator Joseph McCarthy, who had sent out a mailing that was possibly financed, in part, at government expense, and was "covering up" the sources of his campaign funds, which Campbell speculated were coming from the CIO.[21] The same charges that Campbell leveled in his letters were later to be found in the public comments of Taft's supporters. Stassen at the time was unaware of Campbell's efforts and when later told of the activities of his former supporter, the Minnesotan shrugged it off. "I'm not surprised, really," he said. "MacArthur and Taft were so close philosophically."[22]

Stassen began his Ohio effort in earnest less than forty-eight hours after his triumph in Nebraska, flying into Cleveland on the morning of Thursday, April 15. Bad weather had forced a cancellation of his initial plans to arrive in the city the night before, to the bitter disappointment of Allen J. Lowe, the managing director of the Hotel Carter, who had prepared a large birthday celebration for the candidate, complete with cake and appropriate accompaniments. Stassen was immediately off to Hiram, Ohio, to address the mock GOP convention at Hiram College.

Despite the cheers with which the students greeted the former governor, in the end their convention nominated Dewey on the fourth ballot with 226 votes to Stassen's 206; Taft was presented with a dismal defeat, mustering only 35 votes on the first roll call and zero on the fourth.[23] After his Hiram address Stassen hurried to Youngstown, via his traditional chartered bus, for noon, afternoon, and evening addresses.[24]

That same day, the Taft forces were heartened by evidence that organized labor was clearly not united in seeking to defeat the father of Taft-Hartley. *The Machinist*, the weekly newspaper of the National Association of Machinists, printed an article in its April 15 issue which bitterly condemned Stassen's labor record in Minnesota. Perhaps more damaging given the Minnesotan's anti–Taft-Hartley pitch to Ohio voters, the paper noted the many positive remarks Stassen had made about the labor law and accused him of hiding an "anti-labor" philosophy for the duration of the presidential campaign.[25]

While union members pondered this allegation, business leaders studied the Minnesotan's record and were not displeased. While no general consensus seems to have formed for or against the Minnesota among Ohio businessmen, executives did express enthusiasm for parts of the Stassen program. For example, Stassen supported federal backing for a proposed Lake Erie-Ohio River Canal, believing that this would fit into a national program of conservation and development. This caught the eye of the Youngstown Chamber of Commerce. H.R. Packard, executive secretary to the chamber, sent a letter to Carl Ullman, president of the Youngstown Dollar Savings and Trust Company and Taft confidant, admitting that Stassen's position on the canal "interests us." Dropping broad hints, Packard noted that the Youngstown Chamber of Commerce had been "unsuccessful" in its efforts to discuss the subject with Taft.[26]

With Stassen campaigning in the Buckeye State, Robert Taft was clearly uneasy and defensive. On April 16, Taft abruptly canceled a scheduled trip to Vermont and flew from Washington, D.C., one day ahead of schedule to meet with his advisers in Cleveland. Accompanying him was Congressman George H. Bender, chairman of the Cuyahoga County Republican Party, which, like other county organizations and the state GOP, was working for Taft. The two men huddled with Taft supporters, all the while protesting that their early meeting did not reflect concern on their part, "Nothing specifically is different," Taft commented innocently, "we just want to intensify our campaign."[27]

The agenda at the Taft meeting was not revealed, but the next day the Ohio Republican State Central Committee, which backed Taft, announced plans to place "challengers" at polling places in each of the eleven districts where Stassen delegate candidates were entered. Under a bizarre Ohio law, a voter could ask for either a Democratic or Republican ballot, but, if challenged, was required to take an oath that he or she had voted for a majority of the party's candidates in the last election. By placing individuals at the polls to challenge voters, the Republicans were attempting to guard against a reported, never substantiated, strategy of Democrats to call for Republican ballots to vote for Stassen in an effort to discredit the Ohio senator.[28]

After a brief swing in Florida, Stassen returned to Ohio on April 21, campaigning through Middletown and Hamilton, near Robert Taft's home, before heading to Dayton for a major address on foreign policy. In his speech the Minnesotan sought to portray himself as a reasonable and thoughtful moderate. There were, Stassen said, two views dominating the discussion of foreign affairs. One side called for appeasement, or granting unilateral concessions to the Soviets; the other side had as its premise that war was inevitable, and therefore urged a drastic program of rearmament. Stassen called for a middle ground, recognizing aggression as characteristic of Soviet policy and taking adequate precautions, which included guarding against Kremlin-led subversion in the United States by outlawing the Communist Party. America had to keep its military strength, even resorting to the draft. Yet, Stassen insisted, negotiations to reduce tension between the two powers should be conducted.[29]

Continuing, Stassen reminded voters that he would release any delegates pledged to him who won in the primary, declaring, "I do not believe in political strings or commitments or deals. I believe in a free people exercising their own judgment upon the questions which affect them in light of the accumulation of facts and or experience." Finally, while noting that he was in almost "complete disagreement" with Taft, Stassen praised the sincerity and accomplishments of the Ohio senator and stated that he was enjoining his delegate candidates never to make a personal attack on Taft.[30]

Not placated, Taft charged in Stuebenville the next day that, in claiming to differ with Robert Taft, Stassen was in fact claiming how he differed with the Republican Party as a whole. Declared Mr. Republican: "Mr. Stassen ... has made the general statement that he is more liberal than I am; he wants the support of the people because he is more liberal.... The fact is that my policies on domestic issues and foreign issues have been the same as the Republican majority of Congress. If he differs with my policy, if he thinks my policies are wrong, then he is differing with the policy developed by the Republican Congress. Well, all I have to say is that if he is in disagreement with me, he is in disagreement with the Republican Party."[31]

Exactly how much Stassen's record differed with Robert Taft's was the subject of an investigation by Thomas E. Shroyer, chief counsel for the congressional Joint Committee on Labor-Management Relations. This committee was chaired by Minnesota senator Joseph Ball, with Robert Taft the second-ranking member. Ball had been appointed to the senate by Stassen in 1940, and the governor had supported Ball for election in 1942. However, Ball and Stassen had a serious political falling out in 1944, when the senator supported Franklin Roosevelt against Thomas Dewey. When FDR carried Minnesota, state Republicans, including Stassen, felt that Ball had "sold out."

Early in 1948, Stassen had reportedly even toyed with the idea of supporting a candidate to oppose Ball in the Republican primary. He decided against it, but the enmity between the two was clear, and Ball made no effort to support Stassen's White House bid. "I was not involved in any way in Harold's 1948 campaign...." Ball recalled years later. "This was due partly ... to the fact that Harold and I had drifted apart politically after World War II and saw very little of each other."[32]

Given the antipathy between Stassen and Ball, it is not surprising that the senator apparently made no effort to prevent Shroyer from using committee resources to benefit the Taft campaign. Although there is no evidence that the Ohio senator actually requested the investigation, on April 23 Shroyer prepared a memo address to Senator Taft. "We have," the congressional committee's chief counsel wrote, "studied the Minnesota labor statutes passed under the administration of Governor Stassen with a view to making a comparison with the restriction upon unions provided by the Taft-Hartley labor law." Shroyer reported that, "generally speaking, the Minnesota law is considerably more drastic in its regulation

Harold Stassen (left) and Joseph Ball, 1946 (Minnesota Historical Society).

of unions" in three areas, dealing with internal regulation, the right to strike and enforcement of labor laws.[33] Shroyer's points surfaced in Taft's public remarks in the closing days of the campaign.[34]

The use of congressional staff for campaign purposes presents obvious questions of propriety. The Stassen forces were unaware of Shroyer's memo. Shown the document years later, Bernhard LeVander noted, "Well, it appears that this was done at a strategic time for Taft.... It shows they had little respect for Harold, anyway."[35]

While Shroyer was typing out his memo on April 23, Stassen was in Akron delivering a political pitch that was increasingly focusing on union members. This tactic was admitted frankly by the former governor, who told an audience at Central High School, "The plea will not fall on deaf ears. Already a large number of labor Republicans have expressed their preference for Stassen over Robert A. Taft ... who was co-author of the nefarious Taft-Hartley law."

Stassen had earlier used words more charitable than "nefarious" to describe the law, but his perception of labor support was not without foundation, as prominent Ohio labor leaders began to publicly express their support for the Minnesotan. John Kumpel, compensation director of the United Rubber, Cork, Linoleum and Plastic Workers of America, speaking at a meeting of the Akron CIO Council, made a plea for all district Republicans affiliated with organized labor to back Stassen. "Organized labor of Ohio," he declared, "has an opportunity to eliminate an anti-labor presidential candidate by giving Stassen a strong vote in the May primary."[36]

On April 24 the Stassen campaign received a shot of adrenalin in the form of a new Gallup poll, which announced that for the first time the former governor had moved into the lead in a survey measuring the national support of each White House aspirant. The poll, conducted April 9 through April 17, only partly reflected the national boost of the Wisconsin and Nebraska victories, and still justified the primary-based strategy of the Stassen effort. The Minnesotan had shot up an astonishing sixteen percentage points, rising from 15 to 31 percent, from a poll taken only one month earlier, moving him from third place, behind Dewey and MacArthur, to first, ahead of Dewey at 29 percent and MacArthur with 16 percent. The poll was hardly good news for Robert Taft, who placed fifth with a dismal 9 percent.[37] Stassen now faced the task of maintaining this lead, which he hoped would impress party leaders at the national convention enough to win their support. Despite his poor showing in the national poll, Taft exuberantly predicted an unambiguous vote of confidence from his constituents, telling reporters on April 23 that he was "considerably more optimistic" than Clarence Brown, who predicted that Stassen might win four to nine delegates out of the twenty-three convention seats he was seeking.[38]

Still, Taft was pulling no punches. On April 25 he announced that Ohio's junior senator, John Bricker, and Governor Thomas Herbert would stump the areas where Taft was being contested for delegates. Also that day, Taft's wife, who had delighted audiences in Nebraska with her razor-sharp wit, took to the stump for the first time in the Ohio race. Appearing alongside her husband, she declared, "Bob beat the New Deal, President Roosevelt, and Santa Claus [she meant the WPA] ... and we haven't got anything harder now." She added, "Stassen talks like a New Dealer."[39]

Meanwhile, in New York, Herbert Brownell was talking to reporters, telling them that he and two other Dewey advisers, Edwin Jaeckal and J. Russell Sprague, had each received telegrams from Stassen requesting a meeting with the New York governor. Brownell told reporters that he had sent Stassen a return wire refusing the request. "I wrote him that I thought it would be misinterpreted," Brownell said. The Dewey adviser made a point of emphasizing "we are not interested in any deals."[40] In separate interviews with this writer, neither Bernhard LeVander nor Stassen could recall requesting an interview with Dewey. There is no record in the campaign files deposited in the Minnesota Historical Society in St. Paul of either Stassen's or Brownell's telegram.[41]

The press reports of an effort by Stassen to seek a meeting with Dewey, and being haughtily refused, certainly was helpful for both the New York and Ohio aspirants. With Stassen sweeping two hard-fought primaries and rising to the top in national polls, the press was increasingly speculating that Dewey and Taft were working together to derail the Minnesotan. The April 26 issue of *Newsweek*, for example, reported, "Political experts now see definite signs of a Dewey-Taft move to gang up on Stassen, based on the theory that any further growth in public favor may make it difficult for the party managers to stop him at the convention."[42] These reports, with their implication of desperation, were damaging to both Dewey and Taft; while the alleged Dewey snub of Stassen increased the New Yorker's stature.

Stassen's energetic campaigning, in sharp contrast to the cerebral style of Taft, drew large and excited audiences and, perhaps, caused the Stassen forces to become overconfident. Nationally syndicated columnist Thomas L. Stokes noted the comparatively lukewarm response that Taft was receiving from his constituents and commented, "Senator Taft attracts smaller and less enthusiastic crowds generally. His appearance here and there causes little excitement.... It is perhaps significant that so few come out for another look, and show no real interest in the distinguished senate leader.... The senator is not an actor, or a dramatic figure ... but prosy and prosaic. Leaving this listless sort of performance to travel about with Harold Stassen, you feel the change immediately.... Harold Stassen is always the center of a crowd ... and radiates his personality."[43]

The Ohio senator revealed no concern, however, and told the *Cleveland Plain Dealer* that he would concede "nothing" to the former governor, including the convention delegation from Stassen's own home state. "I understand the Minnesota situation would be very favorable to me," Taft boasted, "just as soon as Mr. Stassen is out of it. And," the senator added, "he'll be out of it, don't worry."[44] Taft was, in fact, making a vigorous effort for the Minnesota delegation, an effort he began several months before Stassen announced he would compete on Taft's home turf. The Minnesotan recalled this years later with perhaps a trace of bitterness and offered it as one justification for his entrance in the Ohio primary beyond his philosophical commitment to liberalizing the Republican party.[45]

In the final days of the campaign, a palpable aura of suspense hung over the state as the outcome seemed to be too uncertain to predict. With six days left, Stassen received an important boost from organized labor when he received an indirect endorsement from William Finegan, the executive secretary of the Cleveland Federation of Labor. Finegan declared that those union members who voted Republican "should vote for Harold Stassen and defeat Robert Taft. If we can give Taft a substantial slap in the face in his own state, his chances of winning the Republican nomination will be very small."[46]

While gathering the labor vote, Stassen more surprisingly seemed to be doing well among other population groups. On May 1, the *Cleveland Plain Dealer* reported the results of a poll they had taken in four of the larger suburbs around Cleveland. Although only Stassen and Taft were on the ballot, the paper asked these suburban residents to choose from the three leading contenders for the nomination. The result was a surprising show of strength by the Minnesotan, with Stassen the favorite in each of the suburbs. Yet with Taft in control of GOP organizations at the state and county level, few observers were willing to predict the final election results.[47]

Both candidates chose to end their campaigns in Cleveland. On Sunday, May 2, Taft appeared before a labor audience and boldly asked for their support based on the merits of the Taft-Hartley Act. "No one today wants to see the law repealed," he asserted flatly. "As the actual provisions of the new labor act have come to be known, opposition has steadily decreased. The country and the labor union members themselves are finding that the Taft-Hartley law is working because it is based on justice and equality...."[48]

As Taft spoke, Stassen arrived in Cleveland from a brief trip to New York. Accompanied in Ohio for the first time by his wife, Stassen held a reception in the ballroom of the Hotel Carter that evening. "We are not relaxing our efforts," Earl Hart said, "optimistic reports and predictions notwithstanding. All through the state workers are continuing their campaign for Mr. Stassen."[49]

A large segment of these workers included the "Paul Revere Riders," who in the final weekend blitzed the state with over two hundred thousand pamphlets touting Harold Stassen. As in Wisconsin and Nebraska, a thousand volunteers, virtually all of them Ohio residents, in two hundred forty automobiles dispensed literature through all eleven districts where Stassen delegates were competing.[50]

Stassen closed his campaign on election eve with a radio address broadcast statewide. The address sought to sum up the differences he had with Taft. Reiterating his objection to certain parts of the Taft-Hartley Act, he went on to discuss other areas of the domestic economy, calling for increased manufacturing output and a fair farm price support system based on parity. He ended the speech with the same invitation to join his bandwagon that he had issued in Nebraska: "I pledge to you that it will be my constant effort in the years ahead to so conduct myself in Republican leadership that the People of Ohio will never have cause to regret their early support of me." Stassen concluded: "Thank you and good night."[51]

When the votes were tabulated the *Cleveland Plain Dealer*, which had endorsed the senator, carried the headline, "With 44 of Ohio's 53 Votes, Taft Staying on Top in G.O.P. Fight." Of the twenty-three convention seats Stassen had competed for, Taft captured fourteen, leaving nine to the Minnesotan.[52]

Was it a defeat for Stassen? In Oregon, where Stassen now headed for the finale of the primary season, Lyle Wilson writing in the *Oregon Daily Journal* felt that the election had served to damage both camps, an opinion which must have delighted Thomas Dewey. While Stassen had received fewer delegates than he had hoped, Taft had been roundly defeated in urban areas, which would be a considerable strike against him at the convention when party leaders attempted to nominate a candidate they thought could win the general election.[53]

Was it, then, a defeat for both candidates? In and of itself, Ohio was in fact an impressive victory for Stassen. While it was commonly noted that Stassen had won delegates in industrial areas, the significance of the victory was overlooked as observers merely wrote off his success to the antipathy organized labor felt for Taft-Hartley. In doing so, party leaders overlooked two vital points, thus delivering to Stassen his ultimate defeat at the convention and delivering to themselves a bitter defeat in November.

First, for whatever reason, Stassen had demonstrated that he could win support in cities. Given the fact that Stassen had already overwhelmingly carried the farm vote, party leaders should have been alert to the abilities of Stassen to compete nationwide in a race against Harry Truman. Skeptics might have objected that Stassen could not possibly be as effective against Truman as he was in industrial areas against Taft because, after all, the president had vetoed Taft-Hartley and had condemned the law in no uncertain terms. Yet the Truman labor record was not without its blemishes, which could potentially have been used effectively against him by a Republican with a history of courting the labor vote. In November 1946, after the UAW had gone on strike against General Motors (GM) and the steel workers voted to call for a national walkout, Truman had requested legislation to prevent major strikes through fact-finding, cooling-off periods, and federal mediation. CIO president Philip Murray expressed outrage, an emotion echoed by labor leaders across the country when, five months later, Truman told his cabinet he believed the government should be able to draft strikers and incarcerate union leaders.[54] With this record, Stassen might have effectively competed for votes in urban areas while coasting to victory in rural areas based on his appeal to farmers.

Second, Stassen had in effect successfully carried out the main component of his strategy, competing against Taft in Ohio using Taft-Hartley as his weapon. The importance of his success lies in the fact that Stassen had no history of support among city dwellers; yet he had picked a daring strategy and effectively carried it out, thus demonstrating a political acumen which would have tremendously benefited the GOP in November. By overlooking this talent, party leaders committed a fatal error.

Finally, the nine-delegate finish was perceived as a defeat when the campaign had originally hoped for nothing better. In February Earl Hart had predicted that Stassen would win "six or eight" Ohio delegates and this would have a "terrific effect nationally." After the Wisconsin primary he boosted the estimate to "ten or twelve" and after Nebraska, Hart was telling reporters that he was sure "a majority" of Stassen's twenty-three candidates would win.[55] Stassen was the victim of rising expectations, an unfortunate result for which Hart bore no little responsibility. In the end, Stassen was not well served by his native Ohio aide.

Next on the political calendar was the May 21 Oregon primary, where Thomas Dewey would be his only opponent, and no "favorite son" would cloud the contest. While Stassen had at least held his own against Taft, in the West Dewey — humiliated in Wisconsin and Nebraska — would strike back.

9. The Decline: Oregon

O Dewey was the morning
Upon the first of May
And Dewey was the Admiral
Down in Manila Bay...
Dewey feel Discouraged?
I Dew not think we Dew![1]

On May 1, 1898, Admiral George Dewey steamed into Manila Bay and for the next seven hours blasted the Spanish fleet from the Pacific surface to the ocean floor. Fifty years later to the day, Governor Thomas Dewey, steamed by the prairie wildfire blazing for Harold Stassen, arrived on the Pacific coast intent on sinking the Minnesotan's candidacy.

Preparing for battle, the dapper New Yorker took off his gloves but — more importantly — he took off his tie and jacket, too. The change in attire impressed veteran politico Raymond Moley, who later reflected, "Only once have I seen Dewey thoroughly disheveled and completely informal. That was in his bitter slugging match with Stassen in the Oregon primary.... Somehow in the fight his instincts got the better of his mind, and this revelation of Dewey as 'regular fellow' won him the state."[2] Happily for Harry Truman, the governor put his business suit back on before the fall campaign.

To a contemporary observer poring over yellowing newspapers and documents of the Oregon slugfest, it is as though, somehow, the identities of the two men had been switched. Dewey suddenly began appearing at local barbecues and state fairs, smiling benignly at small children and hanging ribbons around prize hogs before showing his teeth to shocked reporters when referring to his opponent.

Stassen, meanwhile, was ... where? In Ohio? West Virginia? Arkansas? With a breathtakingly overcrowded schedule, he was not — until the last moment — in Oregon. Rather, Stassen was fiddling in relatively unimportant contests while his chances in crucial Oregon burned to the ground. "We kept telling him, screaming at him, to come out there," Bernhard LeVander recalled ruefully. "When he finally came, he was in bad shape physically ... he was a sick man, running a hundred two degree temperature."[3] Suffering from the flu and wearied by an impossibly hectic schedule, Stassen could not make up the ground he had lost to Thomas Dewey — territory Stassen had commanded only weeks before the primary. Indeed, the New Yorker had considered abandoning the Oregon contest, thinking it hopeless.[4] The discouragement Dewey felt is understandable, for in Oregon, unlike any other primary state, the New Yorker had made an early start at organizing his campaign, not without difficulty. Yet when Dewey arrived on May 1, Stassen was the favorite to win the contest.

According to Dewey biographer Richard Norton Smith, in July of 1947, well before there is any record of the remotest interest in Oregon by the Stassen campaign, Herbert Brownell met with Ralph Moores, a well-connected veteran of politics in the Pacific Northwest. Moores left the meeting with the promise of one thousand dollars a month from the Dewey treasury in exchange for establishing a campaign organization for the New Yorker. By March 1948 the organization, like Dewey himself, had yet to appear in an impressive way before the state's voters, causing the governor's assistant Paul Lockwood to rush to the West Coast to patch together a campaign structure.[5]

Lockwood need not have hurried, given the leisurely pace of the Stassen forces at that point. Overwhelmed with a nationwide effort, precious months slipped by before an organization was established in Oregon. Not that Stassen was an unpopular figure in the Pacific Northwest; the former governor had caused great excitement when he traveled to Oregon in September of 1947.

Arriving in Pendleton for the Northwest Cow Country Annual Rodeo, Stassen clambered onto a horse and rode among the delighted crowd. "At least I've ridden a little more than Admiral Halsey," he offered.[6] Yet it was not until late November that Stassen selected his state campaign manager, Robert A. Elliot. Even then Stassen was unsure about whether he would even compete in the primary. "I have decided to place you in definite charge of our campaign in the state," the former governor wrote Elliot. Curiously, Stassen asked Elliot to "proceed with your organization quietly and effectively. It seems quite clear to me that we will enter the Oregon primary, but I am not ready for an announcement, nor am I ready to make a firm decision. I wish to watch the national developments in the next few months."[7]

Three months later Stassen had seen enough and arrived in the state for a brief campaign swing. The trip was vintage Stassen and tremendously effective. He talked to school assemblies, shook hands with scores of farmers, lingered in front of a hardware store to chat with passersby, and told local reporters that the primary would have national significance.[8]

The excitement Stassen stirred by his visit, and a return trip in March, helped compensate for gains Dewey has made through the admittedly limited organizational efforts of Ralph Moores. Larry Smyth, political writer for the *Oregon Daily Journal*, observed in April that "the signs point to Stassen holding the advantage in Oregon. Last January it appeared that Dewey was the strong man. Then Stassen moved in to tour the Willamette Valley. He made good headway.... Now, with his victories in Wisconsin and Nebraska, the sentiment for him ... is increasing. The situation has Dewey's managers worried."[9]

It was this fear that drove Lockwood to Oregon, carrying with him enough funds to set up a campaign headquarters in Portland's Multonomah Hotel. The hotel quickly turned into a replica of the Pillsbury Building in Minnesota, home of the Stassen campaign, as it worked with the New York office to pull together and mobilize virtually every conceivable voter group in the style of Neighbors for Stassen. Brooklyn realtors who supported Dewey, for example, were put in contact with realtors in Oregon, as were members of the American Federation of Teachers (AFT) and the Railroad Brotherhood. Oregon's twelve thousand black voters received literature detailing the New Yorker's support for civil rights. According to Richard Norton Smith, "Dewey men even threw cash into betting establishments, reversing the pro–Stassen odds and altering the psychological climate of the campaign."[10]

Slow to start, the Dewey campaign had become a formidable organization, as both campaign and candidate seemed to mimic, quite effectively, the Stassen style. Dewey had made faltering attempts to copy the Minnesotan's techniques late in the Nebraska contest. According to Larry Smyth, "Reports from Nebraska indicate Dewey had abandoned his old-style idea of making set speeches in large centers. He is going out into the rural areas for informal meetings, chatting with the people, shaking hands and submitting to questions. That is a technique Stassen had perfected."[11]

Old habits die hard, though. At the beginning of April, Oregon Senator Wayne Morse invited Dewey to come to the state to speak before the Oregon Young Republicans. "Too busy," the New Yorker had snapped.[12] Yet on April 20, Dewey announced that he would campaign in Oregon for ten days beginning with a speech in Portland on May 1.[13]

Stassen would not arrive in the state until May 16 — or so he had planned. Faced with the Dewey offensive, the Minnesotan's advisers pried several hours loose from the candidate's schedule and announced to the press, ten hours after Dewey's announcement, that Stassen would fly into Portland on April 25 at 11:35 P.M. The next day he would speak at 8:00 P.M. at a local college, his only public appearance before leaving the next morning.[14]

When a bleary-eyed Stassen arrived at the Portland airport, he was greeted with refreshing news: The Oregon Public Opinion Panel had conducted a survey of Republican voters in Portland and reported that he held nearly a two-to-one lead over Dewey. Not surprisingly, the panel noted that the youthful Stassen held an edge among young voters, while proportionately more women supported the New Yorker. With Stassen receiving 57 percent, Dewey 29 percent and undecided 14 percent, in the Portland area the Minnesotan seemed undefeatable.[15]

Another good omen was secured by Robert Elliot, who told reporters that he had just made arrangements to open a new Stassen headquarters in Suite 234 of the Imperial Hotel in Portland. This was the same room where several prominent Oregon politicians, including Charles McNary, had based their campaigns. Elliot had secured the room when state senator Guy Gordon, facing no primary challenge, moved out.[16]

Stepping off the airplane, the Minnesotan was greeted by a crowd of Stassen-buttoned supporters, as well as an official delegation of neutral state party leaders, including GOP national chairman Ralph H. Cake. Stassen, who had during his March visit set the number at two hundred, confidently told the crowd that he expected that he would receive three hundred delegates on the first role call at the national convention in Philadelphia.[17]

The next night an estimated one thousand frustrated Portlanders were turned away from a capacity-filled auditorium in Benison Technical College, where Stassen made his first and only appearance of the trip. Those who squirmed their way inside witnessed what was to be a serious mistake from a candidate who had not made very many errors to that point.

With the Oregon primary less than a month away, and with state and national attention riveted on the new front runner, Stassen had a unique opportunity to set the agenda through his choice of issues in his speech that night. Unfortunately, the Minnesotan chose to emphasize his proposal to outlaw the Communist Party in America and allied nations, a proposal which Oregon voters and opinion leaders would ultimately look askance at.

The idea was the central theme of his speech, which included a devious implication when he mentioned the opposition of Harry Truman and Dewey to the communist ban. "The President of the United States," Stassen intoned, "and the distinguished governor of New York are undoubtedly sincere when they both defend the legality of the Communist party. But I believe they are wrong."

Anticipating the objections that the New Yorker would raise on the stump and in his radio debate with the Minnesotan, Stassen argued, "It is said that if the Communist Party is outlawed, it will go underground and that it is better to give the party legal standing and defeat it in elections. But ... when the Communists are given legal standing to operate above ground, they nevertheless operate underground. They use every legal advantage and at the same time carry on subversive and deceptive underground tactics."[18]

To document his argument Stassen pointed to recent uprisings in Bogota, Colombia, where he said the Communist Party was recognized. Yet, Stassen went on, its members did not accept defeat in elections and did everything they could to upset the victors. The infiltration of communists in Czechoslovakia was similar and more tragic, he said. "In our own country," Stassen continued, "particularly New York, it is evident that the Communists have used every legal advantage and at the same time continued to work underground, so that today more than one-fourth of the known communists in the entire nation are in New York. Their newspaper is published in New York. Most of their infiltration in labor organizations stems from New York. In the light of these facts," Stassen concluded, "I urge my countrymen, do not coddle communism with legality. Outlaw the Communist Party above ground and vigorously dig the communists from underground."[19]

Politically disastrous, the anticommunist speech was not delivered without serious thought. Quite certainly it was no mere tactical expedient, no political life raft lunged for by a sinking candidate. Still the front runner, Stassen did not need to act desperately. The proposal to outlaw communism was an idea to which Stassen had devoted considerable study some time before, examining its implications and resolving, in his mind at least, potential contradictions with the rest of his political program. He had first broached the subject in a substantial way in an address in Washington, D.C., and broadcast nationally by NBC on June 14, 1947, almost one year before the Oregon primary. Unspectacularly reciting conventional wisdom that labor disputes could be traced to Communists, Stassen at this early date depicted New York as the seed bed of Red agitation.[20]

The response Stassen outlined was a twelve-point program, envisioning coordinated action from federal, state and local law enforcement officials. The program was targeted at New York City, but the specific points directed at the Big Apple could be applied elsewhere as circumstances warranted. Speaking of New York, Stassen called for a "bi-partisan" program developed and implemented "through the cooperation of the President and the Attorney General of the United States, the Governor and the Attorney General of the State of New York, the Mayor and the Prosecutor of the City of New York." These officials would busy themselves with exposure and prosecution. Communists would be barred from public employment and labor disruption, among other crimes. Point nine was, "Do not lightly use the charge of 'Communist' against anyone unless we are certain of the evidence, then present the evidence with the charge."

Point twelve read, "Take all these actions with complete respect for civil liberties and for equal rights." As evidence that such a program could work, Stassen noted that he had carried out a similar program on his own in Minnesota. "In 1937 and 1938," he recalled, "Minnesota had one of the centers of Communist activity in the United States." He asserted that as governor he had removed Communists from public payrolls, reduced their influence in labor, and generally defeated them. "And now," he boasted, "for years Minnesota has had less than her share of the national Communist difficulties."[21]

In emphasizing how he had single-handedly saved Minnesota from Communist insurrection, and by centering on New York, Stassen obviously was taking aim at Governor Dewey. Yet the proposal should not be written off as complete political boilerplate. During the Oregon primary mention of involving federal officials in New York anticommunism was conspicuously absent. Also, Stassen had in fact avoided contradiction with his objection to Taft-Hartley's ban on Communist labor leaders. In Taft-Hartley, as in his twelve-point program, he was objecting not to removing communist officials so much as to what he saw as insufficient attention to civil liberties. His labor policy required that proof be presented against the accused, rather than requiring self-incrimination or promoting perjury; his anticommunism program had the same emphasis. The point that should be remembered is that, while Stassen clearly saw his stand as an anti–Dewey tactic, it was not a reckless, off-the-cuff proposal to win over voters. It was, for better or worse, a well thought out and serious proposal.

In Oregon the anti-communist thrust was happily promoted by Don Kennedy, a sales promotion manager of the Jantzen Knitting Mills and a shipmate of Stassen during World War II. Late in February, Robert Elliot announced that Kennedy would head the Oregon Veterans for Stassen. For his part, Kennedy insisted that he had been on the job for his former naval colleague since Thanksgiving Day 1944. At a large shipboard dinner that evening, he said, Kennedy had sat next to Stassen as Admiral Halsey addressed the group, telling them to "help Harold in his cause after the war."[22] On April 27 Stassen boarded an early flight for Ohio; he was not scheduled to return to Oregon until May 16.

On May 1 a feisty New York governor arrived in Portland for a scheduled ten-day tour which would carry him to thirty-one cities and towns during the first week alone. Stepping off his plane at 7:05 A.M. after an overnight flight from New York, a grinning Dewey told a welcoming crowd that he was ready for "some good old-fashioned campaigning, because that is what I enjoy."

Later, at a press conference at his hotel, he explained that "now that the New York legislature has gone home ... I can really get into the campaign."[23] The statement was a tacit admission that his opponent had preempted the New Yorker's candidacy with his barnstorming style, and Oregon waited intently to find out if the New Yorker could match the Minnesotan's pace. The difference between the two styles was observed by the *Oregon Daily Journal*, which, with rather tortured syntax noted, "Stassen is the pure quill of peripatetic spellbinders.... His method of campaigning is not only from town to town but ... from person to person.... The cumulative gains by Harold Stassen ... help to explain the arrival in Oregon of Governor Thomas Dewey. [And] there will be a first-class demonstration of how to win support and influence voters."[24]

Wasting no time, Dewey, on his first day, in a speech before the Oregon Jaycees, launched into Stassen's proposal to ban the Communist Party. The New Yorker called instead, for keeping communists out in the open and under the spotlight. "I have seen a good deal of communists during my eleven years as public prosecutor and six years as governor," he said. "They have fought me every time I ran for office and as of this moment their influence is at the lowest point in its history. We have diminished their influence, discredited them, exposed them and defeated them because at all times we kept a spotlight on them.... I am greatly concerned, however, about some hysterical suggestions that have been made about handling communists."[25] He did not mention Stassen's name.

It was an impressive first performance for the governor, although his erstwhile haughtiness had its consequences even as he adopted a new warm campaign style. Six days after Dewey made his address before the Jaycees, a miffed past vice president of the organization, Walter Finke, wrote to Robert Elliot informing the Stassen manager that years before Dewey had not bothered to respond to a letter from the Jaycees informing him of his selection for the Distinguished Service Award. Finke then went to Dewey's New York office and waited many hours before Paul Lockwood told him that Dewey was being offered honors by many organizations, colleges, and so forth and, as he had to draw the line somewhere, could not accept the award. An indignant Finke still resented it.[26]

The next day, Sunday, Dewey attended services at Trinity Episcopal Church in Portland before driving to the Bonneville Dam for a "non-political" tour. Campaign aides assured reporters that the governor would not profane the Sabbath with such temporal matters as the presidency. The next day he appeared at West Linn for a breakfast meeting at 8:00 A.M. before showing up at a Canby Street corner to talk with locals. Two hours later he was at a high school in Woodburn encouraging young people to apply their youthful energy to the noble profession of politics. The suddenly indefatigable New Yorker squeezed in four more appearances before addressing an audience at Oregon State College that evening.[27] Stassen, meanwhile, was in Cleveland.

It was as if Dewey had been suddenly transformed into William Jennings Bryan. Significantly, the man Alice Roosevelt had said looked like "the groom on a wedding cake" was pictured on the front page of a newspaper smiling kindly at a young child. Directly lifting a line from Harold Stassen, Dewey explained his intensive campaign appearances as an effort to let the people know exactly "where I stand," which must have galled supporters of the Minnesotan who had read his book of the same title.[28] Moreover, the New Yorker's style was generating intense waves of excitement among voters, who mobbed Dewey as if he were a glamorous movie actor. At one appearance, for example, the auditorium was jammed one hour and twenty minutes before he spoke.

At the conclusion of the address, Dewey, in a maneuver Stassen had adopted long before but which was new to the New Yorker, hurried around to the back to greet the exiting audience. No sooner had he appeared when the delighted crowd, squealing with excitement, surged toward him, pushing him off the sidewalk and onto the wet grass, where the governor slipped and landed on his backside in a mud puddle. Picked up by his aides, Dewey maneuvered to the rear door of the auditorium, where he commenced autograph signing, a task he did not abandon until the last fan had been satisfied.[29] The formerly cold New Yorker had suddenly become transformed into a warm and sympathetic human being. The next night, when his chartered bus, another Stassen tool, hit a dog belonging to a woman from Salem, Dewey wired her expressing his remorse: "I am deeply distressed and extend my profound regrets. Will you not let me send you a puppy which I hope grows in your affection and replaces your loss?"[30]

Worried about a possible loss of their own, by May 8 the Stassen campaign broke down and announced that the Minnesotan would arrive in Oregon three days before his original plan of May 17. Stassen, in Washington, D.C., for an appearance on *Meet the Press*, explained that the change in plans was made in order to allow for a debate between the two candidates. Learning of this, Paul Lockwood snorted that a debate was just "an excuse to bring him back to Oregon earlier than he planned because he fears the gains that Dewey is making in the state." He also made it clear that the New York governor was not interested in a debate, believing that his intensive campaign would be sufficient to inform voters of his policies.[31]

With Stassen unavailable, other Minnesotans were brought in to campaign in lieu of the candidate. On May 4 three Minnesotan women who had campaigned in Wisconsin and Nebraska arrived in Oregon to stump for their former governor. Mrs. Richard Gale, wife of a former congressman and cochair of "Citizens for Stassen," proudly explained: "We believe our Citizens for Stassen organization is unique in political history because it is entirely voluntary."[32] Four days later Minnesota governor Luther Youngdahl arrived in the state, telling voters that the presidential primary system should be expanded to make the nomination more democratic.[33]

On May 10 the *Oregon Daily Journal* carried the headline "Stassen OK's Debate Here with Dewey." The article explained that Stassen had accepted an invitation by Dr. Peter H. Odegard, president of Reed College, to meet Dewey "in a discussion of campaign issues." Stassen had wired Odegard, saying, "I will accept your kind invitation for a joint discussion of the vital national issues under the sponsorship of Reed College at the Portland Auditorium and will adjust my schedule to be present on any date between now and the election."[34] The short headline belied an intense effort behind the scenes to arrange the debate.

The chief instigator of the proposed debate was Tom Swafford, a young and recently hired program director at radio station KPOJ in Portland.[35] As his station carried a Dewey speech in which the New Yorker attacked the proposal to ban the Communist Party, Swafford mused, "That's the only thing these two guys have disagreed on. They ought to debate it." Swafford carried the idea to Philip L. Jackson, the publisher of the *Oregon Daily Journal*, which owned the station. "You forget, young man," the publisher told Swafford, "the *Journal* is a Democratic paper. We're not interested in helping Republicans settle family squabbles."

But Jackson was nevertheless intrigued, and called Dr. Odegard at Reed College. With the debate under Odegard's aegis, the radio station was set for a major coup.[36] Unhappily for Swafford, Dewey rejected the idea. In his wire to Odegard, the New Yorker, whose feelings seem to have been hurt, complained, "I have been debating the vital issues of our time before the people of Oregon in the smallest and largest communities for the last ten days on this, my first opportunity." But Dewey was not opposed to the idea of a debate — not entirely: "While I usually disapprove personal debates between Republicans because they tend to weaken and divide the party, I regard the proposal to outlaw the Communist Party as so dangerous ... that I think a full discussion of it under the auspices of the Multonomah County Republican Central Committee, is essential...."

Dewey was rejecting the sponsorship of Dr. Odegard. Further, he wanted to limit the discussion to Stassen's proposal to outlaw the Communist Party. Finally, Dewey insisted that the radio debate was to be strictly a studio affair, no audience would be allowed. With these demands, Dewey remained in Oregon should Stassen agree to debate.[37]

In other circumstances, these three demands would have stretched the patience of any candidate; yet Stassen was slipping, and he knew it. So did Bernhard LeVander, who recalled, "We did make a lot of concessions, but we saw it [a debate] as an opportunity to make up the lost ground."[38] While staff members from the two camps continued to negotiate the terms of a debate, Stassen returned to the hustings. On May 12 he told reporters that he did not believe the result in Oregon would be conclusive in deciding the Republican nomination but that it would "be very important." Apparently forgetting the New Hampshire primary, Stassen said, "If I win ... that would make the score 3 to 0." That night a slim crowd turned out at the Portland ice arena, where Stassen drew rounds of applause when he asserted that while the Constitution guarantees the right of free speech, it does not "give the right to destroy."[39]

Two days later, the mayor of Cascade Locks issued an invitation to Thomas Dewey to visit the city and declared a school holiday to enable the children to meet the governor. Later in the day, when the mayor learned that Stassen would be in the area, he extended an invitation to the Minnesotan, too. Conscientious advance men for Stassen promptly rushed to the town to distribute pictures of their candidate, who arrived to a huge crowd of eager schoolchildren. As Stassen and his young fans stood by the side of the road, a police car with flashing lights slowly approached followed by the Dewey bus, which slowed, then resolutely proceeded down the road past a fuming mayor. "I don't think it was very fair to us after all I did for him," the mayor complained, referring to his declared "school holiday." An obviously amused Stassen turned to the children as the bus drove by and laughed as he said, "We'll wave him up the highway. What do you say?" The young fans dutifully waved to Dewey.[40]

As it happened, arrangements had been made that morning to give Dewey a chance to wave back. A determined Tom Swafford called on Stassen at the candidate's room at the Multonomah Hotel to prod the former governor into granting Dewey his three demands. The interview, as Swafford later recounted in an engaging article in *American Heritage*, actually took place in the hotel room's bathroom. Sporting green pajama bottoms, Stassen was shaving and at first in no mood to compromise. "No," he grumbled, "I've given on every point. Let him give on this one." The point he referred to was whether an audience should be present during the debate; he had earlier relented on the issue of sponsorship and limiting the debate to the proposal to ban the Communist Party. "Governor," an exasperated Swafford responded, "if you can beat Dewey in a debate, does it make any difference whether you do it in front of a live audience?" Stassen put down his razor and grinned. "All right," he said. "I'll debate that little son of a bitch anywhere, anytime, on any subject."[41] Swafford later reflected that Stassen, green pajamas notwithstanding, had "an almost regal manner" about him, and seemed "terribly overconfident."[42] Bernhard LeVander, in contrast, implied that the decision to concede to Dewey's demands and hold the debate on the New Yorker's terms was almost an act of desperation as the Minnesotan's fortunes seemed to ebb. Whether motivated by cockiness or concern, Stassen in consenting to the debate had made a fatal mistake.

The encounter was scheduled for May 17. On May 16, Stassen arrived in Portland nearly an hour behind schedule. After hastily greeting six hundred persons at the airport, he left for Le Grande. On the bus a reporter gave him a red balloon, which broke free and floated along the roof. Asked if it were a trial balloon, Stassen quipped, "It is — on the red question." The day was crammed with six major appearances, and apparently no time for rest and study for the debate.

Larry Howes, a reporter for the *Oregon State Journal* observed, "Although still energetic, Stassen was beginning to show the strain of ... campaigning."[43] Bernhard LeVander noted Stassen's poor health, and Stassen himself recalled that he had contracted the flu as early as the Nebraska primary. It is possible that Stassen's poor performance during the debate was due, as LeVander believes, to his poor physical condition. There is no direct reference to Stassen's poor health in Oregon newspapers, although it was reported early in the month that Dewey had a slight cold. Tom Swafford, who produced the debate and was in the studio at the time, expressed surprise and incredulity when told of Stassen's flu.[44] The reason for Stassen's unusual poor performance remains a mystery.

On May 16, Ronald R. Van Boskirk, chairman of the Multonomah County Republican Central Committee, issued a press release explaining the format of the debate. The two candidates were to limit their discussion to the question, "Shall the Communist Party be outlawed in the United States?" Stassen would speak for twenty minutes in the affirmative, followed by Dewey speaking for the opposing point of view, also for twenty minutes. Stassen would then have eight and a half minutes for rebuttal, followed by an equal time for Dewey to respond.[45]

A crestfallen Tom Swafford was informed that his dream of a KPOJ radio station exclusive would not come true. The candidates had allowed the debate to be carried nationwide by all the major networks, and only CBS declined. Nine hundred radio stations carried the discussion, and millions of listeners tuned in nationwide. When the debate began, telephone operators reported that long distance calls dropped 25 percent.[46]

When the two candidates arrived for the encounter, Stassen seemed to make a point of walking over to the New Yorker to shake hands, while cameras clicked away; as Stassen stood perhaps a foot taller than Dewey, the implied message was unmistakable. "Good evening, Tom. We certainly stirred up a lot of interest," the Minnesotan chirped. Dewey replied evenly, "We sure did." "We have seen a lot of Oregon," Stassen went on pleasantly. "I'll say we have," came Dewey's response; he was in no mood for small talk. The two candidates parted and sat down at their respective tables.

At Stassen's table sat Ed Larson, Portland businessman Ted Gamble, who would later head up the Stassen campaign when it moved to Philadelphia for the national convention, Fred Seaton, manager of the Nebraska campaign, and Senator Joseph McCarthy. With Dewey sat Paul Lockwood, Elliot Bell, New York state superintendent of banks, and Robert Ray, a University of Iowa professor and Dewey advisor.[47]

In his opening statement Stassen, according to a charitable newspaper account, ran "a bit far afield" in mentioning campaign issues other than communism. Returning to the point, Stassen reiterated his belief that communists were determined to work underground to destabilize democratic institutions even as they took advantage of the protection afforded them in a free society. Interestingly, the Minnesotan went out of his way to praise the Nixon-Mundt bill, implying that the proposed law would outlaw the Communist Party.[48] A surprised Karl Mundt, a Republican congressman from South Dakota, told reporters that the bill would not outlaw the Communist Party, but would only control "certain of its activities." For his part, Congressman Richard Nixon trumpeted that the "clear winner of the Dewey-Stassen debate was the Mundt-Nixon bill." Asked if his bill outlawed the Communist Party, Nixon replied, "It outlaws the subversive activities of communists, communism and/or the Communist Party."[49]

As Stassen read his opening statement, Tom Swafford stood in the glass-enclosed control room, his attention riveted on Thomas Dewey. Swafford later recalled: "I was fascinated by Dewey's attitude. He sat there, hands folded in his lap, staring off across the studio, totally composed, almost detached. If he'd had a cigar, you'd have expected smoke rings.... When it was time for him to speak, he did so without a note. As he began, his voice, a deep baritone, was pitched at its lowest register. His pace was deliberate; his tone thoughtful. He built in temp and voice level slowly.... At one point in the control room, I asked of no one in particular, 'Did Stassen forget what a hell of a prosecutor this guy was?'"[50]

When the New Yorker completed his statement, Stassen rose for his rebuttal clearly feeling the dread of impending defeat. According to Swafford, Stassen "was wearing the kind of half smile a boxer puts on after taking a damaging blow when he wanted the judges to think it didn't hurt. The radio audience couldn't see that, of course, but it could hear the uncertain, diffident delivery that had replaced the earlier booming confidence.... I thought at the moment that we were watching a man who had not done his homework and was now aware of it, a man who had been so certain he could whip Dewey ... that he'd completely underestimated his opponent."[51]

It is difficult to determine exactly how much of Stassen's defeat at the polls was due to his poor radio performance and how much was due to his absence from Oregon for so much of the last month of the campaign. What can be said with certainty was that the Dewey camp was tickled with their candidate's performance, with good reason. Bradley Nash, a former secretary to Herbert Hoover who was in Oregon running a Dewey phone bank, directed his operators after the debate to ask the registered Republican voters whom they called to indicate which candidate they would vote for. Nash remembered later that, on the basis of this informal poll, the Dewey campaign was comfortably predicting victory before the polls opened.[52]

The prediction was correct. On May 21, in a heavy voter turnout, Dewey garnered 113,350 votes to Stassen's 104,211.[53] The next morning at 11:00 A.M. Stassen, at his home in St. Paul, conceded the election to Thomas Dewey. Warren Burger quite reasonably blamed the defeat on "the most monumental campaign we have yet been up against."[54]

Oregon marked the end of the presidential primary season, and the candidates and their supporters headed toward Philadelphia for the national convention. Minimize it as they might, the Stassen campaign could not dispel the notion that their balloon had been punctured. In one primary, a pioneering and wondrously successful effort to circumvent party kingmakers had fizzled.

10. The Decline: Republican National Convention

In December 1946 Harold Stassen had set out to win the Republican nomination using presidential primaries as a fulcrum to pick up the support of party leaders. Regrettably for him the time had not yet arrived when primary voters would decide which candidate would receive the presidential nod; of the 1,094 delegates to the GOP national convention in Philadelphia, only seventy-seven were chosen to support specific candidates by primary voters. Of these, forty-five had been won by Stassen, with Dewey collecting eighteen and Robert Taft fourteen. The balance of the delegates had largely been chosen by party conventions and were usually controlled by the state GOP leaders who were more sympathetic to Dewey than the liberal and independent-minded Stassen.

The Stassen strategy had centered on entering primaries, not to collect enough delegates to win the nomination outright, but to demonstrate superior vote-getting skills. In this task Stassen succeeded. In the five contested presidential primaries the former governor won a total of 806,906 votes; more than any other candidate.

Thomas Dewey did not compete in the Ohio contest; yet even removing the votes Stassen received in the Buckeye State, Stassen still won more popular support than Dewey in the four states in which they competed against each other, receiving 446,419 votes to Dewey's 345,440. Stassen's victories had propelled him to the forefront among Republicans nationwide. By May 1948 he had surged to an impressive lead in a Gallup poll measuring support for each candidate, leading second-place Dewey 37 to 24 percent.[1]

The Oregon primary, however, had removed any aura of invincibility Stassen had generated. In a state uncluttered with favorite sons, with neither candidate enjoying a regional advantage, Dewey had won decisively. As a result, delegation chairmen saw little reason to support a candidate more liberal than themselves and who had conscientiously tried to wrest their nominating power from them by creating a public demand for his selection.

Nevertheless, the Stassen forces stuck to their guns to the end. An intricate organization was established in Philadelphia to promote the Minnesotan, headed by Portland businessman Ted Gamble. Bernhard LeVander and Warren Burger arrived in the convention city fifteen days before the opening ceremonies, with Burger in charge of rounding up new delegates while keeping allies on the reservation. It was difficult going, as a newly invigorated Dewey campaign, with substantial support among party regulars and a huge treasury, flooded the city with pro–Dewey workers. "I remember they had guys doing nothing but riding elevators all day," LeVander recalled. "They'd stand there and say things like, 'Well, I guess he'll go over the top on the first ballot,' all that kind of stuff, just putting out that propaganda all the time." In the face of this, "it was kind of tough keeping our forces buoyed up," LeVander admitted.[2]

In an effort to corral the convention into a Stassen nomination, the Minnesotan's supporters arranged a "spontaneous" demonstration such as the one which led the 1940 convention toward Wendell Willkie. LeVander laid careful plans for this clamor. In a June 9 memo to Ted Gamble, the campaign chairman stressed this point: "It ... will be of great importance that we put on an outstanding demonstration on the convention floor.... It will need to be exceptionally well-coordinated and planned out in advance."[3]

Under Vic Johnston's aegis, the demonstration was carried out flawlessly. According to *Newsweek*, "for sheer noise and circus tactics the Stassen demonstration outdid all others." Fired with a zeal missing in other camps, the youthful Stassenites screamed themselves hoarse, released scored of balloons, and paraded a pretty girl in a boat ("Man the oars, ride the crest, Harold Stassen, he's the best!")[4]

On Thursday, June 24, when the convention settled down to begin casting ballots, Dewey immediately captured the lead and remained there through three roll calls. Stassen won 157 votes on the first ballot, far behind the New Yorker with 434 and Robert Taft with 224. On the second ballot Stassen slipped to 137 while Dewey rose to 515 and Taft to 274. The New York governor was only thirty-three votes shy of the nomination.

At this point the Taft campaign moved for a recess, obviously to buy time to round up more delegates. To the astonishment of many of his supporters, the Dewey campaign acquiesced in the request. Yet what seemed to be a foolish risk on the New Yorker's part was in fact a diplomatic concession. The Dewey campaign, confident of the loyalty of their delegates, had been informed that the Connecticut, Arizona and Michigan delegations would switch to the governor on the next ballot. With a surfeit of delegates, Dewey had no taste for a procedural battle over a recess.[5]

Unaware of the impending rush to Dewey, Robert Taft contacted Stassen, and the two men negotiated possible efforts to stop Dewey. Stassen wanted Taft to join him in an effort to nominate Arthur Vandenberg; Taft wanted Stassen to support Taft. Hours later Taft withdrew, as did Stassen and two other candidates whose names had been entered, Earl Warren and Arthur Vandenberg. On the third roll call Dewey was nominated unanimously. Harold Stassen's pilgrimage had come to an end.[6]

After securing the nomination, Dewey returned to his hotel and convened a group of party leaders to seek their advice on a running mate. Shortly after 4:30 A.M. Dewey called Earl Warren, promised to make the vice presidency an office with more responsibility, and offered the California governor the post. Warren wanted to think it over, and promised a reply by 11:30 that morning. At 9:30 A.M. a second meeting was held, and the group debated calling Harold Stassen and offering him the spot should Warren refuse. However, at 11:00 A.M. the Californian accepted, and the call to Stassen was never made.[7] Dewey later regretted his selection of Warren, calling his running mate a "dumb Swede."[8]

His best chance for the Republican nomination lost, the most significant accomplishments of Stassen's career were still before him. Still, the next four years would be an interlude, and an awkward one at that. Having become an instinctive political animal, Stassen would have to make the adjustment to the private life of an academic. It would not be an easy adjustment.

11. President Stassen

In a sense, the Stassen campaign pilgrimage was not unsuccessful, as he left Philadelphia as a presidential nominee. The presidency, though, was that of the University of Pennsylvania, and, actually, the nomination was not quite his yet, since the board of trustees still had to give its official nod. Yet from the moment when the university's chairman of the board of trustees, Robert T. McCracken, tapped him on the shoulder at the close of the convention, both the nomination and the office were securely in Stassen's future.

Four years of accomplishment loomed ahead. Still, although Stassen claimed that "my devotion to American education has been life-long,"[1] so, too, had been his devotion to political activities. Stassen's years in the political wilderness had created an untamable animal. Given high marks for the time he spent at his desk, tensions arose as Stassen essentially attempted a two-front career battle — as university president and as political activist.

The observant could have discerned the coming tension in Stassen's letter of acceptance to the trustees, as he noted, "I will continue a vigorous interest in public questions." Even his starting date at the university would be, he cautioned, "subject to the fulfillment of my speaking schedule on behalf of Governor Dewey."[2] Alumni, trustees, administrators and students leaped to praise the Stassen appointment; nevertheless, there were murmured misgivings about a politician president.[3]

Still, as Martin Meyerson, a succeeding university president who served on the faculty during Stassen's tenure reflected in 1981, Stassen did more for the University of Pennsylvania than Eisenhower did for Columbia. "I think he was a man who had tremendous imagination in everything he did," Meyerson added, calling Stassen "astonishing."[4]

Overall, Stassen's service at the university was a time of accomplished administration that often required significant courage. It was also a time in which Stassen devoted increasingly serious thought, and activity, to national issues. Finally, it was occasionally a time of frantic headline hunting.

Befitting the political atmosphere in Philadelphia in June 1948, the rumor mill began churning almost as soon as Stassen and McCracken took leave of each other. One local paper reflected that Stassen had directed much of his two-year presidential campaign at young people, drawing them into national issues with his Republican Open Forums and utilizing their vitality in his grassroots campaign. "He lost no opportunity," the paper noted, "to appear on college campuses or among students and other young people."[5]

The office which Stassen was rumored to have been offered was becoming vacant; Dr. George William McClelland, the incumbent, had warned the trustees earlier in the summer that his increasingly unpredictable health would soon force his resignation. Unlike Stassen, McClelland was a career academic, having served as president since 1944 after a career at the University of Pennsylvania dating back to 1911, when he had arrived as an instructor in

English. McClelland would be named chairman of the university when Stassen assumed the presidency.[6]

The Pennsylvania post was not Stassen's only option; he had been approached by Johns Hopkins and Northwestern as well. He had also been sounded out by insurance, manufacturing and law firms, yet appointing national figures to academic posts seemed to be in vogue. With Eisenhower at Columbia, Pennsylvania officials had earlier approached Lewis W. Douglas, the U.S. ambassador to Great Britain, who declined.

The need at Pennsylvania, as at other institutions, was fundraising. Having announced its commitment to a thirty-two million dollar postwar expansion program, which envisioned raising twenty million in the next five years alone, the university was seeking not an academic but a prominent and aggressive executive.[7]

Upon leaving Philadelphia after the convention, Stassen returned to Minnesota, while the trustees swung into action. Excited by the conquest, the trustees had to run a gauntlet of two board meetings, one to nominate Stassen and one to elect him. Noting that lawyers dominated the board, William Dubarry, a university official, explained: "This may seem a strange way to do things, but lawyers are strange."[8]

While these machinations proceeded, Thomas Dewey announced that he had invited a willing Stassen to his Quaker Hill farm to discuss the "situation in the country in general," obviously meaning GOP harmony in November — quite a concern, since the top two Republican primary vote-getters were reportedly "only on speaking terms."[9] Perhaps this animosity is why, with Dewey evidently on his way to the White House, there were few objections that President Dewey would call President Stassen to serve on his cabinet, thus leaving the university in limbo.

Apparently, one of the few groups to insist on getting Stassen's post–November intentions straight were the students, who, because of the mid-summer nomination, could not address the matter until after Stassen had assumed office in September. In an interview with the editors of the *Daily Pennsylvanian*, the student newspaper, Stassen in "a statement marked by quiet firmness: declared that the prediction by Drew Pearson that he would be appointed Secretary of State was 'utterly without foundation.'" Stassen strongly implied that, cabinet offer or no cabinet offer, he would remain with the University.[10]

Untroubled by Dewey's appointment plans, or assured by Stassen that he would not abandon them, the trustees went public on July 28. They had, they owned, informally offered Stassen the job on July 12, and he had accepted. On July 29 a special meeting of the trustees convened at 3:00 in the afternoon in Houston Hall, where Stassen was formally nominated.

Duly informed, the Minnesotan telegraphed: "After careful consideration, I have decided to accept your nomination to Presidency of the University of Pennsylvania. I look forward with enthusiasm to join with you in carrying on the superb tradition of the University." In announcing Stassen's formal acceptance, Robert McCracken lauded Stassen's "civil and military record," as well as his "intense interest in higher education."[11] There is no record that the trustees, while voting for Stassen, were crossing their fingers; rather, they seemed confident of their nominee. The *Philadelphia Inquirer* observed that "a sharp change in the direction" of the university could be anticipated.[12]

As usual, it was the students who raised the tough questions, despite the fact that by the time they convened the nomination was a fait accompli. An editorial in the *Daily Pennsylvanian* observed that Stassen's nomination "caught most of us by surprise.... The questions that arise from this unforeseen action are, of course, what manner of man is he and what will he do? The latter question, only time can answer...." Still, the students were upbeat. Concerning the "manner of man" question, the editorial declared, "We feel him to be among the foremost younger statesmen of the world." They even proclaimed to be proud of Stassen's intention to continue to be active in public affairs. Addressing the criticism that the former governor was using the university as a stepping-stone to the White House, the students were philosophical. "We can only point out," they noted, "that should Mr. Dewey be elected ... it will be by political custom, eight years before an opportunity will come to Mr. Stassen.... What free man can say what he will be doing eight years from now?"[13]

The nomination sailed through with unanimity. Yet as Robert McCracken reported, there was one "discordant note." Unexpectedly, Earl G. Harrison, who for four years had been dean of the law school, resigned to join a law firm. McCracken suspected that Harrison was miffed because he had been passed over for the presidency. "Your first job," McCracken wrote the incoming president, "therefore, will be to turn over in your mind some names for a new Dean of the Law School."[14]

As Stassen's nomination was secured, congratulations poured in from across the nation, including one from former secretary of state and fellow United Nations charter delegate Edward Stettinius on August 2. "Congratulations on your appointment," the statesman telegraphed.

In addition to congratulations came advice. Most notable in this regard was a detailed memo from Congressman E. Wallace Chadwick, a university alumnus and U.S. representative from the nearby Seventh Congressional District. Assuring Stassen his "decision to come to Pennsylvania was a matter of most profound personal satisfaction to me," the congressman proffered five points to help Stassen acclimate himself to Philadelphia and to the university. The thrust of the memo was to urge Stassen to relocate the university to Valley Forge, where it owned property thanks to a benefactor. This removal would rescue the College of Liberal Arts from an "inundation of day students from Philadelphia" which drove respectable students to other institutions where "the personnel of the undergraduate body are more congenial."[15] This proposal had been rejected several years before by the university. Stassen politely thanked the congressman for his memo, noted that "Mrs. Stassen and I" were looking forward to the new job, and ignored the recommendation.[16]

Stassen was officially elected by the board of trustees on September 17 and began his duties three days later. It was reported that his salary was $22,000 a year and additional preparations were made to befit the president's economic and social status. Even before his official election, Donald Angell, who was to serve as Stassen's assistant, wrote to his future boss in St. Paul informing him "an order has been placed for a black Buick five-passenger sedan, and we are assured that it will be ready for delivery between September 10 and 15."[17] The university then proceeded to remodel a house it owned at 8212 St. Martins Lane in Chestnut Hill to serve as the executive mansion. Pennsylvania's executive vice president, William Dubarry, huddled with his staff on the subject of Stassen's social life. "After discussion," he wrote the new president, "we believe that you should be put up for membership in the following organizations...." He then proceeded to list eleven groups ranging from the Philadelphia Museum of Art to the Zoological Society of Pennsylvania. "These institutions are the cultural institutions of Philadelphia," he stressed, "to the point that no proper University president could do without an affiliation with them."[18]

Yet, before his introduction to Philadelphia society would come his introduction to the university community, and the institution's staff labored over the proper form of this academic coming-out party. The executive vice president's office finally produced a script in the form of a memo sent to the trustees and university staff "to suggest a plan for the introduction of Mr. Stassen to the University." "Of course," the memo noted, "much more thinking will have to be done before any final plan is prepared, but this memorandum may at least serve as a point of departure." The plan identified six "purposes to be served," all of which seemed aimed at the final point: "To have as one of its ultimate effects the greater support of the University." Twelve groups were to be favored with a presidential meeting, ranging from the trustees, group number one, to the general public, which ranked number twelve. "Students" ranked number seven on the presidential priority list, right behind "faculty wives." The introduction was a twelve-point program as well, complete with dinners, press conferences, teas and receptions. While the program was only a proposal ("others will have better ideas"), it was closely followed as Stassen assumed office.[19]

It seemed to have its intended effect. Acclaim for the new president was rampant as even the students, perhaps not aware that they had ranked only seventh on Stassen's guest list, expressed enthusiasm. After a presidential appearance before the *Daily Pennsylvanian* Senior Board during registration week, students patiently told themselves that the reason for "Dr. Stassen's [Stassen had been granted an honorary degree by his new employer] few campus appearances was his commitment to campaign for Governor Dewey." They remained apprehensive over what Stassen's schedule would look like after the election; but by December the student paper noted that the president's "announcement of a reception for male undergraduates prior to Christmas vacation coupled with recent dinners and public meetings has done a great deal to assuage fears of 'absentee administration.'"[20]

Almost immediately a wary cordiality was established between Stassen and the university press. Neither was above a little sniping, especially as the paper increasingly grumbled about "absentee administration," assuaged fears notwithstanding. For his part, Stassen was careful to make sure his young reporters minded their manners. In May 1951, for example, the president wrote a letter to the dean of student affairs, in which he indicated that he "assumed" that a student writer for the *Daily Pennsylvanian*, Kenneth Simsarion, would no longer write a column in the paper. Simsarion, it appears, had written a rather lewd article mocking female members of the dormitory staff. The article was an "interview" with a fictitious "Miss Dusteaser." Accordingly, Simsarion's column, "Through the Keyhole," did not appear again. Yet Stassen was a reasonable man. In October 1951 the paper's editor wrote Stassen to plead that Simsarion be permitted to write a column with a different name and format. Stassen agreed, adding, "I have no personal objection to Mr. Simsarion's doing such writing as you wish him to do."[21]

Harold Stassen was thus ushered into office, encouraged by the confidence of the board of trustees, basking in the light of carefully orchestrated, favorable publicity, and at least delicately in good standing with the student body. With this auspicious beginning, President Stassen turned toward his duties.

Stassen had no sooner buckled down to business in Pennsylvania than Joseph McCarthy made his fateful trip to Wheeling, West Virginia, in February 1950. The infamous "I have in my hand" speech focused an already vibrant anticommunist hysteria and led to nervous hand-wringing on university campuses. Loyalty oath requirements, accusations, tenure battles, and firings left many administration buildings running red during the second Red Scare.

As a presidential candidate Stassen had done his bit in Oregon and elsewhere to frighten voters over the Communist menace. Still, as noted, the former governor had been more loyal to civil liberties than one might have expected of one who wished to outlaw the Communist Party.

Stassen's conduct as president of a university during the second Red Scare was that of a quiet and effective, and firm, defender of academic freedom. Thirty years after his departure from the university, Stassen reflected, "I think the matter of emphasis on academic freedom was one of the most important things we did."[22] It is a difficult assertion to deny.

Predictably, it was apparently the students who first thought to quiz the Nixon-Mundt bill supporter about the rights of campus Communists. In his inaugural interview with the *Daily Pennsylvanian* Stassen was asked, "Do you believe Communist or Communist youth groups should organize groups on campus?" The president replied evenly that he did not think it compatible with freedom to suppress any group that honestly declared its stand. What he opposed, he insisted, were "false fronts; or organizations with "questionable" aims. "There is," he asserted, "a separation between the matter of individual expression and that of a group taking instructions from foreign powers." If a group was freely expressing its ideas rather than subverting the Constitution, he had no objection to its operating on campus.[23]

Sufficiently alert to ask the question, the young reporters were apparently not alert enough to question the answer. Who would determine if an organization had "questionable" aims? What would constitute proof that a group was taking "instruction from a foreign power?" Still, in retrospect Stassen's reply can be seen as the beginning of an increasingly strong emphasis on civil liberties, at least where the University of Pennsylvania was concerned.

It was a guarded, quiet move, and the effort if not the intent was to lower the blood pressure of Pennsylvania's faculty and trustees. That Stassen never fought a bitter, tooth-and-nail battle to save an accused Communist faculty member is a testament not to evasiveness, but to diplomacy. In an age of campus witch hunts, there was not one case of a university faculty member being reprimanded in any way for the expression of political opinion.

One example of McCarthy-era suspicions and the low-key Stassen response came in April 1949, when Reverend A. Wallace Copper of Sellers Memorial Methodist Church in Upper Darby, a western suburb of Philadelphia, wrote to the Pennsylvania president to complain about a professor. Donald Harter, of the Political Science Department, had appeared in an Upper Darby "Town Meeting on Foreign Policy," jointly sponsored by the Foreign Policy Association, the League of Women Voters, and the United Nations Council. After one speaker had blasted the Soviet Union, exclaiming, among other things, "my mind is closed in respect to Russia and I am proud of it," Harter was called upon to comment. He had six minutes to do so, to the other speaker's forty. According to the indignant Copper, "Doctor Harter took the position that what Russia was doing was our fault." "I need not tell you," Reverend Copper went on, "that this is basically and unalterably false. Anyone who knows the history of Communism and its present achievements ... recognizes the untruth of Doctor Harter's position."

With Copper a prominent member of the metropolitan community, Stassen had to tread lightly. Quietly, within the councils of the university, he initiated an inquiry into the case by C. Canby Balderston, dean of the Wharton School. Balderston provided Stassen with information on who sponsored the meeting and who attended. He also unobtrusively spoke with others who were at the function to determine exactly what Harter had said. This included, as it turned out, support for the Marshall Plan, support of a strong armed forces — "We must keep our powder dry," Harter had insisted — support for the United Nations and use of the United Nations as a vehicle for discussion with the Soviets. Apparently, Harter's most controversial point was to question the NATO Pact, as Balderston paraphrased, "because of possible misinterpretation by Russia." Balderston added that "the majority of the audience was not in a mood to receive Dr. Harter's remarks because of the strong emotional appeal [against the Soviet Union] that had just been made." Before Balderston had presented his report, Stassen wrote a three-sentence, nonchalant letter to Copper, promising a "careful inquiry." With that promise, Stassen apparently closed his correspondence with the reverend. The matter was dropped.[24]

Perhaps such silly criticism as Copper's could have had no other response; yet in the supercharged Cold War climate career-disrupting charges were often silly. Stassen refused to grandstand his opposition to Communism. Nor did he create a ruckus with outspoken support of the unjustly accused. His tight-lipped response was typical of his approach, and given the national anticommunist hysteria, perhaps the wisest policy. He simply refused to get into a brawl.

One alumnus, A.W. Coombs, wrote Stassen vigorously asserting his belief that Communists not be allowed to teach. He also asserted that university hiring decisions should be made by the trustees rather than the faculty. Where, Coombs demanded, did Stassen stand on this issue? The president's noncommittal, one-sentence reply observed, "New members of the Faculty are chosen by a combination of the Trustees and the Faculty."[25] The man who had as a presidential candidate prided himself on directly confronting issues had discovered that, sometimes, discretion was the better part of valor.

At the beginning of his tenure Stassen had hedged his answer to the *Daily Pennsylvanian* concerning Communist groups on campus. There is no record that Stassen actually had to confront such a nuisance; yet by the spring of 1949 he was confronted with faculty members associating themselves with "questionable" organizations, and the case revealed how far Stassen had gone in the direction of genuine tolerance. In April 1949 a University alumnus wrote to Stassen to complain about two Pennsylvania professors who were members of the National Council of the Arts, Scientists and Professions, which he referred to as a "thinly vailed [sic] Communists [sic] front organization." The president responded: "I thoroughly disapprove of this organization, but I believe we must maintain academic freedom with reference to our faculty and act only on matters which affect their competency to teach the subjects assigned to them."[26] Stassen was becoming increasingly relaxed about alleged "Communist front" groups.

One sensitive flash point for the anticommunist crusade on American campuses was whether to require "loyalty oaths" of faculty members. In 1949 the National Education Association sponsored a report by a panel whose members included representatives of higher education, including Columbia president Dwight Eisenhower and James B. Conant of Harvard, which declared Communists "unfit" for the classroom. With a budding consensus on the "fitness" issue, it was a short leap to the position that faculty members must declare, in effect, that they were fit to teach. The issue quickly became national in scope. In September 1949 forty-eight courses had to be dropped from the curriculum of the University of California at Berkeley when faculty members refused to sign such an oath. To them, loyalty oaths were an unambiguous subversion of free thinking and association, and their refusal to sign amounted to an entrenched, Maginot line for academic freedom.[27]

In this, Harold Stassen stood as an ally. As a matter of policy, he squelched any move to require loyalty oaths of Pennsylvania's faculty. However, the Pennsylvania legislature had other ideas. By the spring of 1951 the state house of representatives had passed a bill requiring loyalty oaths of faculty members at state-supported institutions. As the senate teetered on the brink of passing the bill as well, the university president rushed to Harrisburg to testify against the measure.

Stassen's remarks to the Pennsylvania State Senate opened on a conciliatory note, with the president assuring legislators that he was in "whole-hearted agreement" with the objective of combating "subversive Communist activity in our country." But he quickly got to the point. The bill, he declared, was "un–American" because it cast all faculty members under suspicion, requiring them to in effect prove their own innocence. Reaching back to his objections to Taft-Hartley, Stassen called for an "American method" to root out subversion. This method would be "to seek evidence, to investigate, and to punish when the evidence is obtained." It is not, Stassen snarled as he became uncharacteristically vehement, "the American method to require all law-abiding and patriotic citizens to file reports that they are law-abiding and patriotic." Such a law would "drop a smothering blanket over the freedom of thinking and of the freedom of speaking that exists at present and should exist on our campuses." For good measure, Stassen added, "Our faculty at the University of Pennsylvania is with us in this respect."[28]

Obviously, Stassen was not adopting a radical civil-libertarian line. He declared that Communists were unfit to teach. Perhaps because of this position, his remarks were favorably received among the members of the legislature and the bill was dropped. With Stassen's blessing, in its place a less stringent law was passed which required that the presidents of state-aided universities certify that they had no Communists in their employ.[29] In his limited demands, in his quick embrace of compromise, Stassen had eased anxieties rather than raised them. The more moderate measure passed by the legislature was clearly preferable to the loyalty oath bill, and Stassen could claim a significant accomplishment.

It should be noted that even the moderate strategy that Stassen employed required courage: appearing before the Pennsylvania legislature to testify against a bill seemingly on its way to passage held obvious dangers for a representative of a state-supported institution. Yet Stassen's refusal to be intimidated was quite in keeping with his belief that governmental aid to education, whether state or federal, should come with no strings attached. Speaking to the opening session of the 36th Annual Conference of the Associated Alumni of the University, Stassen emphasized the policy. He also made clear that, while the University of Pennsylvania strove to recruit accomplished and promising students, his goal was that the student population be broadly representative of all economic, racial and religious groups.[30]

This goal was no empty shibboleth. Stassen during his tenure at the university did, in fact, work vigorously to ensure that his institution did not discriminate on racial or ethnic grounds. This was compatible with his record as governor of Minnesota, where he had established a moderately progressive record on civil rights. Nor did he backtrack while in Philadelphia. His support for federal anti-lynching and anti-poll tax legislation, as well as a Federal Fair Employment Practices law with provisions for compulsory compliance, placed him as stronger on civil rights than either the Democratic or Republican platforms of 1952.[31] Stassen's actions at the University of Pennsylvania were sensitive to racial and ethnic discrimination.

On February 19, 1949, the *Pacific Citizen*, the official publication of the Japanese-American Citizens League, reported that a Nisei woman's application for admission to the University of Pennsylvania "apparently was ignored as were a number of other Nisei applications." Stassen sent a concerned memo to Henry Oberly, dean of admissions. "What does this refer to?" Stassen inquired. "Do we have Nisei here as students? If necessary," the president directed, "phone the magazine for info."

Apparently not content to wait for the dean's reply, Stassen fired off a letter to the *Pacific Citizen*, based in Salt Lake City, via air mail. Requesting further information, including the woman's name, he added, "I am confident that you will be very willing to cooperate with me in trying to be certain that any prospective applicant is not treated unjustly." Seeking yet more information, Stassen also contacted a University alumnus living in Salt Lake City and asked him to investigate.

Stassen was right to be concerned. As he was taking these actions, the article was attracting widespread notice. In Minnesota the St. Paul Council of Human Relations, at the direction of its vice president, Warren Burger, wrote to Stassen to express concern.

The uncovered facts of the case indicted American society and the U.S. government, but largely exonerated the university. According to an internal university memo, during World War II the War Department "made the direct request that the University of Pennsylvania should not enroll Japanese-American students." This request was lifted in 1944 and the university resumed admitting Japanese-Americans. No explanation was provided by the War Department for its request; yet the university conducted defense research and was located in close proximity to the Philadelphia Navy Yard. This, the memo reasoned, was a likely explanation. The specific case referred to in the *Pacific Citizen* was unrelated to the wartime discrimination. The case involved an applicant who had not taken the College Board Examination, which the University required as a matter of policy. After the exam had been completed, her case was reviewed by a committee on admissions, and she was accepted on July 28, 1948. By the time the *Pacific Citizen* article appeared, she was enrolled and doing well. It was the one-year delay in admittance, before she had taken the College Board Exam, that had caused the impression of being "apparently ignored." In a subsequent letter to the editor of the paper, Stassen reviewed the World War II policy, emphasizing that the university had now "reverted to its traditional policy of being completely open regardless of race, color, creed, religion or individual status."[32]

While the *Pacific Citizen* case required no policy decision by Stassen, his vigor in pursuing the matter with evident good faith demonstrated a commendable sensitivity to discrimination. Certainly his handling of the affair was above reproach. Indeed, throughout Stassen's tenure occasional charges of discrimination were made, sometimes becoming nasty battles fought out in headlines and editorials in the *Daily Pennsylvanian*. Overall, Stassen should get high marks for acting where necessary to defuse the situation and get a clear accounting of the facts. For example, on one occasion the Committee on Fair Educational Opportunities of the Philadelphia Fellowship Commission conducted a survey of the admissions policies of area professional schools. Some university students quickly got the impression that the survey revealed discrimination on the part of their university. It did not. Stassen met with both the committee and the students, made the facts clear, and the issue faded. In 1950 the Anti-Defamation League of B'nai B'rith published a report which listed the University of Pennsylvania as one of several "great institutions" which placed "no racial or religious barriers upon admission."[33]

With Stassen's policies regarding civil rights and academic freedom, two hot buttons of the intellectual community, operating smoothly, Stassen maintained vigorous action in an area dear to the hearts of trustees—financial affairs. Months after arriving on campus Stassen pushed the alumni annual giving campaign into high gear. At a December 1948 dinner and meeting at the Bellevue-Strafford Hotel, Stassen announced a drive to top the previous year's record of $165,534 and hammered the alumni to be forthcoming. He stressed to the university's graduates that their alma mater was spending far more per student than the tuition covered. "Do not underestimate the importance of your task," he warned the potential contributors.[34]

Upon his departure from the university, Stassen would confess that he had been "somewhat impatient because the rate of growth" of Pennsylvania's financial assets had not been greater; still, solid and substantial progress, and responsible financial management, could not be denied. In each of Stassen's four fiscal years the budget was balanced. This had not been easy, "The most rigid economies," Stassen correctly reflected, had been observed. There had also been two increases in tuition, which grew from $550 for undergraduate schools to $700 in 1953–1954. Yet these increases did not keep pace with inflation. More revenue was obtained from Stassen's successful quest for alumni contributions, which netted $722,596 over the four years of Stassen's reign. Thus, by 1953, despite tuition increases, the percentage of the university budget contributed by students had decreased from 34 percent to 28 percent. The annual budget had increased, meanwhile, from $19,220,000 to $23,610,000. The total assets of the university increased from $80,000,000 to $98,400,000. Of this, $12,000,000 came from new assets, with the remainder from appreciation.[35]

One of the motives behind the trustees' selection of the erstwhile presidential candidate was the presumption that, as a national figure, he would be a successful fundraiser. While the Stassen record in this area was not spectacular, it was in fact quite respectable. In 1948 "Gifts and Grants" of $950,000 represented 5 percent of the university's budget. In 1952 funds from this source provided $1,620,000, or 7 percent of the budget. Funds from various other sources increased from $6,520,000 to $8,810,000. According to Stassen, the university's development fund, targeted for the expansion of plant and equipment, showed an impressive increase from $5,719,783 to $9,414,000. This met the original goals for the construction of two new buildings, Gates Pavilion and Dietrich Hall. However, as construction of these buildings proceeded, costs grew beyond original calculations. When Stassen resigned the presidency, he could only note that funds were "currently being sought" to cover the increases. Stassen was notably effective in soliciting corporate contributions. During his four years a hundred ninety-nine corporations donated $3,263,832. Of that total, eighty-five had never contributed to the university before. Also, eighteen "corporate-related" foundations gave $686,045. Twelve of these foundations had never before made University of Pennsylvania contributions.[36]

It was a substantial, though perhaps not spectacular, financial record, and Stassen received high marks for his fiscal management. The most prominent critic was Stassen himself. In 1953 he complained that "living in the Philadelphia area and closely associated with Philadelphia and its traditions are many families and individuals who could easily" have facilitated more rapid expansion. "It is," he remarked, "a matter of deepest personal regret that during the past four years I have been unable to persuade any of these individuals or families to make this vital connection" (with university goals).[37]

The halls of academe had not softened the political ambitions and interest in national affairs of the former governor. He was, after all, still a national figure, and the university president had no intention of leaving the spotlight. His associations and contacts alone guaranteed that nonacademic interests would act as a centrifugal force, driving him away from the university that nonetheless had become his political base. Political and military acquaintances came to call, as did the ambassador to Pakistan, whom Stassen entertained at a private luncheon in Houston Hall.[38] For over a year after his arrival at Philadelphia, though, Stassen focused on his university duties. The lure of national affairs, however, was to become increasingly irresistible.

On September 20, 1950, Stassen was forced to deny rumors that he would succeed Francis Matthews as secretary of the Navy; White House press secretary Charles G. Ross made the same denial. Significantly, Stassen had to deny the rumor not from Philadelphia but from New York, where he was addressing the National Industrial Conference Board.[39] That Stassen was in New York was symptomatic of the fact that he was becoming increasingly preoccupied with public affairs. This involvement was not headline-hunting, at least not always. Stassen spent his years grooming his political program, studying issues in a characteristically intensive way and moving, just slightly, to the right.

A good example was national health policy. Stassen had addressed the issue only in a sort of obligatory way during his presidential campaign, as one who recognized that he had to have a policy yet was not deeply enamored of the subject. At the time he was moderately inclined to negotiate the form of some fashion of limited, national health care insurance. In *Collier's* in 1946 Stassen, while cautioning that a national Republican program would not disrupt "existing medical and hospital insurance plans," still expressed an activist approach. Without providing details, he asserted as a goal governmental action to "seek to safeguard small and moderate income families from the crushing effects of extended illness and serious injuries." An important aspect of this program would be "establishment of a universal health and dental annual checkup, with consequent professional advice not limited by the means of the individual." He called for governmental assistance to promote the extension of hospital facilities, coordination of health programs, prevention, and federal, state and local cooperation.[40]

In his remarks on health care, candidate Stassen chose to accentuate governmental activism, with little more than a reassuring nod toward the political right. By 1950, however, this pattern would be reversed, with Stassen now becoming something of a national spokesman for the anti-health insurance forces. His new emphasis was part political hyperbole, part serious thought and investigation.

In late 1949 Stassen embarked on a trip to England to investigate the British Health Program, which went into effect on July 5, 1948. The British plan provided health care to all citizens at a nominal charge. In England Stassen consulted doctors, administrators and public officials. Returning to the United States he wrote a series of *Reader's Digest* articles on national health insurance, beginning with an article unambiguously entitled, "Never! Never! Never!" In the article Stassen blasted the year-old British system as costly, inefficient and utterly ineffective. The article compared health statistics in the United States and England from July 1948 to July 1949, and found the British system wanting. He ended the article on an ominous note: "The additional tombstones in the British cemeteries," he gravely observed, "72,125 more than the year before the National Health Program went into effect — are grim signposts on which we can read: 'Never take this road for a national Health Program.'"[41]

The tombstone statistic was, of course, a bit of specious exaggeration befitting a *Reader's Digest* article. Reading the article in his office, Senator Claude Pepper of Florida, a member of the Senate Committee on Labor and Public Welfare and coauthor of the Truman-supported National Health Insurance Bill, sputtered with rage. When NBC's *American Forum of the Air* invited Pepper to debate the issue with Stassen, the irascible senator could hardly say "yes" fast enough.

The two men faced off before a packed Continental Room of the Wardman Park Hotel in Washington, D.C., on January 29, 1950. Speaking first, the senator cried foul to Stassen's *Reader's Digest* claim that Pepper's bill was similar to the British system. He then rather inappropriately quoted Winston Churchill in support of the Pepper Bill. Next, he went after the tombstone target. "The Governor and I are in politics, or we have been, he may still be," Pepper tartly commented, asking if "it is likely that Winston Churchill ... if he believes, and if the British people believe, that a national health scheme in effect was causing more tombstones," would wish to maintain the National Health Service? A speechless Stassen let the point slide. The senator could notch an oratorical victory in his belt after the debate.[42]

Another issue that Stassen had devoted only modest attention to during the campaign was federal aid to education. After 1948 the politician-turned-educator invested increased study, and breath, to the issue.

In June of 1949 Stassen received a letter from a friend and prominent Chicago attorney, Glen A. Lloyd. "I don't recall that we ever talked about the proposal pending in Congress for Federal aid to education," Lloyd reflected, adding, "I hope you will oppose it and think it would be a good thing if you would make your position known to those considering the subject in Congress." Lloyd needn't have worried. Stassen had already gone to Washington, D.C. to lobby Republican members of the House Committee on Education and Labor, and was "confident that they will unanimously oppose this legislation."[43]

The legislation in question was backed by Stassen's old nemesis, Senator Robert Taft. In 1948 Taft, lending a bipartisan cast to President Truman's call for federal education aid, had steered an education bill through the Senate by an impressive fifty-eight to twenty-two margin. It was the first time in sixty years that the Senate had approved general federal aid to education. Although the bill died in the House, by 1949 Taft and Truman had renewed the battle. Again, the Senate passed an education bill, this time by a fifty-eight to fifteen margin. Again, opponents retreated to the House. On May 9 Congressman John Lesinski, a labor-boosting Democrat from Detroit, assigned the bill to a subcommittee headed by Graham A. Barden, a conservative former schoolteacher who supported federal aid for public education.[44]

With battle lines thus established, Stassen increasingly spoke out against the measure. Yet, as in the case with Taft-Hartley, Stassen's opposition to the specific bill obscured the fact that he agreed with much of the underlying philosophy. While Stassen believed "it would be most desirable if there were no Federal Aid to Education at all," he nonetheless allowed that it would "be reasonably acceptable to have a Federal program in assisting with the construction of needed school houses in poor districts." Poor districts, to Stassen, were districts in the South, where federal aid "should be confined."[45]

Meanwhile, congressional passage of an aid bill grew dimmer when the Barden sub-committee reported a bill which, unlike the Senate bill, denied federal funds to Catholic schools and did not require a "just and equitable" distribution of funds between white and black schools. The fragile consensus between the National Education Association and the National Catholic Welfare Conference was shattered as the NEA, getting greedy, pushed for the Barden plan over the Senate bill, which it had previously supported.[46] Thus, Stassen was only driving a nail in the education aid coffin when he traveled to Houston, Texas, to speak before the fifty-fourth annual convention of the Southern Association of Colleges and Secondary Schools, to grumble about national federal aid.

Still, the address usefully outlined the extent to which Stassen did support federal aid targeted at the South. To his receptive audience Stassen emphasized the national responsibility in raising low standards of living and education traceable to the Civil War. "A major, continuing national investment should be made," Stassen declared, "in building up the resources, facilities, industries and schools in the South." Nevertheless, the university president made clear that he remained an inveterate foe of opening up the federal spigot for public school funding on a national basis. Educational policies of non-southern states, he insisted, "should be to concentrate upon stimulating and securing adequate local support, rather than upon the opening up of direct channels of funds to the central national Treasury."[47]

Were the speech and the policy merely a ploy for southern delegates to the 1952 Republican National Convention? The *Atlanta Constitution*, approving of the policy, suspected as much. Not that it minded. On the contrary, it said, "Of all the Republicans who aspire to be President, Mr. Stassen is the only one who so far has given any indication of going after the Southern vote."[48] Politically motivated or not, the Stassen education policy was detailed and thoughtful, representing much more analysis on the issue than was evident during his presidential campaign.

Foreign policy, though, remained Stassen's primary interest, and the subject on which he spent increasing amounts of time, to the dismay of many University of Pennsylvania devotees. Actually, Stassen's renewed vigor in foreign affairs, requiring extended globetrotting, was part of his increasing willingness to travel to distant areas and immerse himself in politics, a point well comprehended by some of his university critics. A large share of his time was spent in seeking to boost the electoral fortunes of Republican candidates. Ironically, in light of their subsequent clash in the Eisenhower administration, Stassen traveled to New York in November 1949 to campaign for GOP senatorial nominee John Foster Dulles, then battling former governor Herbert Lehman.[49] Not that Stassen neglected Republicans in his new, nominal home base. After a series of Stassen campaign appearances for local candidates, James Finnegan, Democratic city chairman of Philadelphia, could stand no more. He lashed out at Stassen for endorsing Philadelphia candidates while not even bothering to change his voter registration from Minnesota to Pennsylvania; a chastened Stassen subsequently did just that.[50]

Of course, the erstwhile presidential candidate still rubbed many conservative Republicans the wrong way, and they were quite satisfied to go without Stassen campaign aid. In September 1950 the university president abruptly cancelled a speech to Chicago Republicans. Democratic Illinois senator Scott Lucas, running for reelection, told the *New York Times*, "I have it on reliable authority that the isolationists in control of the Republican party in Illinois demanded that he not come because Stassen stands firm with Vandenberg."[51]

Stassen had a different, though esoteric, explanation. "Unforeseen developments," he said, "connected with an important national move make it impossible for me to complete my engagement."[52] He did not say what this "unforeseen development" was, and the mystery was not revealed in a subsequent *New York Times* story entitled "Stassen Planning Change in Activity." Stassen merely told the paper that he would have an announcement "within ten days" of his appointment to a post having both international and domestic importance. Refusing to explain further, he would only reveal that the new activity would not be an appointment by the Truman administration. A broad hint, however, was dropped when Stassen said he "might do some traveling."[53]

The suspense was broken on October 4, 1950, with a two-part Stassen press release. Part one was a copy of a letter Stassen had sent to Joseph Stalin, chiding the Soviet leader for international aggression. Part two, apparently Stassen's "national move," was his announcement of extended foreign travel. "It is my ... intention to take a leave from my duties as President of the University of Pennsylvania in November and December," Stassen declared, "and, with the support of one of the major Foundations of our country, travel to Asia to personally study conditions there."[54]

Critics quickly pointed out that Stassen had begun his 1948 presidential campaign with just such a globetrotting performance and speculated that the scenario was repeating itself for 1952, which of course, it was. Many Pennsylvanians, whether associated with the university or not, were insulted. One typical get-back-to-work letter Stassen received expressed the point succinctly. "I'm a taxpayer and you work for a state-aided college," it snapped, "so it would be a good idea if you tended more to your work for which you are being overpaid instead of going around criticizing your betters."[55]

Actually, Stassen was not paid during his Asian trip; the leave of absence the board of trustees granted, to begin December 3, 1950, was without pay.[56] On that date Stassen clambered aboard a United Airlines flight to Detroit, en route to Minnesota, from which he departed to Alaska on his way to Asia. His trip included stops in Japan, Siam, Indonesia, Malaya, India, Pakistan, Israel, South Africa, Portugal, and England. An exhausted Stassen returned to New York on January 9.[57]

If the expedition was meant to garner headlines, it was unsuccessful; the trip achieved only modest publicity in and of itself. Upon his return, however, Stassen stirred widespread interest with his "reports." Appropriately, the first report was to his employer, the board of trustees of the University of Pennsylvania on January 22. To the trustees Stassen affirmed that "knowledge without a sense of direction, without the foundation for a purposeful life, is not only inadequate, but has proven harmful." It was with this conviction that Stassen during his trip "sought out Dr. Albert Schweitzer in the jungles of Central Africa." Rising to the philosophic subject, Stassen called Schweitzer "the greatest living philosopher. His philosophy of 'reverence for life,' his concept of the 'ethics of civilization,' his evolution of the significance of the 'will to live' in all mortal beings, are inspiring." Stassen called the time he spent at Schweitzer's missionary hospital "treasured hours."[58]

Yet Stassen the would-be philosopher was also a practical man-of-affairs, and his subsequent addresses were more grounded in geopolitical reality. Such was the thrust of Stassen's address to the Executive Club of Chicago on March 30. Significantly, recalling Scott Lucas' September remarks, Stassen began his speech by asking, "May I say, in a lighter vein, that I am aware of the fact that all of the men of Chicago have not always agreed with me on foreign policy?" The university president then went on to call for what he called "A Common Sense Foreign Policy." Actually, much of the policy was merely common. Still, there was a great deal of substance to his remarks. Speaking with great detail about NATO military forces, Stassen called for dispersed global firepower of a hundred ninety to two hundred divisions. He also called for increased vigor in weapons research and development. He placed "long odds" on war with the Soviet Union, largely because of his prediction of increasingly vocal independence movements in the Soviet Republics of the Ukraine, Latvia, Lithuania and Estonia, and in occupied Europe.[59] To an extent not evident before 1949, Stassen balanced his call for military superiority with sensitivity toward the sensibilities of foreign nations. In a Howard Crawley Memorial Lecture at the Wharton School, Stassen identified racial problems as an urgent but little-attended-to subject of U.S. foreign policy. In the address he blasted South Africa for its "effort to turn the clock back — set up complete segregation." He decried this effort, which he called an "explosive and tense situation," and called for racial equality. The rest of his address, which also included a discussion of Asia, centered on the need for land reform, improved standards of living and health care.[60]

Despite this welcome attention to the needs of foreign peoples, Stassen was not detached from the military fixations and anticommunist obsession of his time, particularly where GOP candidates were concerned. Such concerns were evident, for example, in a nationally broadcast radio address before a Connecticut Republican rally on November 4, 1950, in New Haven. Pausing to commend the Secret Service for defending President Truman during the attempt on his life, Stassen ripped into the Democratic Party for "five years of building up Chinese Communist strength through the blinded, blundering, bewildering American-Asiatic policy." It had been, he charged, "five years of coddling Chinese Communists, five years of undermining General MacArthur [odd words from a man who had done his bit to undermine MacArthur in Wisconsin in 1948], five years of snubbing friendly freedom-loving Asiatics, and five years of appeasing the arch–Communist Mao Tse-tung." He added that the Truman administration was "socialistically inclined."[61]

If Stassen indulged, in the midst of generally thoughtful public addresses on foreign policy, in an occasional partisan free-for-all such as the New Haven address, so, too, did his critics, who saw Stassen's increasing devotion to public activism and absence from the university as an unprotected flank in Stassen's political armor. In a strategic position to send chills down the spines of trustees, Hiram C. Andrews, the Democratic minority leader of the Pennsylvania State House of Representatives, launched an assault on the university president. Upon Stassen's return to the United States Andrews attacked Stassen what he called "political globetrotting." In an address to the trustees, Andrews warned that the University of Pennsylvania was not "cultivating goodwill, legislative or otherwise, by continuing to employ and apparently encourage a perambulating, migratory president."[62]

Andrews' comments had to be taken seriously by the trustees. Under the Pennsylvania constitution a two-thirds vote was required to approve all appropriations for schools such as the University of Pennsylvania. Although the Republicans controlled the state house, their number fell eighteen short of the two-thirds mark; Stassen and the university needed Democratic support.[63] Despite the animosity of the house minority leader, Stassen did in fact do a credible job in soliciting state funds. Appropriations from the state increased from $1,920,000 in 1948 to $2,860,000 in 1952, marking an increase from 10 percent to 12 percent of the budget.[64]

Still, Stassen was vulnerable on the time-on-the-job issue, a problem that only increased in the ensuing months as Stassen's extracurricular activities increasingly vexed university supporters and brought Stassen a significant amount of negative publicity. From October 1951 through January 1952 he rubbed many partisan nerves the wrong way in a rancorous tussle with the State Department, involving charges, countercharges and fully five appearances before a Senate Foreign Relations subcommittee considering Truman's nomination of Philip Jessup to the post of United Nations delegate.

The battle began when Stassen appeared before the subcommittee to oppose the Jessup nomination. In the course of his testimony, the university president told of a White House conference with congressional leaders and State Department officials. Stassen said that the late Senator Arthur Vandenberg had told him that secretary of state Dean Acheson and ambassador-at-large Philip Jessup had proposed halting aid to Nationalist China. "I fear Mr. Stassen's memory is playing him tricks," responded State Department press officer Michael McDermott, who denied that such a conference had taken place. However, days later a red-faced State Department acknowledged that there had, after all, been such a meeting. According to the department, the senior U.S. military representative in China had proposed at a meeting to halt U.S. aid, a proposal rejected by Truman. Still, the State Department emphasized that Jessup was "not involved in any way" in the proposal. Stassen, though, encouraged by the department's reversal, continued to insist that both Jessup and Acheson had been in favor of cutting off aid to the Nationalists.[65]

Thus began an interminable battle, with Stassen calling for Acheson's resignation. Initial press reaction in light of the State Department's fumble over whether any meeting had taken place was supportive of the university president. "Why the State Department didn't check up first, before practically charging Stassen with falsehood, is difficult to understand," grumbled the *Philadelphia Inquirer*.[66] Yet as the issue dragged on it was increasingly ignored by the press, which became bored with Stassen's endless promises of "new evidence." President Truman eventually gave Jessup a recess appointment to the U.N. post. One group not ignoring Stassen's role, though, was the trustees of the University of Pennsylvania, who wondered when Stassen would get back to full-time work. As it turned out, he wouldn't, or not for very long. With the 1952 presidential election looming, Taft had announced his candidacy on October 16, 1951, and Stassen directed his attention toward another White House bid.

As early as November 1951 Stassen began preparations for yet another leave of absence, although it appears he was reluctant to ask for one. By December 1 his staff had prepared an up-to-date memorandum on procedures of administration during the absence of the president, under University statutes. The memorandum went on to envision that the members of the executive committee of the university each take turns of "Special Executive Duty" during the president's absence, and went so far as to list the rotation of duty, with Stassen assistant Donald Angell taking the first turn.[67]

What is interesting about the preparations Stassen was making is that he had not yet informed Robert McCracken, chairman of the board of trustees, of his desire to take a leave. Indeed, when he so informed McCracken on December 26, the president could not bring himself officially to ask for a leave of absence. In his letter to McCracken, Stassen announced that he was presenting to the chairman "a special situation which has arisen due to circumstances which were not anticipated when the Trustees elected me and I accepted in September, 1948." Stassen went on to explain:

A number of citizens in various states, including the official Republican Convention of my native state, have asked that I give my consent to their presentation of my name for the Presidency in the primaries and conventions of 1952.

It has not been an easy question to answer, and I have considered it long and prayerfully in search of the right thing to do. I have now concluded, with humility, that in view of the policies in which I believe, in the light of the orderly process by which our citizens reach their decisions under our constitution, and in careful consideration of all other information available, it is my clear responsibility to permit those who believe in the policies I represent to present my name.

In view of this decision it is my earnest wish that action be taken that is the best for the University with respect to my relations to it. I therefore place myself entirely in the hands of the trustees for their decision as to the wise course for the University to take under these conditions.[68]

The trustees must have been tipped off about Stassen's "earnest wish," for on the very next day the trustees unanimously agreed to grant a leave of absence without pay.[69] A grateful Stassen on January 15 sent letters to all trustees expressing his "deep appreciation." One of his letters was addressed to Francis Henry Taylor, the director of the New York Metropolitan Museum of Art. Taylor obligingly wrote back:

This is to acknowledge your thoughtful and informative letter of January 15th in which you tell me of your proposed political activity....

Perhaps you have not been informed ... that I submitted my resignation from the Board of Trustees on October 18th and it was accepted at the meeting of the Board on October 22nd, 1951. The reason for my resignation was not made public although I had gone to Philadelphia the previous week to protest to Mr. McCracken as Chairman of the Board your exploitation of the presidency of the University for your own political ends. I was informed by Mr. McCracken that the policy of the Board appeared to be to allow you to continue to prostitute the University in this fashion and there was nothing further left for me to do but resign.

Since you have been able to give so little time to the University in recent months that you have not learned of my resignation, I take the liberty of writing you to say how deeply I deplore your conduct as President of the University.

Very truly yours,
[signed] Francis Henry Taylor[70]

Taylor's charge was particularly devastating because it hit an essential truth: Stassen had attempted a two-front career battle, and despite his great skill and energy as a university president, he was simply overextended.

The dilemma of an able officer who, in effect, frequently called in sick was nicely captured by the student writers of the *Daily Pennsylvanian*. "It is difficult," the paper reflected, "to reconcile the fact that during his reign here he has inextricably confused political ambitions and actions with pure educational administration." Nevertheless, the paper found much to praise in the Stassen administration, describing his university actions as being marked by "intellectual superiority, and dynamic character."[71]

Indeed, on balance Stassen received more praise than blame for his four years at Pennsylvania. This included receiving the National Award for Outstanding Leadership as an Education Administrator, conferred by the American Association of School Administrators in 1950.[72]

As Stassen departed Philadelphia for Washington, D.C., after the 1952 Republican National Convention when President-elect Eisenhower appointed him as Mutual Security Administrator, the Trustees adopted a statement of effusive praise: "President Stassen brought to the office of administrative head of the University a rich and varied experience in executive work; a broad vision; a deep insight into the fundamentals of American life; a lively interest in the problems of education and an unusual capacity for decisive action." The statement also praised Stassen for invigorating the alumni, gaining the support of "prominent citizens and great corporations" and publicizing the University.[73]

Was the praise warranted? Stassen's direction of university finances was at least respectable, if not spectacular. During his presidency, measures were adopted to ensure student participation in university management. The All-University Student Council was established to provide the means for university-wide participation in university affairs. Members of this council were joined by the Undergraduate Council and the Senate of the Women's Student Government Association at annual dinners in Stassen's home. He also met regularly with individual students and the student newspaper. Enrollment at the university upon Stassen's arrival stood at a dizzying 19,761, reflecting the postwar boom. Before the war, enrollment had stood at 14,664. In 1952–1953, the figure stood at 15,905. Scholarship awards increased from 1,127 awards in 1948–1949 to 1,577 in 1952–1953. The record, then, shows little to complain about concerning Stassen's policies toward students.[74]

The faculty undoubtedly benefited from Stassen's refusal to allow the university to be drawn into the McCarthy-era witch hunts on American campuses. Yet the number of full-time faculty members at the university plummeted during Stassen's tenure by 98 percent, more than enough to match the decline in enrollment. Moreover, even Stassen admitted that salary increases, which lagged behind inflation, were "not as great as I wish they could have been." Still, to encourage research among the faculty that remained, Stassen in July of

1949 created the position of Director of Sponsored Research. University-sponsored research contracts subsequently increased from $2,500,000 in 1949 to $3,500,000 in 1952. Stassen called this a "splendid increase in research projects," and there is no record that anybody objected to this view.[75]

Ultimately, Stassen's performance was praised and damned — praised for its vigor and initiative and damned for its neglect of the university when Stassen was preoccupied with public affairs. The latter time was often well spent, though, as Stassen engaged in a generally thoughtful study of national issues, only occasionally dirtying himself with partisan wrangling. Moreover, he had, during the McCarthy era acted as a moderating force in hysterical calls for campus Communist witch hunts, thereby demonstrating genuine fortitude and courage. On balance, Stassen could be proud of his service in Philadelphia.

12. The Rationale

Internationalist-minded Republicans in the fall of 1950 could expect that their thrice-failed effort to elect one of their own as president would in 1952 finally succeed. In September George Gallup reported that among Republican voters Dwight D. Eisenhower was the runaway favorite for the GOP nomination, with a 42 percent preference rating. The internationalists were encouraged; whatever views Ike may have held, he was not Senator Robert Taft, who as the GOP's second choice was a full twenty-seven percentage points behind Eisenhower and only one point ahead of Thomas Dewey and Harold Stassen, who were tied for third place.

Yet from this pinnacle of popularity Eisenhower began a slow descent, maintaining his lead but with less stratospheric popularity ratings. His support among GOP voters fell from September's 42 percent to 38 percent in April of 1951. In June of that year Gallup reported that Eisenhower was the choice of 30 percent of GOP voters. By November of that year the general's share would drop to 28 percent. Senator Taft's support climbed steadily to 22 percent.[1] Taft, having learned from Stassen in 1948 the advantages of a vigorous and early campaign, announced for the presidency on October 16, 1951. Yet, he had been an unannounced candidate for some time. In a memorandum to General Lucius Clay in June Thomas Dewey, an early supporter of General Eisenhower, grumbled that Taft's "agents are conducting a very effective campaign in all forty-eight states, backed by immense resources which are being spent quite without scruple."[2] "I am encouraged," admitted the Ohio senator in February 1952, "because the results of polls taken among Republican party leaders seem to show that a large number of them favor my nomination."[3]

Still, Dewey in his memorandum demurely purred that he did not "share the hysteria which some are expressing that if great activity does not occur immediately" Taft would wrap up the nomination in short order.[4] Harold Stassen, being chronically prone to "great activity," was less sanguine, and called for a meeting of his political associates and advisors in the Clarksboro, New Jersey, home of Amos Peaslee in late June of 1951.

Thus began Stassen's complex and controversial actions in the 1952 Republican presidential nominating campaign. Stassen later claimed that his goal was not to nominate himself, but to ensure the nomination of Dwight Eisenhower by challenging Robert Taft. Stassen was running not for president, but for Eisenhower, whose position as NATO supreme commander required that he remain silent as Taft actively campaigned.

The record makes clear that Stassen's activities were for the most part consistent with this aim. Yet the effort was hampered by distrust between the Minnesotan's supporters and the avowedly pro–Eisenhower backers, led by Senator Henry Cabot Lodge and Thomas

Dewey. Stassen was alarmed at Taft's successful, and for the most part unchallenged, bid for GOP delegates; further, he was suspicious of the ability of eastern Republicans associated with Dewey to make a credible pro–Eisenhower campaign. From this premise, Stassen concluded that an independent effort on his part was desirable because he could effectively challenge Taft in the primaries, keeping the Ohio senator on the defensive; also, he would not be forced to support campaign policies with which he did not agree. "I did not want to be under their direction," the Minnesotan recalled, referring to Dewey and Lodge. "I thought they'd make mistakes. And if you're in a team you've got to go with them on mistakes, so I wanted to keep my own position."[5] Finally, it seems certain that Stassen was not unaware of the fact that in a deadlocked convention the Republican party might well turn to the Minnesotan. While his actions were rarely inconsistent with the purpose of nominating Dwight Eisenhower, they also were clearly designed to keep his own options open, a point not lost by the Eisenhower campaign staff.

For their part the Dewey-Lodge forces recognized that Stassen would be helpful. "We all agreed," Dewey wrote Clay, "that it was quite important to avoid letting [Taft] take" important state primaries "by default." Indeed, Dewey averred, "We might have to ask [Stassen] to run in them."[6] Clay agreed, noting that Stassen could "be very valuable."[7] Yet Stassen could be valuable only so long as he remained non-threatening, so the national Eisenhower forces kept a wary eye on him. On occasion, actions designed to keep Stassen politically manageable would harm their ultimate purpose of nominating Dwight Eisenhower.[8]

The meeting at Clarksboro consisted of forty-one prominent Republicans, not all of whom would eventually choose to support the Stassen initiative in 1952, but all of whom had done so in 1948. Among current or former Republican officeholders at the meeting were Senators Ed Thye of Minnesota and Fred Seaton of Nebraska, Congressman Walter Judd of Minnesota, Lieutenant Governor Gordon Allot of Colorado, Governor Walter Kohler of Wisconsin, and former governor Huntley Spaulding of New Hampshire; also present was Warren Burger.[9]

The group mulled over possible avenues either to thwart Taft or to "moderate his views" by joining the senator's bandwagon at an early date. The group arrived at a consensus that Eisenhower should be nominated and, according to Stassen, it was "decided that because of my earlier work with Eisenhower, I should go to Paris to encourage him to run as a Republican, and to assure him of our support if he would consider running."[10]

Yet the group also prepared for the contingency that Eisenhower would either not run or procrastinate so long as to make a Taft nomination likely. In that case, Stassen was to be a candidate. It was also decided

Dwight D. Eisenhower, ca. 1950s (John F. Rothmann collection).

that Bernard Shanley, a New Jersey lawyer, would serve as campaign manager. Later, Shanley recorded in his diary a "statement which was generally accepted by" the group at Clarksboro. This statement indicated that a campaign would "be instituted for the election of H.E.S. to the Presidency." However, plans might be modified after obtaining information whether General Eisenhower was a Republican, and would run on the Republican ticket in 1952. Should this be true, the Stassen campaign would throw its support to Eisenhower at an "effective" time. In the absence of an Eisenhower candidacy, the "emphasis will be on the candidacy of H.E.S. and no other candidate."[11]

Stassen was emphatic that he not be perceived as a stalking horse, that his candidacy not be viewed as simply an attempt to garner support that would inevitably be thrown to Eisenhower. Moreover, in such a role his room for maneuver would be limited, and he would be viewed as an underling and thus would have to act more cautiously than if he were working on his own behalf. Yet it was precisely this independence which alarmed the Eisenhower forces almost immediately. Indeed, the seeds of misunderstanding had already been sown by the time of the Clarksboro meeting. The week before, Stassen had traveled to New York for a conference with Dewey, Herbert Brownell and Russell Sprague. "It was a frank, useful, working meeting," Dewey exclaimed. "The most significant highlight was that [Stassen] said that he pledged himself 'one thousand percent' and with no reservations to the movement so long as our friend [Eisenhower] was available and said all he wanted was cooperation and orders."[12]

While it seems unlikely that Stassen would have played the eager junior to Thomas Dewey, cheerfully requesting orders, it seems quite plausible that he did in fact pledge "one thousand percent" cooperation. Dewey perhaps confused subordination with cooperation; certainly Lodge, Clay, Brownell and others would be quick to accuse Stassen of reneging on his commitment. Still, it seems clear that Stassen made reasonable efforts to ensure effective communication between the two camps; he informed Dewey of the events at Clarksboro and designated Shanley as the official Stassen liaison to the Eisenhower group.[13]

Meanwhile, the Stassen for President campaign began to take shape. Early in August Shanley appointed an executive committee consisting of Elmer Ryan, Warren Burger, Daniel Gainey, Amos Peaslee and Bud Mackay, executive vice president of Northwest Airlines. All were veterans of the 1948 campaign. Meeting in Minneapolis, the group labored over timing, office location, staffing, and other details of running for president. According to the minutes of the meeting, Stassen "appreciated the necessity of having campaign moves emanate from his friends and supporters rather than directly from the candidate." Insiders in the campaign were assigned responsibilities for coordinating "relationships with other candidates." To Elmer Ryan went the task of winning over a wavering Senator Thye into the Stassen-for-Eisenhower strategy. To Shanley went the task of conferring with Senator Frank Carlson of Kansas, who was soon to be appointed executive director of the national Eisenhower for President Committee, on "the relationship of the Stassen and Eisenhower campaigns, particularly as to Presidential Primaries" which would "if possible" be "correlated."[14]

Correlation, however, was proving to be difficult, and among the Stassen and Eisenhower forces private grumblings about the other camp could already be heard. In late August, Eisenhower wrote Clay a letter expressing appreciation that Stassen had not made over-zealous efforts to see him up to that time, and "was one of the few who have not attempted to dictate some type of time schedule. He "seem[ed] to comprehend clearly" that until Eisenhower's agenda for NATO moved forward Eisenhower could not "give consideration to taking any other position or responsibility." Eisenhower noted with satisfaction that

Stassen insisted to the general's other would-be backers that "it was up to everybody to adopt their hopeful planning to the compulsions placed upon me by the requirements of this position."[15] Reading this, Clay must have reddened with indignation; he was mindful of the compulsions of Robert Taft. When Stassen departed for Europe in early December to finally sound out the general, Clay pleaded to his old friend Eisenhower: "Please be careful with him.... No one, I repeat no one, of your group trusts him fully."[16]

Nor was the Stassen group entirely delighted to fully cooperate with a rival. This was especially true of the occasionally over-eager Shanley, who in September of 1951 confided to his diary that he was not especially inclined to proffer advice to the Eisenhower forces about the appropriate time for an Eisenhower for President campaign announcement. "I do not think," Shanley mused, "it is fair to either Harold or the General that we do so, as Harold has only taken the position that if the General enters the race at an *effective* time, he will not oppose him but will support him. I am loathe to give this advice primarily because by the time the first four primaries are history, I believe that Harold will have sufficient strength to defeat Truman handily, and as I believe and many of the top leaders in the Republican party believe, Harold is the best-equipped man in the country to be president."[17]

One "top leader" who did not feel this way was Russell Sprague, who was already suspecting the worst of Shanley and Stassen. In July, Sprague hinted to Shanley that the effort to stop Taft could be undone by "selfish interests." Shanley hastened to reassure Sprague that of the Stassen personnel "our own personal interests were not selfish and we had no intention of making them such."[18] But Sprague was not reassured and informed Dewey of his suspicions. A few months later, former U.S. senator Harry Darby of Kansas informed an increasingly exasperated Dewey that Stassen's supporters were spreading the word that Stassen was *really running for president*. Dewey promptly called a meeting with Stassen and asked, "Is your commitment still good?" Specifically, Dewey demanded to know if Stassen would throw his strength wherever possible to Eisenhower. "Tom," Stassen declared, "I want this clearly understood—I have no commitment."

Stassen proceeded to explain in lawyer-like and, one suspects, pedantic fashion that he and his supporters had, from the beginning, and as a matter of policy, decided that they would throw their strength to Eisenhower at an *effective* time. Further, Stassen explained that Dewey had received no promises from him and therefore the use of the word "commitment" was inaccurate.[19] Tom exploded. In June of 1951 he had written to Clay that "despite the aspersions cast upon him by many—as happens to everyone in public life—I think he is undoubtedly a solid, experienced and intelligent man.... I was ... impressed with his sincerity."[20] Now he complained to Clay: "Beyond a doubt his attitude is markedly different from the pledges he gave in June." After describing the encounter with Stassen, Dewey grumbled that the Minnesotan "refused to be nailed down."[21] Clay lost no time in informing Eisenhower.[22]

The general was calm. He patiently reminded Clay that Stassen had always indicated that he could be no stalking horse if he were to effectively challenge Taft. Stassen had also personally assured the general that "I shall not only become your lieutenant, but shall deliver to you, so far as it is possible, all the strength that has been pledged to me." "A letter received today from a friend of mine," Eisenhower soothed, observed that Stassen "has just reiterated this purpose."[23]

Clay and Dewey remained edgy, soothing general notwithstanding. Shortly before Stassen left for Europe in early December, Dewey passed on to Shanley, and hence to Stassen, the interesting information that Eisenhower would be out of uniform and available to campaign within sixty to ninety days.[24] This information, as it turned out, was inaccurate by up to four months. Regrettably, there is no record of where, or whether, Dewey received this information. It is conceivable that it was a ruse to discourage the Minnesotan. What is indisputably true is that on December 27, 1951, after Stassen had come and gone from Europe, Eisenhower reminded Clay that "an added consideration for my aloofness from the current American scene is found in the following paragraphs from Army Regulations: 'AR600–10.18 Election to, and performance of duties of, public office.... Members of the Regular Army, while on active duty, may accept nomination for public office, provided such nomination for public office, provided such nomination is tendered without direct *or indirect* activity or solicitation on their part. They may then file such evidence of their candidacy as required by local law.'"[25] Barring retirement, Eisenhower could not campaign. And if he could not campaign, Stassen was convinced, he could not be nominated.

It seems clear that as of December Eisenhower did not envision returning to the U.S. to campaign for the nomination. Stassen, leaving for Europe, may have hoped that Eisenhower would not change his mind, giving the Minnesotan time to build a viable candidacy. Or he may have hoped that Eisenhower would not run at all. Still, Stassen, according to both his recollection of his meeting with Eisenhower and the general's diary entry of that day, pressed the general not only to jump into the race, but also to do it soon. Stassen went on to explain that in the meantime he would campaign for himself, making as his primary purpose the thwarting of Robert Taft. "Do as you please," Eisenhower responded. "I shall never, in advance of a convention, indicate a political intention."[26]

If Stassen's presidential ambitions were truly still alive, his heart must have leaped at these words; the convention would have been far too late to mount an effective campaign. Even if Eisenhower entered at the last minute, Stassen, by swinging his support to the general at the convention, might be in an effective position for the vice-presidential nomination. This had been Shanley's hope and expectation for some time; in October he had written a former law partner: "Confidentially, my present thinking is that ... Harold will be the #2 man. If the General is not available ... it is pretty hard to know where the Party would turn except to Harold."[27] Now, on December 12, as Stassen and Eisenhower conferred outside Paris, Shanley in New Jersey could barely contain his excitement. "Today is a very important day in the history of the world," he exuded in his diary. But he tried to remain calm: "I don't feel that the General will make any promises to Harold relative to the vice-presidency, but he will indicate that he will expect him to take a very high place in his administration." Promises or no promises, "my guess is that the candidacy in '52 will be given to Eisenhower and that Governor Stassen will be his vice-president."[28]

On the night of December 12 Stassen and his wife, Esther, joined the Harrimans for dinner at the Eisenhowers' home. The Stassens then hurried back to the United States to announce for the presidency. Awaiting his arrival at the McAlpin Hotel in New York were Burger, Peaslee, Ryan, Gainey and Shanley. Stassen had assured Eisenhower that the details of their conference would remain secret; and so they were, even to Stassen's closest associates.[29]

This is curious because before, Stassen left for Europe, he and Shanley had worked out a code for Stassen in sending a telegram after the meeting with Eisenhower. These codes would indicate the various contingencies they envisioned.[30] Yet Stassen remained mute to his own staff, telling them only that he thought the general would accept the nomination but underestimated the threat posed by Taft. Further, Stassen told them he believed Eisenhower would not return any time soon to the U.S. "For all practical purposes," Stassen wrote years later, "Taft's speeches and statements ... would go unchallenged. Merely entering the General's name in the state primaries would not automatically win him the nomination."[31]

Although Stassen has claimed that at the McAlpin Hotel, "we decided that I should become Taft's main challenger in the primaries,"[32] the final decision to run, presumably absent a surprise announcement by Eisenhower that he would immediately return to the U.S. to campaign, had been made at least one month before. Thomas Coleman, party leader of Wisconsin, had written to Minnesota national committeeman, and Taft supporter, Roy Dunn on November 23: "There is no question that [Stassen] is going to run delegates in Wisconsin because he told me so when he was here a week ago last Saturday for the Penn game."[33]

The campaign announcement was scheduled for December 27. At 7:00 P.M. a testimonial dinner would be held at the Warwick Hotel in Philadelphia. Invitations promised coyly that Stassen "will make a significant address based on his findings [in Europe] and indicate his position in the national campaign" of 1952.[34] Prior to the dinner a press conference was planned. When alarmingly few members of the press seemed disposed to travel to Philadelphia to cover the conference, Stassen obligingly traveled to Washington, where he could be more accessible.

Standing before a hundred twenty-five members of the press, Stassen announced that he would be a candidate for president in 1952. Discarding the brash tone of impatient youth that he had used so effectively in 1948, the Minnesotan's announcement was quiet and elderly statesmanlike. He outlined an unspectacular four-point program calling for "an honest administration of the national government," a "modern gold standard" and an "up-to-date American foreign policy." The fourth and most specific plank called for the encouragement of voluntary profit-sharing plans for corporations through favorable tax treatment. In contrast to 1948, when Stassen had portrayed himself as a potential martyr to the cause of forthrightness, the announcement was uncommonly bland. A copy of the announcement distributed to the press merely promised that "it will be explained in detail in a series of major speeches on television and radio during the Presidential campaign."[35]

"This was a new, conservative Stassen," *Newsweek* observed. "His role in the Republican Party until recently had been that of Spokesman for young, Western, discontented elements. Now he seemed to be offering himself as a peacemaker at home and abroad, an open-minded leader who would resolve disagreements over national policy and as a possible compromise Presidential nominee if the Republican convention should deadlock between Taft and Eisenhower."[36] Unimpressed reporters yawned through the opening statement and then bombarded Stassen with questions, not about his campaign but about his meeting with Eisenhower. Was his announcement the result of anything discussed in his conference with the general? The reporters were not pleased with Stassen's position that the conference was private and he was not at liberty to reveal what they had discussed. Shanley noted that "it was indicated in some of the antagonistic columns the next day that it was the first time in eleven years that Stassen would not be completely forthright with the press."[37] One such columnist was Walter Lippmann, who sneered that the Minnesotan "is fervently, boldly, uncompromisingly for all the abstract nouns which nobody would dream of disputing."[38]

Eisenhower was not any more forthright. During a brief trip to the United States in late 1951 he kept reporters baffled about his presidential intentions; but unlike Stassen, who faced the complaints of "antagonistic columns," the press was enamored. He kept his position secret, the *Washington Post* marveled, but did so "with eloquence and charm."[39] Ten days before Stassen announced for the presidency, Senator Frank Carlson of Kansas was named executive director of the Eisenhower for President Committee's Washington, D.C., headquarters. He was so named by Senator Henry Cabot Lodge, who served as campaign manager of the movement. Both men acknowledged that their "draft Ike" effort was moving into a new stage, that of delegate canvassing.[40]

The claim that delegate canvassing represented a "new stage" for the Eisenhower movement was somewhat disingenuous. Bernard Shanley, with Lodge's full knowledge and approval, had been crisscrossing the country lining up favorite-son candidates in order to amass a field of delegates that could be brought to bear at the convention.[41] In this, Stassen was squirreling away a delegate base that could be used either for the general or for himself; the Eisenhower forces could be contented with a delegate block not directly committed to Taft nor to the unpredictable Stassen.

Yet the time was fast approaching when voters in state primaries would have to choose delegates pledged to one candidate or another. As in 1948, the first two primaries would be held in states which could be considered the "back yard" of one of the candidates, thus presenting the dangers of a demoralizing defeat early in the game.

13. New Hampshire

The first contest was New Hampshire. In 1948 that state's primary had not sent much of a signal. With Stassen obtaining two delegates, he could plausibly claim a moral victory; Dewey, capturing the remaining six, could just as plausibly claim a mandate. Knowledgeable state leaders recognized that neither assertion was very convincing; voters had been forced to choose not presidential candidates, but candidates for delegate. The local popularity of the would-be delegate, not the presidential aspirant, often most directly affected the outcome.

By 1952 the state legislature had revamped the presidential primary with the aim of making it more of a bellwether signaling presidential candidate strength. This was done by stapling onto the existing primary law a "beauty contest" or preferential vote provision. Apart from the race for delegates, a candidate could enter his name on the ballot. The voters could then directly vote for the presidential aspirant of their choice.[1] The decision of the Eisenhower forces to compete in both the beauty contest and the race for delegates was natural; Dewey maintained a powerful political army in the state, and eastern, liberal Republicans were Eisenhower's natural constituency. More surprising was Taft's decision to enter both the delegate race and the preference vote.

This decision had not come about without agonizing soul-searching on the part of the Ohio senator. Indeed, he had initially decided against the New Hampshire contest, planning to compete only in Wisconsin, Ohio and Illinois. According to Taft, his decision to compete actively in New Hampshire came about "inasmuch as my supporters in New Hampshire have seen fit to file petitions placing my name in the preferential presidential primary."[2] By "supporters" Taft may have meant first and foremost William Loeb, publisher of the *Manchester Union Leader* and the *New Hampshire Sunday News*, and Wesley Powell of Hampton Falls, a former administrative assistant to New Hampshire's senior United States senator Styles Bridges. Loeb had used his newspapers to try to minimize Eisenhower's support, and had published straw ballots purporting to show either Douglas MacArthur or Taft to be the overwhelming choice of the state. It is likely that either Loeb or Powell, the latter having failed to encourage Bridges to run as a favorite son, encouraged the filing of four delegate candidates "favorable" to Taft.[3]

Still, Taft could have requested that the delegates be withdrawn. Instead, he entered the "beauty contest" as well. His decision to compete actively in New Hampshire may have stemmed from his belief that Stassen would enter in the primary, thus at least partially splitting the liberal Republican vote for Eisenhower. Stassen did not file until the last minute, and then only in the preferential contest; he filed no delegate slate. The latter may have come as a surprise to Taft, but Stassen's interest in the state was probably well known in political circles.

Stassen's refusal to file a delegate slate worked in the interest of Eisenhower; the Minnesotan was given entrée to campaign against the Ohio senator, but would not draw away delegates. But available evidence somewhat clouds Stassen's claim that he entered the New Hampshire primary in order to "go after" Taft for Eisenhower's benefit. Long before there was any hint that Taft would compete in New Hampshire, Stassen and his associates had been assiduously courting Governor Sherman Adams, who played the political coquette, encouraging Stassen up to the moment he declared for Eisenhower. Adams had been invited to the Clarksboro meeting, but had been unable to attend. Shanley was convinced that Adams had sincerely wanted to attend. Three weeks later Adams contacted Shanley and asked him to fly to Concord for a conference. At this meeting Adams assured Shanley that if Eisenhower did not run, Adams would support Stassen in the primary.[4] Quickly, Stassen zeroed in on the governor. Early in September Stassen traveled to Concord. Adams told Stassen that he would "do everything possible" for Stassen and would run at the head of a ticket of delegates for him if Eisenhower was not in the primary. Coyly, Adams hinted that he did not believe that Eisenhower would either enter the primary or, in fact, be a candidate at all. Over dinner that evening Stassen spoke expansively of his campaign efforts throughout New England. Carefully, Stassen said that he wanted Adams to assume leadership of Stassen's political fortunes throughout the region. Finally, Stassen declared that he was looking to the East for the vice presidency and wanted the governor to feel that he would be under very serious consideration. Stassen emphasized, however, that Adams would have to demonstrate leadership in order to justify being on the ticket.[5]

Adams hesitated but kept the door open. As late as September 27 Shanley received a note from Adams enclosing a newspaper editorial favorable to Stassen, which Shanley took to be a sign of good will and possibly of support.[6] Three days later, however, Adams announced to the press that he was supporting Eisenhower, being "almost sure" the general would allow his name on the New Hampshire Republican ballot.[7] Even then, Adams kept a foot in the Stassen camp, indicating to Shanley and John Guider, who would shortly be named to reprise his 1948 role as Stassen's New Hampshire campaign manager, that he would "talk up" Stassen as well as Eisenhower if the Stassen campaign provided him with "such ammunition as polls indicating Stassen strength."[8]

With or without Adams, Stassen pressed ahead in the Granite State. The avowedly pro–Eisenhower forces, however, ran straight into an insuperable barrier. Under the state's 1949 revision of its presidential primary laws, a presidential candidate could be entered in the preference primary upon the filings of petitions carrying signatures of fifty qualified voters in each of the state's two congressional districts. The problem was that any petitioner offering the name of a presidential candidate was required to affirm under the penalties for perjury that he was a "member of the same political party as the proposed candidate."[9] Since Eisenhower's political affiliations were not widely known, this presented a dilemma for Republicans seeking to file the general in the GOP primary.

Among friends and associates, Eisenhower had long indicated an affinity for the Republican Party[10]; yet this was not common knowledge, and as Eisenhower was ever-mindful of Army regulations against campaigning, only silence emanated from NATO headquarters. Finally, after a Grafton County Democratic vice-chairman began steps to file Eisenhower as a Democrat, Henry Cabot Lodge wheeled into action.

"I consider it incumbent on me to divulge certain conversations I had with General Eisenhower," Lodge unburdened himself in a letter to Governor Adams, "while he was serving in a civilian capacity at Columbia University." Lodge was careful to observe the requirements of Army regulations. "During these discussions," Lodge went on, "he specifically said that his voting record was that of a Republican. He also pointed out that his political convictions coincided with enlightened Republican doctrine." Therefore, signers of Republican petitions in New Hampshire "are completely secure in their signed sworn statement that General Eisenhower is a member of their party." Lodge added that "the Democratic petitioners are swearing to something that is contrary to fact."[11] It appeared on the surface that on the basis of cocktail party chitchat Lodge was assuming responsibility for the New Hampshire campaign of Dwight Eisenhower.

Any doubt, however, was dispelled on January 7, when Eisenhower issued a statement backing up the Massachusetts senator. Senator Lodge's announcement, the general declared, "gives an accurate account of the general tenor of my political convictions and of my Republican voting record." Even so, Eisenhower went to great lengths to emphasize that, "under no circumstances will I ask for relief from this assignment in order to seek nomination to political office and I shall not participate in the pre-convention activities of others who may have such an intention with respect to me."[12]

Eisenhower's apparently unshakable determination to "not participate in pre-convention activities" meant that in effect only his name would appear in primaries; there would be no rebuttal to the campaign of Taft. This delighted the senator's supporters. In Washington, D.C., John Hamilton, former chairman of the Republican National Committee and Taft campaign manager, snickered, "This is the first time I have ever known anyone to find cause for jubilation in having the rug pulled out from under him." Hamilton went on to explain that since the general had made clear his determination not to campaign, "the Eisenhower Committee does not have a candidate."[13]

Hamilton had a point. Because Eisenhower could not or would not defend and promote his policies Stassen's plan of challenging the Ohio senator in the primaries became all the more compelling. Thus, on the same day Eisenhower's statement was read to the press, John Guider announced that Stassen's name would be placed on the New Hampshire preference ballot.[14] The task of challenging Taft appeared more urgent on January 7, and not only because of Eisenhower's stated refusal to campaign. *Newsweek* on that day reported: "Taft is far ahead of his rivals in number of convention delegates already pledged. His managers claim four hundred of the six hundred-odd needed to nominate." The magazine added that while Eisenhower backers did not believe the Ohioan would be successful in his drive for a first ballot nomination, "they weren't certain."[15] Somebody had to get busy to stop Taft, and even to his detractors, Stassen had a talent for staying busy.

This was fortunate, for Wesley Powell promptly filed as a Taft delegate candidate, bringing with him a field of "young Turks," exuding energy and conservative indignation against the alleged "me-tooism" of "eastern establishment" Republicans, and the vacuity of the unstated Eisenhower platform. "These times are too treacherous and the issues confronting us too vital to our country's future for the Republican Party to select its standard bearer blindly," Powell sputtered.[16] Powell and other Taft delegate candidates soon began sponsoring a series of debates across the state, attracting increasing attention. The senator himself soon arrived in New Hampshire on a whirlwind tour worthy of Stassen at his best; the Ohioan made some thirty speeches in three days.[17]

Stassen arrived in New Hampshire in mid–February, promising that if elected he would save the New England textile industry by directing the military to concentrate its purchases in the region. He dismissed Taft as being "out of touch." Also, in a declaration that must have caused considerable irritation in the Eisenhower camp, he predicted that the General would not win the Republican nomination because he was "too close to the administration."[18] For the most part, however, the Minnesotan was deferential to Eisenhower, concentrating on attacking Taft for his isolationist views.[19]

The Minnesota primary followed the New Hampshire contest by only one week, and the erstwhile Minnesotan felt obliged to attend to his former home turf. For this reason, Stassen ultimately was to spend less time in the Granite State than Taft and had far less of an impact. That Taft's campaign was effective was underscored by an Associated Press poll taken at the end of February. This poll had Eisenhower with only a narrow lead over Taft. Some reporters concluded that Taft could win as many as four of New Hampshire's fourteen delegates. "The final outcome," the *Concord Daily Monitor* speculated, "may be decided by the effect of Taft's appearance here next week."[20]

Coincidentally, less than twenty-four hours after the Associated Press showed Taft within striking distance of Eisenhower in New Hampshire, Henry Cabot Lodge innocently observed to the press that the general could return to the United States "quite soon."[21] A clearly nervous Lodge went on to claim indignantly, "I cannot understand the reasoning that says winning one quarter [of the New Hampshire delegation] would constitute victory. The only victory is for the man who gets the greatest number of delegates." The senator apparently was referring to statements by Taft that if they could manage to win four of the fourteen delegates they would consider it a victory.[22] This claim was recognized by the press for what it was, alibi preparation for a strong showing by Taft. Leon Anderson, columnist for the *Concord Daily Monitor*, which supported Eisenhower, remarked that Lodge in his statement had "pulled a boner," and observed, "The big league out-of-state newspapermen laughed up their sleeves [at the senator's disclaimer]."[23]

Stassen did what he could to help, although his capability to be of service in the Granite State was steadily shrinking. For one thing, he was being massively outspent. Eisenhower and Taft spent a record $30,000 in the last week of the campaign alone. For the primary, the general's supporters spent some $65,000 and Taft $50,000.[24] The sum spent by Stassen in New Hampshire is unclear from available records, but he was clearly outclassed. His national organization did not budget any money specifically for New Hampshire, and the amount raised by state campaign manager Guider appears negligible.[25]

However, Stassen's primary asset had always been his indefatigable penchant for campaigning. On March 3, according to Stassen's recollection, he "dropped everything and matched Taft city-for-city, speech-for-speech."[26] He arrived at Dover to begin a six-day tour, beginning at Concord in a Republican rally at the city's municipal auditorium.

This rally, filmed for Edward R. Murrow's *I Can See It Now* television show, was not a stellar event for the Minnesotan. Stassen was the only presidential candidate to appear, with Congressman Christian Herter, recently announced candidate for governor of Massachusetts, speaking for Eisenhower and Congressman William Ayers of Ohio speaking for Taft. Stassen's strategy for the evening appears to have been to let Herter and Ayers fight it out between themselves, with Stassen confining himself to quiet generalities. The strategy appears to have backfired; one spectator said loudly that no man could possibly live long enough to deliver all the promises Stassen had made. Neither did Stassen's longtime aide Ed Larson have a successful evening, he spent much of it pawing around in the darkness of the wings of the auditorium stage looking for Stassen's hat, which the candidate had misplaced. Stassen explained that he had always taken a size seven and seven-eighths, so nobody should think it was politics that gave him a big head.[27]

The above-the-fray posture Stassen occasionally took did not signal a total abandonment of his mission to blast away at Taft's noninterventionist record; Stassen vigorously did so, adding to that his criticism of Taft's proposal to provide aid for public schools.[28] The Minnesotan charged that Taft had been "wrong in the vital matters of foreign policy for the past twelve years," citing the Ohioan's statements and votes which Stassen said added up to "isolationist" views.[29] On the evening of March 10, the night before the election, Stassen took to the airways on station WKBR of Manchester for one final blast. Concentrating his fire almost exclusively on foreign policy, he reminded his audience that New Hampshire's two senators, Bridges and Tobey, had consistently voted against Taft's position in the Senate on foreign policy matters. "The new American foreign policy," Stassen concluded, "presented by our Republican Party should be a strong and vigorous policy. It should be based on the best ideas of Senator Vandenberg and of General Eisenhower."[30]

Election day, March 11, initially brought good news for Robert Taft. A steady, cold rain and freezing roads threatened to reduce voter turnout, thought to be a boon to the Ohio senator and his committed, ideologically charged supporters. Yet voters proceeded to the polls in record-breaking numbers in spite of the weather, apparently due to the fact the vote coincided with the traditional day on which town meetings were held. In the preference "beauty contest," Eisenhower cruised to a victory with 46,661 votes to Taft's 35,838. Stassen limped home third with 6,574. The entire Eisenhower slate of delegates was elected.[31]

Stassen called the results "gratifying," although it is not clear why. While it is conceivable that Stassen's attacks on Taft could have caused some potential Taft supporters to switch to Eisenhower, there is no evidence that this was a significant occurrence. It was, however, something of a minor personal (as opposed to Eisenhower), victory for Stassen; he had garnered twice as many votes as expected.[32] Moreover, while no names had been entered on the preference ballot for vice president, 5,876 voters had written in Stassen's name, just slightly less than favorite son Styles Bridges, who had received 6,535 write-in votes.[33]

Stassen's impact on either his own presidential ambitions or Eisenhower's in New Hampshire had been minimal. Yet the Minnesotan had in fact suspected such an outcome. In a February 22 letter to Henry Cabot Lodge, who had tried to persuade Stassen to withdraw from the New Hampshire contest, the Minnesotan argued that having decided to challenge Taft in Midwestern presidential primaries, he could not easily avoid the Granite State. For one thing, Stassen noted, he would be immediately dismissed as an Eisenhower stalking horse. Since he had competed in New Hampshire in 1948, ducking the contest in 1952 would have sent a signal that he was not a serious candidate. Also, Stassen noted, "A small number of New Hampshire voters would nevertheless write in my name and the unfriendly section of the press could then claim that I only had a blank number of supporters in the entire state." This, Stassen felt, would have damaged his effectiveness in later primaries. Finally, Stassen ruefully pointed out, "My name would tend to be dropped from national stories, cartoons, and comment in the period leading up to the New Hampshire primary. I have," the candidate added, "a difficult enough time in this respect."[34]

From the tenor of Stassen's letter, one may surmise that Stassen looked upon the New Hampshire primary as a necessary chore. The next week in Minnesota, presumably, his impact would be greater. Yet even as voters in the Granite State were trudging through the rain and ice to the polls, events in Stassen's abandoned home state were slipping out of his control.

14. Minnesota

Like New Hampshire, Minnesota had in 1949 revised its method of selecting delegates to national political conventions. Unlike the Granite State, Minnesota had one candidate in mind when it rewrote its election laws: Harold Stassen.

Minnesota elections laws in the twentieth century had followed national trends. During the progressive era the state, inspired by the presidential primary instituted in neighboring Wisconsin under Robert LaFollette, passed a presidential primary law. In the years prior to World War I, however, national interest in progressive reform began to wane; most presidential primaries fell into disuse. Some states, including Minnesota in 1917, repealed their laws altogether.[1]

In 1949 the presidential primary was resurrected in Minnesota as the Republican-controlled state legislature sought to anticipate Stassen's needs in 1952. By implementing a state primary early in the season, Stassen could be provided with a convincing statewide victory, thereby boosting his chances. Yet the assistance did not end there. The law provided that to appear on the primary ballot, the presidential candidate himself could file. Also, any state resident who was a member of the same political party as the White House aspirant could place the presidential contender on the ballot by filing petitions bearing at least one hundred voters from each congressional district with the secretary of state. What made the law unique, and of potential benefit to Stassen, was that should a presidential candidate not wish to appear on the ballot he would have to sign an affidavit that he would *not* accept a nomination even if it were offered him. This was a direct effort to thwart, or at least flush out, Dwight Eisenhower or Douglas MacArthur or both. If their supporters put them on the ballot they would be faced with the choice of either withdrawing from the presidential contest entirely or, presumably, suffering an electoral drubbing in Stassen territory. Two delegates were to be chosen in each congressional district and three delegates elected at-large.[2]

As the filing period of January 15–February 15 approached, the central preoccupation of state politicians was whether or not the Eisenhower campaign would enter the Minnesota primary. State Eisenhower enthusiasts had been organizing for some time under the leadership of Bradshaw Mintener of Minneapolis, an attorney and vice president of Pillsbury Mills. In December Mintener had offered to step aside from his position as Minnesotans for Eisenhower Committee chairman in favor of Stassen, who politely refused the honor.[3] From the Washington, D.C., headquarters of the National Eisenhower for President Committee came what was thought to be the definitive word. Frank Carlson announced that the general would not be entered in the Minnesota primary out of deference to Harold Stassen.[4]

Robert Taft, who had not received much deference from Stassen in 1948, seriously considered making a bid in Minnesota. Taft had a clear base of support within the state from which to build, evidenced by a poll of county commissioners in February. In this poll Taft was the choice of eighty-eight commissioners, followed by Stassen with seventy-four.[5] A prominent Minnesota Republican political consultant, Walter Quigley, confidently predicted, "There are six or seven Congressional Districts here, which Taft can carry even against Stassen."[6] Stassen was up to the challenge. Three days after the county commissioners poll was published, the former governor wired the Ohio senator daring him to enter the contest. According to Fred Neumeier, state political writer for the *St. Paul Minnesota Pioneer Press*, "The Stassen challenge to Taft is seen as a move by the former Minnesota governor to get something 'to shoot at' ... in the opinion of observers. He doesn't want to bombard Gen. Eisenhower, they believe, and he's looking for something to sensationalize in the campaign."[7]

Early indications showed that Taft was ready to pick up the gauntlet. In late 1951 he had made a tour of the state, probing for support. He found it. Republican National Committee committeeman and Minnesota State house majority leader Roy Dunn, an Old Guard conservative and inveterate opponent of Stassen, pleaded with Taft to enter the contest.[8] Returning to Washington, Taft consulted with advisors who were connected with midwestern politics, most notably Tom Coleman, chairman of the Wisconsin GOP. Taft decided to leave his options open. On November 29 he wired Dunn a two-sentence telegram: "I would like you to handle all of my affairs in Minnesota. I am looking forward to working with you in the campaign." Dunn could hardly wait to accept.[9] Dunn was convinced that a Taft delegation stood "at least a fifty-fifty chance of winning" and began organizing an intensive advertising effort. But Taft was dubious, as early as December 30 privately telling Dunn that he did not want to enter a delegate slate.[10] Taft announced his intention to forego the Minnesota contest on February 10. "I do not approve of entering the home state of another bona fide Republican candidate," Taft stated perfunctorily. He pointedly reminded the press, "Mr. Stassen has chosen to enter Ohio."[11] The Taft-directed and Dunn-operated advertising campaign in Minnesota would seem to belie Taft's claim that he was forgoing the contest out of deference. There is another more plausible explanation for the decision.

While Taft indeed had a foundation of support upon which to build in Minnesota, it was by no means certain that the edifice could be constructed. Although Stassen's influence in Minnesota was clearly waning by 1952,[12] he had nonetheless completely transformed the Minnesota GOP since 1938. His internationalist perspective was still more representative of the state's Republican party in the 1950s than Taft's viewpoint would have been. Anti-Stassenites might be drawn not to Taft but to the ever-popular Eisenhower, whose name might yet be placed on the ballot. Winning, or even doing well, in Minnesota was by no means a sure thing. "Because of Stassen's continuing influence here, you will have a tough fight in Minnesota," admitted William H. Rentschler, editor of the *Minneapolis Star and Tribune* and Taft supporter.[13] Eisenhower was a better bet to defeat Stassen than Taft, who could find himself presented with a humiliating third-place finish. Still, to yield to Eisenhower in Minnesota might bring complications of its own — the general might win. Since Eisenhower ultimately was a greater threat than Stassen, this outcome would have been unbearable.

There is evidence that the Taft campaign resolved the dilemma by using Eisenhower as a Trojan horse, inside which were ensconced pro-Taft delegate candidates. With the Ohio senator out of the race, Taft supporters quietly joined forces with the Minnesotans for Eisenhower Committee, working with Bradshaw Mintener to place the general on the ballot and to field a slate of delegate candidates.[14]

Mintener needed help. Quite simply, his was an amateurish organization, low on political experience and even lower on funds. And he received no help from the national Eisenhower campaign; on the contrary, Frank Carlson and Henry Cabot Lodge frantically pleaded with Mintener *not* to file Eisenhower in the primary. Initially, this policy of nonintervention stemmed from their fear that the liberal Republican vote would be split between Eisenhower and Stassen, thus paving the way for a respectable showing by Taft. With the Ohio senator off the ballot, they still recognized that Stassen would have his uses in upcoming primaries, notably Wisconsin, Nebraska and Ohio, and did not wish to defeat the still-useful Minnesotan. And, of course, if Stassen won, the defeat would tarnish the general. Carlson sternly refused Mintener's requests for help.[15]

In Minnesota, George MacKinnon, former U.S. congressman and long-time Stassen supporter, eyed Roy Dunn suspiciously. Having served with Dunn in the state legislature in the late thirties and early forties, MacKinnon was well acquainted with his conservative views. When Dunn began organizing an Eisenhower delegate slate, MacKinnon suspected a plot. Specifically, MacKinnon feared that ostensible Eisenhower delegates would at the convention publicly switch their allegiance to Taft. "Properly played," MacKinnon feared, "that could cause a stampede."[16]

Nor was Taft's behind-the-scenes maneuvering limited to "cooperation," or rather co-optation, with the Eisenhower forces. While the pro–Taft *Minneapolis Tribune* reported after the Senator's withdrawal that the Taft campaign was "taking a 'hands off' attitude toward the primary,"[17] this does not appear to have been the case; rather, the Taft organization seems to have been cooperating with the forces of Douglas MacArthur.

Immediately after the filing period had opened, supporters of MacArthur entered the general's name on the ballot. Yet MacArthur was worried about a crushing defeat by Stassen — he was remembering Wisconsin in 1948 — or Eisenhower. He requested that his name be withdrawn without signing the required affidavit that he would not accept nomination. The issue went to the state attorney general, who ruled the affidavit provision of the 1949 primary law invalid, and MacArthur's name was withdrawn.[18]

Promptly, a Minneapolis schoolteacher, Edward Slettedahl, state chairman of the "Fighters for MacArthur," filed as a presidential candidate himself, explaining that he was a "stand-in" for the general.[19] While it is unclear whether the general encouraged Slettedahl, it is very clear that he took a great interest in the fate of the Slettedahl delegation. On January 31 MacArthur and General Courtney Whitney met with the Wisconsin GOP chairman, who was a Taft supporter, Tom Coleman, at the Waldorf Hotel in New York City. According to a memorandum of the meeting written by Coleman, MacArthur and Whitney were "keenly interested" in the Minnesota primary and requested Coleman to provide them with further details of developments in the state. Coleman was only too happy to oblige and called Roy Dunn for a report. The next day, Coleman phoned Whitney with a status report.[20]

Three days after the close of the filing deadline of February 15, James Fetsch, a St. Paul attorney, retained lawyer William Green to challenge the legality of the petitions placing Eisenhower on the ballot. Green submitted a three-page letter to secretary of state Mike Holm, protesting against the petitions filed on behalf of the General and demanding that Eisenhower's name be removed from the ballot. When asked about his motivations, Fetsch declared himself to be an Eisenhower supporter who did not feel that participation in the Minnesota primary would be in the general's interest. "I have nothing to do with Harold Stassen," he insisted.[21]

Fetsch was not telling the whole truth. Earlier, a desperate Frank Carlson had contacted George MacKinnon to inquire about the chances of keeping the wildcat Eisenhower group in Minnesota from successfully entering the general's name in the primary. Alert to the sudden conversion of Roy Dunn to the Eisenhower cause, MacKinnon was already exploring options and requested from secretary of state Mike Holm photostatic copies of the Eisenhower petitions.[22] MacKinnon found the petitions full of irregularities, including several signatures in obviously the same handwriting. He forwarded the copies to the National Eisenhower Campaign, which provided them to Fetsch.[23] Publicly, Stassen denied any involvement in the effort to remove Eisenhower from the ballot.[24]

Minnesota attorney general J.A.A. Burnquist, reviewing Fetsch's petition, ruled that Eisenhower's name should remain on the ballot "unless the Supreme Court shall otherwise order."[25] It did. In *Fetsch v. Holm*, the state tribunal ordered Eisenhower's name struck from the ballot, on the grounds that since the nominating petition from one congressional district did not contain the signed oath required by the 1949 law, that petition "was fatally defective, and the whole nominating petition was vitiated."[26] The decision triggered an uproar throughout the state. Within an hour state representative William Carlson of St. Paul delivered a letter to Governor Elmer Anderson requesting that the governor call a special session of the legislature to repeal the 1949 presidential primary law. Carlson argued that a special session would cost the state only $25,000 compared to the $300,000 to $350,000 of holding the primary. With Harold Stassen the only bona fide presidential contender on the ballot, the cost of a primary was simply not justified. Anderson, a long-time Stassen supporter, summarily refused.[27]

In the aftermath of the court's decision Stassen's state campaign chairman, Bernhard LeVander, cheerfully called for all Republicans to unite in supporting the former governor as a method of promoting Stassen's momentum going into the Wisconsin primary.[28] The Stassen forces were simply oblivious to the outrage seething in the state among voters who felt they were being muzzled and stifled, not by an obscure Eisenhower supporter named Fetsch but by a behind-the-scenes play by Stassen, whose denials of involvement in the Fetsch case were ridiculed. One group that not only understood this resentment but personified it was the Minnesotans for Eisenhower Committee. Stunned by the Supreme Court's decision, the committee spent several days in disarray and confusion before pulling together and developing a plan to strike back, announcing on March 13 that it would conduct a last-minute drive for a write-in vote for Eisenhower. Leonard Linquist, an Eisenhower delegate candidate, summarized the bitterness felt by both the general's supporters and many previously indifferent state voters when he spoke of the write-in plan. "The Eisenhower sweep in voting in New Hampshire is the kind he would have had in Minnesota if the Stassen followers had not maneuvered Ike's name off the ballot," he complained. "The people of Minnesota can get back by writing in the name of Eisenhower."[29]

The Stassen forces yawned, indifferent to this late threat to their fortunes. "Now," exclaimed Warren Burger, "we can swing to Wisconsin and fight our real opponent–Taft!" With six days left to election day, it was not even clear that write-in votes could be legally counted in the final tabulation. It would be March 14 before attorney general Burnquist ruled that the votes must be counted.[30]

Clearly, Stassen did not believe that the write-in effort warranted time out from his campaign in Wisconsin. On March 1 Stassen made brief appearances in Minneapolis, Edina, Golden Valley and Richfield.[31] He did not return until after the New Hampshire primary on March 11, and then only for two days. During this swing Stassen was plagued by persistent rumors that he had promised to deliver his delegation to Eisenhower. "There is nothing to that story," the former governor snapped. "I never tie up my supporters as to what they should do. I never try to put them in a bag and try to deliver them here or there."[32] With that, Stassen blithely scampered to Wisconsin.

Election Day, March 18, dawned cold and drizzly, yet voters defied the elements and stormed to the polls in record numbers. Precincts began running out of ballots; in some cases voters were forced to wait until nine at night for police officers to arrive with more ballots. In other precincts impatient election officials provided scratch paper instead of ballots. And the voters were bringing pencils. To write in a candidate was not an easy task — not by accident, some Eisenhower supporters darkly insinuated. The voting machines used in St. Paul required that the voter write in a candidate's name on a slant, five feet nine inches from the floor at the low end and six feet at the high. Some voters complained that they were simply not physically able to scrawl in the candidate's name. And then there were the instructions: "To vote for a write-in candidate," the voting machine informed, "push up the slide over the office — write in name or use prepared sticker. Do not push up slide unless you intend to write-in a vote, as pushing up slide locks candidate pointers below." Many voters complained that they found these instructions and the voting machines confusing.[33]

Those voters who successfully mastered the art of writing in, cast their votes for "Ihenhawer," Eizinhower," or, occasionally, Dwight D. Eisenhower." The total Eisenhower vote ran to 108,692, not far behind Stassen, who technically won the primary with 129,076 votes. The name of Robert Taft was written in by 24,093 voters, allowing the Ohioan to edge out Slettedahl, the MacArthur stand-in who appeared on the ballot and received 21,712 votes. MacArthur himself and Warren received a smattering of write-in votes.[34]

That Stassen's victory was merely technical was immediately apparent, especially to Dwight Eisenhower, who at Rocquencourt two days after the primary admitted, "The mounting number of my fellow-citizens who are voting to make me the Republican nominee are forcing me to re-examine my present position and past decisions."[35] By "past decisions," the General presumably meant his refusal to return to the U.S. to campaign for the nomination. The *St. Paul Pioneer Press* pronounced Eisenhower's interpretation "correct."[36] It was Eisenhower, not Stassen, who got top billing in the *New York Times* on March 19. "Without exaggeration, a political miracle," the *Times* exclaimed.[37]

In Wisconsin, where Stassen had been concentrating his energy for the April 1 primary and hoping for a major assist in the form of a Minnesota mandate, the *Milwaukee Journal* felt the primary pushed the Eisenhower movement into first place and "pretty well sank Harold Stassen's hopes."[38]

On March 18 Stassen was in LaCrosse, Wisconsin, and called himself "very pleased." In two respects this emotion was well founded. When Stassen had become a force in the Minnesota GOP in 1938 it had embraced an isolationist, conservative position on foreign affairs. Now, in 1952, Stassen and Eisenhower had both overwhelmed the MacArthur "stand in" and the write-in votes for MacArthur himself and Robert Taft. Internationalism had triumphed in the Minnesota GOP. Moreover, although Stassen had declared himself pleased before Eisenhower's Rocquencourt statement, the Minnesotan had set the stage for the general's ultimate return to the U.S. and thus made more likely an Eisenhower nomination. Although hometown humiliation had never been part of the scenario, Stassen had inadvertently furthered the cause to which he insisted he was committed.

Stassen had done this by working with George MacKinnon and the national Eisenhower for President campaign in the successful effort to remove Eisenhower from the ballot. Stassen denied, incorrectly, attempting to push Eisenhower off the ballot and also denied, more accurately, opposing the write-in campaign. Nonetheless, the situation looked suspicious to Minnesota voters, who accused the former governor of trying to rig the election. According to a survey of state newspaper editors, up to 42 percent of Eisenhower's vote could be attributed to either a protest against Stassen or resentment over primary manipulation.[39]

Harold Stassen's actions in the Minnesota primary, including the effort to remove Eisenhower from the ballot, were consistent with his stated goal of winning the nomination for Eisenhower. As George MacKinnon later said, "Everything we did was cleared with Frank Carlson."[40] Moreover, Stassen moved decisively to keep the peace when Bradshaw Mintener demanded that the four delegates from the two congressional districts where Eisenhower had placed first be pledged to the general. This demand rested on dubious legal ground; nonetheless, Stassen granted his wish. Thus, four of Minnesota's twenty-eight delegates went to the convention prepared to vote for Eisenhower on the first ballot. Still, Stassen's actions were also consistent with his unstated but likely goal of keeping open the possibility for the nomination of Harold Stassen. The result of these actions was unforeseen. Undoubtedly, the Minnesotans for Eisenhower campaign benefited from being denied a place on the ballot; many indifferent or lukewarm Eisenhower supporters were driven into the general's camp by righteous indignation against election manipulation. Similarly, the national Eisenhower for President Committee unexpectedly was presented with a watershed event in the primary season — an event which propelled their candidate back across the Atlantic. In Minnesota a prairie fire had started for the general. But prairie fires tend to burn out quickly, and the next few primaries would not blaze so hot for Eisenhower.

15. Wisconsin

Like New Hampshire and Minnesota, Wisconsin revised its primary election law in 1949; unlike New Hampshire but similar to Minnesota, the impetus behind the reform was the candidacy of Harold Stassen. His supporters in the state legislature shepherded to passage a bill repealing the state's preference advisory poll and pointedly omitting any provision for write-in votes. Having been nearly burned by the MacArthur candidacy in 1948, the goal was to eliminate candidates who were not active. The new, stripped-down law was a pure primary in the senses that its sole purpose was to select delegates to the national conventions. Two years later MacArthur supporters pushed their own primary election bill through the legislature. This second revision reflected the MacArthur forces' concern that under the 1949 law only a candidate himself could place his name on the ballot, thus ruling out a White House aspirant who wished to remain coy about his intentions. The MacArthur-inspired revision allowed state activists to file a candidate on their own initiative. Still, in order to win the acceptance of the state legislature, a provision was inserted in the bill requiring that before a candidate's name was placed on the ballot the presidential hopeful explicitly had to give permission.[1]

The first candidate explicitly to give permission and to work to round up support in the state was Robert Taft, who by mid-1951 had decided to make Wisconsin a do-or-die primary.[2] His cultivation of state leaders was astonishingly successful — and at the expense of Harold Stassen, as he drew into his entourage state party boss Tom Coleman and Vic Johnston. Both men had been active and decisive players in Stassen's impressive 1948 triumph in the state. Their defection left Stassen with a still considerable base of popular support but little leadership, while the Taft campaign worked hard to draw away what support remained for Stassen.[3] After his miserable showing in the New Hampshire primary on March 11, Taft redoubled his already considerable energies in the state. The initial Taft strategy was now irrelevant. Events, more than the Ohio senator, made Wisconsin a make-or-break affair. "If we were to be beaten badly in Wisconsin," said national Taft campaign manager David Ingalls, "the senator might as well get out."[4]

Following the Minnesota primary Stassen was in much the same position, not only in terms of his own potential nomination, but also in terms of his effectiveness in combating Taft. His efforts to defeat Taft in Wisconsin and thus weaken him nationally might have succeeded but for the presence on the ballot of Earl Warren. "For reasons that I still do not understand, the Dewey-Lodge-Brownell committee urged California Governor Earl Warren, Dewey's running mate for Vice President in 1948, to enter" the primary, Stassen recalled in his memoirs. "I suggested that the better strategy would be to let me take on Taft alone in this state abutting Minnesota; but Warren entered."[5] There is no clear-cut evidence that the Eisenhower for President Committee "urged" Warren to enter Wisconsin, but Stassen's point is accurate. The *New York Times* noted that "Senator Taft cannot fail to profit greatly from the split in the opposition.... Both of Mr. Taft's major opponents — Governor Warren and Mr. Stassen — are seeking Eisenhower votes."[6] The result was not only an electoral disaster but a farce, with roles for both Warren and Stassen. For his part, the California governor conducted what can only be described as a two-faced campaign, a bald attempt to have it both ways, a candidate in his own right and a "stand-in" for Eisenhower.

Not only did Warren deny that he was in any fashion a "stand-in" for Eisenhower, he repeatedly and unequivocally emphasized that he had no right to speak for the general, had never discussed any issues with him, and did not know where Eisenhower stood. He added that he had made no secret commitments for his delegates and was "not responsible for what they said concerning their relationship with the General." "Not responsible" was an appropriate choice of words; Warren did not repudiate or ask his delegate candidates to refrain from insisting that "a vote for Warren is a vote for Eisenhower."[7] Indeed, quite irresponsibly the California governor appeared to wish to ride the general's coattails to a Wisconsin victory. There is no other explanation.

If indeed a vote for Warren was a vote for Eisenhower, Warren should not have been there. Although his strength had clearly waned since 1948, Stassen still had widespread contacts — a base upon which to build an anti–Taft campaign. If Warren was running for himself he should have recruited a delegate slate loyal to him. Stassen only made matters worse. In a March 25 speech in Sheboygan, as the nation was refocusing on the Republican nomination battle after the stunning Minnesota outcome, Stassen simply took leave of his political senses. In a move that totally overshadowed his criticism of the isolationist policies of the Ohio senator, the Minnesotan gamely declared that he aimed to elect all thirty delegate candidates on his slate, after which "I have decided to give my permission to one-half of this group of thirty to vote for General Dwight D. Eisenhower on the first ballot." The ever-conscientious Stassen thoughtfully provided the press with an advance copy of his speech, and the next day his proposed "split" received front-page headlines around the country. Little notice was made of the rest of the text, in which Stassen blasted Taft's foreign policy.[8]

The Stassen proposal elicited consternation in the Warren camp and gleeful mockery from Robert Taft. The California governor, on a campaign swing through southern Wisconsin two days after Stassen's speech, emphasized again that he had no connection with the Eisenhower campaign and haughtily refused to get into a "bidding war" for the General's supporters. Unperturbed, his delegate candidates continued to stress their support for Eisenhower.[9]

Robert Taft could barely contain his delight. Noting Stassen's offer to give away half his delegates and Warren's delegate candidates' expressed loyalty to Eisenhower, Taft exclaimed, "One of my opponents has run out on his delegates; the other has had the delegates run out on the candidate."[10]

With Stassen and Warren, or at least Warren's delegate candidates, squabbling over Eisenhower's support, Taft was free to flail away at his two rivals for not addressing the serious issues of the day. Looking calm and presidential during an appearance in Milwaukee, Taft observed "that the other candidates in Wisconsin say nothing" on foreign policy. Speaking gravely to an audience comprised largely of Polish-Americans, Taft noted that "no peoples have suffered more from this Administration than the Polish people. The agreements made at Yalta betrayed every interest of the Polish people as if they had never existed. Our representatives accepted Stalin's promises that he would restore liberty to Poland and the

Balkan states, although he had never kept a promise and although every well-informed person knew that he did not intend to keep that one."[11]

Taft was free to promote his candidacy and his foreign policy virtually without challenge. The time Earl Warren could devote to the Wisconsin electorate was limited by the fact that the California legislature was still in session; the governor was reduced to weekend forays into the Badger State. While Stassen, according to the *New York Times*, was "everywhere" in the state, the press was preoccupied with his proposed delegate split. Reporters peppered the Minnesotan with questions, not about his foreign policy but about what came to be known as the "Stassen-Eisenhower" ticket. Often both Stassen and Warren were ridiculed as "EisenStassen" and "Warrenhower."[12]

Inevitably, Stassen and Warren began bickering over who best represented the views of Eisenhower. The argument was to some extent meaningless, the general's views were not known in any detail. Moreover, it is difficult to see how either Stassen or Warren could have been more like Eisenhower than the other, since the two were in general agreement on foreign and domestic matters. Both candidates regarded themselves as pro-conservation and endorsed farm price supports, public power projects, a permanent Fair Employment Practices Commission, subsidized federal housing, the Marshall Plan, NATO, and revisions in the Taft-Hartley Act. While there were nuances of disagreement in some of these areas, both men clearly belonged in the moderate-to-progressive wing of the Republican Party.[13]

Yet Warren's political associations in Wisconsin did raise legitimate questions about his commitment to an internationalist foreign policy. The California governor's chief sponsor in the state was Philip LaFollette, three-times governor and cofounder in 1934 of the state's Progressive party and, since 1946, a Republican. Considered an isolationist on foreign policy issues, in 1948 he had worked energetically on MacArthur's behalf.[14] A related factor which plagued the Warren campaign was the charge, stressed by Taft, that a vote for Governor Warren would help to restore the "LaFollette dynasty" to political power. Since the LaFollette wing—comprising old progressives and hankering for domestic reform and foreign policy isolationism—was anathema to the Tom Coleman "regular Republicans," this accusation undoubtedly damaged Warren and thus Eisenhower.[15]

Election Day, April 1, brought the inevitable result of the Stassen-Warren folly. Their vote was split, allowing Taft and the Tom Coleman faction of the Wisconsin GOP to capture twenty-four of the state's thirty delegates, with Warren capturing the remaining six. Taft received a plurality, but nowhere near a majority of the votes cast, totaling 315,541, or 40.6 percent. Earl Warren captured 262,271 votes, or 33.7 percent, while Stassen placed third with 169,679 votes, or 21.9 percent. Predictably, Taft had benefited from a split in the opposition.[16]

The "default" nature of Taft's victory received great attention from the national press[17] and somewhat vitiated the psychological impact of the triumph; nevertheless, the costs to Dwight Eisenhower's candidacy at the Chicago convention were tangible. The twenty-four Taft delegates provided Taft with one of his most enthusiastic and hardworking groups of supporters. Tom Coleman became the Ohioan's floor manager. And, despite their claims that "a vote for Warren is a vote for Eisenhower," Wisconsin's Warren delegates, the only delegate block for the Californian outside his home state, refused to switch to the general's column before the vote was made unanimous.[18]

The Wisconsin primary was a disaster for both Stassen and Eisenhower. His campaign in the state would be the last one in which he was viewed with any seriousness. With his defeat, the political career of Harold Stassen as an effective campaigning politician was over.

16. The Nomination of Dwight Eisenhower

The Nebraska presidential primary was held on April 1, the same day as the one in Wisconsin. Although his name appeared on the ballot, Stassen ignored the state. However, supporters of both Taft and Eisenhower waged a furious last-minute write-in campaign, with the result that Taft won an astounding victory with 79,357 votes. Eisenhower finished second with 66,078 write-in votes, while Stassen, whose name was on the ballot, trailed with 53,238.[1] The next week Taft cruised to victory in Illinois, picking up forty-nine of the state's fifty delegates; the remaining delegate went to Eisenhower on the basis of write-in votes. By mid–April the Taft for President Committee was crowing that their candidate "has had more votes cast for him in the five states in which Republican primaries have been held than the total given all his opponents combined."[2]

The avowed rationale behind Stassen's candidacy was that while Eisenhower remained incommunicado in Europe the Minnesotan could, through vigorous personal campaigning prevent the primary elections from going by default to Robert Taft. By mid–April Stassen had failed dismally, with Senator Taft cruising to victory in three of the four primaries in which he had competed. With the exception of Minnesota, Stassen had finished third in all the primary elections. He no longer commanded the slightest attention from the national press, except in the form of ridicule. "Wake up to the facts, Mr. Stassen," the *Philadelphia Inquirer* urged. The paper grumbled that the absentee president of the University of Pennsylvania "seems to be about the only one left who is not convinced that his candidacy can no longer be given serious consideration."[3] Even the supportive *Philadelphia Evening Bulletin* spoke pointedly in the past tense when it in April observed of Stassen, "During the months of uncertainty over whether General Eisenhower would consent to run kept the country alert to the danger of an isolationist program such as Senator Taft has advocated." "Mr. Stassen," the paper concluded, "probably realizes that so far as personal ambition is concerned he may be pursuing a forlorn hope. But he did keep the ball from being stolen at a time when few other guards were on hand."[4]

From mid–April to the time of the Republican convention in July Stassen kept frantically busy, with no visible impact. His most serious effort, in the Ohio primary, was a pale reflection of his 1948 challenge. Spending a mere $4,485, to Taft's $58,000 and launching no major statewide effort, all of Stassen's delegate candidates finished a distant second in every district.[5]

Taft's success in rounding up delegates meant that as the Republican convention approached he had a clear lead in delegates; still, he was short of the six hundred four needed to nominate. According to Stassen, seventy-two of Taft's five hundred thirty delegates were from contested delegations, principally those of Texas, Louisiana and Georgia. These contested delegations held the balance of power and raised the possibility of "fierce battles that could end in deadlock."[6]

Toward the end of June this looked like the most appetizing prospect the Eisenhower forces could hope for. Guy Gabrielson of Minnesota was chairman of the Republican National Committee, and had been working with Roy Dunn since at least December 1951 for a Taft nomination.[7] With a much-publicized air of magnanimity, Gabrielson offered to split the sizeable Texas delegation, twenty-two for Taft and sixteen for Eisenhower. Lodge, with the apparent support of Warren Burger, summarily refused.[8]

An alternative to the Gabrielson "compromise" was drafted by a meeting of Republican governors immediately prior to the convention, when the GOP state executives issued a "manifesto" laying the bases for an effective challenge to the Taft forces over the contested delegations. In essence the Republican governors' plan would have barred the contested del-egations from voting until their status was resolved by the convention. This would have represented an abrupt change in rules not only from 1948, but from every convention since 1860, and Taft supporters could barely contain their indignation. "Contrary to every principle of parliamentary procedure," the Senator himself snapped.[9] Stassen wasted no time express-ing his support for the plan in the form of a telegram sent to the governors, a copy of which he thoughtfully sent to Taft along with the rather audacious request that Taft recommend the rule change to the convention.[10] Whatever the Ohio senator may have murmured under his breath upon receipt of the Minnesotan's telegram he quickly realized that the Eisenhower forces, packaging their effort to change the rules as "Fair Play," were scoring a propaganda coup. In a convention carried on national television, this was a serious matter.

Hence ensued a change in strategy. No sooner had Governor Arthur Langlie of Wash-ington proposed the rules change than congressman Clarence Brown of Ohio leaped to his feet demanding recognition. Brown proposed a substitute to the Langlie initiative that in effect would have granted the Eisenhower forces sixty-one of the sixty-eight contested del-egate seats. The Taft campaign was making a strategic retreat. Appearing gentlemanly and compromising, the Ohioan was merely asking that seven delegates from Louisiana who had not been contested before the national committee be seated. The seven delegates were trivial, as everyone knew; the Taft forces were trying to win over moderate and uncommitted del-egates by making the Eisenhower forces in their demands for all sixty-eight delegates appear greedy. The effort failed. The Brown amendment was defeated on a roll call, 658 to 548, and the Langlie substitute was accepted by voice vote.[11] Throughout the credentials battle Stassen and the Minnesota delegation remained in harness with Eisenhower, despite the efforts of Robert Taft to lure Stassen into his fold with promises of the vice presidency.[12]

As the convention settled down to the business of nominating a president, Stassen was watched with deep suspicion by the leaders of the Eisenhower campaign and, surprisingly, by his own campaign manager. For several months Bernard Shanley had been wary of his candidate's intentions; by late June he was beside himself with anxiety. "I am more worried than ever about our general situation," Shanley confided to his diary, "because I can't help believe Harold is going to play for a deadlock and may very well attempt to force one, which if he does, whether it misses or doesn't miss, I think would be fatal to the country, the party and certainly to Harold Stassen." By the time they reached Chicago Shanley was ready to interpret any slight to him by Stassen as a move to subvert the will of the convention. When Stassen requested that Shanley move out of the suite they shared at the Blackstone Hotel into an office of his own, Shanley "wondered if he felt it wiser to get me into another suite so that I would not be listening to plans for deadlocking the convention."[13] It is not clear why Shanley had come to harbor such doubts about his candidate. It is plausible that the Newark-based lawyer had come under the influence of Dewey, Herbert Brownell and Russell Sprague, who were intensely suspicious of the Minnesotan.

Their suspicion was ill founded. When the convention began the roll-call vote for the presidential nomination on the fourth day, Stassen was ready to strike for an Eisenhower nomination. According to Minnesota's primary election law, Stassen's delegates were required to vote for Stassen until his share of the total convention vote slipped below 10 percent, implying that on the first ballot the Minnesota delegation was "stuck" with Stassen. Searching for options, Warren Burger, co-floor manager, along with Daniel Gainey, for Stassen, met with convention chairman Joseph Martin. Could Minnesota change its vote on the first ballot? According to Burger, "Martin said that until his gavel went down announcing the first ballot vote, any delegate or delegation could change. He smiled and said he would keep that in mind in light of our conversation."[14]

Actually, five[15] Minnesota Stassen delegates had already announced their intention to support Eisenhower on the first ballot — primary law notwithstanding. This had come over the vigorous opposition of Stassen, whose truculence in the matter was later cited by some of the delegation as evidence that Stassen was still hankering for his own nomination.[16] This is flimsy evidence; Stassen believed quite reasonably that a sudden shift of the state's delegation as a block would have greater psychological impact on the convention. Moreover, it contradicts Warren Burger's account of the event. According to the former chief justice, "Stassen emphasized the crucial need for decisive action on the floor. He said in case communication was delayed ... he would expect us to move swiftly to shift his delegates to the General whenever that would ensure his nomination."[17]

That moment occurred in the closing seconds of the first ballot. At that moment Eisenhower had 595 votes — just nine short of the 604 required for nomination; Taft held 500. After a frantic conversation with Burger, Senator Ed Thye screamed into a microphone, "Mr. Chairman! Mr. Chairman!" Granted recognition by the forewarned Martin, Thye announced, "Minnesota wishes to change its vote to twenty-eight for Eisenhower." Eisenhower was nominated.[18]

The next day William Dubarry, acting president of the University of Pennsylvania, sent Stassen a one-sentence telegram: "You are a patriot."[19] Certainly Stassen was quick to express his delight and sense of accomplishment. "The six months of effort in the public responsibility which I undertook last December culminated in an unbelievably successful and dramatic manner," Stassen exuded to Robert McCracken, chairman of Penn's board of trustees. "I feel very happy about it," Stassen added, "and have the deep quiet sense of satisfaction which comes at the favorable conclusion of a long and frequently misunderstood project."[20] The Minnesotan sent out gilt-edged certificates to each of the delegates who voted for him on the first ballot — a group he referred to as "The Minnesota Nineteen." "May It Be Ever Known," the certificate trumpeted, "That [blank] ... remained loyal and stalwart in my support in the face of very extreme pressures and through many days of discouragement, until ... in complete accord with my basic publicly announced policies, and without any deals of commitments whatsoever ... [they] cast their votes then and there for General Eisenhower."[21]

It is altogether possible that Harold Stassen was not in 1952 running for Eisenhower but rather for himself. His denials to the contrary, he may have secretly hoped that the general would not run or, failing that, that the convention would deadlock and turn to

Stassen. Yet the Minnesotan's actions in the campaign were consistent with his avowed goal of nominating Eisenhower.

If his actions were well intended, they were also ineffectual. If anything, Taft's political strength increased in the months following the Minnesotan's entry into the presidential race. After the Wisconsin primary Stassen continued to flail at Robert Taft but, simply, nobody cared. Had Earl Warren not entered the Wisconsin primary, it is just conceivable that Stassen could have won in the Badger State and then, propelled by two straight victories, effectively challenged Taft in Ohio and elsewhere. Warren's entry in Wisconsin damaged Eisenhower and thoroughly destroyed Stassen.

Stassen returned to Philadelphia to face a board of trustees and a student body impatient with their absentee president. Nor did the Eisenhower campaign show any initial inclination to include Stassen in the general's fall "crusade." No matter how pleased he claimed to be, Stassen must have left the Windy City with a heavy heart.

17. Managing Foreign Aid

"I should like to have a long talk with you," Dwight Eisenhower said in a letter to Harold Stassen on November 10, 1952. "I will look forward with pleasure to seeing you," replied Stassen.[1]

He understood what the president-elect's letter portended, and he was not pleased. In his College Hall office at the University of Pennsylvania, Stassen grumbled to his assistant, Robert Matteson, that "the Dewey crowd" was trying to maneuver him into the Labor Department, a position Stassen did not want and, he told Matteson, would not accept.[2] While Stassen understood that John Foster Dulles had the inside track on the position of secretary of state, in the days since the election he had missed no opportunity to remind Eisenhower of his interest and expertise in foreign affairs.[3] When the two met on November 20,[4] Eisenhower reassured Stassen almost immediately. "I'm not going to give you a regular cabinet post," he declared, "as that would be too limiting for what I have in mind." To his infinite relief Stassen was offered a job well-tailored to his interests, that of director of the Mutual Security Administration (MSA).[5]

As Mutual Security administrator, Stassen would be in charge of both economic and military aid programs. While MSA was nominally part of the State Department, Stassen was to be a member of the cabinet and the National Security Council and would have direct access to the president. He was delighted. "Thank you very much," he exclaimed in a letter acknowledging the appointment. "My predominant emotions are those of humility and determination — humility before the task which you have asked me to do — and determination to carry this Mutual Security Program forward for you and your high objectives."[6]

Those "high objectives" were a matter of interpretation. Both Eisenhower and John Foster Dulles approved of MSA because, among other reasons, it was cheap way to provide for defense. "And so," Emmet Hughes observed, "when the banner of Mutual Security fluttered aloft over Administration deliberations, it rather became the most rare of all pennants if its time — the standard saluted with equal respect by those most preoccupied with foreign policy and those most obsessed with domestic economy."[7] While this was an exaggeration (treasury secretary George Humphrey found MSA no more palatable than any other kind of deficit-inducing expenditure), Hughes was essentially correct. In seeking the "great equilibrium" between a healthy domestic economy on the one hand and a well-provided-for military on the other, bolstering the ability of friendly nations to defend themselves without the presence of American troops was to Eisenhower and Dulles a shrewd, self-interested proposition.[8]

Stassen concurred, but his policy orientation toward mutual security had a tinge to it for which Eisenhower had at best lukewarm sympathy and Dulles outright antipathy. For the president, mutual security programs were advantageous to the degree they provided

Harold E. Stassen (right) with John Foster Dulles (left) and Dwight D. Eisenhower, 1953 (Minnesota Historical Society).

cost-efficient defense, tangibly calculated. "That meant," according to Stephen Ambrose, "specifically that he wanted more funds for MSA, so that he could distribute military hardware to the Koreans, to the NATO allies, and to other friends around the world...."[9] The secretary of state added that nations benefiting from mutual security programs should show their gratitude in the form of a clearly articulated allegiance to the West. Dulles proudly announced in January 1954 that, "broadly speaking, foreign budgetary aid is being limited to situations which clearly contribute to military strength which also helps us."[10]

Stassen was in fundamental agreement, but he was less sure it was always possible to discern which nations would "clearly contribute" to the United States' position in the Cold War. Moreover, he was not certain that "strength" necessarily had to be "military" in nature. Whereas Dulles sought reassurance in alliances, Stassen privately explained to Eisenhower that a more realistic Cold War strategy involved capturing the "friendliness" of the nine hundred million of the brown, black and yellow people outside the Iron Curtain."

Couching his foreign policy vision in realpolitik language suitable for a former army general, Stassen argued his case. "In the cold war struggle versus Kremlin-directed communism," he noted, "the Atlantic Pact nations are our main center force, the nations of Asia and Africa with their colored population are the left flank." Maintaining the allegiance, or at least avoiding the hostility, of the left flank was made easier by a strong U.S. economy, which through properly directed trade policies would provide the carrot of economic growth to Asia and Africa. However, the left flank could not be held together through economic policies alone. "In fact," Stassen observed, "there is a considerable resentment of the wealth and success of America among this colored population. There is also an intense pride and extreme sensitivity, fed by memories of, or present experiences with, imperial domination." Therefore, Eisenhower needed immediately to establish contact with Asian and African leaders, making clear American "respect for their dignity." In direct opposition to Dulles, Stassen urged Eisenhower that "regard for an independent third position in world affairs on their part, and gradual assistance in their progress toward better economic conditions and successful self-government, are all essential." He specifically pleaded that Eisenhower understand that Nehru was the recognized leader among "this nine hundred million of colored population" and should be treated accordingly.[11]

Stassen had proffered this advice on November 13, 1952, even before being appointed to the administration. His views were in basic harmony with Eisenhower's. In his inaugural address the president stated, "Honoring the identity and the special heritage of each nation of the world, we shall never use our strength to try to impress upon another people our own cherished political and social institutions."[12] Eisenhower proudly noted that "among all the powerful nations of the world the United States is the only one with a tradition of anti-colonialism." Within his narrow definition of the term, as president he endeavored to keep it that way, refusing for example, to send American forces to Indochina without an explicit pledge by the French to grant independence.[13]

Both Eisenhower and Stassen had limits to their liberalism, however, and, of the two, Eisenhower was the more conservative. A dainty concern for world opinion, for instance, would not convince him that the Guatemalans and Iranians should not be provided with new governments, something Stassen would have never considered. Eisenhower was instinctively less sympathetic and more easily annoyed than Stassen by the charge of colonialism. It especially vexed him that, while the West was viewed by the developing world with unceasing suspicion because of past imperial acts, the Soviet Union could continue to practice in eastern Europe without reproach, as though "colonialism is not colonialism unless it is a matter of white domination over colored people."[14]

While Eisenhower to some extent recognized the importance of flexibility and the necessity of thinking beyond the East-West conflict, Dulles was flatly unmoved. "Where Dulles scorned neutralism," Herbert Parmet has noted, "Stassen emphasized the need of the underdeveloped nations for food, technical skills and literacy as prerequisites for ideological compatibility. Where Dulles thought in terms of the deterrent uses of power, Stassen looked toward breaking the nuclear deadlock and reducing the arms race."[15] Consistently doctrinaire and uncompromising, the secretary of state would not be convinced that acceptance of neutrality was not assent to a compromise with evil.[16] Although Stassen's association with Dulles dated to the United Nations Charter Conference in 1945, and he had enthusiastically supported Dulles' 1950 senate campaign and admired his background in and knowledge of foreign affairs, working with Dulles proved impossible. Stassen regarded Dulles as too quick to rely on military strength, too narrow in his thinking about world issues, and, above all, unable to reach out and establish a dialogue with any nation but the most overtly friendly.[17]

Stassen and Dulles were destined to come to loggerheads even without their differing foreign policy orientations. Neither man was easy to get along with. Dulles, at least, was protected by the fact that he obviously held the confidence of the president; conversely, few leaders in the administration, including the president, were fully convinced that Stassen had not been out for himself rather than Eisenhower at the 1952 Republican National Convention. As a result, Stassen was isolated among the cabinet almost from the beginning. While the President had great personal respect for Stassen's abilities,[18] according to Sherman Adams one cabinet member told Eisenhower that "you could put all of Stassen's followers into a small closet and you wouldn't have any trouble shutting the door."[19]

Compounding the problem was Dulles' determination that no interloper infringe on his foreign policy turf. Having watched the fate of his uncle, Robert Lansing, when Colonel Edward House took on foreign policy assignments; being aware of how Franklin Roosevelt had ignored Cordell Hull while conferring with Sumner Wells; and knowing of Harry Hopkins' supplanting of Edward Stettinius, Dulles unceasingly maneuvered to keep Stassen under control.[20]

Ultimately Dulles, who is regarded as having enjoyed his greatest success in the arena of bureaucratic politics,[21] succeeded in driving Stassen from the administration. Still, for over five years Stassen labored in the cabinet and often succeeded in achieving presidential approval for his policies. "Whether by design or not," Robert Divine has written, "Ike pursued a series of peaceful initiatives from the White House that contrasted sharply with the suspicious and aggressive policies that Dulles propounded in the State Department. The result was to give American policy a schizophrenic appearance, with the Secretary of State waging a Cold War and the President searching for detente."[22] Eisenhower sought to provide himself with breadth and alternatives in the advice and policies suggested to him, and for a time the system worked as Stassen and Dulles checked and even occasionally reinforced each other. Still, Eisenhower had appointed incompatible men with opposing philosophies to mutually overlapping assignments. It was an arrangement that could not last.

Stassen and Dulles were thrown into uneasy proximity immediately after the inauguration by the imperative of maintaining European anticommunist unity. Eisenhower's concern for the European alliance was one of long standing; indeed, it had been a central factor in his decision to seek the presidency. A major threat to the alliance, the president believed, was a sustained, Kremlin-directed effort to sow "division and suspicion" within NATO, an effort Eisenhower had seen behind the mass protests he had encountered during a tour of NATO capitals in January of 1951. While he had faith that NATO leaders had shrewdly perceived the source and inaccuracy of the anti-alliance agitation, he worried that as elected politicians they could not "ignore the effect upon many of their less-informed citizens."[23]

Communist-inspired division threatened Eisenhower's most urgent NATO-related goal: the ratification of the European Defense Community (EDC). The EDC was designed to strengthen and supplement NATO by integrating western European armies and rearming West Germany while depriving it of a general staff. Eisenhower saw in the EDC three desirable outcomes. First, western European nations would be further bound together in an anti–Soviet posture; second, the economy and population of West Germany would strengthen the anticommunist alliance; and finally, the United States would save money and manpower as the Europeans picked up a larger share of the defense tab. Yet the likelihood of the plan's adoption was in question. At the time of Eisenhower's inauguration, the treaty had not been ratified by West Germany, France, Italy, Belgium, the Netherlands, and Luxembourg. The treaty's fate was in particular doubt in France. While foreign minister Georges Bidault had assured Eisenhower of his government's support for the treaty, the president realized that anti–U.S. mass protest made parliamentary support problematical.[24]

Eisenhower's concern for shoring up the U.S. image in Europe was influenced by personal pique as well as geopolitical concerns. "Most of the published attacks were directed more against me than against NATO," the president complained later. "They charged that I was a cruel, military type, coming to Europe to start an aggressive war no matter what the cost in European lives."[25] In an effort to counter Kremlin-directed propaganda and convince Europeans of the peaceful, accommodating nature of the United States, Eisenhower hit upon the unlikely idea of sending John Foster Dulles on a public relations tour of European capitals.

Given the goal of calming European nerves over the possibility of war, the president could not possibly have made a worse choice. "Mr. Dulles is not very well liked here," observed *New York Times* correspondent Raymond Daniell in London, "either by the Conservative Government or the Labor Opposition.... His expressed idea that United States propaganda should and could be used effectively to undermine Soviet influence in the satellite states has been received here with suspicion and fear as likely to yield no results other than to increase the danger of world war." In France, Dulles generated little good will by his blunt threat, delivered hours before he departed from the U.S., to "give a little rethinking" about the American relationship to western Europe should the treaty fail.[26]

In Eisenhower's first case of foreign policy schizophrenia, he ordered Stassen to accompany Dulles on the European tour. Such a plan appealed to the President's chain-of-command sense of order: while Dulles as secretary of state was to assure the allies of American commitment to Europe, Stassen as Mutual Security administrator was to preach the necessity of an open market and deal with economic problems between the continent and the United States. The president also wanted the conciliatory Stassen to balance the more strident Dulles. Yet the result was a mess. While he had sent the secretary of state to Europe to "make it clear that we're in Europe to stay, that it's in our best interest to be there, no matter what some of the Republicans in the Senate say," he remained silent as Dulles attempted to coerce the Europeans into ratification with the threat of U.S. abandonment, this while Stassen was charged with the task of steering the Europeans away from excessive nationalism.[27]

Stassen and Dulles, after breakfasting with the president, departed for Rome on January 30, 1953, the first stop on their nine-day tour. In France, the second nation on the seven-nation journey, Ike's emissaries listened with interest as U.S. ambassador James Dunn explained that the French would ratify the EDC under the conditions that Germany accept the treaty first and the U.S. support France in Indochina. Until Dien Bien Phu surrendered in May of 1954 the EDC and Indochina were linked, as Dulles and Stassen agreed with Dunn's assessment. Stassen's support for the French cause demonstrated the limits of his international liberalism; more idealistic than his colleagues, he nonetheless held fundamental Cold War assumptions.[28] Returning to the U.S. on February 9, Dulles proclaimed the trip a success in a tone that was, according to the *New York Times*, "much friendlier, much quieter" than the secretary had previously used.[29]

Stassen had remained uncharacteristically silent on the trip; inwardly he was deeply troubled. First, it was not clear that the trip had done anything to improve the U.S. image in Europe, let alone dispel anxiety over the emphasis on "liberation" Dulles had written into the 1952 Republican platform. Second, the EDC was no closer to ratification. Stassen privately felt that Dulles was too rigid and demanding in his relationship with the allies. One member of Stassen's staff characterized Dulles on the trip as "slow" and "stern," qualities not associated with Stassen. For ideological and professional reasons, it had become clear to Stassen that the two men would have a trying time working together.[30]

In addition to revealing to Stassen the difficulty of working with the secretary, the trip also set the tone of what was to follow for the next five years. While Eisenhower was not the genial, absent-minded president his critics made him out to be, neither did he restrain his strong-willed secretary from changing the nuance, if not the actual structure, of his orders concerning the European mission. Stassen, who was instinctively closer to Eisenhower's foreign policy views, had remained quiet; in this case his objection to Dulles was not, he felt, compelling enough to declare intramural war. Indeed, Stassen had quietly reminded the West Germans that economic aid to their country would be contingent on acceptance of the EDC, a pressure tactic quite agreeable to the secretary of state. But Stassen was worried about Dulles' readiness to threaten publicly and to bully privately. To the Mutual Security administrator, this demonstrated a worrisome insensitivity. So long as his complaint with Dulles was limited to a rather hazy objection to the secretary's "attitude," Stassen quietly acquiesced. But his objections would not always be so limited.[31]

Stassen had left for Europe only two days after being unanimously confirmed by the Senate as Mutual Security administrator.[32] Upon his return on February 9 he launched an effort to quiet congressional critics of the U.S. "give-away program" by streamlining MSA and refashioning it to suit changing foreign policy requirements and the policy choices of Dwight Eisenhower.

Under Stassen's predecessor, Averell Harriman, the agency's finances had been chaotic, leading to congressional irritation toward a program which in the best of circumstances was enormously difficult to push through the legislative branch. In preparing the initial 1954 budget Harriman had envisioned an appropriation of $8 billion. When the Bureau of the Budget slashed this figure to $5.8 billion, Dean Acheson had joined with Harriman in successfully pleading with Truman to restore the appropriation request to $7.6 billion. Even had the Republican Party not captured both houses of Congress in the 1954 elections there was no chance of such a large appropriation passing legislative muster. The Truman administration's budget request in 1952 had been reduced by $2.2 billion, to $7.3 billion, while the 1953 request had been cut by $1.9 billion to $6 billion.

To a large extent MSA under Harriman had only itself to blame for these budgetary cutbacks. Particularly infuriating to members of Congress was the desultory pace with which MSA spent the funds it obtained, leading to enormous budgetary surpluses in the agency's spending power even as it requested ever more funds. By 1954 these unspent funds totaled an estimated $10.5 billion. The reason for this, Eisenhower's director of the Bureau of the Budget, Joseph Dodge, explained, was that "for several years the approach to the MSA budget request was in terms of appropriating a larger amount than it was intended to spend, for its psychological effect on foreign nations."[33] Although Dodge did not say so, bureaucratic turf-building was also a factor. Neither Eisenhower nor Stassen had much enthusiasm for reducing MSA appropriations. Asked by *Newsweek* in December 1952 if foreign spending could be cut "soon," Stassen pointedly sidestepped the question.[34]

To avoid a budgetary bloodletting Stassen attempted to establish the credibility of MSA as an efficiently run and frugal agency. Even before his departure for Europe Stassen established a task force to review the workings of the agency. After the fashion of government commissions from time immemorial, it was composed of prominent and well-regarded individuals. After the fashion of the Eisenhower administration most, though not all, of these individuals were prominent businessmen. Led by Clarence Francis of General Foods Corporation, the commission sent out teams of investigators to the nations receiving U.S. economic and military aid. Their task was to evaluate the efficiency with which

U.S. aid was distributed and utilized by the recipients. All of the team leaders were industrialists or bankers. Stassen's goal, in addition to streamlining the agency, was to garner the support of businessmen for U.S. foreign aid programs by giving them a voice in its organization.[35]

Having launched the Francis commission, Stassen held long discussions with Robert Matteson during his European trip with Dulles. A close friend and confidant whose opinion Stassen respected enormously, Matteson had been appointed by Stassen as assistant director for research; yet Matteson held a position in MSA far more influential that his title implied, and would play a key role in all of Stassen's activities throughout the 1950s.

Matteson's career, both before and after his association with Stassen, was as remarkable as his employer's. A graduate of Carlton College and Harvard University, Matteson had resigned a post as desk officer in the State Department to fight in World War II. Turning down a commission, he enlisted as a private in the 80th Infantry Division. Promoted to counter intelligence in the waning days of the war in Europe, Matteson had hunted down and single-handedly captured Gestapo chief Ernest Kaltenbrunner, his aide, Arthur Scheidler, and two SS guards on top of a mountain in the Bavarian Alps. Awarded the Silver Star, Matteson returned to his native St. Paul, Minnesota, where he began working for Stassen as a research assistant. When Stassen assumed the presidency of the University of Pennsylvania, Matteson served as his top assistant while teaching international relations part-time. More liberal than Stassen, Matteson had a habit of writing "personal to Harold Stassen" memos in which he urged his boss toward liberal policies, with varying degrees of success. Matteson remained in government service until 1970, when his opposition to the Vietnam War in general and the Cambodian invasion in particular led to his forced resignation by Richard Nixon.[36]

The two men agreed that MSA and its far-flung operations had become bogged down in bureaucratic inertia, becoming ponderous and incapable of creative thinking. Stassen directed Matteson to establish the Bureau of Research, Statistics, Reports and Evaluation. Under Harriman a previous version of this office had provided factual information regarding U.S. foreign aid programs. RSRE would now be expanded to serve as a think tank, evaluating the data it generated and producing new ideas. While the office was being set up, the restless Stassen exhorted the agency simply to work harder. In this he was astonishingly successful; in his first six months on the job the amount of foreign aid deliveries almost doubled. There would be no unspent funds or excess capacity at MSA on Stassen's watch.[37]

The aid which Stassen was eager to expedite took three forms. The first, military aid, was controlled by the Department of Defense (DOD), with MSA's role essentially being one of coordination. This aid consumed 70 percent of the Mutual Security Program when Eisenhower took office, Stassen was skeptical of the ability of tanks and guns to ensure security. In a major foreign policy address in 1951 Stassen had warned that in the developing world generally and Africa particularly problems of racism, overpopulation, poverty, and underdevelopment presented opportunities for Communist agitators. Security in Africa, he emphasized, "will depend upon what is done about land, water, and population pressures, and finally about the relationships between the peoples of different colors."[38] From the beginning he urged within the councils of the administration a shift toward programs to assist nations in their bid for economic self-sufficiency and social stability. In this effort he was only modestly successful. While he reported to Eisenhower in 1955 "an increased proportion of total funds are being used for economic purposes,"[39] this was just barely true: military aid as a proportion of total aid had dropped only 10 percent.[40]

Stassen took a special interest in technical assistance, the second form of aid. In his first year he successfully lobbied within the administration to have the whole authority of this program shifted to his jurisdiction; he had previously shared responsibility with the State Department. Technical assistance comprised a myriad of activities initiated by the International Development Act of 1950, popularly known as Point Four. "Our projects ran the gamut of human activity," Stassen recalled, citing efforts ranging from constructing fertilizer plants to sending doctors and medical technicians to needy nations.[41] Under Stassen's direction, technical assistance became a more vital aspect of mutual security as the number of American technicians abroad increased from 1,350 to 1,950 and the number of trainees arriving in the U.S. rose from 1,600 to 4,800 — this while the overall Mutual Security budget was deeply slashed. This aid was increasingly focused outside Europe, reflecting the success of the Marshall Plan and Stassen's interest in Africa and Asia. By 1955 the proportion of nonmilitary funds devoted to areas outside Europe rose from 32 percent to 95 percent, with 64 percent going to Asia.[42]

Throughout his political career Stassen had learned the importance of one-on-one communication; his effort to apply this lesson to foreign aid was one of his finest moments. In an effort to solidify the reputation of the United States in recipient counties, he sought to broaden contact beyond that of the previous government-to-government relationship. In one example of this, Stassen reached out to foreign universities to contract with academic specialists in foreign countries to join with their American colleagues to tackle specific developmental problems, particularly in the area of education. The number of such contracts when he assumed office was sixteen; by the time he left the foreign aid field in June of 1955 the number of such contracts had grown to sixty-three, with forty-three different universities working in more than thirty different countries.[43]

In a separate move to bolster the U.S. image Stassen commissioned an artist to design a logo which would be placed on every item shipped to foreign countries in the technical assistance program, including packages of food, grain, powdered milk, tractors and a wide range of other items. The logo the artist produced was a design of a shield, divided into three segments. The top third held a blue field supporting four white stars; in the middle two hands clasped in a gesture of comradeship, under which was printed "United States of America." The bottom third contained thirteen red-and-white vertical stripes. "As you know," Stassen told agriculture secretary Ezra Taft Benson, "the emblem has great psychological value in our relationship with other countries." The logo was still in use decades later.[44]

The third and final form of mutual security was economic assistance, a type of aid neither Stassen nor anyone else especially liked. In a *Foreign Affairs* article in April of 1954 Stassen approvingly observed that it was an "axiom" of U.S. foreign policy that the "economic health of the free world must be built upon the resources and efforts of the citizens of each country, and not on repeated extraordinary grants of aid from the United States."[45] During Stassen's tenure economic aid to western European Marshall Plan nations was phased out. While small funds continued to be spent in Spain, Yugoslavia and Berlin, and while Stassen increased economic aid to Asia, he was for the most part happy to let the Export-Import Bank take the lead in foreign economic aid.[46]

When the Francis Commission made its report in March 1953, Stassen eagerly adopted its recommendation. Concentrating mutual security planning in the government's top security policy groups, he streamlined consideration of MSA programs throughout the government, concentrating its final review in the planning board of the National Security Council, of which Stassen was a member.

In areas where Stassen's jurisdiction overlapped with cabinet departments such as State or Defense, formalized structures were put in place for policy review. Finally, MSA's overseas staff was more closely integrated with the Washington, D.C., office. By 1954 Stassen could report that he had "cut to a minimum any duplication of effort and overlapping of jurisdiction."[47]

Members of Congress were impressed, and the stock of MSA and Stassen himself rose perceptibly.[48] "Mr. Stassen is beginning to justify some of the promise of his boy-wonder days," James Reston observed in April then added, "[He] is turning out to be the 'surprise' of the Eisenhower team."[49] With this bolstered public image, Stassen on May 5 presented his first budget request. Aware of the hostility in Congress to Harriman's tactic of requesting lavish appropriations for diplomatic and bureaucratic effect, Stassen adopted a "no games" approach, requesting that Harriman's proposed level of funding for 1954 be cut by roughly 25 percent, to $5.8 billion.[50] "I'm terribly worried about this," complained Douglas MacArthur II. "There's no water in the $5.8 billion figure, and if we don't get all of it, we're in *real* trouble."[51]

Given the desire of congressional unilateralists to do away with MSA entirely and the overall Republican desire for a tax cut, even with the intensive assistance of Eisenhower Stassen was unable to prevent a 22 percent cut in his own proposed spending authority for 1954. Whether or not "real trouble" resulted, Stassen continued the policy he began with for the next two years: realistic budget proposals coupled with a low-key approach in his lobbying for funds. Avoiding public brawls with congressional leaders, he would limit his lobbying to private sessions with congressional leaders.[52] On the face of it his strategy was a failure. Spending for Mutual Security plummeted by more than half, from just over six billion dollars in 1953 to just under three billion in 1955, when Stassen left the foreign aid program.

This trend, however, had begun in 1952. Moreover, Stassen made the most of the funds with which he was provided. As the *New York Times* pointed out, those who "feared that a Republican administration would mean ... the beginning of the end in foreign aid were dead wrong," citing Stassen's successful effort to integrate foreign aid into the long-term foreign policy of the United States.[53]

Throughout the early months of the administration, Nelson Rockefeller's Advisory Committee on Governmental Organization directed its attention to mutual security. More interested in policy development than in the operational chores of foreign aid, Dulles had indicated that he had no desire to keep MSA within the State Department. On June 1, 1953, Eisenhower announced that the agency would be abolished. In its place would be the new, independent Foreign Operations Administration (FOA), headed by Stassen.[54]

The move was bureaucratic in nature and did not have an impact on Stassen's relative power within the administration. On paper, FOA director Stassen did have authority which he had not previously had, namely to direct an agency located outside of State and to administer technical aid; but in fact he had been assuming these "new" responsibilities all along, given Dulles' boredom with the topic, Stassen's eagerness to take on the task, and Eisenhower's often unclear goals concerning the tone and direction of his foreign policy. The president claimed that the new organization chart repaired the duplication and overlap which had prevented a "balanced program." It did nothing of the kind.

Stassen's role in foreign policy continued to be ambiguous. His status as a member of the cabinet, the National Security Council (NSC), and the Council of Economic Advisors suggested a free hand; the reorganization, however, authorized the secretary of state to provide "guidance" to the FOA director, who would serve at the secretary's pleasure.[55] Despite these restrictions Stassen apparently chose to regard his status as head of an agency located outside of State to mean greater freedom to speak his mind about Dulles' policies, which he proceeded to do in gradually louder tones. The reorganization drew battle lines as well as organization charts.

18. Managing McCarthy

By 1953 Stassen had already demonstrated a remarkable dexterity in handling the anti-communist issue. In 1948, while careful to praise the Nixon-Mundt bill — which would have declared the Communist Party USA the "agent of a foreign government" but would have not outlawed the party[1] — Stassen rivaled Nixon in anticommunism. Yet while serving as president of the University of Pennsylvania, where he could have worked no end of mischief against campus liberals, he worked conscientiously to protect academic freedom. Instead, he thundered about foreign Communists and the need to stop shipments of war-related material to communist nations.[2]

Appointed to the Eisenhower administration, however, Stassen was shocked to discover McCarthy "headline hunting" with anticommunism and became embroiled in a series of disputes with the Wisconsin senator.[3] Meanwhile he moved to protect, at considerable political risk to himself, government workers unjustly accused of softness or sympathy toward Communism.

"In 1953," Richard Rovere wrote, "the very thought of Joe McCarthy could shiver the White House timbers and send panic through the whole executive branch."[4] Despite Robert Taft's cheerful prediction in January that by maneuvering Taft into the Government Operations Committee "we've got McCarthy where he can't do any harm," by mid-year McCarthy had managed to remove three U.S. Information Agency officials, insert Scott McLeod in the State Department and seriously jeopardize the confirmation of Charles Bohlen as ambassador to the Soviet Union.[5] As the Bohlen nomination moved toward a vote in March, staff members of McCarthy's Permanent Investigation Subcommittee appeared at the Rochambeau Office Building, about one block from the Executive Office of the president.

While Stassen and Matteson held offices on the second floor of the Executive Office Building, it was in the Rochambeau that the bulk of the MSA/FOA staff was situated, including Kenneth Hanson, acting deputy for MSA. McCarthy's representatives quizzed Hanson at length about U.S. government efforts to block trade between American allies and communist nations. Hanson reported that the State Department was closing in on an agreement with the Greek government to prevent such trade in ships flying the Greek flag. Knowing that communist trade was being carried out by Greek-owned ships carrying the flags of other nations, the State Department was systematically signing agreements to close this loophole; agreements were already signed with Panama, Costa Rica and Honduras. In the meantime the U.S. was negotiating with the British and French governments to prohibit Greek or other ships to be admitted to British or French ports if they were engaged in sending strategic materials to communist China. Hanson conceded that some shipowners were "under investigation" for illicit trade.

On March 21 McCarthy called on Stassen himself and inquired about communist trade; Stassen repeated what Hanson had told the subcommittee's investigators.[6] An unimpressed McCarthy promptly announced that his Permanent Investigation Subcommittee would hold hearings on communist trade and issued a subpoena to Kenneth Hanson to appear before the committee on Monday, March 30.[7]

Stassen now faced a decision. He was supremely aware of the nature of McCarthy's public inquisitions, having been an accomplice during the Truman administration.[8] He was also aware that Hanson had a spotless record, having directed MSA personnel director Tom Naughtin to review the acting deputy's past.[9] Stassen could have easily stood aside, a posture practically invited by McCarthy's having issued the subpoena to Hanson rather than Stassen. Further, since it was the State Department rather than MSA that was charged with negotiating communist trade prohibition agreements (MSA's role was hazy, having to do with "coordination") Stassen could have quite easily passed the buck should evidence of continuing trade surface.

As Stassen mulled over this situation, McCarthy announced to the press on Saturday, March 28, that he had "negotiated" an agreement from Greek owners of 242 merchant ships to stop trade with North Korea, the People's Republic of China and the far eastern ports of the Soviet Union. McCarthy knew full well, because Hanson and then Stassen had made it perfectly clear, that his agreement was superfluous, given the government-to-government agreements engineered by the State Department. Still, he argued that "the immediate effect will be ... a substantial reduction of materials, goods and supplies that are now being carried in and out of these Communist ports." It was clear that his real target was John Foster Dulles. Bent on revenge after his defeat over the Bohlen nomination one day earlier, McCarthy made comments to the press that were loaded with sarcastic references to the State Department.[10]

Since Dulles was a Stassen rival, it must have been sorely tempting for him to leave the secretary and Hanson to their fates. Stassen was aware that in taking on McCarthy he would get no help from the president. The previous week he had gone to Eisenhower to tell him of Hanson's subpoena and his intention to accompany his deputy to the hearings. Eisenhower's response was extraordinary. As Stassen remembered it, the president made this incredible statement: "I, as you know, was in Europe when the McCarthy thing really got going. I didn't hear much about it until I returned home last June. Ike continued: "Of course, I couldn't escape it then or in the campaign." Then went on to criticize Truman for playing into the senator's hands by conducting a public feud with him. "Now," the president soothed, "you go on up there with your man, Hanson, and you can protect him, and do whatever you think is smart. But," he said, "be sure everyone knows you're speaking for yourself and not for me." Stassen thought this a remarkably astute presidential policy.[11]

Sunday night was not too late to back out; still, Stassen made his final decision to appear with Hanson before the Permanent Investigations Subcommittee Monday morning. He would have been better off calling in sick. Within a few minutes Stassen succeeded only in rescuing the State Department by diverting attention to himself by accusing McCarthy of "undermining" the foreign policy of the Eisenhower administration.

Stassen pointed out that McCarthy, by commending the Greek shippers, made it more difficult for the administration to crack down on the illicit trade in which some were engaged. He also explained that under the Constitution the executive branch and not the legislature was charged with foreign policy. By emphasizing that what remained of Greek-owned ships engaged in communist trading would be virtually shut off once the agreements with the British and French took effect, Stassen made clear that the shippers had agreed to what was inevitable, playing McCarthy for a fool.[12]

If Stassen expected gratitude from either Eisenhower or Dulles he was to be disappointed. On April 1 the secretary of state serenely invited McCarthy to lunch, thanking him for his efforts while mildly warning him of the "dangers" of foreign policy interference. The two then issued a joint statement that McCarthy's actions were "in the national interest." The senator pronounced this "perfectly satisfactory."[13]

No one in the administration defended Stassen. "I'm not saying boo about Senator McCarthy," stressed State Department press officer Lincoln White, which was unusual only in that the senator's name was mentioned at all.[14] The president finally broke the silence on April 3, when he told his weekly press conference that he thought Stassen was speaking of an "infringement" on foreign policy rather than an undermining. He added that McCarthy couldn't possibly have conducted negotiations since senators had no power to do so.[15] The next day Stassen agreed that he had indeed meant to say "infringe" rather than "undermining."[16]

In 1984 Stephen Ambrose called Eisenhower's policy in the Greek shippers case a "policy of denial—denial that McCarthy had any right to negotiate with foreign governments, denial that he had done so, denial that Stassen had said what he said, denial that there was any difference on basic issues between himself and McCarthy."[17]

In 1990 Stassen provided a denial of his own, denying in his worshipful book on Eisenhower that the president had rebuked him. Writing off Eisenhower's insistence that Stassen had meant "infringe" rather than "undermine" and how "writers, analysts, Truman, other Democrats, and later historians" interpreted this as a rebuke, he exclaimed, "Thus are mountains of character diminution built from semantic molehills!"[18]

Stassen was not cowed by McCarthy. If anything, he became bolder with respect to the Wisconsin senator. In 1954, a State Department land expert, Wolf Ladejinsky, attempted to transfer to the Agriculture Department. Ezra Taft Benson initially refused to hire him, apparently because Ladejinsky had relatives in the Soviet Union. Stassen came to his support, and Ladejinsky moved to the Agriculture Department but continued to be a storm of controversy. In September Stassen put an end to it by informing Secretary Benson that Ladejinsky's services were required in FOA. Explaining that a land reform specialist was needed in Vietnam, he declared, "No one except Mr. Ladejinsky possesses what we believe are the necessary qualifications." He strongly implied that if the transfer was not made Vietnam would fall to communist domination as a result. Benson was only too happy to oblige.[19]

Stassen took this action knowing he was already open to the charge of harboring communist sympathizers as McCarthy defined them. Robert Matteson, as a youth, had served internships with Ernest Lundeen, who once rode with Earl Browder in a Communist Day parade; he had also at age twenty-two attended a Communist Party cell meeting with the daughter of Senator Burton Wheeler and had dinner with Nathan Fine, a Russian-born labor leader. Moreover, he had attended Harvard. Finally, Matteson was an open advocate for U.S. recognition of the People's Republic of China. McCarthy never took on Matteson, but he would have been an easy target. That Matteson was a decorated World War II veteran might not have helped him any more than it had helped George Marshall. Given the times, Stassen was taking his chances in adopting Ladejinsky.[20]

Almost immediately after the Greek shippers case Stassen began firing direct potshots at McCarthy, ostentatiously pointing out the benefits of nonstrategic trade with communist nations, an issue sure to provoke McCarthy's wrath.[21] This was odd for an official who had just been publicly rebuked by the president, but it reflected Stassen's overwhelming confidence in himself.

Stassen did not accept defeat gracefully; he simply did not accept it at all. He was incapable of admitting even to himself that he had been beaten. Like McCarthy and unlike Richard Nixon, Stassen never seems to have been pushed into introspection and reappraisal by a personal or professional misfortune. Trained by his early success to think of himself as being on an irresistible trajectory toward greatness, he could not believe he had been foiled. As a result, he saw no reason to reevaluate his methods, to examine where he had made mistakes. But as a subordinate in the turbulent U.S. capital, Stassen could no longer control events and define battles as he could as governor and lone political operator. His new circumstance required a heretofore unthinkable sense of caution.

19. "Secretary of Peace"

If Eisenhower was not an unintelligent man, neither was he a rocket scientist, something that quite literally would have been most helpful to Harold Stassen in the early summer of 1957. By then Stassen stood at the brink of a significant arms-control treaty with the Soviet Union, having handled not only Khrushchev but also Dulles, Atomic Energy Commission chairman Lewis Strauss and Joint Chief's chairman Arthur Radford. In this, the president had not been particularly helpful and Stassen not especially skillful; but Eisenhower genuinely desired a reduction in superpower tension and Stassen's epic effrontery in pursuing a treaty threw his opponents off balance. Ironically, it was this effrontery that caused Stassen to fail.

By 1955 a decade of disarmament deadlock mingled with radioactivity from nuclear tests to produce dangerous political fallout in the United States. The deadlock resulted from the degree of emphasis the U.S. and the Soviet Union placed on each corner of the triangle of salient issues involved in arms control: inspection, disarmament and limitation. The first two issues had been the cornerstone of American proposals since November 1945, when the heads of government in Canada, the United Kingdom and the United States called for a system of international controls to assure the peaceful use of nuclear energy and the prevention of nuclear weapons development.

The Baruch Plan introduced to the United Nations the next June codified this thinking into a set of proposals for the control or ownership of all atomic energy material by the International Atomic Development Authority. Atomic weapons production would cease and a system of "control, inspection and licensing of all other atomic activities" would be instituted. All existing nuclear weapons would then be destroyed. The UN General Assembly endorsed the essential elements of the Baruch Plan in 1948, leading to an inevitable Soviet veto in the Security Council.[1] Obviously tailored to an age of U.S. nuclear monopoly, the emphasis on literal disarmament became more urgent with the 1949 Soviet detonation of an atomic device.

The United States government by 1955 was perfectly aware that the idea of total nuclear disarmament had been rendered absurd by the course of the arms race, yet it was unable to develop alternative proposals. J. Robert Oppenheimer in July of 1953 publicly revealed a major finding of the advisory group to which Eisenhower had appointed him: It was difficult to account for fissionable materials used in the production of atomic weapons, a realization that obviously doomed the Baruch Plan.

Two months later Eisenhower appointed a committee comprised of State, Defense and Atomic Energy Commission (AEC) representatives to review U.S. arms control policy with special reference to the international control of atomic energy, which went to work with the "growing belief in certain quarters that the verification and disclosure procedures of the

U.N. plan supported by the U.S. were no longer feasible and, therefore, undesirable for continued U.S. support." The committee got nowhere, reaching an impasse by the fall of 1954 largely because no one could agree on the desirability of the trip.

While the State Department argued that "a program for the progressive control of armaments [i.e., arms limitation] is feasible, and in the U.S. interest," DOD's representative on the committee was not listening: "The U.N. plan, or any presently conceivable disarmament plan, is unfeasible and contrary to the security interests of the U.S., because it is improbable that any technical means can be designed to detect Soviet diversion, or secretion, of nuclear materials."[2] Unable to agree that any proposal was desirable, the lower levels of the U.S. government were trapped in the tomb of the Baruch Plan.

Dwight Eisenhower was not, and he edged toward the third issue of arms control: limitation. His December 1953 "Atoms for Peace" proposal, which, significantly, he had to dream up himself, dodged the issue of abolishing weaponry in its call for nations to make joint contributions of fissionable materials to an international atomic energy agency. Still, this evasiveness signaled that the president, if not all of his subordinates in the U.S. government, was open to partial rather than comprehensive measures.[3] Comprehending the dangers of nuclear stockpiles and the risk of war, and worried that a sustained arms race threatened the U.S. with bankruptcy, Eisenhower was committed to pursuing some form of arms control and reducing superpower tension.[4] While the U.S. and Soviet Union remained deadlocked unrestricted nuclear testing produced worrisome political fallout.

By February of 1955, fifty-seven announced tests of nuclear devices had been conducted by the United States, the Soviet Union and Britain, which had exploded forty-eight, six and three bombs, respectively.[5] Public anxiety about fallout became a serious issue. On February 14, one day after Eisenhower had approved yet another series of atomic tests, the *New Republic* carried a detailed description of this "new dimension in killing power." Two days later the AEC issued a long-delayed report on nuclear fallout that simultaneously scared the wits out of people by announcing that one nuclear blast could threaten seven thousand square miles and enraged scientists for being too conservative in its warnings. The report stressed the importance of continued testing, averring, "If we had not conducted full-scale thermonuclear tests ... we would have been in ignorance of the extent of the effects of radioactive fallout." One day later Winston Churchill proudly announced that Britain was producing a hydrogen bomb.

On February 23, a reluctant Eisenhower was forced to publicly defend continued testing, arguing that the U.S. could not halt such tests without a workable disarmament agreement with effective international inspection, something the U.S.S.R. was on record as opposing. By early March the AEC found itself conducting a frantic public relations campaign for continued testing. Eisenhower's devotion to arms control was genuine, but even a more skeptical president would have realized the necessity of appearing to work for arms control.[6]

Eisenhower ordered Robert Bowie, chief of the State Department Policy Planning Staff, to come up with options. It was Bowie who conceived of the unique idea of creating the cabinet-level position of Special Assistant for Disarmament. Recognizing that a central difficulty in pursuing arms control was the inability of the various governmental agencies to agree on a unified position, Bowie envisioned that the disarmament adviser's staff would comprise officials drawn from the existing security-concerned agencies, including State, AEC, and Defense, as well as career officials from each branch of the military. The disarmament adviser would develop a unified, consensus-driven U.S. policy proposal. Bowie presented this idea to Eisenhower during a meeting of the National Security Council on February 10, 1955.[7]

Ike immediately consulted Dulles. While Stassen later expressed the belief that his appointment had come over the objection of the secretary of state,[8] Dulles not only approved of the concept of disarmament advisor but also expressly agreed that Stassen be asked to accept the assignment. Indeed, after Eisenhower drafted a letter to Stassen offering him the job he sent it first to Dulles, asking for comment. Dulles inserted a reference about the need to appear "before the nation and the world" as having a firm and single basic policy on "the question of disarmament" (Dulles struck out the word "great" before "question"). Eisenhower accepted all of Dulles' changes and sent the letter to Stassen in the form of a cable to Karachi, where the FOA director was visiting as part of a three-week trip to inspect the U.S. overseas assistance agencies. Stassen cabled back his inclination to accept but held off from a commitment until "after discussion with you personally and with my Esther."[9]

That Stassen would accept was a foregone conclusion, simply because he had nowhere else to go. In October of 1954 Herbert Hoover, Jr., had been appointed under-secretary of State and established the Overseas Economic Operations Task Force to evaluate the foreign economic programs of the government, including foreign aid. The task force comprised the inevitable leading businessmen and lawyers; but these members served only as a window dressing, having little time for the actual work. The real decisions were made by the staff, which was headed by John Hollister, a former law partner of Robert Taft and reputedly no friend of foreign aid. Christian Harter, Jr., a former Nixon aide who had become disillusioned and enlisted under Stassen as FOA's general counsel, checked up on the task force and warned Robert Matteson that FOA's prospects were not good. Matteson appeared before the task force on January 7, 1955, and complained that the task force was a charade, meant only to ratify the conclusion already arrived at by the staff: abolish FOA.[10]

To Stassen, who was in Paris at a NATO meeting, Matteson urged an all-out campaign to save FOA. Failure to do so, he pleaded, would lead to the abolition of FOA, which "would be to seriously weaken the U.S. potentiality for free world leadership.... Some of the prompt, bold actions taken during the last two years would never have been taken."[11]

Curiously, Stassen seems to have refused to fight for his agency. Congress, accepting the commission's findings, mandated that FOA be abolished and its activities divided. Military aid programs were to be concentrated in the Defense Department while other economic and technical assistance was to return to the State Department in a new International Cooperation Administration, to be headed by John Hollister. Stassen's reluctance to lead a public charge in his agency's defense may have been due to the fact that, as Matteson observed, it would have required seeking support from other cabinet members, including Dulles, and Stassen knew there was precious little goodwill for him in that body.[12]

Indeed, John Foster Dulles had a distinctly low opinion of Stassen's performance at FOA, or at least privately said he did to Eisenhower. According to Dulles, FOA's reduced appropriations reflected the enemies that Stassen had made on the Hill over the years.[13] There is no evidence that this was the case. Indeed, Representative Walter Judd thought that Stassen had earned a great deal of respect in Congress.[14] It was more likely that Dulles' comments reflected the growing professional and personal dislike and rivalry between the two men.

It was because of, rather than in spite of, this rivalry that Dulles supported Stassen's appointment as disarmament advisor. Aware of the apparently implacably opposing views of State, Defense, and the Joint Chiefs on arms control and the directive that the disarmament adviser hammer out a consensus position, Dulles was sure that it was a highly technical dead-end job — just the place for Harold Stassen.[15] Eisenhower selected Stassen because he believed him "energetic and imaginative." According to Sherman Adams, although he was "well aware" of Stassen's personal unpopularity with many members of the cabinet, Eisenhower felt that Stassen's dogged perseverance would be valuable in this field where little had been accomplished up to that time.[16] Andrew Goodpaster observed that the president was annoyed that disarmament plans were not being forwarded to him, as lower-level officials deadlocked during discussions.[17]

Eisenhower announced[18] the appointment of Harold Stassen as "Special Assistant for Disarmament"[19] on March 19, 1955, while White House officials pointed out that "no world power has ever had an official of such rank as Mr. Stassen holds devoting his time solely to the possibilities of world disarmament and policies aimed in that direction." The *Washington Post*'s response was typical: "Former Governor Stassen is well-equipped for the undertaking," although "his new position is not one that is likely to give much play" to his presidential ambitions.[20] The *New York Times* in a lead editorial referred to Stassen as the "Secretary of Peace." Dulles, reading the editorial in his State Department office, growled to assistant secretary of state for Europe Livingston Merchant, "What am I? 'Secretary of War?'"[21]

In the ensuing months the strained cordiality between Dulles and Stassen would snap; when Dulles had approved of Stassen's disarmament post he never dreamed that Stassen might actually be successful. Still, both Stassen and Matteson were wrong to characterize Dulles as a knee-jerk obstructionist.[22] What Dulles feared with unreasoning blindness was not arms control, wary though he was, but Stassen. The secretary's relationship to disarmament was complex. Whereas at the outset he opposed the separation of political questions like German reunification from arms control, at a crucial moment in early 1957 he showed a marked flexibility on the subject, at least as it related to a test ban. While Dulles feared Stassen as a rival, the military worried about what Stassen might do to the U.S. security position.[23] The secretary of state — once Stassen was finally disposed of in 1958 — became a constructive, if exacting arms control negotiator.[24]

On April 15, 1955, the first meeting of the White House disarmament staff convened in Harold Stassen's second-floor office in the Executive Office Building. In attendance, in addition to Stassen and Robert Matteson, whom Stassen had appointed director, were the officials "loaned" to the disarmament staff by each branch of the military, the State Department, AEC, DOD, and CIA. Stretching the spirit, if not the letter, of his powers, Stassen informed the "loaned" staff that they were to regard themselves not as representatives from their home agencies but as part of the disarmament office; they were to speak their own minds, not their agency's.[25] With one breathtaking exception Stassen was to get his wish.[26]

Stassen made two further announcements. First, he directed his staff to assemble at the Marine base at Quantico, Virginia, on April 15. Stassen desired "fresh thinking" and wanted a coherent policy thrashed out in seclusion. Second, he announced that he was appointing a citizens advisory committee to undertake a study of the vexing question of inspection. Eight task forces would be appointed to coincide with each aspect of inspection. In two of the most important appointments, Stassen selected James Doolittle to investigate aerial inspection and Dr. Ernest Lawrence to study the inspection and control of nuclear materials.[27]

While the citizens' advisory committee began its work, the disarmament staff convened at Quantico. It was to be an important event. Stassen had already had a profoundly significant conversation with James Doolittle. The retired General, according to Stassen, "made the simple statement that in today's world of the most destructive weapons of all time, the most important consideration is the mutual, reciprocal fear of all nations of a surprise attack. If all nations could be protected from surprise attacks, it would quiet world tensions and go a long way toward preventing the need for a continuing increase of armaments.... Conversely, if we could not develop some formula to prevent surprise attacks, we would end up spinning our wheels on all other disarmament discussions.... One way to calm those mutual fears of all nations," he continued, "would be a formula to permit each side to fly over the other at any time, to be sure that no new military buildings developed, no armies massed for movement.... I told General Doolittle that his idea of 'flyovers' impressed me greatly and would become one of our crucial disarmament 'texts.' I told him I would fight for his idea."[28]

There is no question that Stassen did so. The report which developed from the Quantico meeting, which Stassen presented to the president and the NSC on May 26, 1955, had two highly significant features. First, Stassen put to rest the goal of eliminating all nuclear weapons. For the first time in the Cold War, the United States would seek arms control rather than disarmament. "It is not possible," the report stated, "by any known scientific or other means to account for the total previous production of nuclear weapons material, and the margin of error is sufficient to allow for clandestine fabrication or secretion of a quantity of thermonuclear weapons of devastating power." Therefore, it was urged that the arms race be leveled off, hopefully through the cessation of all nuclear production, limited production of conventional weapons, for replacement only, and no further expansion of foreign bases.[29]

Second, since the Soviet Union would "attain during the next ten years, and probably within the next five years, such capability of thermonuclear weapons and of air, missile, and naval delivery methods, that it will have the power to destroy effectively the United States through surprise attack," a primary objective of U.S. policy should be to eliminate the ability of either side to launch a preemptive, surprise strike. To this end, adopting the Doolittle recommendation, the report urged that the International Armaments Commission be established, "with the right to observe and inspect by land, sea, or air."[30]

Subsequently, Eisenhower and Stassen would squabble over who deserved credit for what came to be known as "Open Skies."[31] Surprisingly, Nelson Rockefeller, who had succeeded C.D. Jackson as special assistant for Cold War strategy and whose claim to having initiated Open Skies is by far the weakest, has generally been given the distinction. According to historian Robert Divine, Rockefeller and "experts" at Quantico "came up with the idea of mutual aerial inspection." Ike was immediately attracted to this new approach.[32] This is manifestly false. Rockefeller did not convene his group at Quantico until June 10 and did not present his report to Eisenhower until July 6; Ike had learned about aerial inspection in extensive detail over a month earlier.[33] Perhaps historians have been bewildered by the fact that two very different meetings occurred at the same place; this is surely true of Stephen Ambrose, who resolves the dilemma by splitting the difference. According to Ambrose, *both* Stassen and Rockefeller were at Quantico, *together*. Moreover, "they" had "the report" ready on June 10. How Ambrose has Stassen and Rockefeller together at Quantico (they never were), what June 10 report he means (there is no arms control report carrying that date on record at the Eisenhower library), and how he explains the May 26 report which quite plainly discusses aerial inspection is unclear.[34]

The erroneous attribution to Rockefeller of Open Skies is unfortunate because of the implicit message that the proposal was merely a propaganda ploy. As Peter Lyon, who assumes unquestioningly that the proposal was generated by Rockefeller, asserted, "On the face of it the logical cubbyhole for disarmament was in the office of Harold Stassen.... It says much for the prospects of disarmament, seriously considered as an objective of the Eisenhower administration, that the project ended up in the hands of the President's special assistant for Cold War Strategy, Nelson Rockefeller."[35]

Meanwhile Stassen, even before presenting his report to the president, was shopping around for a venue in which Eisenhower could present the Stassen arms control plan. Stassen telephoned UN ambassador Henry Cabot Lodge, one of the few Stassen supporters in the cabinet, early in May for advice. Lodge vigorously asserted that the General Assembly of the UN would be "by all odds the best forum for the President to use." Yet, since Stalin's death, Stassen's first choice had been a superpower summit.[36]

At the worst possible time Stassen learned that he was to get his longed-for summit, if not an arms control announcement. To have any value, the Stassen disarmament report would have to win the approval of John Foster Dulles, who was not disposed to do him any favors and was an unabashed opponent of a superpower meeting.

Seven days before Stassen was to present his plan, Eisenhower turned to Dulles during an NSC meeting and said, according to Stassen, "in the firmest 'command tone' I ever heard him use, 'Foster, I have decided to instruct you to proceed — to let the other countries know that if they want a summit, I am ready to go to one.'" Dulles accepted the order, but he voiced reservations, arguing that such a meeting would provoke American anticommunists while handing the Soviets an opportunity for propaganda. Ike remained adamant.[37]

Significantly, it was at this moment that Dulles' hostility toward Stassen boiled over. The next day the two men met at the secretary's Foggy Bottom office. A furious Dulles objected to the phrase "Secretary of Peace," which he accused Stassen of promoting, and made it clear that Stassen was to be more accountable to State and the foreign service. By his own account, Stassen refused to be a loyal lieutenant to Dulles and argued that he was merely furthering the president's policies.[38]

When Stassen presented his report to the NSC and the president the next week, Lodge was quick to voice his enthusiasm. "Governor Stassen," he told Eisenhower, "has rendered a great service in developing a scheme which holds out the prospect of bringing this desperately and vitally important matter to a head."[39] Dulles, however, was in no mood to be persuaded, except toward a harder line. Whereas earlier State had been more accommodating than the AEC or the Joint Chiefs, Dulles now reacted with such sputtering outrage that Arthur Radford was content to sit back, reflecting that allowing the secretary of state to shoot down the Stassen plan was a "nifty way" in which he could oppose the report without being the spearhead of the opposition.[40]

During the next three weeks Stassen conducted follow-up discussions with security-related officials, seeking their specific criticisms. Dulles complained about the shift away from the goal of eliminating nuclear weapons. Allen Dulles thought the whole exercise pointless because the Soviets were sure to reject it due to Stassen's heavy emphasis on inspection.[41] The Joint Chiefs complained that there was too little emphasis on inspection.[42]

Faced with either debilitating or contradictory advice, Stassen resubmitted his report at a June 30 NSC meeting virtually unchanged, gambling that the president would overrule his hawkish subordinates. Eisenhower, ignoring a glowering secretary of state, was enthusiastic about arms control, as opposed to disarmament, but agreed with the Joint Chiefs that the report's inspection provisions were inadequate.[43] With that the president launched into his final preparations for Geneva, at which, ironically, he would present a watered down version of Stassen's inspection proposal in the form of Open Skies.[44]

Eisenhower went to Geneva undecided whether to follow Dulles' advice or Stassen's. Wanting both within earshot at the summit, but unwilling to deliver a second rebuff to his prickly secretary, who did not want Stassen and Rockefeller in his way, Eisenhower developed the curious scheme of having Stassen, Rockefeller, Radford and Robert Anderson go to Paris rather than Geneva. This had the advantage of keeping Dulles' feelings from being hurt but required a frantic phone call and flight to Geneva when Eisenhower, in the second day of the conference, decided to present his aerial inspection plan after all.[45]

Actually there was no aerial inspection plan, at least in a form suitable for delivery at Geneva as an issue separate from arms control. How the plan developed in the hours after Andrew Goodpaster called Stassen at the Hotel de Crillon in Paris to pass on Ike's order to go to Geneva will probably never be known with certainty. Stassen, Eisenhower and Rockefeller all remembered the events differently, although Rockefeller's version is least probable. Stassen claims that he drafted the proposal alone "through the long hours of the night of July 19–20."

Stassen's memoir, *Eisenhower: Turning the World Toward Peace*, contains a photostat of what he claims is the first page of his longhand draft of Eisenhower's July 21 presentation.[46] Eisenhower's 1963 memoir, *Mandate for Change*, is ambiguous about Open Skies authorship,[47] although in a 1964 interview Ike remembered it as his idea. "I talked to some people in Defense, to what's his name, Radford. I said we ought to look at having some air and ground inspection on our side and on theirs. Defense said they thought this would be to our advantage. I brought it up and there were some brief studies." He did not mention anyone drafting his July 21 proposal.[48]

Nelson Rockefeller advanced the doubtful assertion that not only did he, Rockefeller, draft Open Skies, he also fought for it over the opposition of Stassen.[49] Given that Stassen had been eagerly promoting aerial inspection since at least May 26, this hardly seems possible. Still, Rockefeller had worked on an Open Skies concept at his Quantico meeting in June, presumably to further study the Stassen plan. Although Rockefeller later claimed to have had no idea Stassen had already developed a plan for aerial inspection, this is highly unlikely, since Rockefeller was a member of the NSC. Robert Matteson had a dim recollection of seeing a late–July letter Stassen wrote to Rockefeller, in which Stassen noted that he had used a paragraph of a Rockefeller memo in the president's speech.[50] The most likely explanation is that Stassen wrote the presentation drawing on language drafted by Rockefeller, and that neither one wanted to credit the other for his help, while Eisenhower blithely took their assistance for granted.

When the summit adjourned, an unhappy Eisenhower told the cabinet that all that had been accomplished was "a new atmostphere."[51] But Stassen carried on as if it had been a major turning point, preaching Open Skies' virtues with evangelical fervor, with Dulles clearly off balance. On August 5 Eisenhower designated his disarmament adviser as the deputy United States representative on the Disarmament Commission of the United Nations.[52] Within four months Stassen had engineered a profound shift in U.S. disarmament objectives; lobbied successfully, as he saw it, for a summit; generated, or helped generate, an exciting new proposal for aerial inspection; and was now poised as U.S. delegate to do some serious negotiating with the Soviets. The next year, however, would see all these gains temporarily evaporate.

At this point, Stassen's relationship with Richard Nixon moved to a critical stage. Richard Nixon first met Harold Stassen in the South Pacific during World War II while stationed at Bougainville in the Solomon Islands. In February of 1944 Nixon wrote to his wife,

Pat: "Today Lt. Commander Stassen came in on one of the ships and I met him and furnished him transportation to his destination. He left this afternoon and seemed appreciative. He is only thirty-five—a big, good-looking Swede—and I was very impressed with his poise."[53] Nixon later recalled how impressed he was with Stassen's handshake.[54]

They were two young men in a hurry. Stassen knew that he was running for president in 1948. He believed that he would be elected and continued to build his base. Nixon was convinced that when he got out of the service and returned home he would have a future in politics. Meeting Stassen, even briefly, offered Nixon a close-up view of a rising political star. Nixon had campaigned for Wendell Willkie in 1940, had toyed with running for the California State Assembly that year, and knew that he wanted to do more than practice law when he returned home. It was no surprise that years later, when asked, Stassen had no memory of meeting Nixon. But Nixon did remember meeting Stassen.

On May 20, 1946, candidate Nixon wrote soon-to-be candidate Stassen reminding him of their meeting two years earlier. "As you may recall, I met you at Bougainville in February of 1944. I was the officer in charge of the SCAT detachment there, and you arrived … on an inspection tour." In that letter Nixon explained to Stassen: "I have been very interested in following your campaign to liberalize the Republican Party because I feel strongly that the party must adopt a constructive, progressive program in order to merit the support of the voters." Nixon enclosed a campaign flyer and told Stassen that he was running against Jerry Voorhis in the 12th Congressional District of California. Nixon asked to meet Stassen when he spoke for the Pasadena Junior Chamber of Commerce on May 28.[55]

Although Stassen was unable to personally campaign for Nixon, he endorsed Nixon and sent him an election morning telegram wishing him "all the best of luck in the election."[56] In the minds of the voters, Nixon was firmly established as an ally of Stassen. In an editorial published on the eve of the election, the *Los Angeles Times* described Nixon as "a friend of Governor Stassen, and his political philosophy is along the lines advocated by Stassen. He is no reactionary in his thinking, but he is distinctly not a leftist or a parlor pink."[57] Nixon's victory in the election brought a firm Stassen ally to the new Republican-controlled 80th Congress.

As Nixon began his congressional service, Stassen prepared to run for president in 1948. California's Governor Earl Warren was also a potential candidate for president in 1948. Nixon and Warren had a strained relationship. While Stassen had gladly supported Nixon in 1946, Warren, following his policy of not endorsing other candidates, declined to endorse Nixon. Nixon felt a kinship with Stassen and wanted to help him win the nomination in 1948. Years later Nixon was to explain: "I supported him [Stassen] in 1948 and believe he would have made a good president primarily because of his enlightened views on foreign policy."[58] Nixon believed "the Republicans needed a fresh face and a change in 1948, and I supported Harold Stassen of Minnesota—the one-time 'boy wonder' of the Republican Party—for the presidential nomination."[59]

Nixon was well aware that many Republican leaders were uncomfortable with Stassen. Stassen's support for Willkie in 1940, his decision to become Willkie's floor leader at the convention, when as keynoter and temporary convention chairman he was supposed to remain neutral, had never been forgiven by the Dewey and Taft campaigns. Stassen was viewed as "too liberal" for the mainstream of the GOP. His repeated declarations that the Republican Party should be the liberal party was the antithesis of what many GOP leaders wanted to hear from a potential nominee for president. Nixon defended Stassen, stating that he was "the most electable candidate and probably the ablest man of the bunch. He is definitely not the left winger that so many party Republicans have labeled him."[60]

As the primary season developed, the two main contenders were Thomas E. Dewey, the governor of New York and the defeated 1944 Republican candidate against Franklin D. Roosevelt, and Harold E. Stassen. As Stassen swept through the first two critical primaries, Wisconsin on April 6 and Nebraska on April 13, he looked like a winner. It soon became clear that the make-or-break primary for Dewey and Stassen would be Oregon on May 21.

The details of the Dewey-Stassen debate and the 1948 campaign are discussed in Section 2. The debate centered on the proposed Mundt-Nixon bill. Dewey opposed the bill, while Stassen favored its passage. Nixon described the bill simply, stating that it would require "Communist organizations to register with the government."[61]

Nixon wrote a brief defense of the bill, which he provided to Stassen before the debate. Nixon later reflected that during the debate Stassen "inaccurately insisted that it [the bill] would outlaw the Communist Party — the same position taken by our left wing critics." Dewey correctly argued that the purpose was not to make it illegal to join Communist organizations, but only to enable the government to identify and publicize Soviet Block support of such groups.[62]

Ezra Taft Benson, for eight years Eisenhower's secretary of agriculture described listening to the debate "under rather elevated circumstances."[63] With his wife, Flora, beside him, he remembered, "We tuned it in while sitting in our car on top of a grease rack. We were getting a 'lube' job while driving from Salt Lake City to Seattle. But we heard every word and at the end, I said to her, 'Dewey will win this primary. He took the debate hands down.'" The rest of the country agreed with Benson. Stassen lost the primary to Dewey and with it his best chance to be nominated for president.

Early in 1949 Nixon decided to run for the United States Senate from California. Many in Stassen's organization in California lined up behind Nixon as he began his campaign. Harold Stassen enthusiastically endorsed Nixon. When Nixon won, Stassen told him that he would no doubt provide "splendid leadership in the Senate as in the House."

As Stassen began his preparation for the 1952 presidential campaign, he turned to Nixon once again. Stassen knew that if Eisenhower decided to run he would be the clear favorite for the nomination. He also understood that if Eisenhower did not run, his own chance for the nomination was possible. Stassen met with supporters and considered his options. He turned to Nixon for two reasons. He knew that to be nominated he would need support from California. He also knew that a balanced national ticket headed by he himself, who in 1952 could claim both Minnesota and Pennsylvania as home [as Eisenhower could claim both Kansas and New York as home], would be greatly helped by a dynamic, young face from the West. Nixon fit the bill.

Nixon had attended the all-important Stassen gathering held at "Justice House," the New Jersey estate of Amos J. Peaslee. Peaslee was an important Stassen supporter who edited a collection of Stassen's major speeches for a book published by Doubleday in 1951 entitled, *Man Was Meant to Be Free*. The book was the opening salvo of Stassen's 1952 campaign.

Following the meeting in New Jersey and confident of Nixon's friendship and probable support, Stassen approached Nixon with an offer he hoped he would seriously consider. Stassen spoke seriously with Nixon about accepting the vice presidential nomination on a ticket headed by Stassen.[64] For Nixon it was a critical moment. While he chose not to play into Stassen's tentative offer, he realized that being offered the possibility of the vice presidency was a serious step up in how he was viewed by national Republican leaders.

Indeed, at the Republican convention of 1952, Richard Nixon was nominated for vice president on the ticket headed by Dwight D. Eisenhower. In fact, Nixon had done for Eisenhower with the delegates from California what Stassen had hoped Nixon would do for him at the convention.

The next critical turn in the Stassen-Nixon relationship took place as the story broke about the Nixon Fund. Nixon was accused of having an eighteen thousand dollar fund for his personal use provided by wealthy campaign fundraisers. As the storm broke over the fund, the question of retaining or dumping Nixon from the Republican ticket was hotly debated. Nixon received an unexpected blow from one he had considered to be a friend. The telegram sent by Harold Stassen from Philadelphia on Sunday, September 21, 1952, was clear and precise — Nixon should quit:

> After a thoughtful review of the entire situation, Dick, I have regretfully reached a conclusion which I feel that I should frankly tell to you. I consider it to be imperative for the success of the Republican campaign to clean out Washington and for your own long-term future that you now send General Eisenhower a message of this nature:
>
>> I deeply regret the embarrassment which has been caused to you and to your campaign by the Dana Smith fund which has assisted in my expenses these past two years. I assure you that I have not personally profited one cent from these funds and my relationship to the committee has been honorable in every way. It is obvious to me, however, that the entrenched opposition will now use this situation to blunt the drive of your superb campaign to clean out the mess in Washington and will handicap the effort to bring in your urgently needed leadership for future peace for America. Above all else your Campaign must succeed for the good of America. My situation must not become a diversion for them to draw across your path. I therefore herewith extend to you my offer to withdraw as your running mate and assure you and the people of my continued devoted efforts to serve our country in the ranks and to defend America against Communist infiltration and subversion.
>
> I do not know, Dick, what the General would then do. If he decided to accept your offer Earl Warren should be named to step in. I am certain that for the success of the Eisenhower campaign he must have the opportunity to make a clear cut decision. Otherwise it will divert and drag from here on for him and for you and above all for the essential movement for good government in Washington. In the long run it will also strengthen you and aid your career whatever may be the immediate decision or results.
>
> With my best wishes,
> Harold E. Stassen

Nixon never forgot the Stassen telegram. He talked about it in the years ahead with some bitterness. Describing it to his political biographer and columnist Stewart Alsop Nixon said, "Then there were telegrams — from Harold Stassen, for example. Have you seen the Stassen telegram? You ought to!"[65] Nixon never forgot or forgave what he considered Stassen's betrayal.

Eisenhower and Nixon won a decisive victory over Adlai Stevenson and John Sparkman and the process of putting together the new administration began. The Stassen-Nixon relationship was to suffer another decisive turn as the team for governing was assembled.

Stassen wanted the job of secretary of state. His old rival Thomas E. Dewey, who had been instrumental in Nixon's selection as the vice presidential candidate in Chicago, backed his old friend and foreign policy advisor, whom he had appointed to fill a vacancy in the U.S. Senate, John Foster Dulles. Dulles got the job.

In 1954 Stassen sought a new job in the Eisenhower administration. If he was not to be secretary of state, Stassen thought he would like to be under secretary of state. Dulles did not want Stassen. He had lived through Stassen's competition with Dewey and did not like or trust him. More important was the role of Richard Nixon in blocking his "old friend" Stassen. Nixon had his own candidate to be under secretary of state. Herbert Hoover, Jr., the son of the former president, was an expert on Europe and the Middle East. It was Nixon who suggested to President Eisenhower that Hoover should get the job and Hoover became under secretary of state.

Nixon never forgave Stassen for his betrayal during the Fund Crisis and Stassen never forgot that Nixon blocked him from getting the job he sought from Eisenhower. The stage was set for what became known as the "Dump Nixon" movement in 1956.

20. Dumping Dick

"For more than a year, a small group of 'liberal' Republicans have been plugging for someone other than Mr. Nixon for second place on the ticket with President Eisehnower."[1] Who was part of this group? Aside from Stassen, it was reported that "others include friends and advisers of the President in and out of government."[2] The first question that has to be posed is what Eisenhower knew and whether he was secretly responsible for the effort to "Dump Nixon." Stassen was always vague about what Eisenhower's role was in the effort. He once cryptically said, "The whole story cannot now be told."[3]

Columnist Stewart Alsop observed that he believed, based on Stassen's comment, it "hints strongly that Stassen did have some reason to believe that the President wished to replace Nixon."[4] Emmet Hughes, an Eisenhower advisor, observed that Eisenhower "showed no sense of regret over Harold Stassen's then-raging campaign to displace Nixon from the 1956 Republican Convention."[5] Raymond Moley believed that "in the first three months of that year [1956], the President, under certain anti–Nixon influences, doubted whether the Vice President should be accorded a place on the 1956 ticket."[6] Lyndon Johnson's aide, Horace Busby, recalled that Johnson never forgot that "a White House cabal had almost succeeded in persuading President Eisenhower to select a new running mate for a second term."[7]

Friends of Eisenhower like George Allen and Howard Snyder supported the idea of an Eisenhower-Warren ticket. The thought that "it is a sure winning ticket" was tempered by the question of "what to do with Nixon." George Allen thought that "the President [could] handle Nixon by agreeing to make him an important person in the administration — possibly in Sherman Adam's place."[8] These thoughts were shared by Eisenhower's close friend Ellis Slater in his diary notes of January 9, 1956. Slater also noted in his diary entry of July 31, 1956, that "Stassen wants Herter in the second place on the ticket because he believes it would be stronger than Ike and Nixon, and he wants to run no risk nationally and feels the Herter substitution would win more Congressional seats. Whether right or wrong, Stassen is sincere, and the President is disinclined as he has been all along, to try to dictate who his running mate should be. He feels Hall has been wrong in running Nixon. That's the job of the delegates at the Convention."[9]

Ed Martin, the brother of former Speaker and Republican leader in the House Joseph W. Martin, Jr., and a Republican insider himself, offered this insight into the "Dump Nixon" effort: "We all felt that Harold was receiving encouragement and financial support from people close to the White House because he was devoting so much time, energy and money to the campaign. The two names most frequently mentioned in this connection were a friend of Secretary of State John Foster Dulles, John McCloy, who was President of Chase Manhattan Bank and the former American High Commissioner to Germany, General Lucius Clay, an Eisenhower friend, who since his retirement was chairman of the Continental Can

Company."[10] Minnesota Republican National Committee member Elisabeth Bradley Heffelfinger thought that Stassen pursued the "Dump Nixon" effort because "he had the go-ahead sign from somebody, and I think it was Sherman Adams, because Sherman Adams had no time for Nixon.... They didn't trust his Checkers speech.... They just didn't trust him [Nixon]."[11]

Without a doubt Eisenhower had misgivings about Nixon. In a conversation that Eisenhower had with Republican National Committee chairman Leonard Hall on February 6, 1956, the president was clear: "I think at this moment, if I could have my favorite fellow, my first choice would be Bob Anderson." Hall told the president, "The easiest thing [would be] to get Nixon out of the picture willingly." Eisenhower responded, "Talk to him, but be very, very gentle." John P. Crecine, dean of Carnegie-Mel-

Richard M. Nixon, ca. 1950s (John F. Rothmann collection).

lon University College of Humanities, released the transcript of the conversation and observed, "He [Eisenhower] didn't want to fire him outright, but Nixon did not take the hint."[12]

James Reston, chief Washington correspondent for the *New York Times* expressed the view of many when he concluded that Stassen's effort to "Dump Nixon" had "Eisenhower's tacit consent."[13] Reston wrote, "It was generally believed by well-informed Republican politicians that while Stassen was not acting at the instigation of the President, he at least had the President's acquiescence in the move for Mr. Herter. This reporter has personal knowledge that if the President had told Mr. Stassen that he was determined to have Mr. Nixon on the ticket, or even that a public move on behalf of Governor Herter would embarrass the President, today's announcement would not have been made."[14]

Based on the observations of the president himself, his friends, his advisors, Republican leaders and the press, it seems clear that, while Eisenhower had doubts about Nixon and would have liked to replace him as the vice presidential candidate, he did not want to deliver the blow to Nixon personally. Many of his key advisors wanted Nixon removed from the vice presidency. Eisenhower believed that Stassen still had political credibility. He knew that tensions existed between Nixon and Stassen. It was not uncommon for Eisenhower to, in Fred Greenstein's well-turned phrase, resort to a "hidden-hand presidency." If Stassen was willing to take the chance, Eisenhower was willing to let him try. Stassen was Eisenhower's cover in a clumsy, ill-conceived effort to remove Nixon from the vice presidency.

Stassen's own comments in later years about the "Dump Nixon" effort provided the continuing cover that Eisenhower sought in his ongoing relationship with Nixon, both political and personal, until Eisenhower's death in 1969. Eisenhower simply felt that there were others who would better serve as president when he left office. The question of whether Eisenhower conspired with Stassen, encouraged Stassen, or simply stood aside and let events take their own course remains an open question. What is certain is that if Eisenhower had gotten his way, Nixon would not have been renominated in 1956. In later years Stassen did not pursue the matter. He never wrote about what transpired behind the scenes. His final comment on the matter was clear and matter of fact: "My biggest disappointment was that I was not able to save the country from the tragedy of Richard Nixon's candidacy. I tried, you know."[15]

In 1989 Stassen summed up his feelings about Nixon in an interview that he gave to the biographer of Senator Styles Bridges, James J. Kiepper. Candidly Stassen said, "I felt Nixon was lacking in what really ought to be in character for a president, and was the first to see through him."[16] Years later, Stassen's son, Glen, would recall his father's distrust of Nixon. "Dad came home from the Cabinet and NSC meetings he had each week that included Richard Nixon saying, 'Richard Nixon has a moral blank where other people have their morality.'" Speaking of his father's move to dump Nixon from the ticket in 1956, Glen reflected, "I think he felt compelled morally to try that desperate move because he knew Nixon well from his own strong moral perspective, and foresaw something like [Watergate]." "What Nixon stood for," Glen added, "and would propagate could be foreseen, since they were together in two meetings each week. I think he sacrificed his political future in that moment to try to avert something like the outcome for the party that we have seen."

As the final preparations for the Geneva summit proceeded in July of 1955, Robert Matteson listened on the back porch of Gabriel Hauge's home, while the assistant to the president for economic affairs ruminated about the following year's presidential possibilities. Eisenhower would not run, Hauge believed, unless there was some emergency, or a realistic possibility of lessening world tensions appeared; he certainly would not run "just to save the G.O.P." Hauge did not know who would; he knew of no governors or members of Congress with the proper credentials. Nor did the administration harbor any prospects, including Nixon, who "lack[ed] stature." "What about Stassen?" Matteson asked. Noting the disarmament adviser's energy and creativity, Hauge asserted that "people around the White House" thought him "too obviously ambitious" and too much in the public eye than was proper for a White House staff member.

Matteson was impressed. Hauge's comments corresponded with what other officials had confided and what Matteson himself observed in his boss.[17] The next day he wrote a brutally frank memorandum reporting Hauge's comments and offering some unsolicited advice. "Subordinate yourself to Eisenhower for your own benefit and for the benefit of the country," said Matteson, urging Stassen to explicitly inform the president of his loyalty. "Impress on him particularly that while you *had* been interested in the Presidency that you no longer have that interest.... Tell him that you realize the hang-over of criticism on the score of being politically ambitious and how this has been a hardship — and tell him that you want to lay that to rest once and for all."[18]

Stassen was an excellent administrator who knew how to reach out for advice on technical issues. But on matters concerning his career he never listened to Matteson, his most valued aide, or anyone else. Matteson attributed this to Stassen's overwhelming self-confidence.[19] More precisely, Stassen suffered from an inability to think introspectively. He was unable to doubt or question himself. His brilliant mind was in that sense shallow; focused on his objective, he could not think reflectively about the wisdom of his method of pursuing that objective. He was a supreme egotist who never thought about himself, and because he could not examine himself, he continued to operate on the lessons he had learned in the 1930s. For Harold Stassen, long odds did not matter; his super-fund of energy would make up the difference.

According to Matteson, Stassen in the aftermath of Eisenhower's heart attack took "preliminary surveys" which revealed a distrust of both Nixon and himself as a presidential candidate.[20] The distrust of Stassen grew from the perception that he still wanted very much to be president. Since this perception was accurate there was little to be done except deny it. By January Stassen had added a stock paragraph to his public speeches:

> Since that dramatic moment when the Minnesota delegates made a first ballot nomination of Dwight Eisenhower a certainty at Chicago in 1952, I have been continually a very happy man and deliberately a relatively quiet man. I have been very happy because I was certain that Dwight Eisenhower's nomination ... would lead first to his decisive election and then to the successful carrying out of a philosophy of government and a program of action of the nature in which I had deeply believed throughout my adult life. I have been deliberately relatively quiet because of my conviction that this was the way to be most effective in the tasks to which the President has assigned me.[21]

From March to May of 1956 Stassen squirmed restlessly in the disarmament talks in London. With Eisenhower recovering from his heart attack and Dulles, Radford and Strauss throwing up obstacles, Stassen had been unable even to piece together a coherent negotiating position. With Britain, France and Canada looking to the U.S. for leadership, the talks essentially became a holding action.[22] Interestingly, an AEC official "loaned" to the disarmament staff, McKay Donkin, told Matteson that Strauss, Dillon Anderson of the NSC and Percy Brundage of the Bureau of the Budget had praised Stassen's performance at the London talks and had spoken not unfavorably of Stassen's "gunning for the vice-presidency."[23]

Since Donkin had reported this to Matteson at the London talks, the comments reflected the assumption that Stassen desired the vice presidency. The president had announced his intention to accept a second nomination on February 29, a symbolic date, coming only once in four years.[24] Certainly, it did not reflect organized activity to dump Nixon, an effort Stassen had yet to launch or even, he later insisted, consider. Stassen claimed that while in London, he "had very little information as to what was happening on the United States political scene." After his return on May 6 at the close of the London talks, he said, "I began to hear from some of my friends in the Republican Party and from some of the independent voters of their misgivings [about Nixon]."[25] There is no evidence that he took any action until Saturday, June 9, when he discussed with Matteson the election and, apparently, the possibility of replacing Eisenhower-Nixon with Eisenhower-Stassen. The day before, Eisenhower had undergone an ileitis operation at Walter Reed Hospital.

On Monday morning, after Stassen had departed for Washington State to speak for the president at the dedication of the Chief Joseph Dam on the Columbia River, Matteson wrote a memorandum on the political situation. Although Matteson was skeptical of the optimistic medical reports coming out of Walter Reed ("this may later be called another 'doctor's plot'") he noted that Eisenhower's nomination was beyond question. Turning to the vice presidency, Matteson observed that with Nixon on the ticket "the G.O.P. stands to have a close contest in November." Matteson listed potential replacements, finding none of them impressive, including Christian Herter, who "is not known."[26] With Stassen replacing Nixon, however, the party's chances "would be much stronger."

But Matteson had great misgivings about an attempt by Stassen to take Nixon's place. A successful outcome, a long shot in any case, required at a bare minimum the support of powerful members of the Eisenhower cabinet. "This is where the Saturday discussion left off," Matteson observed, "when you changed the subject.... It's no help to you if this is not faced up to and if one holds back stating it frankly." Matteson stated the situation as he saw it. Noting that members of the administration valued Stassen's creativity, energy and competence, he emphasized, as he had nearly a year before, that "they also see you as a man who is extremely ambitious — who wants to be President — and some, as I said Saturday, go so far as to indicate personal power above everything else. Finally, they see you as an independent, unpredictable, fast-moving person. [This causes] fear, sometimes mistrust and doubts about judgment.... To some extent, jealously and competition enter in — but more than that — as an additional factor — is resentment at what they consider to be a domineering 'I know it all, I was right, I have the answer' attitude. I have been told this by a number of people."

"If the above is correct," Matteson concluded, "the answer to what you do yourself to either secure your own place on the ticket or, failing that, to simply dump Nixon, would be nothing."[27] Stassen ignored Matteson's comments, including the warning that "Herter is not known." It is unclear at what point he seized on the former Massachusetts governor as Nixon's replacement, but it was certainly within days of Eisenhower's ileitis operation.

The base of operations for the Eisenhower-Herter campaign was the 5020 Glenbrook Road NW, Washington, D.C., home of Matteson. There Stassen would regularly meet with Christian Herter, Jr., who, Matteson recalled, "was serving as a go-between for Stassen and his father."[28] Although the press as yet suspected nothing, word somehow leaked through Republican circles; as early as July 1 no Republican politician would sit next to Stassen at the National Press Club. Matteson was pressed into service.[29]

On July 7 a group of Young Republicans at Trinity College in Hartford, Connecticut, announced the formation of a movement to nominate Harold Stassen for vice president, or as head of the GOP ticket if Eisenhower chose not to run. "It has become more and more obvious that there is a tremendous lack of confidence and belief in Nixon," said Arthur Phelan, the group's vice chairman.[30] Stassen claimed to have no idea what the students were up to.[31]

Vice President Nixon recalled in his memoirs that he steadfastly refused his "many supporters" who urged him to ignore the disarmament adviser's effort to remove him from the ticket, because "I knew that Stassen was a clever man and, except when blinded by ambition, a very able one."[32] Nixon had not noticed blind ambition in Stassen's move to dump him. Therefore, he moved in mid–July to solidify his position.

On July 13 he and Republican National Committee chairman Leonard Hall called Herter to ask him to place Nixon's name in nomination for vice president at the convention.[33] Herter said he would think about it and let them know on July 24. He then called his son, who called Stassen, who the next day called the White House to set up an appointment to see the president, which was granted for July 20. On the 15th, according to Matteson, Stassen called Herter, Sr., although both men would later deny that they had consulted each other before the move became public.[34]

At 9:30 A.M. on Friday, July 20, Stassen entered the Oval Office and got straight to the point. Nixon's name on the ticket would cost at least six percentage points.[35] Nixon's strongest opposition came from independents and younger, well-educated voters, who would take offense at Joseph McCarthy's "strong support" for the vice president. On the other hand, Christian Herter had well-recognized "integrity and strength of character," making it likely he would "maintain a very high favorable rating as he becomes better known."

Therefore, Stassen would seek to have the convention substitute Herter for Nixon. He would also publicly request that those individuals and groups who sought to nominate him for the vice presidency switch their support to Herter, "it being clear to me that my name for different reasons would also detract a few important percent of votes because of the strong adverse feeling toward me on the extreme right of our Republican Party." Stassen did not ask for the president's approval or support; he was merely "informing" him. Eisenhower told Stassen that he could do so as an "American citizen," though, awkwardly put, not as a presidential spokesman.[36]

Historians have tended to take Eisenhower at his word that he was innocently unaware of the Stassen-Herter-Nixon-Hall machinations before July 20,[37] but the accounts of Eisenhower, Nixon and Sherman Adams differ just enough to call this statement into doubt. Eisenhower recalled that he found the idea "astonishing," presumably meaning, in part, surprising. Nixon recalled, "Eisenhower later said that he found this proposal 'astonishing' — not least because he knew that a week earlier Len Hall and Jim Hagerty had received a tentative agreement from Herter to place *my* name at the convention."

Did Eisenhower really know this? If so, someone must have told him about the offer without telling him why it was made, which, given the potential of the convention erupting in civil war, seems unlikely. Adams says Eisenhower did not know; but Adams' credibility is doubtful. He implies that Hall did not ask Herter to make the nomination until July 20; he even says *Nixon* was unaware of Stassen's action until he directed Jerry Parsons to tell the vice president on the morning of July 20, after Stassen passed through his office on the way to see the president.[38]

The question of what Eisenhower knew and when he knew it is important because, implicitly, he excused himself for letting the situation get out of control by saying that on July 20 he was preoccupied. "Mr. Stassen's attitude was astonishing to me, but because I was at that moment hurrying to leave Washington for Panama, I said, 'You are an American citizen, Harold, and free to follow your own judgment in such matters.'"[39] Ike was not in too much of a hurry to speculate about politics with Arthur Larson, who was the first to see him after Stassen. As Larson recalled their conversation:

> After a few tours around the Oval Room, punctuated by an occasional glare through the windows at the Rose Garden, Eisenhower wheeled on me with an expression in his highly elastic face that somehow managed to combine genuine agitation with a trace of sly amusement. "Art," he demanded, "have you ever been Nasserized and Stassenized on the same day?" [The previous day the U.S. had withdrawn an offer to help finance the Aswan Dam.]
>
> He then started talking about the vice presidential nomination. The *New York Times* had reported that the rock-and-roll set went strongly for Eisenhower, but simply did not go for Nixon. Eisenhower, preoccupied with winning over the younger people, was perplexed and disturbed by this.... He said that a "professional politician" had just told him that Nixon's presence on the ticket would cost him four percent of the popular vote. "And you know," he continued, "when the margin of victory is just something like six percent, that's serious."[40]

It is plausible that Eisenhower knew of Stassen's plans beforehand, and that his implied "go-ahead" was a premeditated, if misguided, move to dispose of his vice president. As Peter Lyon observed, it was the classic Eisenhower formula, "to allow some other to loose a trial balloon and then, if it were shot down in flames, to turn, palms up spread and jaw unhinged, the picture of wondering innocence."[41]

After his meeting with the president, Stassen walked back to the Executive Office Building and asked for an appointment to see Richard Nixon, whom he wanted, incredibly, to consider "taking the initiative in the nomination" of Herter. He was told to come back on Monday morning, July 23. Stassen obligingly deferred his press conference while Nixon busily lined up further support. Instead, he attempted to see GOP chairman Leonard Hall and was told that the chairman would not be available until the 24th. Stassen called Governor Herter. Herter repeated what he had already told Stassen; he was not a candidate, but if the nomination was offered to him, he was, naturally, willing to do his duty. In other words, Stassen was on his own, but would not be undercut by Herter.

On Monday morning Stassen walked into Nixon's office only to be told that the vice president was "engaged" and it was not clear when he would be available. Returning to his office Stassen fired off a letter to Nixon explaining his decision to support Herter, and then he held a press conference.[42] To the few reporters who bothered to attend (there had been rumors of a coup attempt against Nixon, but Stassen's name had not been connected with it) the disarmament adviser repeated what he had told the president: Nixon would cost at least six percent of the vote; Herter would reassure anti–Nixon voters and should be nominated; and, finally, he, Stassen, would not accept the vice presidential nomination.[43]

Stassen's selection of Herter was not, as Stephen Ambrose claims, "one of the worst possible choices Stassen could have made." While Ambrose cites Herter's age of sixty-one and arthritis,[44] the *New York Times*, calling Herter a "persuasive politician," dismissed the latter: "The arthritis can be painful at times, but the condition is not progressive. His personal physician has assured him he can tackle any assignment." The *Times* ignored the former.[45]

Independent voters were more concerned about Nixon's anticommunism than about Herter's liabilities. Adolph Toigo, a Republican pollster who was a veteran of the 1952 Eisenhower-Nixon campaign, reported on August 17 that all potential running mates were a weight on Eisenhower's stratospheric popularity ratings, but Herter less so than Nixon.[46]

During his press conference, when asked, "Did you inform Governor Herter of your intention to make this announcement?" Stassen replied evasively: "I intend to confer with Governor Herter within the next few days." Actually, he had tried to contact Herter that morning, but the governor was watching a golf tournament and could not be reached. When chased down by reporters, Herter disingenuously claimed "complete surprise" at Stassen's statement, which was patently false given their conversations and the Stassen-Herter, Jr., discussions.[47]

The next morning, as Stassen was busily opening an Eisenhower-Herter headquarters at 1610 K Street, NW, in Washington, D.C., Robert Matteson wrote a memorandum urging his boss to "Keep Herter informed of the facts so he doesn't get cold feet from pressure from Hall, Dewey, etc."[48] In fact, Herter's feet on the 24th were already frozen, particularly after Sherman Adams told him "that, in making his future plans, he could take into account the fact that he would be given favorable consideration for a position of responsibility in the State Department,"[49] a veiled threat that Herter, whose longing for a foreign affairs position was intense, took seriously.

Obediently, Herter authorized Hall to brag to the press that, "Governor Christian Herter of Massachusetts telephoned me this morning to say that he would consider it a 'privilege' to nominate Dick Nixon at the Republican National Convention in San Francisco." As James Reston wryly observed, Stassen's effort had turned into the "deadliest boomerang in recent American political history."[50]

"It has now ... become clear," the *New York Times* editorialized the next day, "that Mr. Stassen did not consult or sound out Governor Herter on his project."[51] Certainly Herter had given this impression, which was absurd. Stassen, aware that any move to replace Nixon would have to take on the aspect of a draft, had allowed Herter to keep his distance; now, Stassen was in effect double-crossed. From this moment it seems that Stassen knew his effort was doomed. Greeted with the Herter-Hall announcement, Stassen practically begged Eisenhower to get them both off the hook, saying that he would abandon his anti–Nixon campaign if the president asked him to do so.[52] The president refused the bait, and instead during a meeting with Stassen on July 30 at Gettysburg announced he was providing a four-week unpaid leave of absence to his disarmament director, to allow him to pursue what had now become a hopeless effort, benefiting only the Democrats.[53]

Since Stassen had ostensibly launched his effort at the behest of independent voters and ominous polls, he could not now simply throw up his hands and say he had been out-classed, although he apparently knew that was precisely what had happened. Lacking a presidential cease-and-desist order, he did the next best thing. On July 26, Stassen declared he would not press the matter until the results of a new poll, which he called a "re-evaluation," were available the first week of August. As it turned out, it was not completed until the convention opened. He never did release the results.[54] Stassen kept his hand in with an occasional dig at Nixon and a letter to convention delegates, but he was clearly aware of the futility of the effort.

In his memoirs Nixon claimed that Stassen kept up the fight to the very morning of August 22, the day the convention was to nominate the vice president. On that day, Nixon wrote, Stassen "produced a letter he planned to discuss with Eisenhower. It was an ultimatum addressed to Hall ... demanding that the nomination for Vice President be postponed until the next day. Adams told Stassen that he would see Eisenhower only if he agreed beforehand to second my nomination.... Stassen finally seemed to get the message and agreed to accept these terms."[55] This is, to say the least, unlikely, although Stephen Ambrose, Herbert Parmet, and Charles Alexander, among others, have virtually copied the tale verbatim, usually crediting the president, not Adams, with the demand that Stassen drop his campaign.[56]

It is not clear why the story has not undergone more scrutiny.[57] What is clear is that on the morning of August 17, just before Stassen left Washington, D.C., to go to San Francisco, where the convention would open August 20, he and Eisenhower discussed the vice presidency.[58] In a memorandum "confirming and supplementing our conference" Stassen acknowledged the "probability of the delegates to the Convention wishing to nominate Richard Nixon." Thus, at an "appropriate time in this event I will say something like this." Stassen proceeded to give a statement that closely resembled the one he actually delivered on August 22: "I am satisfied that the elected delegates to the Convention have concluded that Richard Nixon is the best available Vice Presidential nominee for 1956. I wholeheartedly accept that conclusion of the delegates of our Republican Party and do so in accordance with American and Republican tradition. I will give complete backing to the Eisenhower-Nixon ticket in November, and urge all those who believe as I did to do the same and to help in getting out the maximum vote for the re-election of our great President Dwight Eisenhower and for continued leadership of our nation on the path of a prosperous peace." Stassen was not quite ready to give up and expressed the hope that Nixon would "step aside." Still, Stassen was clearly ready to bow to the inevitable. Remaining noncommittal, Eisenhower told Stassen to keep Lucius Clay informed of his actions.[59]

Three days later, in San Francisco, Stassen had all but thrown in the towel. In another memorandum to the president, Stassen noted, "there has been no important change in the delegations toward a new Vice Presidential nominee, with the support for Richard Nixon held firm by Leonard Hall, Tom Dewey, William Knowland and a number of others." Stassen was still wary of Nixon, but was clearly willing to abandon his campaign should Eisenhower direct him to do so.[60] On August 22, Stassen walked down from his ninth-floor room at the St. Francis Hotel to Eisenhower's sixth-floor suite. It is unlikely Stassen put up much, if any, fuss about seconding Nixon's nomination.[61]

Quixotic though Stassen's effort had been, it had received tacit presidential approval; one stern phone call from Ike would have put an end to it. An unanswered question is whether Stassen was encouraged by Eisenhower or other presidential associates to undertake the effort in the first place. Publicly, he denied that he had received support in his campaign from any of the president's entourage.[62] Privately, he told Jay Cooke that "the White House" was behind the effort.[63]

Certainly the vice president thought so. As early as December 26, 1955, when Eisenhower had suggested that he accept a cabinet post rather than renomination, Nixon suspected a plot. "For the first time," he recalled, "I began to understand what was behind this conversation. Eisenhower's staff or his friends had evidently been sowing doubts in his mind, suggesting not only that I might lose if I ran on my own, but that I might be a drag on the ticket if I were his running mate again. It was hard not to feel that I was being set up."[64] In fact, he was not being set up, despite his feelings and despite Stassen's bragging. No link between Stassen and the White House concerning the dump Nixon movement can be uncovered.

Lacking a presidential order, Stassen's motivations were rooted in his own ambitions and his inability to listen to advice when it concerned his career. He knew that a Nixon replacement would have to be the object of a draft, and he knew nobody would draft him. He knew that in suggesting Herter nobody would go further and suggest Stassen, indeed, in his eagerness to deny any interest in the vice presidency, he went overboard and said on July 29 that he was foreclosing any interest in either the vice presidency or presidency "for ever and ever."[65] This overstatement notwithstanding, Stassen must have known that in 1960 Herter, who would be sixty-five and who was already arthritic, would not be in his way, whereas Nixon would if not disposed of. Matteson pleaded with him to put his ambitions aside; Stassen could not listen. He knew that his plans had been laughed at in Minnesota, and he had become a famous and successful governor. So too, now, would he overcome the odds.

When Eisenhower-Nixon were safely reelected in November, Matteson closed a letter to Stassen with a quotation from Psalm 37 that came probably less as a comfort to his boss (Stassen never needed comforting) than a confirmation of what he knew and how he perceived himself: "Though he fall, he shall not be utterly cast down; for the Lord upholdeth him with His hand."[66] Stassen failed to dump Nixon, but he did not feel defeated. Insofar as the abortive anti–Nixon move had an impact on him, it was to make him more fiercely determined to achieve an arms control treaty in 1957. That year, Stassen believed, would be the last chance for the U.S. and the Soviets to bring the arms spiral under control; and a Stassen treaty, he also knew, would be his last chance to win the praise which could still make him president.

21. "And then the heavens fell in..."

Harold Stassen was never a man to look backwards. His eyes were always on the future. As 1957 dawned Stassen was only 49 years old. In his public life he had excelled. He had been acclaimed as "the boy wonder" of American politics. Walter Lippmann had hailed him as "a recognized American leader high up on any list of those whom the country can and will count on." Arthur Krock observed that "Mr. Stassen to me is an inspiring American figure. He is bold and compassionate. He knows life's struggle and has conquered it." It must have crossed Stassen's mind that if he had been nominated for president and defeated Harry Truman in 1948, the one year when he had a real shot at the White House, he would just be completing what he truly believed would have been a successful presidency. Had Stassen been president he would have moved swiftly to strengthen the United Nations; after all, he was a key architect of that organization. He would have moved to achieve a disarmament agreement with the Soviet Union. Stassen believed with perfect faith that he would have been able to achieve that historic agreement. Certainly John Foster Dulles would not have been secretary of state. Dulles would never have been in a position to block Stassen's effort to achieve such an agreement. Had Stassen been elected president, he would have directly challenged his former supporter in the 1948 campaign, Senator Joseph McCarthy. Stassen believed that as president he could have derailed McCarthy's hate-filled anticommunist crusade. If he had been president, true to his own deeply held convictions, Stassen would have moved the country forward on the road to true racial equality and a truly effective civil rights bill. Had Stassen been elected, Richard Nixon, his one-time protégé, would most certainly not have been on the path to the presidency. Stassen had come to realize that with all of Nixon's outstanding qualities, there was a flaw in him that went to the heart of his character. On January 20, 1957, Dwight D. Eisenhower would take the oath of office for the second time. Stassen believed that Eisenhower had been an outstanding leader. He had made Stassen a part of his team. Stassen was grateful that he had had the opportunity to make a difference for the good in a troubled world. Despite his service to Eisenhower, in the back of his mind, Stassen must have considered what might have been if only he had been inaugurated on January 20, 1949.

The year 1956, which had brought Stassen a frustrating arms control deadlock and the Herter campaign, was not through torturing him after Eisenhower's reelection. On December 13 the disarmament adviser told reporters in Washington that the U.S. was prepared to explore the proposal by Nicolai Bulganin, contained in a letter to Eisenhower, to reduce troop levels in central Europe.[1] This was the most respectful statement that the administration had yet made about Bulganin's November 17 letter; still, it was an innocuous comment. In

183

February Stassen had within the administration proposed, and the president had not rejected, a limitation on U.S. and Soviet force levels to 2.5 million men as part of a seven-point arms reduction package. Dulles and Arthur Radford had howled with protest, to little effect. Now, however, Dulles claimed that Stassen's press briefing undercut his authority, since at that moment Dulles, secretary of defense Charles Wilson and secretary of the treasury George Humphrey were attending a NATO meeting in Paris where Dulles was calling for increased pressure for a united Germany.[2]

Eisenhower agreed. In much the same way that his view of Nixon was ambiguous, so too was his opinion of Stassen. He valued Stassen's energy, creativity and, often, political acumen. Much as Eisenhower used Nixon as a campaign hatchet man, as recently as two months before, he had Stassen respond to Stevenson's call for a nuclear test ban.[3] Later, he would defend Stassen against Dulles.[4] Yet Ike was also suspicious of a man he regarded as a "professional politician," a term of disdain which could not be applied to the secretary of state. Eisenhower sided with Dulles, bluntly telling Stassen that Dulles was his superior. This the secretary regarded as an inadequate response. On February 5 the president, at Dulles' urging, went further and informed Stassen that the disarmament office would be moved from the White House to the State Department, where he would more directly answer to Dulles. Stassen would retain the title of special assistant to the president, but would not be permitted to attend cabinet and NSC meetings unless Dulles deemed it appropriate. The transfer would be announced March 1.[5]

Stassen was realistic enough to know his days in the administration were numbered and immediately began to put into effect his contingency plan of running for governor of Pennsylvania. He leaked his intention to James Reston, and the *New York Times* on February 14 announced that Stassen "has told President Eisenhower of his plan to resign," citing "friends of Mr. Stassen."[6] The next day Earl Mazo bluntly, but accurately, shot down Stassen's trial balloon with an unambiguously titled article, "No Chance Is Seen for Stassen in Pa."[7] Someone at the State Department furthered the humiliation by leaking Stassen's demotion to the *Washington Post* on February 24. The White House immediately denied the story and continued to deny it right up to the afternoon before the announcement was made on March 1.[8]

Coming as it did a mere eighteen days before the U.S. Disarmament Subcommittee was to re-convene in London, the move severely undercut Stassen's position and sent a disappointing signal to arms control advocates. As the *Washington Post* observed, the prospect that disarmament efforts "may now be buried and forgotten in another State Department bureau will be dismaying to the world."[9] "Seldom has an Ambassador gone on a peaceful mission with so many strikes against him," correspondent Joseph Harsh said. "His quest is almost a hopeless one."[10] Yet Stassen thrived on hopeless quests, and in the next two months nearly achieved his longed-for arms treaty.

Weakened though his position was, Stassen held some aces. First, the Soviets genuinely feared a rearmed Germany and Britain's continued development of atomic weapons. Second, world public opinion was becoming more sensitive to the dangers of nuclear fallout, and Eisenhower was sensitive to the dangers of adverse public opinion. Finally, Dulles, Radford and Strauss underestimated Stassen's determination to succeed.

In June 1954 Eisenhower had agreed to an interdepartmental recommendation that the U.S. not agree to a test moratorium without a comprehensive disarmament treaty. He reiterated this policy in a February 1955 press conference when he rejected a call by the Communist World Peace Council for an immediate test ban. Reviewing Stassen's June 1955 arms control policy report, Eisenhower agreed that a moratorium on H-bomb testing "would not be in the interest of the U.S. and should not be agreed to except as part of a comprehensive safeguard disarmament agreement."[11] When Adlai Stevenson called for a test ban in 1956, Ike dismissed it as a "theatrical national gesture."[12]

But the president began to have doubts after the election. Robert Divine has noted that, while the sense of danger in the world after Hungary and Suez doomed the test ban in 1956, by early 1957 concern with nuclear fallout had generated a new political climate. "The outcry over radiation led to a reconsideration of American policy on nuclear testing.... President Eisenhower, disturbed by the fallout problem, began to place greater weight on the need to reassure world opinion than on the military's pleas for continued testing."

Dulles' position on a test ban moratorium was complex. In May 1954 he had recommended a halt in nuclear testing provided the U.S. could be assured that a recent series of tests had guaranteed a firm lead over Soviet technology and that the moratorium could be effectively policed. Soon afterward he again opposed a test ban treaty, convinced by Radford and Strauss that it would severely damage weapons development, be impossible to monitor, and lessen pressure on the Soviet Union to withdraw from East Germany.[13] But by early 1957 Dulles began to wonder if a test ban treaty was not desirable after all. Alarmed over Soviet propaganda victories, he began to lower his opposition to a test ban.

Neither the president nor the secretary of state was eager for a test ban moratorium, but signs of flexibility began to creep into their discussions within the administration. Thus, by the spring of 1957 only Strauss and the Pentagon were firmly in favor of continued testing.[14]

Since assuming his arms control post, Stassen had agreed that a test ban should come only as part of a definite disarmament package. His May 26, 1955, *Report* envisioned a test ban taking effect at "the same fixed date the arms race is stopped" (i.e., after the cessation of nuclear production and the establishment of a rigid system of control).[15] But Stassen had always been flexible; and now he was desperate. A Stassen arms treaty would revive his reputation and his presidential aspirations. Early in March, he suddenly seized upon a long-shot chance at success.

Bulganin's November 17, 1956, letter to Eisenhower proposing a variety of arms control measures had at the time been haughtily dismissed by the administration, including Stassen, as a propaganda ploy of the meanest sort, intended to distract attention from the Soviet oppression in Hungary. But now Stassen considered the letter again. In addition to proposals for troop cutbacks, the letter advocated an immediate ban on testing, production, and use of nuclear weapons, as well as the destruction of nuclear stockpiles. Also, the letter accepted an earlier Stassen proposal to allow aerial inspection in preselected zones, providing a "keyhole" look at military preparations.[16] Driven by his personal ambition Stassen looked at the letter in a more constructive vein.

His second look was perceptive. His first battle as arms control adviser had been to bring U.S. proposals up-to-date with contemporary arms realities, changing the focus from disarmament to arms limitation. Now he began to wonder if he had not gone far enough. The chief difference between the Bulganin proposal and the American position was the timing of a test moratorium. The Soviets wanted a test ban to come first, in conjunction with aerial zone inspection; the U.S. wanted it to come third, after inspection mechanisms and the reduction, or perhaps control, of existing stockpiles.[17] Stassen now believed that the U.S. position, much as its pre–1955 proposals, sacrificed realistic goals for idealistic schemes. A test ban would slow the arms race; moreover, it was apparently obtainable. That Stassen's impatience was fueled by his presidential ambitions made his ideas no less worthy.

To succeed, Stassen needed to overcome or circumvent the anti-treaty bias of the AEC, the Pentagon and to some extent the State Department; convince the entire administration that a separate test ban treaty, detached from larger arms limitation issues, was desirable; convince the Soviets to accept more comprehensive aerial inspection zones; and convince the allies, including the British and French, that a test ban and an aerial inspection zone over Europe would be in their interest.

That he came tantalizingly close to achieving a treaty with the Soviets is largely attributable to the fact that his opponents within the administration were caught napping. Radford and Strauss appear to have simply not considered that Stassen, weakened by the Herter campaign and his demotion and facing a defensive and discredited post–Hungarian invasion Soviet Union, could possibly succeed in achieving an arms agreement. Dulles, unsure exactly what he thought about a test ban, and smugly secure in his role as chief foreign policy adviser now that the disarmament adviser was clearly his subordinate, dropped his guard. For both these reasons, Dulles permitted Stassen to present to Eisenhower on March 6 a proposal for the U.S. arms control position for the upcoming London talks.

At this meeting Stassen again discussed his proposal for aerial inspection, beginning with zones of Europe and the Bering Straits, to be gradually enlarged to the Soviet Union and combined with ground inspection. All future production of fissionable materials would then be used or stockpiled exclusively for non-weapons purposes under international supervision, followed by the reduction of nuclear stockpiles. Once production was controlled, the U.S. would then seek to "limit, and ultimately to eliminate, all nuclear test explosions." Pending this comprehensive test ban, the U.S. would be "willing to work out promptly methods for advance notice and registration of all nuclear tests ... and to provide for limited international observations of such tests." The U.S. would also seek reductions in armed forces' manpower.

Eisenhower accepted Stassen's recommendations, but insisted that a proposal for a European inspection zone would have to come from the Europeans. Seemingly as an afterthought, Stassen asked for permission to explore Soviet intentions in private bilateral discussions, presenting ideas "for illustrative purposes on a personal basis," not as official positions for the U.S. government. This Eisenhower agreed to, with Dulles, Radford and Strauss in tacit acceptance; it was the most fateful decision of the March 6 meeting.[18]

The day before the London talks were formally to commence, the U.S. and Soviet delegations held a luncheon. By coincidence, Robert Matteson was seated at the table next to Igor Usachev of the Soviet contingent. Matteson was quick to note how Usachev turned the discussion to "shop talk" and the constructive tone of his remarks. Usachev emphasized that the two superpowers were moving closer in their respective positions and hinted that agreement could be reached on at least a few points of their separate comprehensive proposals even if an entire disarmament framework could not be agreed to. He wondered why the weapons-rich U.S. would not agree to an immediate test ban, and called attention to the fact that Bulganin's November 17 letter moved the two countries closer together on aerial inspection.[19]

Usachev, of course, knew perfectly well why the U.S. was reluctant to pursue an immediate comprehensive test ban, it was for the same reason the USSR desired such a moratorium, the continuing development of nuclear capability by the British. Yet a test ban seemed the most likely area of agreement, and Stassen thus began an attempt to steamroll a moratorium over the allies as well as over Radford and Strauss. His method was to stretch to the breaking point his authorization to advance "personal" ideas to the Soviets.

On March 28 Stassen asked of the subcommittee his "personal" question about the possibility of achieving some sort of "limit" to nuclear tests prior to the cessation of all nuclear tests under adequate safeguards as defined by the U.S., meaning intensive ground and aerial inspection. He had no explicit authority to seek such a measure; but he did have the authority to present "personal" ideas. No one seemed to object.

On April 8 he presented further "personal" ideas concerning reductions in conventional weapons and inspection zones. This was followed up with further "non-official" ideas presented privately to the Soviets on April 9. Stassen's volubility began to have effect. On April 10 the chief of the USSR delegation, Ambassador Valerin Zorin, told Stassen the Soviets were giving "serious attention" to his proposals.[20]

By the time of the April recess Stassen, barely a month earlier discredited and in a seemingly hopeless position, had fundamentally changed the prospects for a nuclear weapons treaty. Robert Matteson has descriptively recalled what had happened: "The sheer boldness and imaginativeness of his approach had left Stassen's opposition flat-footed and almost speechless. In one month's time, Stassen had written into the official UN record to be interpreted as U.S. policy, personal ideas which went beyond anything authorized as U.S. policy. And governments were responding to the ideas as if they were U.S. policy. He was weaving draft treaty language into the verbatim record that had never been seen or discussed by the President and Secretary of State."[21] Prior to the Easter recess the Soviet delegation had been cautious, apparently unsure whether Stassen was advancing genuine proposals or simply playing them for fools. By the time the subcommittee reconvened on April 25 they decided that Stassen was serious, and they were ready to do business.

On April 26, during a bilateral session requested by the Soviets the previous day, Ambassador Zorin handed Stassen a new position paper. The paper emphasized that a treaty was unthinkable without both a cessation of nuclear tests and a declaration not to use nuclear weapons. This Stassen had already understood. The critical part of the paper was a call for an inspection zone even larger than the one the U.S. had proposed, covering a more comprehensive region of the Soviet Union, from Lake Baikol to the Bering Straits. Stassen was simply beside himself with joy.[22]

The Soviets formally introduced their proposals to the full subcommittee on April 30. Dulles immediately demanded to know what was going on. Stassen responded with a purposely long and complicated three-part cable.[23] For help in trying to figure out what he had said, the State Department could not even look to Stassen's own staff. Those officials who remained in Washington were, as late as May 1, gravely discussing whether the U.S. should pursue a test ban. Stassen should have kept in better contact with his office. On the same day that he was beside himself with joy over the Soviet proposal for an expanded aerial inspection zone, Colonel Thomas Abbott, the disarmament official "loaned" from the Defense Department, warned that the Pentagon had never agreed to an aerial inspection plan and would, presumably, oppose such a treaty provision.[24]

But by early May Stassen probably would not have listened to any warnings; by then, the dark side of his energy and creativity had taken over. In combination with his blindness to obstacles, his overwhelming self-confidence, and his inability to take counsel when the advice was to be cautious, his native intelligence had been overtaken by his native ambition.

On May 25, at the White House Stassen lectured the president, Dulles, Radford, Strauss, deputy secretary of defense Donald Quarles, and national security adviser Robert Cutler on the desirability of a temporary test ban agreement with the Soviets as the first phase of a comprehensive agreement. This was a complete shift in the U.S. position. But Eisenhower, catching Stassen's enthusiasm, approved. Fatally, he also approved of Stassen's presenting his ideas to the Soviets in the form of an "informal memorandum," which would reflect unofficial suggestions, not official U.S. proposals, as a means of testing Soviet intentions.

Ike sternly instructed Stassen to clear his unofficial ideas with the NATO allies before turning them over to the Russians. He also reminded Stassen that European inspection zones would have to be initiated by the Europeans. Finally, the proposed U.S. treaty was an all-or-nothing proposition; no treaty would be accepted that dealt with only part of the larger disarmament picture.[25] There is no record of the extent, if any, to which Dulles, Radford and Strauss objected to the change in negotiating positions and to the authority given to Stassen. Very likely they assumed the NATO allies would shoot down the whole idea, since a test ban would presumably thwart the nuclear ambitions of Britain and France.

Stassen knew this, too. When he presented the ideas to NATO on May 28, he presented his package in its entirety: A temporary test ban as a first step, followed by a limited aerial inspection system with ground inspection, exchange of blueprints, reduction of armaments and manpower and a cutoff of fissionable material production.

There was no immediate objection, and the NATO members respectfully indicated that they would ask their governments if they wished to suggest to the Disarmament Subcommittee a European inspection zone as part of a first disarmament step. Stassen had now carried out the letter of his instructions from Eisenhower to "consult" with the allies; now he hurried back to London to get an agreement before the allies could formally reject the proposal. That NATO had not rejected the idea out of hand is probably attributable to the fact that Stassen did not mention that he was going to indicate to the Soviets that agreement on any *one* issue might be reached apart from the others. Simply put, NATO had no idea Stassen was so close to an agreement.[26]

Back in London Stassen began the final phase of his arms control railroading. On May 30 he contacted Matteson and U.S. ambassador Amos Peaslee and told them, and only them, that he was going to give the Soviets an informal memorandum. He did not say on what or when, although Matteson later learned that Stassen had contacted Zorin on May 28 and requested a bilateral meeting on the 31st.

Stassen then went back to his room at the Westbury Hotel and dictated his "informal memorandum" to the Soviets. The text of the memorandum failed to make clear that the ideas presented were Stassen's — not official U.S. government proposals. On the contrary, the opening paragraph implies that it was an official government document:

> The Chairman of the U.S. Delegation is pleased to inform the Chairman of the U.S.S.R. Delegation that following a recent thorough review by the U.S. Government of the various questions and proposals in relationship to disarmament and decisions by President Eisenhower during the recent recess of the Sub-Committee, the U.S. Delegation is authorized to resume negotiations in an endeavor to conclude a partial agreement for a sound safe-guarded first step in disarmament. In these resumed negotiations the U.S. Delegation is further authorized to meet half-way on a reasonable basis the positions and proposals of the other members of the Sub-Committee including the U.S.S.R.

The paper then casually hints at the unofficial nature of the proposals: "The Chairman of the U.S. Delegation therefore in this first substantive discussion since the recess presents this informal memorandum to the Chairman of the U.S.S.R. Delegation and engages in this discussion between the two delegations."

The paper covered the gamut of arms control issues, including reductions of manpower and strategic nuclear delivery systems. Armaments would be placed in depots under international supervision. On the key issues of nuclear tests and aerial inspection zones, Stassen's proposals were indeed efforts to meet the Soviets half-way: "The United States Delegation is prepared to favorably consider the acceptance, within a partial agreement, of the U.S.S.R. proposal for a temporary cessation of nuclear tests, provided the U.S.S.R. is prepared to favorably consider the acceptance of the U.S. proposal for the cessation of the manufacture of fissionable material for nuclear weapons, both reached through detailed arrangements...."

Thus far, Stassen's paper was safely within U.S. policy as cleared by the President and the NSC. On page eight of the sixteen-page memorandum, however, Stassen began skating on thin ice:

> "[I]t is recognized that there are some disadvantages in waiting for the installation of an inspection system, after the conclusion of a partial disarmament treaty before there is a cessation of testing. Therefore, for this part of a partial agreement the United States Delegation would be prepared to favorably consider the cessation of all nuclear testing by all parties for an initial ten-month period, commencing immediately upon the effective date of the partial agreement, combined with the commitment of the parties to cooperate in the design and installation and maintenance of an inspection system."

Stassen was moving dangerously away from the U.S. demand that strict verification measures be in place *before* a test ban. Most dangerously, with his mention of "partial disarmament treaty" he was implying that a test ban treaty could be achieved separate from a treaty dealing with other relevant issues, including force levels and international control of fissionable materials. In fact, Stassen had been expressly told at the May 25 White House meeting that the U.S. position was one inseparable package, with every proposal conditioned on the acceptance of every other proposal.

Moreover, in a move guaranteed to evoke the wrath of the British, French and Germans, Stassen indicated that the U.S. was willing to cooperate in the establishment of initial zones of aerial and ground inspection in both a European-Russian zone and a U.S.-Canada-USSR zone, without defining the exact boundaries. In fact, the May 25 White House meeting had expressly instructed Stassen to *not* propose a European zone unless the Europeans themselves made the proposal. Stassen was perhaps drawing an exegetical distinction between presenting ideas informally to the Soviets in a private bilateral session and formally to the official Subcommittee.[27] Clearly, he was attempting to railroad an arms treaty, building the treaty's momentum to the point where it would be unstoppable by any of his opponents.

Stassen finished the final version of the paper at 10:30 P.M. and handed it to his assistant Ed Larson, who took it back to the U.S. office where secretaries worked until two in the morning typing it and running off copies. Seven hours later Stassen appeared at the regular morning meeting of the U.S. delegation and distributed copies of the memorandum to the members. He announced that he was going to give the paper to the Soviets at an 11:00 A.M. bilateral meeting and asked for comments.

The stunned members had time to do little more than skim the contents of the sixteen-page document, but to a man the delegation opposed giving it to the Soviets without first presenting the document to the allies, let alone the U.S. government. When the meeting broke up Stassen made arrangements for the memorandum to be hand-carried to the Western members of the subcommittee. Incredibly, he did *not* at the same time have it cabled to the U.S. State Department, which for the moment had no clue what was about to take place.[28]

Stassen, accompanied by Matteson and four other members of the U.S. delegation, then went to the residence of the U.S. ambassador in London, where the bilateral meeting would be held. Stassen then spent the next hour reading into the record his memorandum. At noon the meeting recessed for lunch. "And then," Robert Matteson recalled in his auto-biography, "the heavens fell in."[29]

Both delegations repaired to the Soviet embassy for lunch. Minutes after they arrived, a call came through for Stassen from a furious Ambassador Arthur Noble, a member of the UK delegation. Noble demanded that Stassen come to the British embassy at once. Stassen complied, taking with him Robert Matteson, to whom he wryly observed, "Well, I'd better take my beating in silence," and remarked that he expected a stern lecture. "Stassen wasn't disappointed," Matteson wrote. "Noble wanted to see Stassen alone. For one hour Stassen sat and listened to Noble's charge that Stassen had violated the understanding with the Western allies that the U.S. would not reveal the new U.S. decisions until they had been thoroughly discussed with the allies."[30]

A seething Harold Macmillan sat down and wrote a blistering cable to Eisenhower: "I would have hoped that we could have examined together the possible consequences of these proposals before they were put forward." He predicted that there would be widespread hos-tility and cynicism throughout the West, based on the suspicion that the U.S. was trying to maintain a world dominated by "two great nuclear powers"; that European nations were being pressured to sign away their right to defend themselves; that the UK would be pre-vented from acquiring a nuclear capability.[31] The French howled about a "crisis worse than Suez." Eisenhower at the time was aboard the aircraft carrier *Saratoga* for a three-day cruise to review naval maneuvers. With him was Arthur Larson, who reported that Dulles was "in a fine fury," although the President was more calm.[32]

Back in London, Stassen finally sent a copy of his memorandum to the State Depart-ment and then returned to the bilateral meeting after the lunch recess, apparently calm and self-assured. He finished reading the memorandum into the record. "I want to make a very important statement," Stassen said as he concluded. He then emphasized that he was pre-senting his memorandum "informally" because it had not been cleared with the U.S. gov-ernment or Western allies. If the Soviets were bewildered by this statement, they gave no indication; Instead, Zorin asked if the proposals in the memorandum were to be taken as a single proposal, or whether agreement could be reached on individual items. Stassen, clinging resolutely to his original intention, indicated that the U.S. would consider the sep-arability of the proposals.[33]

If nothing else, the May 31 bilateral meeting awoke the slow-witted Radford and Strauss to the fact that people were talking about a test ban, a proposal they found horrifying. Thus began a two-pronged attack, with Radford and Strauss working on the still test-ban-friendly Eisenhower, and Dulles, who had not decided that a test ban wasn't worth the trouble of provoking the allies, reigning in Stassen.

On June 24 Strauss marched a team of scientists led by Ernest O. Lawrence and Edward Teller into the Oval Office, where they proceeded to explain to a bewildered Eisenhower that the U.S. with more testing could develop a "clean" atomic bomb. This device, free of nuclear fallout, could obliterate specific targets but spare general populations, making it a more credible weapon. Even at this late date the president could have built on Stassen's efforts by working out a compromise with the allies. Instead, at a press conference the next day Ike backed away from his prior support, expressed as recently as six days before,[34] for a separate test ban, falling back on the traditional U.S. position that such a treaty would have to be part of a comprehensive disarmament effort.[35]

In his memoirs, the president stated that a test ban treaty was not possible anyway, charging that the Soviet response to Stassen's May 31 memorandum "largely negated the suggestions it contained.... The Soviet response made it clear that the premises on which the Stassen memorandum had been submitted, i.e., that the Soviets would be genuinely interested in progressive disarmament and protection against 'fourth country' nuclear capabilities, were not valid."[36]

This is simply wrong. The Soviet response clearly indicates that on the central issue of a test moratorium, the U.S. and Soviet positions were not far apart. The chief difference between the two positions was in the length of the test ban. The Soviets desired a two-year to three-year ban, the Americans a ten-month to twelve-month moratorium. On the issue of international control, the Soviets made the following tantalizing statement:

> Taking into account the desire, contained in the American memorandum, for international control over the observance of an agreement on the cessation of nuclear weapons tests, the Soviet Government expresses its readiness to establish such control. This purpose would be served by establishing, on a basis of reciprocity, control posts in the territories of the Soviet Union, the United States, the United Kingdom, and in the area of the Pacific Ocean to observe the fulfillment by States of commitments relating to the cessation of atomic and hydrogen weapons tests.[37]

This was in response to the following statement in Stassen's memorandum: "In an agreement all signators should specifically recognize the essential requirement of an effective inspection system to verify and guarantee in the case of all states alike the fulfillment and observance of each commitment, and each signator should undertake to cooperate in the thorough reciprocal installation and maintenance of such inspection."[38]

The efficacy of inspection stations would have depended upon their number and location; yet the Soviets were clearly not rejecting the idea out of hand. While Eisenhower, in a reversal, had on May 10, 1955, rejected comprehensive on-site inspection. ("Are we ready to open up every one of our factories, every place where something might be going on that could be inimical to the interest of somebody else?" the president had asked rhetorically.[39]) The viability of scientific stations to monitor nuclear explosions remained to be fully explored.[40]

Dulles, meanwhile, was busily making hash of Harold Stassen, and in the process making the United States government look ridiculous. On June 4 he cabled Stassen that since he had not been authorized to give the informal memorandum, which Stassen now began calling a "talking paper" to the Soviets, he was to go to the Russians and ask to have it back. "You will notify Mr. Zorin at the earliest possible moment that the memorandum you submitted to him was not only informal and unofficial, but had no approval in its submitted form, either by the President or the State Department, and that there are some aspects of the memorandum to which this government cannot agree at this moment. Therefore, you will request that Mr. Zorin return the memorandum."[41] Stassen meekly went to the Soviet embassy and requested that Zorin return the paper. A surprised Zorin explained that he had already sent it to Moscow.

Dulles responded by ordering Stassen to return to Washington. On June 7, when the Soviets presented their response to Stassen's informal memorandum/talking points, the disarmament adviser was forced to call Dulles and ask if he could accept a response to a proposal that had not been made. Dulles said yes, but to make sure there was no misunderstanding. He ordered Stassen to send a cable to Zorin explaining that Stassen's paper was not to be viewed as a communication between governments.[42]

Zorin responded on June 16, expressing "perplexity" and complaining bitterly that movement toward a treaty had been abruptly thwarted by the U.S. "After both sides have exerted certain efforts in searching for the bringing closer together of the positions of the United States and the U.S.S.R. on disarmament questions," Zorin complained, "the American side suddenly declares the United States memorandum of May 31 as being 'non-existent.'"[43]

When Stassen returned to Washington he received a sound verbal thrashing from Dulles on June 11. He was not fired, apparently because Dulles felt that such a move would harm Konrad Adenauer's chances in the upcoming German elections; instead, Dulles assigned his assistant Julius Holmes to accompany Stassen back to London, in effect to baby-sit him. "Should there be differences of opinion between you and him with respect to the handling of disarmament matters with NATO, the difference will be referred here to the Department for decision before there is any action," Dulles snapped. He added, "I have told Mr. Holmes that he, like you, is free to telegraph me directly through the Embassy if there should be, in his opinion, any occasion for this."[44] Holmes later told Robert Matteson that Dulles was surprised Stassen did not immediately quit.[45]

It is, in fact, surprising. The abuse Stassen was receiving from the secretary of state was almost matched, publicly, by Eisenhower, who in a June 19 press conference insisted that while Stassen had not been reprimanded, "we cannot allow anyone to stray off the path one single iota, taking any chances of it and that is the reason we have them back so much to talk to him about such things."[46] Ike's syntax was typically confused, but his meaning was clear — Stassen was not a proper team player.

On July 28 Dulles himself arrived in London to take over the negotiations. Demanding a complete disarmament package, he got nowhere. On August 27 the Soviets walked out of the talks. The chance for a test ban treaty in 1957 was lost. And whatever lingering hopes Stassen may have had for the presidency were doomed forever.[47]

22. Childe Harold

"Dulles wanted to fire you [after the May 31 bilateral]," Robert Matteson reflected to Stassen in July of 1957. "Every day that goes by he wishes that he had taken the bit in the teeth and done it then." Matteson then speculated that the secretary of state "is now waiting for you to step over the line he has drawn so that he can lower the boom. If you don't he will try to accomplish the same end in other ways."[1] Matteson hoped that Stassen would fight Dulles and continue to work for an arms treaty; for once, his boss was the more realistic. Stassen knew that he had to go.

The question was, to where? For almost three years Matteson had listened with horror as Stassen spoke with increasing regularity of running for governor of Pennsylvania. Word of Stassen's intentions began to spread, largely because Stassen was leaking the story to anyone who would listen. In late October Jay Cooke, a Republican National Committee member from Pennsylvania who had accompanied Stassen to the Soviet Union in 1947 and had been a major financial contributor to Stassen's 1948 and 1952 presidential campaigns, invited Matteson to Philadelphia. There Cooke, seconded by his wife, Hannah, pleaded with Matteson to talk Stassen out of a gubernatorial effort. "Jay said that you had no support at all from anyone that he knows of in Pennsylvania," Matteson reported to Stassen. "He wondered how you could even think of financing a campaign.... He said the *Philadelphia Inquirer* was going to murder you if you came in. I asked what he thought your chances would be in winning through an appeal to the people on the issues and he said that it would not be one chance in one million, but perhaps one chance in ten million."[2]

Unconvinced, Stassen resigned from the Eisenhower administration on February 14, announcing that same day his intention to seek the Republican nomination for governor of Pennsylvania.[3] On May 31 he was swamped in the Republican primary by Arthur T. McGonigle, a former pretzel manufacturer with no previous experience in politics.[4]

At the time he left government service Stassen was fifty years old, a time of reflection for most men. But Harold Stassen, for all his brilliance, was not reflective; for all his tendency to think of himself, he could not think about himself with the same dispassionate analysis that, in his better moments, he could bring to bear on substantive governmental issues. For the better part of his adult life he had been on a sort of mental automatic pilot. At an early age he had learned that he was riding an irresistible trajectory toward greatness; all of the major events in his early career seemed to confirm this. Against overwhelming odds he had succeeded at virtually everything he had attempted. At some point, at some level of consciousness, he ceased to wonder at his success. For Harold Stassen long odds did not matter, only determination. Incapable of dejection, he never suffered through a period of agonizing reappraisal. This protected him against the psychological effects of misfortune — depression, self-pity — but denied him the benefits that could have come from a serious re-evaluation of his direction, goals and tactics. Unlike Harry Truman or Franklin Roosevelt, he never emerged stronger from a calamity. His brilliant mind was ultimately a shallow one when the subject at hand was Harold Stassen. His view of himself was formed during a period of unusual success at an immature age and was never questioned thereafter by Stassen himself. Eisenhower's characterization of him as a mere "professional politician" was unfair. If Stassen thrived on popular acclaim, if he was sometimes blatantly opportunistic, he was also honest, supremely hardworking and, at least when it mattered most, sincere.

In the course of his career he was an anticommunist who avoided witch hunts, a liberal in conservative times, and, at his very best, a zealot in the pursuit of hopeless causes: the defeat of Joe McCarthy at the peak of his power; the well-being of labor unions at the time of Taft-Hartley; civil rights at the time of Strom Thurmond; the respectful attention toward nonaligned nations at the height of U.S. arrogance; U.S.–Soviet rapprochement at the time of John Foster Dulles.

Perhaps the strain of the relatively abrupt end of his presidential aspirations at a young age, after having been a rising star for over two decades, caused him more mental anguish than he could acknowledge even to himself. His quixotic campaigns beginning in 1959 for offices ranging from mayor of Philadelphia to president of the United States suggest a man desperate to appear relevant; an explanation more likely than his own assertion that he merely wanted to discuss and advance important issues. It is this pathetic bid to appear relevant that has made him appear to be a buffoon. For this reason his accomplishments, particularly his pioneering role in presidential campaign strategy, and his service in the Eisenhower administration have been forgotten.

Like Byron's Childe Harold, Stassen continued his quest as long as he was physically able, suppressing even to himself the "strange pangs" of "disappointed passion." He was more accurate than anyone could have dreamed when on May 21, having been utterly defeated for the Pennsylvania gubernatorial nomination, he said, "When God ends my life, that's when my career will end."[5]

Harold Stassen, 1958 (John F. Rothmann collection).

23. Into the Shadows: The Perennial Candidate

In the space of three short years Harold Stassen went from a major force in American politics to being humiliated, marginalized and ridiculed. The failure of the "Dump Nixon" movement in 1956 was a complete humiliation for Stassen. His defeat in the Republican primary for governor of Pennsylvania on May 20, 1958, by pretzel manufacturer Arthur R. McGonigle was decisive. McGonigle got 578,286 votes (54.52 percent), while Stassen received 344,043 votes (32.44 percent).

His defeat was to begin his slide into being marginalized as a political force. Stassen's defeat for mayor of Philadelphia on November 3, 1959, opened up the floodgates of ridicule. He was defeated by Richardson Dilworth, the incumbent mayor, who received 438,278 votes (65.6 percent) while Stassen received 229,818 votes (34.4 percent). As 1960 dawned, Stassen had been labeled by a term that would follow him for the rest of his life. He became known as the "perennial candidate." Stassen continued to take himself seriously and the media still viewed him as fodder for a good story.

On November 12, 1958, at 9:45 A.M., Stassen began a White House meeting with President Eisenhower. Stassen and Eisenhower spent about an hour together. The content of their conversation has never been revealed. What we do know is that when he emerged from the Oval Office, Stassen wanted to talk politics with waiting reporters: "There are a number of men who could lead our Republican Party to victory in 1960." Stassen proceeded to list "Ambassador [Henry Cabot] Lodge, Governor [Nelson] Rockefeller, Secretary [of Treasury] Bob Anderson, and Secretary [of the Interior] Fred Seaton." A reporter asked Stassen if he could think of any other potential candidate. Another reporter asked directly about Vice President Richard Nixon. Stassen replied firmly, "I think that this election of 1958 speaks for itself in that regard. I will be doing what I can to keep the way open for these four men."[1]

On November 14, Stassen was back in Pennsylvania and appeared on a television panel in Harrisburg. During that appearance, he fine-tuned his thoughts, which were reported as three clear points:

1. Nixon was "the principal architect of defeat" in 1958.
2. Nelson Rockefeller, suddenly alone among Stassen's four alternatives, was "the man the Republican Party should nominate in order to win."
3. Pennsylvania's seventy-odd vote delegation to the G.O.P. Convention in 1960 "should be led either by Senator-elect Hugh Scott or by Harold Edward Stassen."[2]

It was reported that a week later in Cleveland, Ohio, Stassen confided to "political reporters ... that he might run himself— not as a selfish matter, of course, but to help Rockefeller win the nomination, just as he had run in 1952 to help Eisenhower win it [the nomination]."[3] Reports of Stassen's activities all concluded that Stassen's real intent was to stop Nixon in 1960. President Eisenhower remained publicly silent, which only added fuel to the political speculation about 1960. In late 1959 Nixon's friend and political biographer, Earl Mazo, reported that, privately, "Eisenhower had telephoned Nixon the day after Stassen's visit [to the White House] to discuss the visit. The President emphatically absolved himself and the White House from any part of what Stassen said and did."[4]

Members of the White House staff were often bemused and amused by Stassen's conduct. E. Frederic Morrow, who was the administrative officer for special projects at the White House from 1955 to 1961, recounted an incident that took place on December 19, 1956. It typified the way in which Stassen was viewed:

> Yesterday I went down to National Airport with other members of the staff to see the Vice-President off on his trip to Hungary, where he is to make observations for the President and report back on the needs of the Hungarians and on the increased possibilities of admitting more of them as refugees than the quota now allows. It was a colorful sight at the airport as the dignitaries gathered. We stood on the ramp near the plane while photographers took their inevitable pictures, and at a crucial moment in the activities Governor Stassen emerged from the crowd, shouldered his way to the Vice-President, grabbed his hand and pumped it vigorously as he wished him well on his trip. Nixon's features did not change at all, and he accepted the wishes with a smile. To some of us in the crowd, however, this was an ironic moment. A short three months ago Stassen had done everything in his power to bring about Nixon's defeat at the Republican National Convention in San Francisco. Some wag in our crowd suggested that perhaps the Vice-President owed a deep debt of gratitude to Stassen for causing Republican delegates to stand together as one and nominate the Vice-President by acclamation. I can never cease to marvel at the gall — some call it courage — of Mr. Stassen. He refuses to be humbled![5]

Stassen had a limited role as 1960 began. Harrison Salisbury, the *New York Times* correspondent, could not help but reflect that had Stassen's efforts in 1957 to achieve an agreement with the Soviet Union worked out differently 1960 might have worked out very differently for Stassen. "With a dime's worth of luck and one clear pat from Eisenhower, he could have had a second shot at the presidency and elbowed Richard Nixon aside. Had he done so," Salisbury observed, "I think he would have beaten John Kennedy in 1960." Salisbury went on to make a point about the Republican Party and the role that Stassen had hoped to achieve in shaping the future of the GOP. Stassen "could have made the Republican Party the vehicle for progress and intelligent change instead of a swamp of opportunism and recurrent know-nothingism under Goldwater, Nixon and Reagan. Stassen would have made it the party of Willkie, Vandenberg, Warren"[6] and other liberal Republicans. By 1960 Stassen's ability to influence the course of the Republican Party had faded to virtually nothing.

Stassen did win one election in 1960. He was elected as one of Pennsylvania's delegates to the national convention to be held in Chicago. He was still determined to prevent Nixon's nomination. On May 25, 1960, Stassen made a bold prediction. He stated that if Nixon was nominated he would carry only five states. Those states, Stassen declared, were Maine, Vermont, New Hampshire, Indiana and Arizona.[7]

When the Pennsylvania delegation met to determine its course of action Stassen was clear about his position. Hugh Scott, elected to the Senate in 1958, was a former Republican national chairman. He remembered Stassen's role and continuing maneuvers:

> Nixon had won ninety-eight percent of the vote in the April 26 preference primary, so there was no shadow of a question where the overwhelming majority of our seventy delegates stood. But

there was considerable question as to who would lead them. I was elected chairman, over State Senate President M. Harvey Taylor, by a vote of 46 to 22.

On the question of endorsements, a Nixon-Scott slate was approved with only one, highly predictable, dissent. It came from Harold E. Stassen, who was one of the Philadelphia delegates and was still on the "dump Nixon" trail he tried to blaze in 1956. He maintained the endorsement should be delayed until after California's June 7 primary so he might have a chance to "adjust" his convictions in the light of the vote in Nixon's home state. In that primary, 1.5 million Republicans voted for a slate pledged to Nixon.

"It's about time somebody clarified the situation," I said with considerable understatement. "I am honored by the resolution endorsing me for Vice President. But I want to make it clear it will be received only as an honor."

Turning directly to Stassen, I continued: "If you want to repudiate the Vice President, this is the time to do it. I suggest we endorse him now." We did, and Stassen stood, as is his wont, entirely alone.

The meeting was barely over before Stassen made public a letter to the sixty-nine other Pennsylvania delegates which declared that Nixon could not win as a Presidential candidate and urged support for any one of four other candidates: Rockefeller, United Nations Ambassador Henry Cabot Lodge, Secretary of the Treasury Robert B. Anderson, or Interior Secretary Fred Seaton.[8]

On July 27, 1960 delegation Chair Hugh Scott announced to the convention that Pennsylvania cast all 70 votes for Richard M. Nixon.[9] Nixon was unanimously nominated on the first ballot. The humiliation of Harold Stassen in 1960 was complete.

1963

Shortly after his election as president of the American Baptist Convention, Stassen demonstrated his active faith and belief in civil rights and social justice by joining the March on Washington led by the Reverend Martin Luther King, Jr. Stassen was deeply moved when, without knowing that they too would be present, he met his own children, Kathleen and Glen, during the march. The Reverend King chose to join the American Baptist Convention in large measure due to Stassen's presence and efforts on behalf of civil rights. Dr. J. Lester Hamish, who served as convention president at the 58th annual meeting of the American Baptist Convention held in San Francisco in May 1965, affirmed the pro-civil rights activism of the convention, noting, "We sent people to participate [in civil rights demonstrations] because we felt we had a mandate from our membership."[10] On May 21 the convention honored Stassen for his leadership "in the drafting and signing of the charter of the United Nations."[11] It was Stassen's active expression of his faith in his public, private and religious life that earned him the respect and admiration of the American Baptist Convention.

1964

In 1964, asked about Stassen's potential presidential ambitions, Charles H. Percy remarked, "The principal problem of Harold Stassen [is] that someone early told him that he should be President and he believed it."[12]

On Sunday August 18, 1963, a Gallup poll was released with the standings of five men who were considered to be potential nominees for the Republican Party in 1964. Gallup reported, "A new name added to the list is former Governor of Minnesota Harold Stassen, who received five percent of the vote of Republicans."[13] It may have been that poll, coupled with the tragic assassination of President John F. Kennedy on November 22, 1963, that triggered Stassen's decision to seek the Republican nomination for president in 1964.

On December 26, 1963, it was reported that Stassen was "considering running for the Republican Presidential nomination next year at the urging of former President Dwight D. Eisenhower."[14] Stassen, appearing in Wichita, Kansas, several days later, said that based on Eisenhower's urging he was "testing the extent of sentiment" for his nomination. Stassen quoted a letter he received from Eisenhower which stated, "You may be sure that there will be no lack of effort on my part to elect the ticket you should be heading." As Stassen considered what to do, he indicated that, in addition to Eisenhower, he had been urged by an "increasing, but limited" number of supporters to seek the nomination.

On Monday, January 20, 1964, exactly one year from Inauguration Day, Stassen held a press conference in Washington, D.C., announcing that he would indeed be a candidate for the Republican nomination in 1964.[15] Stassen stated, "I basically seek to enlarge the debate within the Republican Party and to enlarge Republicans' opportunities for decision in the coming year.... I will not attack any other Republican candidate during the campaign and will make only kind comments about them personally.... I will support any candidate the Republican convention nominates."[16]

Stassen indicated his intent to run in the New Hampshire primary where his goal would be to win a minimum of 10 percent of the vote. While running in other primaries, he stated, his ultimate goal was to win the winner-take-all California primary with eighty-six convention delegates at stake. Stassen felt it necessary to clarify that, while President Eisenhower had encouraged him to run, Eisenhower "believed a number of Republicans should actively enter the race and present their views. He included me in that number."[17] His platform, he said, would be a "projection of the successful Eisenhower program known as 'peace, progress and prosperity,'" and stated that he would "carry forward the best portions of President Kennedy's administration." With that, Stassen was off and running.

Stassen's run in New Hampshire was described by one observer as "the most tragic ... candidate in modern times.... No longer a candidate with any semblance of political organization and with only limited funds, Stassen cut a pathetic figure in the primary campaign.... Pushing through New Hampshire towns, Stassen spoke briefly over a public address system carried in an accompanying automobile. But his amplified remarks fell on few ears. Occasionally, someone would pause to listen from the distance, but no crowds gathered to hear him. The lonely Stassen walked through stores, shaking hands with people and chatting with them."[18]

On Election Day Stassen received 1.4 percent of the primary vote. As Henry Cabot Lodge, Jr., swept to an unprecedented write-in vote primary victory, with his picture on the cover of the March 26 issue of *Life* magazine, Stassen was not entirely forgotten. In that issue of *Life*, Loudon Wainwright wrote a full-page poignant article entitled, "A Dignified Loser Drops One More." It was a graceful yet candid view of Stassen's ill-fated New Hampshire run. How did Stassen view the outcome of the New Hampshire primary? Wainwright quoted Stassen as saying, "I welcome the result of this election. It opens the field and clearly rejects any narrowing down to the two men who were most active in the primary [Barry Goldwater and Nelson Rockefeller]. I believe I now have a real prospect of winning in the California primary in June and then being named the Republican Party nominee."[19]

On the way to California Stassen stopped to participate in the Indiana primary set for May 5. Only two major names appeared on the Indiana primary ballot, Senator Barry Goldwater and Harold E. Stassen. In his best showing of the 1964 primary season, Stassen received 107,157 votes (26.8 percent). Goldwater received 267,935 votes (67.1 percent).

Stassen's major effort in 1964 was focused on the California primary. On February 29, 1964, Stassen arrived at the San Francisco Airport Hilton to appear at the endorsement meeting of the California Republican Assembly (CRA), a major volunteer arm of California Republicans. He answered, in seven pages, a detailed series of questions presented to him by the CRA. The CRA endorsed Goldwater. Stassen moved on to try to qualify for the June primary ballot. He put together a slate of eighty-six individuals who agreed to serve as delegates if Stassen won the primary. In order to qualify for the primary ballot, Stassen had to collect 13,702 certified signatures of registered California Republican voters by April 3. He made clear that he expected to qualify along with Goldwater and Rockefeller. "The importance of my delegation is daily becoming more evident," he said. "The results of the New Hampshire primary makes [sic] it doubtful that either of the two early active candidates ... will be nominated in July."[20] As he filed his slate of delegates in Sacramento on March 17, 1964, Stassen declared:

> This morning I have filed with the Secretary of State in Sacramento the names of the 86 Republicans who will be the California delegation to the Republican National Convention in San Francisco if our movement attains the largest number of votes of the three in the June 2 primary.
>
> The delegation is a Republican "Citizens Delegation" broadly representative of the occupation, ethnic backgrounds and diverse parts of the entire population of this great State.
>
> May I now state publicly the answer which I gave to the Republican county chairmen at Fresno at their closed session of March 13, in response to their questions. This delegation will present my name, and the program which I believe our Republican Party should adopt, to the Republican National Convention in San Francisco.
>
> If it then appears that I would not win the nomination for President, the delegation would invite to meet with them, separately, the other four Republican leaders who are being nationally considered for the nomination but are not on the California Ballot. These are Richard Nixon, Ambassador Henry Cabot Lodge, Governor William Scranton and Governor George Romney.
>
> Then I will ask the delegation to confer with former President Dwight Eisenhower. The delegation would then decide how their 896 votes will be cast for President.
>
> The importance of the proposed California delegation which I am filing this morning is daily becoming more evident. The results of the New Hampshire primary makes [sic] it doubtful that either of the two early active candidates, Governor Nelson Rockefeller or Senator Barry Goldwater, who received only 23 percent and 20 percent of the New Hampshire vote, will be nominated in July and that the final choice will center in the other five names under continuing consideration.

The Field poll released on April 3 showed Goldwater with 43 percent, Rockefeller with 31 percent, Stassen with 10 percent and "don't know" with 16 percent.[21] Stassen may have been behind, but he was determined to catch up. He dispatched Roger A. Johnson, described as "a long-time associate and member of Stassen's Philadelphia law firm,"[22] to advance Stassen's pending trip to California.

Johnson explained that "anything can happen in politics. The situation is extremely fluid. It could change in a moment." Johnson described Stassen's candidacy as motivated by idealism: "Stassen believes in the primary system. He believes that the issues should be discussed in the primaries, and that it's his duty to bring them up." Was Stassen motivated by ambition? Johnson responded, "Well, yes, there is always that. That's bound to be a part of the makeup of any candidacy for the presidency, but any man who wants to be president is bound to be a highly complex individual with highly complex motives."[23]

On April 9, 1964, Stassen sent a letter to all eighty-six members of his delegate slate.

He conveyed to his delegates the news that they had qualified for the ballot and explained his vision of their future course of action.

Stassen's 1964 campaign in California defined his entire approach that year. "America," he said, "should move forward along the broad middle way, avoiding extremism of both the left and right." He believed that the greatest dangers facing the Republican Party and the American people could be simply defined as ABC: Atheism, Birchism and Communism. Stassen went further and said that if he were nominated at the San Francisco national convention, he would seek legal action to bar adherents of these philosophies from running for office under the Republican banner.[24]

Perhaps the most interesting element to Stassen's plan for victory was what was called "Stassen's 4-in-1 Plan." Stassen maintained that a vote for him in the June primary would actually be a vote for Henry Cabot Lodge, Jr., Richard Nixon, William Scranton and George Romney, all viewed as potential alternatives to the conservative Goldwater and the liberal Rockefeller. Stassen summed up his position by explaining: "I don't feel that California [Republican] voters want to support either Barry Goldwater or Nelson Rockefeller. My candidacy gives them another choice."[25]

On April 9, the *San Francisco Examiner* scoffed at Stassen's "4-in-1 Plan," editorializing that "never has one horse offered to stalk for so many so eagerly."[26] Stassen had decided to run for all and by doing so win the primary. Alas, it was not to be. California Secretary of State Frank M. Jordan announced that Stassen had in fact failed to qualify for the June ballot. Stassen accused Jordan of applying a double standard to his petitions and stated that Jordan had invalidated many of his more than twenty thousand signatures because they were undated on the petition. Pointing out that Jordan was pledged to support Goldwater, Stassen petitioned U.S. District Judge Lloyd H. Burke to issue a temporary injunction to halt further preparation of the ballot for the primary. Stassen appealed to the California State Supreme Court and they turned down his appeal. Stassen then turned to the United States Supreme Court for relief. The court turned Stassen down by a six to three vote, without comment.[27] Stassen's hopes to appear on the California ballot were dashed.

Stassen's name was still a factor as the convention approached, if only as the butt of humor. "Stop Stassen" buttons became very popular. Jokes became common. "Have you heard the latest elephant joke?" "Harold Stassen," was the punch line. Even Stassen's nemesis, Richard Nixon, got into the act during an appearance in Baltimore. Under the title "Nixon Cuts the Varsity," the *United Press* reported that former Vice President Richard M. Nixon narrowed the GOP presidential field to one man. He took himself out of the running by telling more than 1000 students and visitors to Johns Hopkins University that he was the "titular leader" of the party. Then he said, "We need to keep the 16 Republican governors we have." This eliminated Pennsylvania's William Scranton, New York's Nelson Rockefeller and Michigan's George Romney. "You really can't spare any of our 33 Senators," he said. Exit Senators Barry Goldwater of Arizona and Margaret Chase Smith of Maine. "The Republicans have only one ambassador — we don't want to lose him," Nixon said. That took care of Henry Cabot Lodge. It appeared, Nixon said, with a smile, there was "only one other person" who could be spared for the party's nomination. "He's a man who has spent years under former President Eisenhower, a lawyer who comes from a populous eastern State ... Harold Stassen," Nixon concluded.

Stassen arrived in San Francisco accompanied by his daughter, Kathleen, and his nephew, Robert Stassen, who joined him for a meeting with President Eisenhower. As late as July 9 Stassen told a press conference, held at 11:30 A.M. at the Hilton Hotel, that Goldwater did not have the nomination locked up. He issued a tally sheet that offered a state-by-state delegate count. Goldwater had 593 first ballot votes, 62 short of the number needed for nomination. Stassen was very direct in his comments. "I would challenge Senator Goldwater to give the delegates their freedom to make a new choice. Not more than 340 would support him if they were released from their early commitments." He conceded that, "since I have only the remotest possibility of being nominated, I would urge delegates not legally bound to Goldwater to cast their ballots for William Scranton, George Romney, Henry Cabot Lodge or Richard Nixon."[28]

Stassen attended the convention, which nominated Goldwater. He had a box at the Cow Palace. On one side of his box sat Senator Margaret Chase Smith of Maine, herself a candidate for president in 1964, and on the other side sat Claire Booth Luce, the former member of the House of Representatives, ambassador, and wife of Henry Luce of *Time* magazine. Throughout the convention, seated right behind the press box, Stassen was greeted warmly by one and all. It was clear to one observer that Stassen was enjoying the spectacle of yet another convention.

The *San Francisco Chronicle* columnist and humorist Arthur Hoppe wrote a column published after the convention entitled "The Candidate Who Was Not a Joke." Hoppe asked Stassen very directly about the ridicule and whether it hurt. Stassen replied with candor: "Sure it hurts. But in politics you've got to be willing to get in there and get knocked around, even knocked flat. These issues are the things I'm living for." Hoppe summed it all up by observing, "No, Mr. Stassen isn't funny. He is sad. But, sad in a very noble sort of way. For unlike a punch drunk fighter, he still has all the attributes of a great man, including sensitivity — all but the protective mantle of success.... I shall think of Mr. Stassen ... and how unforgivably cruel politics is to those it passes by."[29] Stassen left the convention defeated but unbowed.

He emerged briefly on December 10, 1964, in an address to the Duke University International Law Society. He advocated for the establishment of a zone of arms control in the Alaska-Siberia area. His comments came as Cold War tensions between the United States and the Soviet Union continued. "It would be a tremendously significant beginning toward the limitation, inspection and control of modern armaments," Stassen proposed.

1966

In 1966 Stassen decided to once again seek the governorship of Pennsylvania. His announcement came in Philadelphia on February 10, 1966. He chose to announce that his major theme in the campaign would be his opposition to the war in Vietnam and ultimately bringing peace to that nation. He said his goal was to make the Republican Party the "peace party." His opponent was lieutenant governor Raymond Shafer. The primary was held on May 17 and the result was another crushing defeat for Stassen. Shafer received 835,768 votes (78.02 percent); Stassen received 172,150 votes (16.07 percent).

1968

Stassen chose to run for the Republican presidential nomination in 1968 as an avowed peace candidate. On the day after his 60th birthday, he affirmed that he hadn't "really reached the state of deciding" whether to run again. He stated clearly that if he ran, it would be as a "peace" candidate. He was clear he believed that "continuation of expansion of the United States military effort will not lead to a solution in Vietnam."[30]

On Tuesday, November 14, 1967, Stassen became the first announced candidate in the 1968 election cycle. Speaking in Milwaukee, he announced that he would enter the Wisconsin primary, the same state in which he had been victorious in the primary of 1948 twenty years before. His statement was clear: "My decision stems from my deep concern over the nation's twin frustrations — the unending Vietnamese War and the violent unrest in our cities."[31] He concluded his press conference with these words: "These grave issues threaten our nation." Stassen also advocated a United Nations that would be modernized and strengthened. He suggested that two Chinas, two Vietnams, two Germanys and two Koreas should be added to the United Nations to "offer a better assurance of peace."[32] In pursuit of his plans to bring peace in Vietnam Stassen stated that he had met twice with presidential assistant Walt Rostow to present his views.

In January of 1968 Stassen visited Vietnam as part of a delegation of the United States Inter-Religious Committee for Peace. Stassen served as chairman of Panel III on Peace Making and Peace Keeping. On Vietnam, the report was clear in its recommendations:

> Make deliberate moves: to stop at once the bombing of North Vietnam; to quiet down and de-escalate the War in Vietnam; to accept both Vietnamese Governments into the United Nations; to place United Nations Police between the North and South; to insure a cessation of hostilities on both sides; to safeguard an honorable ending of the war through new United Nations or Geneva Conference solutions; and to rebuild the war damage in both North and South Vietnam.

Stassen clearly stated his position on Vietnam in campaign literature circulated in Wisconsin in advance of the primary:

> 1. End the American war drive, with its terrible casualties and destruction; stop the bombing; promptly re-locate the American forces in powerful reserve positions near the sea-coast around major cities and rice bowls; follow the recommendations of the distinguished retired generals, Matthew Ridgway, James Gavin, and Lauris Norstad.
> 2. Invite both North and South Vietnam into membership in the United Nations; work through the United Nations to rebuild the war damage; place UN police forces between North and South Vietnam and win the young men of Vietnam toward nation-building policies used in the Philippines and in Malaya which stopped Communism and established peace in those countries.
> 3. Do not foster any coalition with the Communists in South Vietnam as they could sabotage the government from the inside.
> 4. Keep America very strong and very alert, but also fair and firm, with top priority for peace.

On March 31 Lyndon Johnson withdrew as a candidate for reelection. On April 2 Wisconsin went to the polls and Stassen came in third with 5.8 percent of the vote.

America was sent reeling by the assassination of Martin Luther King, Jr., in Memphis. Stassen had attended the March on Washington in 1963 and King had joined the American Baptist Convention because of Stassen. Stassen was deeply affected by King's death. In June, Robert F. Kennedy was assassinated in Los Angeles following his victory in the California primary. Stassen issued a statement saying, "The deep tragedy of the assassination of that courageous, charismatic, young leader, Senator Robert F. Kennedy, intensifies the current crisis in America." Stassen said that the policies advocated by the late senator "could lead America away from this terrible crisis to a new and better day at peace, at home and abroad."[33]

On June 12, Stassen held a press conference in Washington, D.C. He pledged that in order to "lift America away from this terrible trend to violence and hatred and lawlessness and war," if elected he would set up a bipartisan administration, "a truly national administration"[34] that would include Democrats and Republicans in his cabinet and other policy-making positions.

On Friday, May 17, 1968, Stassen was briefed by Secretary of State Dean Rusk on issues dealing with foreign policy, as were all of the presidential candidates. As he headed for the Republican convention in Miami, Stassen was asked in a radio interview, "Don't you feel foolish running for the presidential nomination again?" Stassen replied, "No, although I enjoy some of the cartoons." When asked when he felt closest to winning the presidency, Stassen replied, "I am inclined to think that may be in the future."[35]

In an article on June 5, 1968, *Time* magazine quoted a Stassen friend saying that Stassen was "implacable as a medium tank." Another friend was quoted as believing that Stassen "has this blind spot, this assumption that he knows more than anybody." Stassen observed about running, "I realize the small power I have within the G.O.P., but I have confidence I can win in November. I steel myself. I've been in the center and out and back. This is part of my life."[36]

Stassen had a number of major write-ups during the 1968 campaign. Most notable was a full feature article in *Esquire* in August 1967. When David Frost interviewed all of the major candidates for president in 1968, he included Harold Stassen in their number. Stassen made clear that he ran to make his views known and certainly all of the attention that he received during the election cycle insured that opportunity.

Stassen was nominated for president at the 1968 convention by his nephew, J. Robert Stassen, a delegate from the state of Minnesota, who was eloquent in his nominating speech. The following is from convention records:

> I also count it a signal honor to place in nomination before this Convention the name of a man who has dedicated his life to the cause of world peace and the freedom of man. A man who is perhaps the most misunderstood and underestimated man in America today. I am humbly grateful for this opportunity to place in nomination the name of Harold E. Stassen as a candidate for the Republican nominee for President of the United States. (Applause)
>
> And with that, it is an honor for me to place in nomination for President of the United States a man who can lead our party to a decisive victory in November, and who would lead our Nation on the path to peace with freedom and justice, the Honorable Harold E. Stassen. Thank you. (Standing Ovation)[37]

Stassen's nomination was seconded by Paul W. Walter, Jr., a delegate from Ohio. He concluded his speech by stating, "I second this nomination as a symbol to all who place ideals above personal considerations, for that is what makes mankind meaningful. Thank you for your attention."

A greeting by Nelson Rockefeller, who was to be defeated for the nomination at the convention by Nixon, was a newsworthy item. "Why Harold, nice to see you. It's a lot of fun isn't it?" said Governor Rockefeller. Stassen replied, "It sure is, but don't you think we're getting a little old for it?" "No," replied Rockefeller, "I never felt younger." Stassen replied, "I'm not so sure I want to do it again."[38] Of course he did!

1972

Stassen did not run for President in 1972. Richard Nixon was in the White House and as Stassen explained, "I never ran against a Republican incumbent even if I disagree with him."

The work that Stassen did on behalf of peace, social justice, and civil rights through the American Baptist Convention was acknowledged in Denver in May 1972. The General Council of the Convention presented Stassen with the Edwin T. Dahlberg Peace Award. Church officials said the award was given to honor Stassen "for his worldwide contribution to the building of a just and lasting international peace, particularly through his development of the United Nations, and for his work for social justice as a private citizen, a public leader and an American Baptist churchman."[39]

The year did not pass without a new term being coined and defined in the vocabulary of American politics. Stewart Alsop wrote a column in *Newsweek* on January 3, 1972, with the title "STASSENIZATION." Describing the meaning of being "stassenized," Alsop explained that "it is a useful verb." Continuing, he offered the following definition: "The word derives, of course, from the sad case of Harold Stassen, who kept on running for President when it had long since become clear to all, presumably including Stassen, that he had not the remotest chance of being nominated or elected. A stassenized politician is one who feels an ungovernable compulsion to become a Presidential candidate even when it is inconceivable that he will ever become President."[40]

1976

In the fall of 1975 Stassen toyed briefly with the idea of running for the United States Senate. It was rumored that the Republican leader in the Senate, Hugh Scott, might not seek reelection. Stassen indicated that he might choose to run for the nomination. "I believe very strongly that I know what domestic and foreign policy would lead to a stable economy," Stassen declared.[41] In the end, he chose not to run for the Senate. He resolved to run for president in 1976.

Even as he prepared to announce his candidacy, he demonstrated both his good humor and his understanding of the political realities. "I've always kept a sense of humor about my political career. At times the press had given me more credit than I deserve, at times less. I feel it all balances out in the end." Stassen could not resist pointing out that his favorite cartoon showed his "supporters holding a convention — in a telephone booth."[42]

In May of 1976 Stassen explained his potential candidacy by saying, "I could unite the Republican Party, unite the country and provide the essential leadership to lift America with full employment, without inflation, and establish conditions of peace with justice and freedom."[43] Only four reporters showed up for his press conference as he announced, "I am considering becoming a candidate for President in 1976."[44] He further explained: "I kept saying no all year to people who asked me if I were going to run. But this is an unusual year, and I may change my mind."[45]

On June 3, 1976, Stassen formally announced that he would run. He would run despite the "ridiculing and joking."[46] It was too late to enter any primaries, so Stassen's appeal for votes at the convention went straight to the delegates via a letter. As neither Ford nor Reagan had the nomination locked up, he suggested, why not consider voting for Stassen "on later ballots if your first ballot candidate" does not win the nomination.[47] Stassen said he understood that his nomination was very unlikely: "I would say it would take a near miracle, but after what the Gallup Poll said, the Republican Party could use a near miracle."

On August 9, 1976, Stassen testified before the Platform Committee at the Republican National Convention held in Kansas City, Missouri. The media focused on one written recommendation that Stassen made to the committee. Richard Nixon's resignation from the presidency had taken place exactly two years before to the day, August 9, 1974. Rather than being critical of Nixon, Stassen offered the following about his former friend and nemesis: "It is my recommendation that our Republican Party should be forthright in meeting the situation arising out of President Nixon's Administration and should adopt a plank in approximately the following terms: 'We hold that the perspective of history will show that much that was good and constructive was accomplished through the Presidency of Richard Nixon; that his resignation was ample punishment for his wrongdoing; that his pardon by President Ford was wise and sound and justified in the national interest of our nation.'"[48]

Stassen's recommendation was not adopted. One editorial gently summed up Stassen's role in 1976 when it observed, "A Republican Convention would really not be official without the familiar apparition of Harold E. Stassen. His benign — it's a bit cruel to say bumbling — presence adds an element of familiarity, nostalgia and mild buffoonery, all in one.... The convention can go on."[49] Indeed, Stassen's "Uncommitted Delegate Headquarters" was reported as being "one of the loneliest places" in Kansas City. The story was poignant: "Mr. Stassen's army of twelve volunteers has managed to give away, mostly to collectors, two hundred Stassen buttons, which cost the Stassen treasury thirty-five cents apiece, and had to order seven hundred more."[50]

1978

On January 23, 1978, having returned to live in Minnesota, Stassen announced that he would seek the Republican nomination for the United States Senate to fill the seat left vacant by the death of Hubert H. Humphrey. He was running, he said, to "carry on Hubert Humphrey's devotion to the well-being of all humanity on this earth."[51] As one editorial remarked, "Without Stassen as a perennial candidate for something, politics would indeed be boring." Running against Rudy Boschwitz in the Republican primary, Stassen was to suffer a crushing defeat, his first in Minnesota. Boschwitz received 185,393 votes (86.81 percent) to Stassen's 28,170 votes (13.19 percent).

1980

On November 9, 1978, Stassen declared his interest in running for president in 1980: "I am serious. We will make this campaign as big as we can, we'll go all out. I want to get up to New Hampshire soon and get things going.... I was the youngest governor of Minnesota and many said I was one of the best. Now I'm trying to be the oldest president and one of the best. I am a realist, but I love campaigning. I go out to win, but I also know that this is the best way to influence public opinion and get your views known. I feel that in every campaign I've been in, some good has resulted. I've always had a constructive influence on the party and on the country and when I lose, I am never a crybaby."[52]

On September 24, 1979, George Gallup released a survey revealing the awareness of voters about potential nominees for the Republican Party in 1980. Ninety-four percent knew the name of Gerald Ford. Ronald Reagan was known by 91 percent. Eighth on the list with 42 percent was Harold E. Stassen.[53]

In October Stassen journeyed to Ames, Iowa, to test the waters of the Iowa caucuses with most of the other candidates. Despite his determination to run in New Hampshire, Stassen soon confronted the political realities. On December 26, Stassen announced that he had failed to collect enough signatures to qualify for the ballot and would therefore spend his energies running in other primaries.[54] As the campaign developed, Stassen stated his position simply: "When the four pace setters [Bush, Reagan, John Connelly and Howard Baker] stumble, when the call is for experience and steady, calm leadership, well, then, here I am."[55]

Running under the slogan "Stassen Can Defeat Carter," his 1980 campaign concluded with a whimper instead of a win.

1984

On September 9, 1983, Stassen announced that he would once again run for president. On December 29 he filed his papers with New Hampshire secretary of state William Gardner to run in the primary.

Stassen decided to run in West Virginia's Republican primary on June 5, 1984. He conceded that "the power of the incumbency is so great." But he went on to explain: "What I am hoping to do is make this campaign a referendum on Reagan's policies. This is so important that somebody has to raise the issues."[56] Remarking on Stassen's explanation, veteran Washington correspondent David Broder postulated what he termed the "Stassen theorem." He defined the theorem in this way: "In its majestic brevity, Stassen's law states: Runners-up are always right."[57]

1986

The year 1986 brought Stassen a political victory. He was chosen to be the Republican nominee for the House of Representatives against Representative Bruce Vento. Stassen said he was "campaigning to win" to represent the people of the 4th Congressional District in Washington, D.C. He did concede that, although he had carried the district when he ran for reelection as governor in 1942, he recognized that, "of course, nearly all of those voters are probably dead and gone to heaven, but maybe they told their children about me before they went."[58] When the votes came in Stassen was defeated in a landslide. Vento received 112,662 votes (72.88 percent) to Stassen's 41,926 votes (27.12 percent).

Reflecting on his latest defeat Stassen said, "Well, Churchill, Eisenhower, DeGaulle — they never went to a rocking chair. I don't suppose I will either."[59]

1988

On September 26, 1987, Stassen announced that he would, indeed, run for president in 1988. It was a surprise announcement, as *NBC Nightly News* had reported during the August 29, 1987, broadcast that Stassen had announced that day that he would not run in 1988. Even as he announced his candidacy, Stassen explained he had decided to run to force a discussion of the real issues confronting the nation. He did state clearly that he did not plan to win the nomination or the election.[60] He was one of those listed in "Quotes of the

Week" in a *U.S. News and World Report*, stating, "The candidates are following the polls rather than leading the people."[61]

Very little attention was paid to Stassen's ill-fated run in 1988.

1992

On December 18, 1991, Stassen decided to run for president again and filed papers declaring his intention to run in the New Hampshire primary. In Minnesota, he actually received the ability to have one delegate on the Minnesota delegation to the Republican National Convention. Even that hope was dashed when another individual won the nod and was elected as the delegate.

1994

Stassen decided to seek the Republican nomination for the United States Senate, but was defeated in the Minnesota primary by Ronald Grams. Grams received 269,931 votes (58.17 percent) to Stassen's 22,430 votes (4.83 percent).

1996

Stassen did not choose to run in 1996. Instead he offered to run with Robert Dole as a candidate for vice president. Stassen said, "The fact that I am eighty-nine and continuing to work productively should provide some support to Senator Robert Dole's view that he is young enough to be a successful President [Dole was seventy-two]. I am confident that a poll of public opinion would show that a Dole-Stassen ticket, could win in November."[62]

Dole chose Jack Kemp to be his running mate in 1996.

1998

On May 29, 1998, the Associated Press reported that Stassen intended to run for governor of Minnesota in the 1998 Republican Primary. Stassen was quoted as saying, "I would focus on the combination of integrity and intelligence in public service."[63] In the end, Stassen decided not to go forward with his candidacy.

In the end, Stassen's continuing to run caused much ridicule. Perhaps a fitting tribute was expressed when it was observed that "once Harold Stassen was a man to be reckoned with.... Stassen had a resume that made George Bush, the 41st President, look like a dabbler. He was a man who could run for President and be taken seriously. But Stassen didn't know when to quit.... Stassen had the bug. He kept on running. He ran for President ... and didn't beat anybody.... Politics without Harold Stassen would be a dull exercise, indeed."[64]

24. Stassen and the Failure of the Liberal Republican Vision

From the very beginning of his political life Harold Stassen proudly proclaimed himself to be a liberal. He believed that the Republican Party should be the torch bearer of that American political tradition. He summed up his philosophy in a speech he delivered to the Princeton University "Students for Stassen" on April 28, 1948. It was delivered at the high point of his bid to win the Republican nomination. For Stassen it was a bold declaration of his essential vision of where he wanted to take the Republican Party:

> If our Republican party measures up, if our policies and program are sound, we will win a victory next November, but even more important, our Republican party will be the means by which this nation successfully meets one of the most critical periods in its history.
>
> Our Republican party must be dynamic in the years ahead, and not static. It must be the party of hope, and not of gloom. It must be constructive and not merely critical. It is my view that we will find our way through to sound policies to meet the challenge of these times if we discuss our proposals openly and forthrightly with the members of the party, and with the people of the country.
>
> It is in this spirit that I present to you tonight my views upon our foreign policy. I do so that others may state their agreement or disagreement, and that through the public discussion there may be an impact upon the decisions of the policy in the Republican National Convention in June.
>
> True liberalism, as I see it, in the best American tradition, is that philosophy which seeks to advance the maximum of individual freedom — economic, social, political, and religious freedom — for each man, consistent with the enjoyment of the same degree of freedom by his fellow man.[1]

The Republican Party in the twentieth century was torn between two distinct and separate visions of what that essential direction should represent. In 1912 the battle was between the liberal beliefs expressed by former president Theodore Roosevelt and the more conservative stance taken by his handpicked successor, William Howard Taft. The resulting battle caused a split in the GOP and ultimately the election of Woodrow Wilson.

The next great battle for control of the party took place in the aftermath of the defeats of Herbert Hoover in 1932 and Alfred Landon in 1936. The Republicans faced the seemingly irresistible force of Franklin D. Roosevelt and the New Deal with confusion and a lack of clear leadership.

As the campaign of 1940 began, the two leading contenders were Thomas E. Dewey and Robert A. Taft. Both Dewey and Taft made a strong case against the New Deal. Both were young and relatively untested as national leaders. The country was deeply divided over America's role in the world. Europe was at war and as the Republicans gathered for their national convention in Philadelphia Hitler's armies swept through western Europe and France fell to Germany. Within the Republican Party the two wings were torn over the question of intervention versus isolationism. The liberal wing of the GOP was clearly more inclined to line up in support of England as it prepared for the ultimate battle under the leadership of their newly named prime minister, Winston S. Churchill.

On April 25, 1940, Wendell L. Willkie delivered an address before the Bureau of Advertising of the American Newspaper Publishers Association at the Waldorf-Astoria in New York. Willkie was viewed as a very "dark horse" contender for the Republican nomination that year. Addressing himself to "Some of the Issues of 1940," Willkie declared, "The liberal is a man who believes in freedom for himself and for other people.... The liberal believes that the purpose of government is to make men free, and thus having freedom, men will be able to build up a productive and prosperous society. The reactionary may desire, with equal sincerity, a prosperous society, but he believes it can be achieved only by the concentration of economic or political power."[2] After winning the nomination, Willkie was to declare in his speech of acceptance, delivered in Elwood, Indiana, on August 17, 1940, that "because I am a businessman, formerly connected with a large company, the doctrinaires of the opposition have attacked me as an opponent of liberalism. But I was a liberal before many of these men had heard the word, and I fought for many of the reforms of the elder LaFollette, Theodore Roosevelt, and Woodrow Wilson before another Roosevelt adopted — and distorted — liberalism."[3]

The nomination of Willkie was a stunning triumph for the liberal vision over the conservative vision within the Republican Party. Willkie supported Lend-Lease, the Roosevelt administration effort to provide England with much-needed support in 1940 and 1941. He supported the establishment of the military draft, a critical move that helped prepare the United States for war.

Willkie took a trip at the behest of President Roosevelt. That journey became known through Willkie's bestselling book *One World*. It helped to force the Republican Party out of the isolationist shadows and into the bright sunshine of international cooperation. It was Willkie's clear vision which brought about near unanimous support within the Republican Party for the United States to join the newly formed United Nations in 1945. Although Willkie was to be defeated when he sought renomination in 1944, his fundamental approach to the world had been accepted by the mainstream of the Republican Party.

In 1948 there were four main contenders for the Republican nomination for president. Three of the potential nominees, Thomas E. Dewey, Harold E. Stassen and Arthur H. Vandenberg, reflected the liberal approach. Only Robert A. Taft spoke for the conservative wing of the GOP. Dewey was nominated for president and chose as his vice-presidential running mate the progressive, liberal governor of California, Earl Warren. The unexpected defeat of the Dewey-Warren ticket in 1948 brought the Republican Party to a crossroad. The Taft wing of the party believed that it was the "me too" approach that caused the Republican defeat. They contended that if the party would only return to its genuine conservative roots it could win a national election.

In 1952 the deep divisions and anger erupted in a titanic battle for the presidential nomination and control of the party. Robert A. Taft sought the nomination for a third time. He was the favorite to win the nomination. With Dewey, a two-time loser, out of contention, the liberal wing of the party needed to find a candidate. Their choice was the genuine American hero Dwight D. Eisenhower. In a very close battle Eisenhower defeated Taft for the nomination. The bitterness at the convention was summed up when Everett

Dirksen pointed his finger at Thomas E. Dewey and declared, "We followed you before and you took us down the path to defeat."[4] Eisenhower's victory at the convention and in the election did not dispel the anger of conservative Republicans over their defeat.

In 1960 the favorite for the nomination was Vice President Richard M. Nixon. Many conservatives preferred Senator Barry M. Goldwater of Arizona. When Nixon flew to New York in advance of the convention to meet with the liberal governor of New York, Nelson A. Rockefeller, in what conservatives called the "Munich of the Republican Party" or "the surrender of Fifth Avenue," Nixon and Rockefeller agreed on the language for the 1960 Republican platform. Goldwater and the conservative Republicans were furious. Goldwater was nominated for president but withdrew his name with this historic declaration: "We are conservatives. This great Republican Party is a historic house. This is our home."[5] Goldwater and the conservatives were more determined than ever to take back the Republican Party. The narrow defeat of Nixon in the 1960 election opened up the party to the great battle for control of the party in 1964.

Since 1936 the liberal wing of the Republican Party had dominated the presidential nominating process. In advance of the 1964 primary season the conservatives raised the cry that was to echo through the spring primaries and caucuses. They demanded "a choice, not an echo." F. Clifton White, a Republican activist who had worked for Thomas E. Dewey, spearheaded the conservative bid to reclaim the party. In his book *Suite 3505: The Story of the Draft Goldwater Movement* he describes in stunning detail the organized effort that was to culminate in the nomination of Senator Barry Goldwater at the San Francisco convention. Goldwater's nomination marked the end of the liberal, moderate eastern Republican control of the party.[6]

By 1964 Harold Stassen was a marginal figure in the contest for the presidential nomination. The moderate/liberal wing of the party was deeply divided. Nelson Rockefeller stumbled in his quest for the nomination. Henry Cabot Lodge, Jr., won the New Hampshire primary on a write-in vote but lost in Oregon to Rockefeller. George Romney declined to run, and Richard Nixon knew that his only chance for the nomination lay in a deadlocked convention. When William Scranton finally jumped in to challenge Goldwater, it was too late to stop the inevitable triumph of the conservative tide. The one hope of the Republican moderates was that Dwight D. Eisenhower would jump into the fray, but Eisenhower would not move to oppose the Goldwater nomination.

When the convention opened at the Cow Palace in San Francisco the Republican establishment was vanquished by the Goldwater revolution. It was a moment of triumph by the right wing of the GOP. Even the landslide defeat of Goldwater in November did not derail the rise of the right. In 1968 Stassen's nemesis, Richard Nixon, was nominated and elected president. When Nixon resigned in 1974 he was succeeded by the moderate Gerald R. Ford. In 1976 the conservative favorite, Ronald Reagan, challenged Ford for the nomination and lost in a very narrow convention vote. In 1980 the right roared back and nominated Reagan for president. With the election of Reagan, the triumph of the right was complete. Although George H.W. Bush would be nominated and elected in 1988, the conservatives believed that he betrayed the Reagan legacy and many opposed him in 1992 when he was defeated for reelection. In 1996 the party nominated Robert Dole. He took as his running mate a conservative favorite, Jack Kemp. The defeat of Dole brought about the last gasp of the moderate Republicans in a presidential battle. The rise of George W. Bush marked the true end of the Willkie, Dewey, Eisenhower, Stassen wing of the Republican Party.

One of the key architects of the philosophy which failed to prevail was Arthur Larson.

Larson served as under secretary of labor during the Eisenhower administration and later served as an Eisenhower speechwriter and advisor. With Eisenhower's full support Larson wrote a book entitled *A Republican Looks at His Party*. Released in 1956, in anticipation of Eisenhower's reelection campaign, Larson stated, "The principles on which our Republic was founded were thoroughly liberal in the real sense of the word and therefore the objective of any true American conservative must be to conserve these liberal traditions."[7]

In 1960 Senator Barry Goldwater responded to the vision articulated by Larson by writing *The Conscience of a Conservative*:

> I am a politician, a United States Senator. As such, I have had an opportunity to learn something about the political instincts of the American people, I have crossed the length and breadth of this great land hundreds of times and talked with tens of thousands of people, with Democrats and Republicans, with farmers and laborers and businessmen. I find that America is fundamentally a Conservative nation. The preponderant judgment of the American people, especially of the young people, is that the radical, or Liberal, approach has not worked and is not working. They yearn for a return to Conservative principles.[8]

Throughout his life Stassen was guided by his faith. His continual runs for political office did not affect his commitment to the causes he valued. He believed that the Republican Party was his home. He never gave up the hope that ultimately the Party would return to the vision that he had battled for throughout his years in politics. For Stassen, the failure of his vision for the party was a great disappointment. He passed away on March 4, 2001. By the end of Stassen's life, the battle for the soul of the Republican Party had come to an end.

Chapter Notes

Chapter 1

1. This is an oft-repeated tale. According to one version, the farmers were going to "lynch" the sheriff or county attorney. See Minnesota Republican State Central Committee Papers, Minnesota Historical Society, box 100, St. Paul, Minnesota, hereafter referred to as MRSCC Papers; Citizens for Stassen, *People Are Turning to Harold Stassen.* See also John Gunther, "Stassen: Young Man Going Somewhere," *Harpers,* January 1946, p. 13.

2. Gunther, "Stassen: Young Man Going Somewhere," p. 12.

3. Larry Smyth, "Swede Voters Hopping to Stassen Bandwagon," *Oregon Daily Journal,* 18 April 1948, sec. A, p. 4.

4. Eleanora W. Schoenbaum, ed., *Political Profiles: The Eisenhower Years* (New York: Facts on File, 1980), p. 573.

5. Gunther, "Stassen: Young Man Going Somewhere," p. 12.

6. Paul Froiland, "The Making of a Visionary," *Minnesota* 86 (May/June 1987), p. 6.

7. Unidentified newspaper clipping, found in box 97, MRSCC Papers.

8. *Time,* 29 April 1940, p. 16.

9. Alec Kirby interview with Harold E. Stassen, 22 February 1991.

10 Walter Davenport, "Stassen's Political Gamble," *Colliers,* May 1946, p. 59.

11. Ivan H. Hinderaker, *Harold Stassen and Developments in the Republican Party 1937–1943,* Ph.D. dissertation, University of Minnesota, 1949, pp. 41–42.

12. *Time,* 29 April 1940, p. 16.

13. *Time,* 26 April 1948, p. 22.

14. J. Alsop and S. Alsop, "One-man Bandwagon," *Saturday Evening Post,* 7 September 1946, p. 15.

15. Gunther, "Stassen: Young Man Going Somewhere," p. 12.

16. Citizens for Stassen, *Stassen Meets the Standards the American People Require,* box 97, MRSCC Papers.

17. Gunther, "Stassen: Young Man Going Somewhere," p. 13; *Time,* 31 October 1938, p. 13.

18. Dale Kramer, "Progress of a Prodigy," *New Republic,* 19 April 1940, p. 16.

19. *Time,* 29 April 1940, p. 16.

20. *Time,* 31 October 1938, p. 13.

21. Ibid.; Barbara Stuhler, *Ten Men of Minnesota and American Foreign Policy 1898–1968,* Minnesota Historical Society, 1973, p. 147.

22. M.W. Halloran, "Candidate Stassen," *Commonweal,* 19 September 1947, p. 552.

23. Alsop, "One-man Bandwagon," p. 109.

24. Walter E. Quigley, "The Truth About Stassen," box 1288, The Papers of Robert Taft, Manuscript Division, Library of Congress, Washington, D.C.

25. Citizens for Stassen, *Stassen Meets the Standard,* p. 1.

26. *Time,* 26 April 1948, p. 22.

Chapter 2

1. Bernard Weinraub, "The 1968 Nomination?" *Esquire,* August 1967, p. 99.

2. Gunther, "Stassen: Young Man Going Somewhere," p. 15.

3. *Time,* 16 April 1940, p. 16.

4. Gardner Cowles, *Mike Looks Back* (New York: Gardner Cowles, 1985), pp. 66–67.

5. Ellsworth Barnard, *Wendell Willkie, Fighter for Freedom* (Marquette: Northern Michigan University Press, 1966), p. 161.

6. Arthur Knock, *Memoirs: Sixty Years on the Firing Line* (New York: Funk and Wagnalls, 1968), pp. 193–194.

7. Joseph Barnes, *Willkie* (New York: Simon & Schuster, 1952), p. 182.

8. Ibid.

9. Steve Neal, *Dark Horse* (New York: Doubleday, 1984), p. 124.

10. Ibid., p. 125.

11. Arthur M. Schlesinger, Jr., "Can Willkie Save His Party?" *Nation,* 6 December 1941, p. 561.

12. Ibid., p. 562.

13. "The Future of the Republican Party," *Nation,* 13 December 1941, p. 609.

14. Ibid.

15. Harold E. Stassen, "Report on a Wakening World," *New York Times Book Review,* 11 April 1943, Section 7, p. 1.

16. Donald Bruce Johnson, *The Republican Party and Wendell Willkie* (Urbana: University of Illinois Press, 1960), p. 236.

17. Ibid.

18. Neal, *Dark Horse,* p. 265.

19. Ibid., p. 311.

20. James L. Wick, *How NOT to Run for President* (New York: Vantage Press, 1952), p. 36.

21. Ibid.

22. Neal, *Dark Horse* p. 312

23. "Proposal for a Liberal Republican Party," *Christian Science Monitor,* 1 December 1945, pp. 17–19.

24. Stuhler, *Ten Men of Minnesota,* p. 148.

25. Neal, *Dark Horse,* p. 100.

26. Ibid.

27. Stuhler, *Ten Men of Minnesota,* p. 150.

28. *Time,* 15 June 1942, p. 10.

29. *Time*, 18 January 1943, p. 23.

30. Alec Kirby interview with Harold E. Stassen, 30 January 1988.

31. Republican State Central Committee, *Minnesota Republicans Endorse Stassen*, November 1943, MRSCC Papers.

32. *Time*, 6 December 1943, p. 17; Barnes, *Willkie*, p. 361.

33. Alec Kirby interview with Harold E. Stassen, 30 January 1988.

34. Ibid.

35. *Time*, 12 March 1945, p. 19.

36. Frost, *The Presidential Debate, 1968*, p. 65.

37. Harold W. Brayman, *The President Speaks Off the Record: Historic Evenings with America's Leaders, the Press, and Other Men of Power at Washington's Most Exclusive Club — The Gridiron* (Princeton, N.J.: Dow Jones Books, 1976), title page.

38. Ibid., pp. 357 – 361.

39. Harry S Truman Library and Museum, Oral History Interview with Harold Stassen by Richard D. McKinzie, Philadelphia, Pennsylvania, 26 June 1973.

40. Ibid.

41. *Time*, 16 July 1945, p. 15.

42. Harry S Truman Library and Museum, Oral History Interview with Harold Stassen by Richard D. McKinzie, Philadelphia, Pennsylvania, 26 June 1973.

43. Eliahu Elath, *Zionism at the UN* (Philadelphia: The Jewish Publication Society, 1976), p. 148.

44. Ibid., pp. 155–156.

45. Stuhler, *Ten Men of Minnesota*, p. 152.

46. Amos J. Peaslee, *A Permanent United Nations* (New York: G. P. Putman's Sons, 1942).

47. Ibid., p. 10.

48. Ibid., p. 7.

49. "The U.N.—A Disappointment at Age 40," *San Francisco Chronicle*, 22 June 1985, p. 5.

50. Harold E. Stassen, "Preventing Third World War," *San Francisco Chronicle*, 26 June 1985, p. A1.

51. Harold E. Stassen, *United Nations: A Working Paper for Restructuring* (Minneapolis: Lerner, 1994), p. 11.

52. Ibid., p. 12.

53. Stuhler, *Ten Men of Minnesota*, p. 152.

54. Ibid.

55. Ibid.

56. *Time*, 25 August 1947, p. 20; *Time*, 26 November 1945, p. 24.

Chapter 3

1. *Time*, 26 November 1945, p. 24.

2. These victories included Harold Stassen as governor; Edward Thye as lieutenant governor; and Joseph Ball as United States senator. See Gunther, "Stassen: Young Man Going Somewhere," p. 11.

3. These victories included Edward Thye's election over incumbent Henrik Shipstead in the Republican senatorial primary; Luther Youngdahl as governor, and Elmer Anderson as lieutenant governor. See Alsop, "One-man Bandwagon," p. 15.

4. "Builds Support for 1948 Republican Presidential Nomination," *Newsweek*, 27 May 1946, p. 17.

5. "Harold Stassen," *Tulsa Tribune*, 28 May 1946, p. 4.

6. R. W. Hitchock to "Fellow Delegates," 3 June 1948, box 1288, The Papers of Robert Taft, Manuscript Division, Library of Congress, Washington, D.C. Hereafter referred to as The Papers of Robert Taft, MDLC.

7. Stuhler, *Ten Men of Minnesota*, p. 124.

8. Stassen was elected county attorney in 1930 and governor in 1938; Ball was appointed (by Stassen) to the Senate in 1940; Judd was elected to Congress in 1942.

9. Interview with Harold E. Stassen, 30 January 1988, Washington, D.C.

10. Milburn P. Akers, "What Are Stassen's Chances?" *Nation*, 29 June 1946, p. 777.

11. Alsop, "One-man Bandwagon," p. 14.

12. "Mr. Stassen's Victory," *Arkansas Gazette*, 9 April 1948, p. 4.

13. Quoted in "How Non-Nebraska Press Views Vote Results," *Milwaukee Journal*, 15 April 1948, p. 10.

14. Thomas Stokes, "More Presidential Primaries Would Be a Good Thing," *Oregon Daily Journal*, 11 May 1948, sec. 2, p. 2.

15. Leslie H. Southwick, *Presidential Also-Rans and Running Mates, 1789–1980* (Jefferson, N.C.: McFarland, 1984), p. 538.

16. James David Barber, *The Pulse of Politics* (New York: W.W. Norton, 1980), p. 159.

17. Barnes, *Willkie*, p. 361.

18. Michael D. Wormer, *Election '84* (Washington, D.C.: Congressional Quarterly, 1984), p. 27.

19. Ibid.

20. Ibid., p. 29.

Chapter 4

1. *Time*, 25 March 1946, p. 21.

2. Alec Kirby interview with Walter Judd, 3 August 1989, Washington, D.C.

3. Alec Kirby interview with Harold E. Stassen, 30 January 1988, Washington, D.C.; Stuhler, *Ten Men of Minnesota*, p. 153.

4. *Newsweek*, 8 April 1946, p. 21.

5. Alsop, "One-man Bandwagon," p. 107.

6. Alec Kirby interview with Harold E. Stassen, 30 January 1988, Washington, D.C.

7. Quoted in *Time*, 1946, pp. 22–23.

8. Akers, "What Are Stassen's Chances," p. 779.

9. Bernhard W. LeVander to Ben Heinzen, 5 December 1946, p. 1, box 97, MRSCC Papers.

10. *Minnesota Letter*, 4 May 1946, box 97, MRSCC Papers.

11. Neighbors for Stassen, *Material Available to All Neighbors for Stassen*, box 97, MRSCC Papers.

12. Edward T. Folliard, "Minnesotan Tosses Hat in Ring Early; Sounds Liberal Note," *Washington Post*, 18 December 1946, p. 1.

13. "Taft Doesn't Consider Himself Active Presidential Candidate," *Washington Post*, 17 December 1946, p. 3; Folliard, "Minnesotan Tosses Hat in Ring Early; Sounds Liberal Note," p. 1.

14. Ibid.

15. Interview with Bernhard W. LeVander, 19 July 1989, Minneapolis, Minnesota.

16. *Time*, 26 April 1946, p. 23; Interview with Harold E. Stassen, 9 August 1989, St. Paul, Minnesota.

17. Alec Kirby interview with Harold E. Stassen, 9 August 1988, St. Paul, Minnesota; James T. Patterson, *Mr. Republican* (Boston: Houghton Mifflin, 1972), p. 511.

18. *Time*, 26 April 1948, p. 24.

19. Richard Starnes, "Minnesota's Favorite Son," *Washington Daily News*, 4 January 1947, p. 9.

20. Alec Kirby interview with Harold E. Stassen, 30 January 1988, Washington, D.C.; Alec Kirby interview with

Bernhard W. LeVander, 19 July 1988, Minneapolis, Minnesota.

21. Bernhard W. LeVander to Warren E. Burger, 19 February 1948; Bernhard W. LeVander to Warren E. Burger, 20 February 1948; Robert Herberger to Daniel Gainey, 4 October 1947, box 7, MRSCC Papers.

22. Alec Kirby interview with Bernhard W. LeVander, 19 July 1988.

23. *Time*, 26 April 1948, p. 23.

24. Ibid.

25. Bernhard W. LeVander, "Stassen for President Volunteers, Minnesota Division," 11 February 1947, box 97, MRSCC Papers.

26. Ibid.

27. Mark Forgette to "Dear Sir," 9 May 1947, box 97, MRSCC Papers.

28. Mark Forgette, "Report to Liaison Men on Neighbors for Stassen," 25 June 1947, box 97, MRSCC Papers.

29. Mark Forgette to Daniel C. Gainey, 3 January 1948, box 97, MRSCC Papers.

30. *Time*, 26 April 1948, p. 23.

31. Minnesota Lawyers for Stassen Committee, "Minnesota Lawyers for Stassen Committee," box 97, MRSCC Papers.

32. Bernhard W. LeVander to Mark Forgette, 18 June 1947, box 97, MRSCC Papers.

33. Marshall W. Houts to Bernhard W. LeVander, 20 March 1947; Bernhard W. LeVander to Mark Forgette, 23 May 1947, box 97, MRSCC Papers.

34. Citizens for Stassen, "How to Organize a Chapter of Citizens for Stassen," box 97, MRSCC Papers.

35. Ibid.

36. Mark Forgette to Harold E. Stassen, 3 December 1947, box 97, MRSCC Papers.

37. Bernhard W. LeVander, "Stassen for President Volunteers, Minnesota Division," 11 February 1948, box 97, MRSCC Papers.

38. Bernhard W. LeVander to Warren Burger, 26 February 1946, box 97, MRSCC Papers.

39. Bernhard W. LeVander, "Stassen for President Volunteers, Minnesota Division," 11 February 1947, box 97, MRSCC Papers.

40. Republican State Central Committee, *Harold E. Stassen: The Man America Needs*, box 97, MRSCC Papers.

41. A copy of the brochure can be found in box 97, MRSCC Papers.

42. Bernhard W. LeVander and Rose Spencer to "Fellow Delegates," 9 February 1947, box 97, MRSCC Papers.

43. Margaret Andrews to "Republican Friend," 15 May 1948, box 97, MRSCC Papers.

44. Unidentified newspaper clipping, 26 July 1947, found in box 97, MRSCC Papers.

45. Bernhard W. LeVander to Contributors, 25 July and 30 July 1947, box 97, MRSCC Papers.

46. Cliff Benson to Bernhard W. LeVander, 27 August 1947; Bernhard W. LeVander to Cliff Benson, 2 September 1947; Harry Kluntz to Bernhard W. LeVander, 4 October 1947, box 97, MRSCC Papers.

47. Daniel C. Gainey to Aaron E. Carpenter, 11 November 1947, box 97, MRSCC Papers.

48. Alec Kirby interview with Bernhard W. LeVander, 19 July 1988.

49. *Minnesota Letter*, 14 August 1946, box 97, MRSCC Papers.

50. Earl Hart to Earl Christmas, 14 February 1946, box 97, MRSCC Papers.

51. *Minnesota Letter*, 7 March 1947, box 97, MRSCC Papers.

52. Ibid.; Clarence Budington Kelland to *Minnesota Letter*, 24 March 1947; Lief Gilstad to Clarence Budington Kelland, 27 March 1947, box 97, MRSCC Papers.

53. *Minnesota Letter*, 7 March 1947, box 97, MRSCC Papers.

54. *Time*, 10 March 1947, p. 21; *Time*, 25 August 1947, p. 18.

55. Gaverrel D. Ra'anan, *International Policy Formation in the USSR* (Hubbardston, C.T.: Anchor Books, 1983), p. 124.

56. Harold E. Stassen, *Where I Stand* (Garden City, N.Y.: Doubleday, 1948), p. 18.

57. Ibid., p. 14.

58. *Time*, 28 April 1947, p. 14.

59. Ibid.

60. *Minnesota Letter*, 30 October 1947, box 97, MRSCC Papers.

Chapter 5

1. "Stassen Optimistic," *Concord Daily Monitor*, 7 January 1948, p. 7.

2. Alec Kirby interview with Harold E. Stassen, 15 July 1988.

3. Albert Baker, "Candid Politics," *Concord Daily Monitor*, 9 January 1948, p. 1.

4. "Nobody Can Stop Trend, Tobey Says," *Concord Daily Monitor*, 10 January 1948, p. 1.

5. "Eisenhower's Reply Awaited," *Concord Daily Monitor*, 12 January 1948, p. 1: "NH Eisenhower Forces Happy," *Concord Daily Monitor*, 13 January 1948, p. 8.

6. "Comment," *Concord Daily Monitor*, 14 January 1948, p. 4.

7. "Stassen Will Tell Policies Here Jan. 27," *Concord Daily Monitor*, 16 January 1948, p. 1.

8. "Dewey Fights Eisenhower for NH Vote," *Concord Daily Monitor*, 17 January 1948, p. 1.

9. Ibid.

10. Southwick, *Presidential Also-Rans*, p. 540.

11. Ibid., pp. 552–554.

12. "Bridges Spikes Move for President Boom," *Concord Daily Monitor*, 19 January 1948, pp. 1 and 8.

13. "Guider Heads Stassen Group," *Concord Daily Monitor*, 19 January 1948, p. 10.

14. "Sulloway Sees GOP Undecided," *Concord Daily Monitor*, 22 January 1948, pp. 1 and 5.

15. "Eisenhower Declines Bid for Nomination in N.H.; Says He's Not Available," *Concord Daily Monitor*, 23 January 1948, pp. 1 and 6.

16. Ibid., 23 January 1948, pp. 1 and 5.

17. Ibid.

18. "Sees Taft and Dewey Deadlocked," *Concord Daily Monitor*, 26 January 1948, p. 1.

19. "Stassen to Be Here Tuesday," *Concord Daily Monitor*, 26 January 1948, p. 1.

20. "Stassen Told Gain in State," *Concord Daily Monitor*, 27 January 1948, p. 1.

21. "Spaulding Tells Why He Supports Stassen," *Concord Daily Monitor*, 28 January 1948, p. 10.

22. "Stassen Tells Varied Views on Problems," *Concord Daily Monitor*, 28 January 1948, p. 1.

23. "Candidate Stassen Explains Hewitt 'Snub' Due to Pledge," *Concord Daily Monitor*, 28 January 1948, pp. 1 and 10.

24. Ibid, p. 10.

25. "Stassen," *Concord Daily Monitor*, 29 January 1948, p. 7.

26. "Blood Unpledged But Favors Dewey," *Concord Daily Monitor*, 2 February 1948, p. 8.

27. Barber, *Pulse of Politics*, p. 48.

28. "Dale Throws Support to Dewey Drive," *Concord Daily Monitor*, 4 February 1948, p. 1.

29. "Dewey Victor in N.H., View of Brownell," *Concord Daily Monitor*, 5 February 1948, pp. 1 and 7.

30. "Dewey Ticket Consolidated," *Concord Daily Monitor*, 11 February 1948, p. 1.

31. Albert S. Baker, "Candid Politics," *Concord Daily Monitor*, 11 February 1948, p. 4.

32. "Stassen Will Make Final Visit to N.H.," *Concord Daily Monitor*, 26 February 1948, p. 1.

33. Leon Anderson, "Stassen May Share Seats with Dewey," *Concord Daily Monitor*, 28 February 1948, pp. 1 and 2.

34. Quoted in "Comment," *Concord Daily Monitor*, 28 February 1948, p. 4.

35. "Dewey for President," *Manchester Morning Union*, 3 March 1948, p. 4.

36. "Dewey Drive to Gain Tempo," *Manchester Morning Union*, 3 March 1948, p. 22.

37. "Stassen Urges Truman Act to Bar New Wage Demands," *Manchester Morning Union*, 4 March 1948, p. 1.

38. "Stassen Talks at Dartmouth," *Concord Daily Monitor*, 4 March 1948, p. 1.

39. "Hopkins Says Stassen Strong," *Concord Daily Monitor*, 4 March 1948, p. 6.

40. Frank O'Neil, "Candidate Addresses Gatherings in Keene and Hanover," *Manchester Morning Union*, 5 March 1948, p. 1.

41. "Stassen Sees Prospects Good," *Concord Daily Monitor*, 5 March 1948, p. 10.

42. "Dewey Rally Held in Springfield," *Manchester Morning Union*, 6 March 1948, p. 5.

43. Leon Anderson, "Edge Seen to Dewey Slate for Tuesday," *Concord Daily Monitor*, 6 March 1948, p. 1.

44. Ibid.

45. Leon Anderson, "Stassen and Dewey Spend $50,000 Here," *Concord Daily Monitor*, 8 March 1948, p. 1.

46. Neal, *Dark Horse*, p. 61.

47. Anderson, "Stassen and Dewey Spend $50,000 Here," p. 1.

48. "Dale Sees 7–1 Dewey Margin," *Concord Daily Monitor*, 8 March 1948, p. 5.

49. Frank O'Neil, "Dewey Candidates Take Strong Lead in Six Contests, May Win Seven," *Manchester Morning Union*, 10 March 1948, pp. 1 and 25.

50. "Governor Dewey Tops Stassen by 6 to 2 in New Hampshire," *Wisconsin State Journal*, 10 March 1948, p. 1.

51. "Nation Studies Primary in NH," *Concord Daily Monitor*, 10 March 1948, p. 10.

52. Frank O'Neil, "Dewey Candidates Take Strong Lead in Six Contests, May Win Seven," *Manchester Morning Union*, 10 March 1948, p. 25.

53. Quoted in "Gov. Dewey Tops Stassen by 6 to 2 in New Hampshire," *Wisconsin State Journal*, 10 March 1948, p. 1.

Chapter 6

1. Richard Norton Smith, *Thomas E. Dewey And His Times* (New York: Simon & Schuster, 1982), p. 483.

2. Bernhard LeVander to Alfred Lindley, 28 April 1947, box 97 MRSCC Papers.

3. Quoted in Ibid.

4. Alec Kirby interview with Harold E. Stassen, 7 August 1988.

5. Vic Johnston, "Plan for Wisconsin," box 97, MRSCC Papers.

6. Ibid.

7. Mark Forgette to Daniel Gainey, 19 June 1947, box 97, MRSCC Papers.

8. *Time*, 1 December 1947, p. 26.

9. Rex Karney, "Bus Solves Stassen's Problem of Transportation," *Wisconsin State Journal*, 7 March 1948, p. 10.

10. Rex Karney, "Stassen Assails Appeasing Reds," *Wisconsin State Journal*, 6 March 1948, p. 1.

11. Rex Karney, "Taft Calls Off Wisconsin Campaign," *Wisconsin State Journal*, 6 March 1948, p. 1.

12. Ibid.

13. "'Mac' Office Open in Washington," *Wisconsin State Journal*, 8 March 1948, p. 5.

14. "2 Labor Leaders Join Campbell Lauding MacArthur," *Wisconsin State Journal*, 8 March 1948, p. 8.

15. "General Says He Would Accept GOP Nomination," *Wisconsin State Journal*, 9 March 1948, p. 1.

16. Rex Karney, "MacArthur Decision May Force Dewey to Campaign in State," *Wisconsin State Journal*, 9 March 1948, pp. 1 and 2.

17. Cabell Phillips, "With Stassen on the Hustings," *New York Times*, 4 April 1948, sec. VI, p. 12.

18. Ibid.; Rex Karney, "Delegate Race Looks Pretty Even," *Wisconsin State Journal*, 10 March 1948, p. 6.

19. "MacArthur Leads Green Bay Straw Vote," *Wisconsin State Journal*, 17 March 1948, p. 21.

20. "'Mac' Petition in Tokyo Gets 35 Signatures," *Wisconsin State Journal*, 17 March 1948, p. 21.

21. "Editors to Interview Stassen on Network," *Wisconsin State Journal*, 10 March 1948, p. 8.

22. Rex Karney, "Dewey Visit Here Seen Likely as Wall Street Aide Eyes State," *Wisconsin State Journal*, 10 March 1948, p. 1.

23. Raymond Moley, *Masters of Politics* (Westport, C.T.: Greenwood Press, 1949), p. 58.

24. "Coming, Tom, or Going?" *Wisconsin State Journal*, 13 March 1948, p. 4.

25. "Stassen Backs Oleo Control in Press Quiz," *Wisconsin State Journal*, 16 March 1948, p. 1.

26. Southwick, *Presidential Also-Rans*, p. 558.

27. Alec Kirby interview with Harold E. Stassen, 7 August 1988.

28. Bernhard W. LeVander to Warren Burger, 22 April 1948, box 97, MRSCC Papers.

29. "New Ike Draft Plan Started," *Omaha World Herald*, 16 March 1948, p. 16.

30. "Stassen Invited Dewey to Discuss Farm Programs," *Omaha World Herald*, 16 March 1948, p. 16.

31. Robert Fleming, "Stassen Uses a Parity Base for Farm Plan," *Milwaukee Journal*, 16 March 1948, p. 1.

32. Robert Fleming, "Hone Farms, Stassen Pleas," *Milwaukee Journal*, 17 March 1948, p. 25.

33. "Stassen Tops Choice of State Farmers," *Wisconsin State Journal*, 1 April 1948, p. 10.

34. Robert Fleming, "Stassen Choice of GOP Group," *Milwaukee Journal*, 21 March 1948, p. 1.

35. "Stassen Raps Policy on Zion," *Milwaukee Journal*, 21 March 1948, p. 19.

36. Rex Karney, "Stassen Assails Truman Policy on Defense, Reds," *Wisconsin State Journal*, 23 March 1948, p. 1.

37. George E. Sokolsky, "These Days," *Milwaukee Sentinel*, 25 February 1948, p. 11.

38. Rex Karney, "Stassen Suggests Mac Join in Radio 'Debate,'" *Wisconsin State Journal*, 24 March 1948, p. 1.

39. "Stassen Hits at La Follette," *Milwaukee Journal*, 27 March 1948, p. 3.

40. "Stassen and MacArthur," *Milwaukee Journal*, 28 March 1948, p. 18.

41. Ibid.

42. "On Past Performance," *Wisconsin State Journal*, 26 March 1948, p. 6.

43. "Who Pays MacArthur Bill?" *Wisconsin State Journal*, 26 March 1948, p. 6.

44. Joseph McCarthy to "Dear Folks," 31 March 1948, box 1288, The Papers of Robert Taft, MDLC.

45. Kirtland King, "Dewey Plans 2 Talks in State Next Week," *Wisconsin State Journal*, 27 March 1948, p. 1.

46. George Gallup, "Dewey Slips, MacArthur Gains," *Wisconsin State Journal*, 28 March 1948, p. 6.

47. Robert Fleming, "Dewey and Stassen Talk Here Thursday," *Milwaukee Journal*, 27 March 1948, p. 1.

48. "Co-op Group Slaps Down Dewey Backers," *Wisconsin State Journal*, 28 March 1948, p. 1.

49. Rex Karney, "Stassen Plans Midwesterner as Ag. Secretary," *Wisconsin State Journal*, 30 March 1948, p. 2.

50. "Oh, Wisconsin," *Newsweek*, 29 March 1948, p. 20.

51. "List Spending in Campaign," *Milwaukee Journal*, 30 March 1948, p. 6.

52. Rex Karney, "Truman Fumbling Can't Avoid War with Reds, Stassen Warns," *Wisconsin State Journal*, 30 March 1948, p. 1.

53. "Investigations," *Time*, 31 May 1954, p. 20.

54. Interview with Harold E. Stassen, 30 January 1988.

55. "War Not Near, Stassen's View," *Milwaukee Journal*, 31 March 1948, p. 12.

56. "'Mac's' Youthful 'Pickets' Get Stassen Buttons," *Wisconsin State Journal*, 31 March 1948, p. 1; Rex Karney, "You Pass on MacArthur, Stassen Tells Voters," *Wisconsin State Journal*, 31 March 1948, p. 1.

57. Marquis Childs, "Words They Wait For," *Wisconsin State Journal*, 1 April 1948, p. 6.

58. "He Lifts Their Hearts," *Wisconsin State Journal*, 1 April 1948, p. 6.

59. Laurence Kelund, "MacArthur 'Myth' Looks Real to Dewey, Stassen," *Milwaukee Journal*, 2 April 1948, p. 10.

60. "Will Continue If Poll Is Lost," *Milwaukee Journal*, 2 April 1948, p. 12.

61. Rex Karney, "Reception in Milwaukee, Results in Iowa and Maine Cheer Stassen," *Wisconsin State Journal*, 3 April 1948, p. 1.

62. "Stassen 'Minutemen' Take Drive to Homes," *Wisconsin State Journal*, 4 April 1948, p. 1.; Smith, *Dewey and His Times*, p. 485.

63. "Mud Called Aid to Stassen; 'He'll Get the Farmer Vote,'" *Milwaukee Journal*, 1 April 1948, p. 28; "Weather Report," *Milwaukee Journal*, 5 April 1948, p. 1.

64. Joe Morgan, "Stassen Holds 19," *Wisconsin State Journal*, 8 April 1948, pp. 1 and 2.

65. "Wisconsin Meaning," *Wisconsin State Journal*, 7 April 1948, p. 6.

66. "Stassen and Candor Win," *Milwaukee Journal*, 7 April 1948, p. 16.

67. Raymond Lahr, "Taft Credits Organization, Stassen Talks," *Wisconsin State Journal*, 7 April 1948, p. 9; Kirtland King, "Still Out in Front, Dewey Tells Press," *Wisconsin State Journal*, 7 April 1948, p. 9.

68. Marquis Childs, "A Minor Revolution," *Wisconsin State Journal*, 9 April 1948, p. 7.

Chapter 7

1. *Time*, 26 April 1948, p. 23.

2. *Time*, 19 April 1948, p. 21.

3. These contests were New Hampshire, Wisconsin, Nebraska, Ohio, and Oregon. "Nebraska Free for All," *Newsweek*, 5 April 1948, p. 22.

4. Ibid., p. 23; "6-Man 'All Star' GOP Primary Assured," *Nebraska State Journal*, 2 March 1948, p. 1.

5. "Vandenberg Like Lincoln, Says Stassen," *Nebraska State Journal*, 13 February 1948, p. 2.

6. Alec Kirby interview with Harold E. Stassen, 30 January 1988.

7. Neal, *Dark Horse*, p. 57.

8. Sinclair Lewis to Arthur Vandenberg, 2 May 1948, box 3, The Papers of Arthur Vandenberg, Bentley Historical Library, University of Michigan at Ann Arbor. Hereafter referred to as the Vandenberg Papers, BHLUM.

9. Arthur Vandenberg to Raymond McConnell, Jr., 1 March 1948, box 3, Vandenberg Papers, BHLUM.

10. Arthur Vandenberg to Arthur Summerfield, (?) January 1948, box 3, Vandenberg Papers, BHLUM.

11. Arthur Vandenberg to Arthur Summerfield, 1 January 1948; Arthur Vandenberg to A.R. Glancy, 12 February 1948, box 3, Vandenberg Papers, BHLUM.

12. Raymond McConnell to Arthur Vandenberg, 1 March 1948, Arthur Vandenberg to Raymond McConnell, 2 March 1948, box 3, Vandenberg Papers, BHLUM.

13. "Vandenberg Entered in State Race," *Nebraska State Journal*, 4 March 1948, p. 1.

14. Alec Kirby interview with Harold E. Stassen, 30 January 1988.

15. "Three GOP Hopefuls Step Up State Race," *Nebraska State Journal*, 5 March 1948, p. 10.

16. *Minnesota Letter*, 25 July 1946, box 97, MRSCC Papers.

17. J.A.W. to Robert Taft, 3 June 1948, box 1288, The Papers of Robert Taft, MDLC.

18. Bernhard W. LeVander to Warren Burger, 17 January 1948, box 97, MRSCC Papers.

19. "Taft Claims 'Liberal' Is GOP Title," *Nebraska State Journal*, 14 February 1948, p. 1.

20. "Taft Greatly Encouraged After Tour," *Nebraska State Journal*, 14 February 1948, p. 1.

21. Thomas Stokes, "Nebraska Illustrates Taft Chain of Command," *Nebraska State Journal*, 18 February 1948, p. 6; "Butler Heads Taft Fight in Nebraska," *Nebraska State Journal*, 28 January 1948, p. 6.

22. "Stassen Lauds 'All-Star' Plan for Primaries," *Nebraska State Journal*, 12 March 1948, p. 1.

23. Ibid.

24. James Keogh, "Fair Farm Share Aim of Stassen," *Omaha World Herald*, 12 March 1948, p. 1; Burt James, "Opposition to Butler, Taft in Open," *Nebraska State Journal*, 13 March 1948, p. 1.

25. Burt James, "Primary Win Is Forecast by Stassen," *Nebraska State Journal*, 14 March, 1948, p. 1.

26. "Stassen Favored in Wayne Voting," *Nebraska State Journal*, 19 March 1948, p. 8.

27. "Taft to Renew State Drive, Will Stress Foreign Policy," *Omaha World Herald*, 18 March 1948, p. 2.

28. "Stassen Worker N.V. Club Speaker," *Nebraska State Journal*, 21 March 1948, p. 4.

29. "Tafts Divide Tour of State," *Omaha World Herald*, 21 March 1948, p. 8.

30. James Keogh, "Stassen Asks Region Control of Missouri," *Omaha World Herald*, 24 March 1948, p. 1.

31. Burt James, "Nebraska Seeing Big Time Politics," *Nebraska State Journal*, 28 March 1948, p. 1.

32. "A Debate Would Be Dandy," *Omaha World Herald*, 2 April 1948, p. 36.

33. James Keogh, "Senator Asks Freedom for Agriculture," *Omaha World Herald*, 6 April 1948, p. 1; Evelyn Simpson, "Test at Hitch-Hiking Faced Mrs. Taft," *Omaha World Herald*, 6 April 1948, p. 1.

34. Burt James, "Taft Raps Nebraska 'All-Star' Primary Ballot as Foolish," *Nebraska State Journal*, 6 April 1948, p. 7; Dean Pholenz, "Mrs. Taft Says 'Free-for-All' Good Idea," *Nebraska State Journal*, 6 April 1948, p. 1.

35. Burt James, "Taft Raps Nebraska 'All-Star,'" *Nebraska State Journal*, 6 April 1948, p. 1.

36. "Three Minnesota Women Arrive to Swing More Support to Stassen," *Omaha World Herald*, 7 April 1948, p. 3.

37. Burt James, "Dewey's First Campaign Talk Raps Foreign Policy," *Nebraska State Journal*, 8 April 1948, p. 1; "2-Day Nebraska Campaign," *Omaha World Herald*, 8 April 1948, p. 1.

38. "Dewey Aims at Rural Vote," *Milwaukee Journal*, 8 April 1948, p. 19; James Keogh, "World Needs Another Big Peace Power," *Omaha World Herald*, 9 April, 1948, p. 1.

39. Harold Anderson, "'Quite Strong' Organization Backs Ohioan," *Omaha World Herald*, 9 April 1948, p. 1.

40. Ibid.

41. "Stassen Refuses to Predict Outcome of Nebraska Race," *Nebraska State Journal*, 9 April 1948, p. 19.

42. "Minnesota's Thye, Youngdahl Cite Qualifications of Stassen," *Nebraska State Journal*, 10 April 1948, p. 14.

43. "Dewey Flays 'Inept' Fight Against Reds," *Nebraska State Journal*, 10 April 1948, p. 7.

44. "Stassen Visits Scribner While Avoiding Dewey 'Clash,'" *Nebraska State Journal*, 10 April 1948, p. 7.

45. "Stassen Says Pick Plan Is Wise Project," *Nebraska State Journal*, 10 April 1948, p. 7.

46. Burt James, "New Yorker Sets, Keeps a Hard Pace," *Nebraska State Journal*, 10 April 1948, p. 1.

47. "Dewey Has Double Trouble in Alliance," *Nebraska State Journal*, 11 April 1948, p. 1.

48. James Keogh, "Dewey Ends Drive in State," *Omaha World Herald*, 11 April 1948, p. 1.

49. "Report of Taft, Dewey 'Deal' Hit," *Nebraska State Journal*, 12 April 1948, p. 1.

50. "Stassen Nebraska Supporters Employ 'Paul Revere Riders' to Garner Votes," *Omaha World Herald*, 12 April 1948, p. 2.

51. "'Big-3' in State 'All-Star' Race Hit Red Policies," *Nebraska State Journal*, 13 April 1948, p. 1.

52. Press Release by Harold E. Stassen, 13 April 1948, box 100, MRSCC Papers.

53. "Stassen Triumphs, Taft a Poor Third," *Nebraska State Journal*, 14 April 1948, p. 1; "9 Votes Pledged to Stassen," *Nebraska State Journal*, 16 April 1948, p. 7.

54. "A Major Contender," *Omaha World Herald*, 15 April 1948, p. 10.

Chapter 8

1. Fred J. Hughes to Bernhard W. LeVander, 22 August 1947, box 99, MRSCC Papers.

2. Alec Kirby interview with Bernhard W. LeVander, 19 July 1988.

3. Earl Hart to Bernhard W. LeVander, 8 December 1947, box 100, MRSCC Papers.

4. Bernhard W. LeVander to Harold Stassen, 11 December 1947, box 100, MRSCC Papers.

5. Alec Kirby interview with Bernhard W. LeVander, 19 July 1988.

6. Earl Hart to Bernhard W. LeVander, 14 January 1948, box 100, MRSCC Papers.

7. George Gallup, "Less Voters Want Labor Law Changed," *Nebraska State Journal*, 18 February 1948, p. 3.

8. Alonzo Hamby, *Liberalism and its Challengers* (New York: Oxford University Press, 1985), p. 105.

9. *Minnesota Letter*, 12 June 1947, box 97, MRSCC Papers.

10. Address of Harold E. Stassen at Macomber High School, Toledo, Ohio, 22 April 1948, p. 10, box 1288, The Papers of Robert Taft, MDLC.

11. For example, the *Summit County Labor News* of the AFL.

12. Address of Harold E. Stassen at Macomber High School, p. 11.

13. Ibid.

14. Unsigned, undated memo to Robert Taft, box 1288, The Papers of Robert Taft, MDLC.

15. "Stassen Draw Lines with Taft," *Wisconsin State Journal*, 19 March 1948, p. 2.

16. Alvin Silverman, "Ohioans Are Impressed by Stassen," *Cleveland Plain Dealer*, 16 April 1948, p. 1.

17. Alfred Lindley to Warren Burger, Leif Gilstad and Bernhard W. LeVander, 1 March 1948, box 100, MRSCC Papers.

18. Unsigned, undated memo to Robert Taft, box 122, The Papers of Robert Taft, MDLC.

19. Dewitt Sage to Robert Taft, 29 March 1948, box 1288, The Papers of Robert Taft, MDLC.

20. Unsigned, undated "Memo on Stassen," box 1288, The Papers of Robert Taft, MDLC.

21. Letters from Campbell found in box 1288 of The Papers of Robert Taft, MDLC, include: to Robert Taft, 20 April 1948; to Robert Taft, 21 April 1948; to Robert Taft, 22 April 1948; to Clarence J. Brown, 24 April 1948.

22. Alec Kirby interview with Harold E. Stassen, 9 July 1988.

23. George Barman, "Hiram Cheers Stassen, Then Picks Dewey," *Cleveland Plain Dealer*, 16 April 1948, p. 1.

24. Alvin Silverman, "Stassen Back on Ohio Trail Today," *Cleveland Plain Dealer*, 15 April 1948, p. 1.

25. "Stassen's Labor Record: Minnesota's IAM Reporting," *The Machinist*, 15 April 1948, p. 3.

26. H.R. Packard to Carl Ullman, 16 April 1948, box 1288, The Papers of Robert Taft, MDLC.

27. Alvin Silverman, "Taft Acts," *Cleveland Plain Dealer*, 17 April 1948, p. 1.

28. Edward Kernan, "Taft Men Look for Switch at Polls," *Cleveland Plain Dealer*, 17 April 1948, p. 4.

29. Address of Harold E. Stassen at Memorial Hall, Dayton, Ohio, 21 April 1948, box 1288, The Papers of Robert Taft, MDLC.

30. Ibid.

31. Address of Robert A. Taft at Grant High School, Steubenville, Ohio, 22 April 1948, box 1288, The Papers of Robert Taft, MDLC.

32. Joseph H. Ball to Alec Kirby, 18 June 1988.

33. Thomas E. Shroyer to Robert A. Taft, 23 April 1948, box 1288, The Papers of Robert Taft, MDLC.

34. See for example, Edward Kernan, "Taft Calls for Stassen Stand on Social Welfare," *Cleveland Plain Dealer*, 27 April 1948, p. 1.

35. Alec Kirby interview with Bernhard W. LeVander, 19 July 1988.

36. "Harold E. Stassen to Ask GOP Labor Aid in Akron Friday," *Summit County Labor News*, 23 April 1948, p. 1.

37. A copy of the Gallup results of 24 April 1948 can be found in box 1288, The Papers of Robert Taft, MDLC.

38. "Taft Glows with Optimism in 'Meet the Press' Quiz," *Cleveland Plain Dealer*, 24 April 1948, p. 4.

39. Edward Kernan, "Taft Heavy Guns Wheel Into Line," *Cleveland Plain Dealer*, 26 April 1948, p. 1.

40. "Dewey Chiefs Veto Stassen Bid for Parley," *Cleveland Plain Dealer*, 26 April 1948, p. 1.

41. Alec Kirby interview with Harold E. Stassen, 30 January 1988 and 9 July 1988; Alec Kirby interview with Bernhard W. LeVander, 19 July 1988. The Stassen campaign files are located in the MRSCC Papers.

42. "The Periscope," *Newsweek*, 26 April 1948, p. 15.

43. Thomas Stokes, "Stassen Sparks Where Taft Doesn't Seem to Click," *Oregon Daily Journal*, 27 April 1948, p. 2.

44. Edward Kernan, "Taft Rules Out Stassen Success," *Cleveland Plain Dealer*, 30 April 1948, p. 32.

45. Alec Kirby interview with Harold E. Stassen, 9 July 1988.

46. Warren Greenwald, "Defeat Taft, Finegan Urges," *Cleveland Plain Dealer*, 30 April 1948, p. 1.

47. "Stassen Up Front in Suburban Poll," *Cleveland Plain Dealer*, 1 May 1948, p. 1.

48. "Taft Defends Act, Asks Labor Votes," *Cleveland Plain Dealer*, 3 May 1948, p. 1.

49. "Stassen Arriving for Windup," *Cleveland Plain Dealer*, 3 May 1948, p. 1.

50. "Stassen 'Reveres' Prepare to Mount," *Cleveland Plain Dealer*, 1 May 1948, p. 4.

51. Press release by Harold E. Stassen, 4 May 1948, box 1288, The Papers of Robert Taft, MDLC.

52. Edward Kernan, "With 44 of Ohio's 53 Votes, Taft Staying on Top in GOP Fight," *Cleveland Plain Dealer*, 6 May 1948, p. 1.

53. Lyle Wilson, "Ohio Results Damages Both Taft and Stassen," *Oregon Daily Journal*, 5 May 1948, p. 18.

54. William Chafe, *The Unfinished Journey* (New York: Oxford University Press, 1986), pp. 95–96.

55. Alvin Silverman, "Stassen Back on Ohio Vote Trail Today," *Cleveland Plain Dealer*, 15 April 1948, p. 1.

Chapter 9

1. Unattributed poem printed in "The People Speak," *Oregon Daily Journal*, 5 May 1948, sec. 2, p. 2.

2. Moley, *Masters of Politics*, p. 58.

3. Alec Kirby interview with Bernhard W. LeVander, 19 July 1988.

4. Smith, *Dewey and His Times*, p. 26.

5. Ibid, p. 489.

6. *Time*, 22 September 1947, p. 25.

7. Harold Stassen to Robert A. Elliot, 19 November 1947, box 100, MRSCC Papers.

8. "Stassen Visits Small Oregon Towns," *Nebraska State Journal*, 24 February 1948, p. 6.

9. Larry Smyth, "GOP Eyes on Oregon Primary in Dewey-Stassen Showdown," *Oregon Daily Journal*, 18 April 1948, p. 1.

10. Smith, *Dewey and His Times*, p. 490.

11. Smyth, "GOP Eyes on Oregon Primary in Dewey-Stassen Showdown," p. 1.

12. Forrest Finely, "Presidential Campaign Spotlight Shifts Here," *Oregon Daily Journal*, 24 April 1948, p. 2.

13. "Dewey to Talk in City May 1, Stay 10 Days," *Oregon Daily Journal*, 20 April 1948, p. 1.

14. Larry Smyth, "Oregon GOP Voters to Get Top Billing," *Oregon Daily Journal*, 25 April 1948, p. 1.

15. Oregon Public Opinion Panel, "Portland GOP Strong for Stassen and Hall," *Oregon Daily Journal*, 25 April 1948, p. 1.

16. Larry Smyth, "They All Say, 'Win with Taft,'" *Oregon Daily Journal*, 25 April 1948, p. 1.

17. Larry Smyth, "Stassen Gives Free for All Query Chance," *Oregon Daily Journal*, 26 April 1948, p. 1.

18. Larry Smyth, "Outlaw Communists, Stassen Pleads Here," *Oregon Daily Journal*, 27 April 1948, p. 1.

19. Ibid.

20. Harold Stassen, "Address of Harold E. Stassen over the National Broadcasting System," 14 June 1947, UPAS 6, University Archives and Records Center, University of Pennsylvania.

21. Ibid.

22. "Stassen Shipmate to Head Veterans for Minnesotan," *Oregon Daily Journal*, 24 April 1948, p. 2.

23. Larry Smyth, "Dewey in Oregon," *Oregon Daily Journal*, 1 May 1948, p. 1.

24. "The Battle of Oregon," *Oregon Daily Journal*, 2 May 1948, p. 1.

25. Larry Smyth, "Keep Strong, U.S. Advised," *Oregon Daily Journal*, 2 May 1948, p. 1.

26. Walter W. Finke to Robert A. Elliot, 7 May 1948, box 100, MRSCC Papers.

27. Larry Smyth, "Dewey Plans Longer Northwest Campaign," *Oregon Daily Journal*, 28 April, p. 5.

28. Larry Smyth, "Dewey Asks Hard-Headed Use for ERP," *Oregon Daily Journal*, 4 May, 1948, p. 1.

29. Larry Smyth, "Keep Reds Out in Open, Dewey Advises," *Oregon Daily Journal*, 4 May, 1948, p. 2.

30. "Dewey Puppy Gift Ok'd," *Oregon Daily Journal*, 5 May 1948, p. 1.

31. Larry Smyth, "Earlier Return Stirs 'Panic,'" *Oregon Daily Journal*, 9 May 1948, p. 1.

32. "Stassenites Invade State for Drive," *Oregon Daily Journal*, 5 May 1948, p. 18.

33. "Governor Here from Minnesota, Boosts Stassen," *Oregon Daily Journal*, 9 May 1948, p. 24.

34. "Stassen OK's Debate Here with Dewey," *Oregon Daily Journal*, 10 May 1948, p. 1.

35. Tom Swafford recounted the debate and the events leading up to it in a fascinating article, "The Last Real Presidential Debate," *American Heritage* 37, February/March 1986, pp. 66–71. Mr. Swafford also provided this writer with additional information during a telephone interview on 28 August 1988.

36. Swafford, "The Last Real Presidential Debate," p. 68.

37. Larry Smyth, "Stassen Will Return, Speak on Wednesday," *Oregon Daily Journal*, 12 May 1948, p. 1.

38. Alec Kirby interview with Bernhard W. LeVander, 19 July 1988.

39. "Stassen Sees State Primary Victory Ahead," *Oregon Daily Journal*, 13 May 1948, p. 1.

40. Larry Howes, "Two Aspirants 'Nearly' Meet," *Oregon Daily Journal*, 13 May 1948, p. 1.

41. Swafford, "The Last Real Presidential Debate," p. 68.

42. Alec Kirby interview with Tom Swafford, 28 August 1988.

43. Larry Howes, "Stassen Arrives Behind Schedule in Pendleton," *Oregon Daily Journal*, 16 May 1948, p. 2.

44. Interview with Bernhard W. LeVander, 19 July 1988; Interview with Harold E. Stassen, 9 July 1988; Interview with Tom Swafford, 28 August 1988.

45. Press Release by Donald R. Van Boskirk, 16 May 1948, box 100, MRSCC Papers.

46. Swafford, "The Last Real Presidential Debate," p. 71; Larry Smyth, "Dewey, Stassen Renew Campaign," *Oregon Daily Journal*, 18 May 1948, p. 1.

47. Swafford, "The Last Real Presidential Debate," p. 70; "We Stirred Oregon," *Oregon Daily Journal*, 18 May 1948, p. 4.

48. Larry Smyth, "Dewey, Stassen Renew Campaign," *Oregon Daily Journal*, 18 May 1948, p. 1.

49. "Bill Held Halfway Between Two Stands," *Oregon Daily Journal*, 18 May 1948, p. 4.

50. Swafford, "The Last Real Presidential Debate," p. 71.

51. Ibid.

52. Alec Kirby interview with Bradley Nash, 22 August 1990.

53. R.W. Hitchcock to Fellow Delegates, 3 June 1948, box 1288, The Papers of Robert Taft, MDLC.

54. Larry Smyth, "The Winners — Dewey and McKay," *Oregon Daily Journal*, 23 May 1948, p. 1.

Chapter 10

1. R.W. Hitchcock to Fellow Delegates, 3 June 1948, box 1288, The Papers of Robert Taft, MDLC.

2. Alec Kirby interview with Bernhard W. LeVander, 19 July 1998.

3. Bernhard LeVander to Ted Gamble, 9 June 1948, box 100, MRSCC Papers.

4. "Republicans: The Party Chooses to Win," *Newsweek*, 5 July 1948, p. 16.

5. Ibid.

6. Ibid.; Bernhard Weinraub, "The 1968 Nomination?" *Esquire* 68, August 1967, p. 100.

7. Smith, *Dewey and His Times*, p. 500.

8. Southwick, *Presidential Also-Rans*, p. 558.

Chapter 11

1. Address of Harold E. Stassen to the Annual Dinner of the American Association of School Administrators, 21 February 1951, University of Pennsylvania Archives and Records Center, hereafter referred to as UPA 4, box 63.

2. Press Release of the Bureau of Publicity, University of Pennsylvania, 29 July 1948, UPS AR File.

3. See, for example, "Criticisms of Appointment of Harold E. Stassen as President of the University of Pennsylvania," UPA 4, box 27; "From the Top — A Thought...," *Daily Pennsylvanian*, 27 September 1948, p. 2.

4. *34th Street Magazine*, 29 October 1981, p. 6. Found in UPA AR File.

5. Unidentified newspaper clipping, UPA 4, box 39.

6. "Dr. George McClelland Becomes Penn. Chairman," *Daily Pennsylvanian*, 24 September 1948, p. 1.

7. Unidentified newspaper clipping, UPA 4, box 39; Herman A. Lowe, "Penn Reported Seeking Stassen as President," *Philadelphia Inquirer*, 12 July 1948, p. 13; "Stassen May Be Named Head of Penn Today," *Philadelphia Inquirer*, 28 July 1948, p. 8.

8. William Dubarry to Mark Kiley, 10 September 1948, UPA 4, box 39.

9. "Dewey to Meet Stassen to Plan GOP Strategy," *Philadelphia Inquirer*, 20 July 1948, p. 1.

10. Herbert Fogel, "Pres. Stassen Says Pearson Prophecy was 'Utterly Without Foundation,'" *Daily Pennsylvanian*, 29 September 1948 p. 1.

11. "Stassen May Be Named Head of Penn Today," *Philadelphia Inquirer*, 28 July 1948, pp. 1 and 8; Press Release of the Bureau of Publicity, University of Pennsylvania, 29 July 1948, UPA AR file.

12. "Stassen Nominated as Penn. President," *Philadelphia Inquirer*, 30 July 1948, p. 1.

13. "1948–1949? Here's a Clue...," *Daily Pennsylvanian*, 24 September 1948, p. 2.

14. Robert McCracken to Harold E. Stassen, 30 July 1948, UPA 4, box 27.

15. Hon. E. Wallace Chadwick to Harold E. Stassen, 16 August 1948, UPA 4, box 27.

16. Harold E. Stassen to Hon. E. Wallace Chadwick, 20 August 1948, UPA 4, box 27.

17. Unidentified newspaper clipping, UPA 4, box 27; Donald Angell to Harold E. Stassen, 17 August 1948, UPA 4, box 39.

18. "Remodeled House in Chestnut Hill Ready for Use by President Stassen," *Daily Pennsylvanian*, 8 November 1949, p. 1; William Dubarry to Harold E. Stassen, 4 October 1948, UPA 4, box 27.

19. "A Suggested Plan to Introduce President Stassen at the University of Pennsylvania," UPA 4, box 27.

20. "From the Top — a Thought," *Daily Pennsylvanian*, 3 December 1948, p. 2.

21. See Ken Simsarion, "Through the Keyhole," *Daily Pennsylvanian*, 22 May 1951, p. 3; Charles Russell to Harold E. Stassen, 12 October 1951; Harold E. Stassen to Charles Russell, 16 October 1951, UPA 4, box 39.

22. *34th Street Magazine*, 29 October 1981, p. 6. Found in UPA AR file.

23. Herbert Fogel, "Pres. Stassen Says Pearson Prophecy Was 'Utterly Without Foundation,'" *Daily Pennsylvanian*, 29 September 1948, p. 1.

24. See A. Wallace Copper to Harold E. Stassen, 1 April 1948; Harold E. Stassen to C. Canby Balderston, 8 April 1948; C. Canby Balderston to Paul Musser, undated; Harold E. Stassen to A. Wallace Copper, 14 April 1949, UPA 4, box 27.

25. A.W. Combs to Harold E. Stassen, 28 March 1948; Harold Stassen to A.W. Combs, 8 April 1948, UPA 4, box 27.

26. H.A. Thomson to Harold E. Stassen, 4 April 1949; Paul Musser to Harold E. Stassen, 8 April 1949; Harold E. Stassen to H.A. Thomson, 21 April 1949, UPA 4, box 27.

27. Richard M. Fried, *Nightmare in Red: The McCarthy Era in Perspective* (New York: Oxford University Press, 1990), pp. 100–103.

28. Memorandum of Presentation of Harold Stassen to a Conference of Members of the Senate and House at Harrisburg with Reference to Senate File No. 27, 30 April 1951, UPA AR file.

29. Harold E. Stassen, "Four Years at Pennsylvania" (a Report to the Trustees of the University of Pennsylvania), UPA 4, box 39.

30. Samuel Lehrer and Fred Forbes, "University Won't Accept Federal Aid with Strings Says Stassen to AUPC," *Daily Pennsylvanian*, 11 November 1949, p. 1.

31. Ronnie Kaplan, "A Talk with President Stassen," *Daily Pennsylvanian*, 23 October 1952, p. 2.

32. "Interpreters of Democracy," *Pacific Citizen*, 19 February 1949, p. 4; Harold E. Stassen to Henry Oberly, undated; Harold E. Stassen to *Pacific Citizen*, 8 March 1949; Lee Lovinger to Henry Oberly, 10 March 1949; Larry Tajiri to Henry Oberly, 10 March 1949; Harold E. Stassen to Larry Tajiri, 5 May 1949, UPA 4, box 27.

33. David Ullman to Harold E. Stassen, 25 May 1949; Harold E. Stassen to David Ullman, 27 May 1949;

Gene Gisburne to Paul Musser, 21 February 1951, UPA 4 box 27.

34. Maurice Kramer, "Stassen Steps Up Alumni Annual Giving Campaign," *Daily Pennsylvanian*, 9 December 1948, p. 1.

35. Stassen, "Four Years at Pennsylvania," pp. 34–38.

36. Ibid., pp. 38–40.

37. Ibid., p. 43.

38. "Stassen to Entertain Pakistan Ambassador," *Daily Pennsylvanian*, 9 December 1948, p. 1.

39. "Cabinet Job Offer Denied by Stassen," *New York Times*, 21 September 1950, p. 13.

40. Extract from Harold E. Stassen, "Program for Progress," *Collier's*, 28 September 1948. Found in UPA 5, box 1.

41. Extract from Harold E. Stassen, "Never! Never! Never!" *Reader's Digest*. Found in UPA 5, box 1.

42. Harold E. Stassen and Claude Pepper, "Do We Want National Health Insurance in the United States?" *American Forum of the Air*, Vol. XII, No.5, 29 January 1950.

43. Glen Lloyd to Harold E. Stassen, 17 June 1949; Harold E. Stassen to Glen Lloyd, 28 June 1949, UPA 4, box 27.

44. Diane Ravitch, *The Troubled Crusade* (New York: Basic Books, 1983), pp. 28 and 33.

45. Harold E. Stassen to Glen Lloyd, 28 June 1949, UPA 4, box 27.

46. Ravitch, *The Troubled Crusade*, p. 34.

47. News Item, *The Kansas City Star*, November 29, 1949, UPA 5, box 1.

48. Quoted in Ibid.

49. Roland Wright, "Stassen Reveals Support of All GOP Candidates," *Daily Pennsylvanian*, 3 November 1949, p. 1.

50. "Finnegan Attacks Prexy for Republican Support," *Daily Pennsylvanian*, 4 November 1949, p. 1.

51. "Reports Stassen Barred," *New York Times*, 18 September 1950, p. 16.

52. Ibid.

53. "Stassen Planning Change in Activity," *New York Times*, 19 September 1950, p. 20.

54. Press Release, 4 October 1950, UPA 4, box 27.

55. Paul Scarmont to Harold E. Stassen, undated, UPA 4, box 63.

56. Harold E. Stassen — personal, undated, UPA 4, box 63.

57. Itinerary of Harold E. Stassen and Robert Matteson, undated, UPA 4, box 63.

58. Address of Harold E. Stassen, 22 January 1951, UPA AR file.

59. Harold Stassen, "A Common Sense Foreign Policy," off-print found in UPA 5, box 1.

60 Harold Stassen, "Some Background for American Policy in Asia and Africa," off-print found in UPA 5, box 1.

61. Harold Stassen, "For the Good of America," off-print found in UPA 5, box 1.

62. "Democratic Leader Attacks Stassen in Speech to University Trustees," *Daily Pennsylvanian*, 9 January 1951, p. 1.

63. Ibid.

64. Stassen, "Four Years at Pennsylvania," p. 38.

65. "Story Vindicated, Stassen Asserts He'll Tell More," *Philadelphia Inquirer*, 4 October 1951, p. 1.

66. "But the State Dept. Still Hasn't Answered Stassen," *Philadelphia Inquirer*, 5 October 1951, p. 24.

67. Administrative Memorandum, 1 December 1951, UPA 4, box 37.

68. Harold E. Stassen to Robert McCracken, 26 December 1951, UPA 4, box 63.

69. Questions Answered by Harold Stassen, 3 January 1952, UPA 4, box 63.

70. Francis Henry Taylor to Harold E. Stassen, 16 January 1952, UPA 4, box 63.

71. "Something for Everybody," *Daily Pennsylvanian*, 25 January 1952, p. 2.

72. Address of Harold E. Stassen at the Annual Dinner of the American Association of School Administrators, 21 February 1951, UPA 4, box 63.

73. Unidentified newspaper clipping, UPA 4, box 63.

74. Stassen, "Four Years at Pennsylvania," pp. 6–7.

75. Ibid, p. 12.

Chapter 12

1. See George Gallup, "Eisenhower Popularity Booms Among GOP Voters in Survey," *Washington Post*, 27 September 1950, p. 18; "Gen. Eisenhower Voted First Choice of GOP for Presidency in 1952," *Washington Post*, 13 April 1951, p. 18; "Ike Still Leads as GOP Choice in '52 But with Lower Margin," *Washington Post*, 15 June 1951, p. 2; "Voters Favor Ike for President Among 18 Men in Both Parties," *Washington Post*, 7 November 1951, p. 13.

2. Thomas Dewey to Lucius Clay, 25 June 1951, box 24, Pre-Presidential Papers, Dwight D. Eisenhower Library, Abilene, Kansas, hereafter referred to as DDEL.

3. Robert Taft to----, 22 February 1952, box 366, The Papers of Robert Taft, MDLC.

4. Thomas Dewey to Lucius Clay, 25 June 1951, box 24, Pre-Presidential Papers, DDEL.

5. Alec Kirby interview with Harold E. Stassen, 22 February 1991.

6. Thomas Dewey to Lucius Clay, 25 June 1951, box 24, Pre-Presidential Papers, DDEL.

7. Lucius Clay to Dwight Eisenhower, 7 December 1951, box 24, Pre-Presidential Papers, DDEL

8. Alec Kirby interview with George MacKinnon, 19 March 1991.

9. Harold E. Stassen and Marshall Houts, *Eisenhower: Turning The World Toward Peace*, (St. Paul: Merril/Magnus, 1990), pp. 6–7.

10. Ibid., p. 8.

11. Bernard Shanley diary, p. 5, box 1, Bernard Shanley Diaries, 1951–1957, DDEL.

12. Thomas Dewey to Lucius Clay, 25 June 1951, box 24, Pre-Presidential Papers, DDEL.

13. Ibid.

14. Outline of decisions and discussion of conference, 3 August 1951, found in box 1, Bernard Shanley Diaries 1951–1957, DDEL.

15. Dwight Eisenhower to Lucius Clay, 24 August 1951, box 24, Pre-Presidential Papers 1916–1952, DDEL.

16. Lucius Clay to Dwight Eisenhower, 7 December 1951, box 24, Pre-Presidential Papers, 1916–1951, DDEL.

17. Bernard Shanley diary, p. 53, box 1, Bernard Shanley Diaries, 1951–1957, DDEL.

18. Ibid., p. 12.

19. Bernard Shanley diary, pp. 49–50, box 1, Bernard Shanley Diaries, 1951–1957, DDEL.

20. Thomas Dewey to Lucius Clay, 25 June 1951, box 24, Pre-Presidential Papers, DDEL.

21. Thomas Dewey to Lucius Clay, undated, box 24, Pre-Presidential Papers, DDEL.

22. Lucius Clay to Dwight Eisenhower, 29 September 1951, box 24, Pre-Presidential Papers, DDEL.

23. Dwight Eisenhower to Lucius Clay, 3 October 1951, box 24, Pre-Presidential Papers, DDEL.

24. Bernard Shanley diary, p. 158, box 1, Bernard Shanley Diaries, 1951–1957, DDEL.

25. Dwight Eisenhower to Lucius Clay, 27 December 1951, box 24, Pre-Presidential Papers, DDEL.

26. Robert H. Ferrell, *The Eisenhower Diaries* (New York: W.W. Norton, 1981), p. 207.

27. Bernard Shanley to Charles A. Foehl, Jr., 4 October 1951, box 1, Bernard Shanley Diaries, 1951–1957, DDEL.

28. Bernard Shanley diary, p. 160, box 1, Bernard Shanley Diaries, 1951–1957, DDEL.

29. Ibid., p. 176.

30. Ibid., p. 162.

31. Stassen, et al., *Eisenhower*, pp. 23–24.

32. Ibid., p. 24.

33. Thomas Coleman to Roy Dunn, 23 November 1951, box 366, The Papers of Robert Taft, MDLC.

34. A copy of the invitation found in UPA4, box 63.

35. "Stassen's Platform," found in box 1187, The Papers of Robert Taft, MDLC.

36. "Stassen Tries Again," *Newsweek*, 7 January 1952, p. 14.

37. Bernard Shanley diary, p. 185, box 1, Bernard Shanley Diaries, DDEL.

38. Walter Lippmann, "Today and Tomorrow," *Concord Daily Monitor*, 16 January 1952, p. 4.

39. Edward T. Folliard, "Eisenhower Keeps Secret in Parting Press Session," *Washington Post*, 7 November 1951, p. 1.

40. Robert C. Albright, "Carlson Named Head of 'Ike' Offices Here; Canvassing for GOP Delegates Under Way," *Washington Post*, 18 December 1951, p. 2.

41. David Horrocks, "Interview with Bernard M. Shanley," 16 May 1975, p. 6, DDEL.

Chapter 13

1. Charles Brereton, *First in the Nation: New Hampshire and the Premier Presidential Primary* (Portsmouth, N.H.: Peter E. Randall, 1987), p. 4.

2. Robert Taft to Vernon Valentine, 7 February 1952, box 366, The Papers of Robert Taft, MDLC.

3. Paul T. David, *Presidential Nominating Politics in 1952, Vol.2*, (Baltimore: The John Hopkins Press, 1954), p. 33.

4. Bernard Shanley diary, p. 11, box 1, Bernard Shanley Diaries, 1951–1957, DDEL.

5. Bernard Shanley diary, p. 92, box 1, Bernard Shanley Diaries, 1951–1957, DDEL.

6. Ibid., p. 110.

7. Brereton, *First in the Nation*, p. 7.

8. Bernard Shanley to Harold E. Stassen, 18 October 1951, box 1, Bernard Shanley Diaries, 1951–1957, DDEL.

9. David, *Presidential Nominating Politics*, pp. 29–39.

10. "I have in the past admitted ... that my family ties, my own meager voting record, and my own convictions align me fairly closely with what I call the progressive branch of the Republican Party," Eisenhower acknowledged to Clay in December. Dwight Eisenhower to Lucius Clay, 19 December 1951, box 24, Pre-Presidential Papers, 1916–1951,DDEL.

11. Henry Cabot Lodge, Jr., to Sherman Adams, 4 January 1952, box 24, Pre-Presidential Papers, DDEL.

12. Text of General Dwight D. Eisenhower's statement of January 7, 1952, box 2, William E. Robinson Papers, 1932–1969, DDEL.

13. Taft Committee press release, 8 January 1952, box 459, The Papers of Robert Taft, MDLC.

14. "Stassen's Name Will Go on Ballot in N.H., Says Guider," *Concord Daily Monitor*, 7 January 1952, p. 1.

15. "National Affairs," *Newsweek*, 7 January 1952, p. 14.

16. "Taft Backers Test NH Vote," *Concord Daily Monitor*, 8 January 1952, p. 1.

17. David, *Presidential Nominating Politics*, p. 36.

18. "Stassen Starts Tour of N. H.," *Concord Daily Monitor*, 15 February 1952, pp. 1 and 2.

19. David, *Presidential Nominating Politics*, p. 36.

20. Relman Morin, "Ike NH Lead Over Taft Is Seen Narrow," *Concord Daily Monitor*, 29 February 1952, pp. 1 and 10.

21. "Lodge Hints Ike May Act, End Silence," *Concord Daily Monitor*, 1 March 1952, p. 1.

22. Ibid.

23. Leon Anderson, "The State Is My Beat," *Concord Daily Monitor*, 3 March 1952, p. 4.

24. Leon Anderson, "$30,000 Barrage of Propaganda To Get Voters Faces NH This Week," *Concord Daily Monitor*, 3 March 1952, p. 1; David, *Presidential Nominating Politics*, p. 37.

25. Bernard Shanley to Harold E. Stassen, 29 August 1951, box 1, Bernard Shanley Diaries, 1951–1957, DDEL.

26. Stassen, et al., *Eisenhower*, p. 30.

27. Leon Anderson, "GOP Opens Final Drive; 850 At Rally," *Concord Daily Monitor*, 4 March 1952, pp. 1 and 8.

28. David, *Presidential Nominating Politics*, p. 36; Stassen, et al., *Eisenhower*, p. 29; Brereton, *First in the Nation*, p. 15.

29. Jack Bell, "Final Bid for NH Votes," *Concord Daily Monitor*, p. 1.

30. Press release of Harold Stassen, 10 March 1952, box 111, Pre-Presidential papers, DDEL.

31. David, *Presidential Nominating Politics*, p. 37.

32. The *Concord Daily Monitor* had on March 1 reported that Stassen "is not expected to pull more than perhaps 2,500 or 3,000 votes." "There's a Laugh Now and Then," *Concord Daily Monitor*, 1 March 1952, p. 4.

33. David, *Presidential Nominating Politics*, p. 37.

34. Harold Stassen to Henry Cabot Lodge, 22 February 1952, quoted in Stassen, et al., *Eisenhower*, pp. 27–28.

Chapter 14

1. "Presidential Primaries," *St. Paul Pioneer Press*, 4 February 1952, p. 12.

2. Donald Ackerman, *The Write-in Vote for Dwight Eisenhower in the Spring, 1952 Minnesota Primary*, Ph.D. dissertation, Syracuse University, 1954, pp. 116–117.

3. Wilbur Elston, "Stassen May Toss Hat in Ring Today," *Minneapolis Morning Tribune*, 27 December 1952, p. 13.

4. Alec Kirby interview with George MacKinnon, 19 March 1991.

5. Fred Neumeier, "Politicians Fearful of 'Stooge' Filings," *St. Paul Pioneer Press*, 1 February 1952, p. 2.

6. Walter Quigley to Victor Johnston, 15 January 1952, box 366, The Papers of Robert Taft, MDLC.

7. Fred Neumeier, "Stassen Wires Taft Challenge," *St. Paul Pioneer Press*, 4 February 1952, p. 1.

8. Alec Kirby interview with George MacKinnon, 19 March 1991; William Rentschler to Robert Taft, 7 December 1951, box 459, The Papers of Robert Taft, MDLC.

9. Robert Taft to Roy Dunn, 29 November 1951, box 366, The Papers of Robert Taft, MDLC.

10. Robert Taft to Victor Johnston, 30 December 1951, box 366, The Papers of Robert Taft, MDLC.

11. Statement of Senator Robert A. Taft, 10 February 1952, box 366, The Papers of Robert Taft, MDLC.

12. Ackerman, *The Write-In Vote*, pp. 154–156.

13. William H. Rentschler to Robert Taft, 4 December 1951, box 366, The Papers of Robert Taft, MDLC.

14. George MacKinnon to Alec Kirby, 5 April 1991.

15. Ibid.; Ackerman, *The Write-in Vote*, pp. 121–122.

16. George MacKinnon to Alec Kirby, 5 April 1991.

17. Rolf Felstad, "Taft Backers Stay Aloof in State Primary Race," *Minneapolis Tribune*, 6 March 1952, p. 17.

18. Ackerman, *Write-in Vote*, p. 121.

19. Carey McWilliams, "Mix-up in Minnesota," *Nation*, 8 March 1952, p. 224.

20. Tom Coleman to Vic Johnston, 4 February 1952, box 366, The Papers of Robert Taft, MDLC.

21. Fred Neumeier, "Eisenhower Filing in State Contested; Removal Asked," *St. Paul Pioneer Press*, 19 February 1952, p. 1.

22. The secretary of state's office confirmed to the *St. Paul Pioneer Press* that it had provided MacKinnon with photostatic copies of the Eisenhower petitions; it denied ever providing them to Fetsch. The newspaper added only that "MacKinnon was out of town and could not be reached for comment." Fred Neumeier, "State Ballot May Have 2 Mac Slates," *St. Paul Pioneer Press*, 20 February 1952, p. 4.

23. Alec Kirby interview with George MacKinnon, 19 March 1991; George MacKinnon to Alec Kirby, 5 April 1991.

24. McWilliams, "Mix-up in Minnesota," p. 224.

25. Fred Neumeier, "Ike Filing to Be Put Up to Court," *St. Paul Pioneer Press*, 22 February 1952, pp. 1 and 2.

26. *Fetsch v. Holm*, 52 N.W. 2d. 113, cited in George MacKinnon to Alec Kirby, 21 March 1991; Fred Neumeier, "Move to Halt Primary Fails," *St. Paul Pioneer Press*, 29 February 1952, p. 1.

27. Neumeier, "Move to Halt Primary Fails," p. 1.

28. Ibid.

29. Fred Neumeier, "Ike Backers to Hear Primary Plan Today," *St. Paul Pioneer Press*, 13 March 1952, p. 1.

30. David, *Nominating Politics*, p. 169.

31. Wallace Mitchell, "Stassen Takes to Sidewalks in Vote Drive," *Minneapolis Star*, 1 March 1952, p. 9.

32. "Stassen Begins Final State Drive," *Minneapolis Star*, 14 March 1952, p. 21.

33. Ackerman, *Write-in Vote*, pp. 129–132.

34. David, *Presidential Nominating Politics*, p. 172.

35. Quoted in Ibid., p. 173.

36. "Ike's New Status," *St. Paul Pioneer Press*, 21 March 1952, p. 6.

37. William Blair, "Eisenhower Vote 'Amazing' in Minnesota Write-In Drive," *New York Times*, 19 March 1952, p. 1 and 19.

38. Quoted in "Editorial Comment on Ike Write-In Vote," *Minneapolis Star*, 20 March 1952, p. 5.

39. This survey was conducted by Donald Ackerman, in *Write-in Vote*, p. 142.

40. Alec Kirby interview with George MacKinnon, 19 March 1991.

Chapter 15

1. The "permission provision" ultimately doomed Wisconsin MacArthur supporters, as the General in 1952 refused to allow his name to be placed on the ballot. David, *Nominating Politics*, pp. 130–131.

2. Robert Taft to Vernon Valentine, 7 February 1952, box 366, The Papers of Robert Taft, MDLC.

3. Ibid., p. 135.

4. "Taft Must Pile Up Primary Votes or 'Get Out,'" *Newsweek*, 24 March 1952, p. 35.

5. Stassen, et al., *Eisenhower*, p. 31.

6. "Wisconsin Primary," *New York Times*, 29 March 1952, p. 14.

7. "Wisconsin Bidding Barred by Warren," *New York Times*, 28 March 1952, p. 17.

8. W.R. Lawrence, "Stassen Bid Made to 'Split' Delegates," *New York Times*, 26 March 1952, pp. 1 and 24.

9. "Wisconsin Bidding Barred by Warren," *New York Times*, 28 March 1952, p. 17.

10. Richard Johnston, "Milwaukee Drive Is Opened by Taft," *New York Times*, 29 March 1952, p. 6.

11. "Taft Scores Rivals on Foreign Policy," *New York Times*, 30 March 1952, p. 49.

12. "Stassen Terms Taft 'Weak,'" *New York Times*, 30 March 1952, p. 49; "Struggle for Wisconsin," *New York Times*, 30 March 1952, sec. E, p. 1.

13. "Four GOP Presidential Hopefuls," *Congressional Quarterly*, 18 January 1952, pp. 29–311.

14. David, *Nominating Politics*, p. 136.

15. "Wisconsin Bidding Barred by Warren," *New York Times*, 28 March 1952, p. 17.

16. David, *Nominating Politics*, p. 138.

17. See: W.R. Lawrence, "Taft Leading in Wisconsin But 2 Rivals Hold Majority; Nebraska Write-In Is Close," *New York Times*, 2 April 1952, p. 1.; "National Affairs," *Newsweek*, 19 May 1952, p. 27.

18. David, *Nominating Politics*, p. 142.

Chapter 16

1. David, *Nominating Politics*, p. 289; William Blair, "Counting of Nebraska Ballots Slow in Neck-and-Neck Race," *New York Times*, 2 April 1952, p. 1.

2. Press Release, Taft Committee, 14 April 1952, box 459, The Papers of Robert Taft, MDLC. The Eisenhower-supporting *New York Times* chose to report this information on the obituary page: "Majority by Taft in Primaries Cited," *New York Times*, 14 April 1952, p. 19.

3. "Wake Up to the Facts, Mr. Stassen," *Philadelphia Inquirer*, undated, found in UPPS 4, box 27.

4. "A Point About Stassen," *Philadelphia Evening Bulletin*, undated, found in UPA 4, box 27.

5. David, *Nominating Politics*, p. 18.

6. Stassen, et al., *Eisenhower*, p. 33.

7. Roy Dunn to Vic Johnston, 5 December 1951, box 366, The Papers of Robert Taft, MDLC.

8. Richard Bain and Judith Parris, *Convention Decisions and Voting Records*, 2d ed. (Washington, D.C.: Brookings Institution, 1973), p. 280; Stassen, et al., *Eisenhower*, p. 34.

9. Robert Taft, "Analysis of the Results of the Chicago Convention," p. 5, box 431, The Papers of Robert Taft, MDLC.

10. Harold E. Stassen to Robert Taft, 5 July 1952, box 1187, The Papers of Robert Taft, MDLC.

11. Bain, et al., *Convention Decisions*, pp. 281–282.

12. Alec Kirby interview with George MacKinnon, 19 March 1991.

13. Bernard Shanley diary, pp. 412 and 415, box 1, Bernard Shanley Diaries, 1951–1957, DDEL.

14. "Chief Justice Warren Burger's Description of the

1952 Republican Nomination of General Eisenhower," Appendix 3, Stassen, et al., *Eisenhower*, p. 374.

15. Minnesota had twenty-eight delegates. Of these Stassen had acquiesced without a fight in the selection of four Eisenhower-committed delegates as a gesture of goodwill to the state's supporters of the General. With the defection of five of Stassen's delegates, nineteen were still committed to the former governor on the first ballot.

16. Stuhler, *Ten Men of Minnesota*, pp. 158–159.

17. Stassen, et al., "Description," *Eisenhower*, p. 375.

18. Stuhler, *Ten Men of Minnesota*, p. 158.

19. William Dubarry to Harold E. Stassen, 11 July 1952, UPA 4, box 27.

20. Harold Stassen to Robert T. McCracken, 21 July 1952, UPA 4, box 27.

21. Found in UPA 4, box 5.

Chapter 17

1. Dwight Eisenhower to Harold Stassen, 10 November 1952, quoted in Stassen et. al., *Eisenhower*, p. 98; Harold Stassen to Dwight Eisenhower, 13 November 1952, box 34, Papers as President, Administration Series, DDEL.

2. Robert Matteson, *A Search for Adventure and Service, Part IV, The Eisenhower Years: 1953–1961* (St. Paul: Privately published, 1985), p. 1.

3. Stassen's letters of November 8 and 13 dealt in a lengthy and detailed manner on the subject of foreign affairs, especially Korea. See Harold Stassen to Dwight Eisenhower, 8 November 1952, re-printed in Stassen, et al., *Eisenhower*, pp. 91–96; Harold Stassen to Dwight Eisenhower, 13 November 1952, box 34, Papers as President, Administration Series, DDEL.

4. Matteson in his highly specific memoir recalls that the meeting took place at the Commodore Hotel in New York; Stassen in his memoir of Eisenhower recalls that the meeting took place in Ike's Morningside Heights home.

5. Stassen, et al., *Eisenhower*, p. 104; Matteson, *Eisenhower Years*, p. 3.

6. Harold E. Stassen to Dwight Eisenhower, 22 November 1952, box 34, Papers as President, Administration Series, DDEL.

7. Emmet John Hughes, *The Ordeal of Power: A Political Memoir of the Eisenhower Years*, (New York: Athenaeum, 1963), p. 81.

8. Stephen Ambrose, *Eisenhower the President* (New York: Simon & Schuster, 1984), pp. 90–91; Charles Alexander, *Holding the Line: The Eisenhower Era 1952–1961* (Bloomington: Indiana University Press, 1975), pp. 42–43.

9. Ambrose, *Eisenhower the President*, p. 90.

10. "Text of Dulles' Statement on Foreign Policy of Eisenhower Administration," *New York Times*, 13 January 1954, p. 2.

11. Harold E. Stassen to Dwight Eisenhower, 13 November 1952, box 34, Papers as President, Administration Series, DDEL.

12. William White, "Unit to 'Clean Up' State Department is Voted by Senate," *New York Times*, 28 January 1953, p. 1.

13. Ambrose, *Eisenhower the President*, p. 177.

14. Ibid., p. 371.

15. Herbert Parmet, *Eisenhower and the American Crusades* (New York: Macmillan, 1972), p. 450.

16. Alexander, *Holding the Line*, p. 30.

17. Stassen, et al., *Eisenhower*, p. 144.

18. "Memorandum of Conversation between Dwight Eisenhower and Robert Matteson," 24 November 1964, box 1, Robert Matteson Papers, Minnesota Historical Society, hereafter MHS.

19. Sherman Adams, *Firsthand Report: The Story of the Eisenhower Administration* (New York: Harper and Brothers, 1961), p. 65.

20. "Memorandum of Conversation Between Livingston Merchant and Robert Matteson," 14 January 1965, box 1, Robert Matteson Papers, MHS; Adams, *Firsthand Report*, pp. 89–90.

21. Ronald W. Pruessen, "John Foster Dulles and the Predicaments of Power," in Richard Immerman, *John Foster Dulles and the Diplomacy of the Cold War* (Princeton: Princeton University Press, 1990), p. 25.

22. Robert Divine, *Eisenhower and the Cold War* (New York: Oxford University Press, 1981), p. 106.

23. Dwight D. Eisenhower, *Mandate for Change* (Garden City, N.Y.: Doubleday, 1963), p. 138.

24. Ibid., pp. 138–140; Robert Branyan, *The Eisenhower Administration 1953–1961: A Documentary History*, Vol. 1 (New York: Random House, 1971), p. 174.

25. Eisenhower, *Mandate for Change*, p. 139.

26. Raymond Daniell, "British Are Wary on Visit of Dulles," *New York Times*, 30 January 1953, p. 1; Ambrose, *Eisenhower the President*, p. 49.

27. Stassen, et al., *Eisenhower*, p. 136. Stephen Ambrose avoids the problem of mixed signals from Eisenhower/Dulles by claiming that the point of the trip was, indeed, to "pressure" the Europeans (*Eisenhower the President*, p. 49). Yet Eisenhower in his autobiography clearly put emphasis on the need to reassure European citizens of the peaceful intentions of the U.S. as the reason for the trip. As evidence for his "pressure" thesis, Ambrose can only cite a February 10, 1953 letter to Alfred Gruenther, asking him to explain to the allies Dulles' January 27 threat to "rethink" American policies concerning Europe. This is flimsy evidence, since Eisenhower obviously had to deal with Dulles' strident remarks once they had been uttered; it does not indicate that Eisenhower ordered Dulles to make them.

28. Robert Eliot Matteson, *The Eisenhower Years: 1953–1960* (Publisher: s.n., 1985), p. 8.

29. Ferdinand Kuhn, "Dulles Home, Hopeful About Allied Army," *New York Times*, 10 February 1953, pp. 1 and 3.

30. Robert Eliot Matteson, *The Eisenhower Years: 1953–1960* (Wisconsin, 1985) p. 13.

31. Stassen, et al., *Eisenhower*, p. 141.

32. Edward Ryan, "Stassen Wins Senate Vote to Head MSA," *Washington Post*, 28 January 1952, p. 1.

33. Joseph Dodge to Dwight Eisenhower, 3 April 1953, box 34, Papers as President, Administration Series, DDEL.

34. "Stassen's Role in Foreign Aid," *Newsweek*, 8 December 1952, p. 25.

35. "MSP Evaluation Project," 5 February 1953, box 34, Papers as President, Administration Series, DDEL.

36. Interview with Robert Matteson, May 30–31, 1991. Matteson's privately-published four-volume autobiography, *A Search for Adventure and Service*, and his papers are available in the Minnesota Historical Society.

37. Matteson, *Eisenhower Years*, p. 16; Harold Stassen to Dwight Eisenhower, 22 August 1953, box 34, Papers as President, DDEL.

38. Harold E. Stassen, "Some Backgrounds for American Policy in Asia and Africa," 19 February 1951, box 4, UPA.

39. Harold E. Stassen, *Report to the President on the Foreign Operations Administration*, 30 June 1955, box 1, Robert Matteson Papers, MHS.

40. "Foreign Aid Comparisons," *New York Times*, 1 August 1956, p. 10.

41. Stassen, et al., *Eisenhower*, p. 149.

42. Stassen, *Report*, pp. 2 and 3.

43. Ibid., p. 7.

44. Harold E. Stassen to Ezra Taft Benson, 7 October 1953, box 1, General Correspondence of the Director 1953–58, R.G. 469, National Archives; Stassen, et al., *Eisenhower*, pp. 151–152.

45. Harold E. Stassen, "The Case for Private Investment Abroad," *Foreign Affairs*, April 1954, p. 402.

46. Stassen, *Report*, p. 5.

47. Ibid, p. 9.

48. Alec Kirby interview with Walter Judd, 3 August 1989.

49. James Reston, "Stassen on the Rise Again After His Political Eclipse," *New York Times*, 27 April 1953, p. 19.

50. Robert Matteson to Harold E. Stassen, 3 May 1953, box 1, Robert Matteson Papers, MHS.

51. Hughes, *Ordeal of Power*, p. 82.

52. Dwight Eisenhower to Harold E. Stassen, 19 March 1954; Harold Stassen to John Taber, 26 March 1954, box 34, Papers as President, Administration Series, DDEL; Ambrose, *Eisenhower the President*, pp. 118–119; Alexander, *Holding the Line*, p. 42.

53. Dana Adams Schmidt, "Eisenhower's Four Years," *New York Times*, 1 August 1956, p. 1.

54. Anthony Leviero, "Eisenhower Moves to Limit State Department to Policy," *New York Times*, 2 June 1953, p. 1.

55. "Eisenhower Message to Congress on Reorganization," *New York Times*, 2 June 1954, p. 24; Edward Folliard, Ike Revamps Information, MSA Setups," *Washington Post*, 2 June 1953, pp. 1 and 13.

Chapter 18

1. Stephen Ambrose, *Nixon: The Education of a Politician 1913–1962* (New York: Simon & Schuster, 1987), p. 160.

2. See, for example, "Reaping the Red Whirlwind," which Stassen delivered over CBS on 15 August 1950, box 4, UPA.

3. "Investigations," *Time*, 31 May 1954, p. 20.

4. Richard Rovere, *Senator Joe McCarthy* (New York: Harper Torchbooks, 1959), p. 16.

5. Richard Fried, *Nightmare in Red: The McCarthy Era in Perspective* (New York: Oxford University Press, 1990), p. 134.

6. Edward Ryan, "Greek Owners of 242 Ships Bar Red Trade," *Washington Post*, 29 March 1953, p. 1; "Athens Agrees to Trade Ban Under Its Flag," *Washington Post*, 30 March 1953, pp. 1 and 2; James Reston, "Eisenhower Official Sees McCarthy Plan on Ships as 'Phony,'" *New York Times*, 30 March 1953, pp. 1 and 14; C.P. Trussell, "Stassen Charges McCarthy Impedes Red Cargo Curbs," *New York Times*, 31 March 1953, pp. 1 and 8.

7. Reston, "Eisenhower Official," p. 1.

8. In 1951 Stassen, at McCarthy's request, testified against the confirmation of ambassador-at-large Phillip Jessup.

9. Stassen, et al., *Eisenhower*, p. 247.

10. Ryan, "Greek Owners," p. 1.

11. Stassen, et al., *Eisenhower*, p. 28.

12. Trussell, "Stassen Charges McCarthy," pp. 1 and 8.

13. Murrey Marder, "Dulles Warns McCarthy on 'Dangers' of Interference," *Washington Post*, 2 April 1953, p. 1; Rovere, *Senator Joe McCarthy*, p. 34.

14. "Greece 6th to Bar Shipping to China," *New York Times*, 31 March 1953, p. 9.

15. "Transcript of President Eisenhower's Conference with the Press," *New York Times*, 3 April 1953, p. 12.

16. Murrey Marder, "Stassen Ends His Tiff with McCarthy," *Washington Post*, 4 April 1953, p. 1.

17. Ambrose, *Eisenhower the President*, p. 63.

18. Stassen, et al., *Eisenhower*, pp. 249–250.

19. Harold E. Stassen to Ezra Taft Benson, 13 September 1954, box 1, General Correspondence of the Director, R.G. 469, National Archives; Fried, *Nightmare in Red*, pp. 180–181.

20. Alec Kirby interview with Robert Matteson, 30 May 1991.

21. "Stassen Sees Benefits in Some Red Trade," *New York Times*, 1 June 1953, p. 5.

Chapter 19

1. Department of State, *Disarmament: The Intensified Effort, 1955–1958* (Washington, D.C.: GPO, 1958), pp. 2–3.

2. Kai Bird, "Stassen Chronology on Arms Control," unpublished, provided to Alec Kirby by Kai Bird.

3. Matteson, *The Eisenhower Years*, p. 71.

4. Divine, *Eisenhower and the Cold War*, p. 105; Ambrose, *Eisenhower the President*, p. 123.

5. William Blair, "U.S. H-Bomb Test Put Lethal Zone at 7,000 Square Miles," *New York Times*, 16 February 1955, pp. 1 and 18.

6. "The New Era in Destructive Capacity," *New Republic*, 28 February 1955, p. 3; "Chronology of events bearing on disarmament," 16 December 1957, box 1, Robert Matteson Papers, MHS; Blair, "U.S. H-Bomb Tests," p. 1; Ambrose, *Eisenhower the President*, pp. 245–246; Robert Divine, *Blowing on the Wind* (New York: Oxford University Press, 1978), pp. 38 and 59.

7. Robert Matteson, "1955 — A Watershed Year in the History of Disarmament Policy," box 1, Robert Matteson Papers, MHS.

8. Stassen, et al., *Eisenhower*, p. 290.

9. Dwight Eisenhower to John Foster Dulles, 28 February 1955; John Foster Dulles to Dwight Eisenhower, 1 March 1955; Dwight Eisenhower to Harold E. Stassen, 1 March 1955; Harold E. Stassen to Dwight Eisenhower, 3 March 1955; box 34, Papers as President, Administration Series, DDEL.

10. Matteson, *The Eisenhower Years*, pp. 58–59.

11. Robert Matteson to Harold E. Stassen, 27 November 1954, box 1, Robert Matteson Papers, MHS.

12. Matteson, *The Eisenhower Years*, p. 59.

13. Memorandum of Conversation between Dwight Eisenhower and Robert Matteson, 24 November 1964, box 1, Robert Matteson Papers, MHS.

14. Interview with Walter Judd, 3 August 1989.

15. Memorandum of Conversation between Dwight Eisenhower and Robert Matteson, 24 November 1964; Memorandum of Conversation between Andrew Goodpaster and Robert Matteson, 15 December 1964, box 1, Robert Matteson Papers, MHS.

16. Dwight D. Eisenhower, *Waging Peace* (Garden City, N.Y.: Doubleday, 1965), p. 469; Adams, *Firsthand*, p. 177.

17. Memorandum of Conversation between Andrew Goodpaster and Robert Matteson, 24 November 1964, box 1, Robert Matteson Papers, MHS.

18. Dulles also approved Eisenhower's statement to the press. See Robert Ferrell, ed., *The Diary of James C. Hagerty:*

Eisenhower in Mid-Course, 1954–1955 (Bloomington: Indiana University Press, 1983), p. 213.

19. Many records of the disarmament office are unaccounted for. When Stassen resigned in 1958 and his office was folded, apparently they were transferred to the State Department and then, in 1961, to the newly-created Arms Control and Disarmament Agency. It is unclear at what point the records were lost. See Finding Aid for White House Office, Office of the Special Assistant for Disarmament: Records 1955–1958, DDEL, p. 2.

20. Charles Egan, "Stassen Named to Cabinet Post on Disarmament," *New York Times*, 20 March 1955, p. 1; "Stassen's New Role," *Washington Post*, 21 March 1955, p. 18.

21. Matteson, *The Eisenhower Years*, p. 68.

22. See: Stassen, et al., *Eisenhower*, p. 144; Matteson, *The Eisenhower Years*, p. 83. Matteson goes so far as to say that there were two foreign policies in the administration: Stassen-Eisenhower's and Dulles.' In 1964, Eisenhower agreed with Matteson that this was the case. Ike was probably referring to the undeniable fact that Stassen and Dulles were in constant disagreement. This alone does not mean that there were *two* foreign policies. At least in the arena of arms control, personal jealousy rather than philosophical disagreement made it appear that Stassen and Dulles were further apart than they actually were.

23. Robert Matteson, "Disarmament Background After 1958," box 1, Robert Matteson Papers, MHS.

24. Ambrose, *Eisenhower the President*, pp. 448–454.

25. Matteson, *The Eisenhower Years*, p. 71.

26. So freely did staff members speak their minds that a panic broke out when the agency was abolished in 1958 and it was learned that the records of the agency were, by order of Under-Secretary of State for Administration Loy Henderson, to be transferred to State. Robert Matteson, knowing that State's "loaned" officials had spoken quite critically of Dulles, stubbornly refused to turn over the documents. Under-Secretary of State Christian Herter sided with Matteson and the papers were destroyed. It is possible that these documents were the "lost" records of the disarmament agency (see note 19). The DDEL has been alerted of this possibility.

27. Matteson, *The Eisenhower Years*, p. 72; Stassen, et al., *Eisenhower*, pp. 294–295; Department of State, *Disarmament: The Intensified Effort, 1955–1958*, (Washington, D.C.: GPO, 1958), p. 9.

28. Stassen, et al., *Eisenhower*, pp. 295–296.

29. NSC Action No. 1328, "Progress Report: Proposed Policy of the United States on the Question of Disarmament," 26 May 1955, pp. 14–18, box 1 Robert Matteson Papers, MHS.

30. Ibid., pp. 11 and 18.

31. Stassen gives the credit for the idea to James Doolittle, but presents himself as the major conduit to the president.

32. Divine, *Eisenhower and the Cold War*, p. 118.

33. Matteson, *The Eisenhower Years*, p. 77.

34. Ambrose, *Eisenhower*, p. 259.

35. Peter Lyon, *Eisenhower: Portrait of the Hero* (Boston: Little, Brown, 1974), pp. 652–653.

36. Henry Cabot Lodge to Harold E. Stassen, 4 May 1955, box 24, Papers as President, Administration Series, DDEL.

37. Stassen et. al., *Eisenhower*, pp. 300–301; Ambrose, *Eisenhower The President*, pp. 247–249.

38. Stassen, et. al., *Eisenhower*, pp. 304–305.

39. Henry Cabot Lodge to Dwight Eisenhower, 14 June 1955, box 34, Papers as President, Administration Series, DDEL.

40. Memorandum of Conversation between Andrew Goodpaster and Robert Matteson, 15 December 1964, box 1 Robert Matteson Papers, MHS.

41. "The security of the United States," the report stated, "should not depend in any essential matter upon the good faith of any other country.... The United States should never agree to and make any reductions or accept any controls in regard to its own armaments unless it has positive proof that the USSR is actually carrying out simultaneously at least comparable reductions or controls." *Progress Report*, pp. 14–15.

42. Matteson, *The Eisenhower Years*, p. 76.

43. Ibid., p. 76.

44. The May 26 Stassen proposal was more comprehensive in that an International Armaments Commission would inspect by land and sea as well as air "with the aid of scientific instruments." The Geneva Open Skies proposal was limited to the exchange of blueprints and overflights. The milder Ike proposals may have been made with the knowledge that Prime Minister Eden would also propose the creation of inspection teams in Europe. See Department of State, *Disarmament*, p. 16.

45. Memorandum of Conversation between Andrew Goodpaster and Robert Matteson, 15 December 1964; Memorandum of Conversation between Dwight Eisenhower and Robert Matteson, 24 November 1964, box 1, Robert Matteson Papers, MHS.

46. Stassen, et al., *Eisenhower*, pp. 326 and "Illustrations."

47. Eisenhower, *Mandate for Change*, pp. 511–512.

48. The quotation is a paraphrase, reconstructed by Robert Matteson from notes he took during a 1964 interview with Eisenhower. Matteson sent a copy of his memorandum of the conversation — including paraphrases — to John Eisenhower for his approval. John struck out "some people in Defense — to what's his name" and inserted "Admiral." box 1, Robert Matteson Papers, MHS.

49. Memorandum of Conversation between Nelson Rockefeller and Robert Matteson, 16 December 1964, box 1, Robert Matteson Papers, MHS.

50. Ibid.

51. Henry Cabot Lodge to Dwight Eisenhower, 4 August 1955, box 34, Papers as President, Administration Series, DDEL

52. Dwight Eisenhower to Harold E. Stassen, 5 August 1955, box 34, papers as President, Administration Series, DDEL.

53. Roger Morris, *Richard Milhous Nixon: The Rise of an American Politician* (New York: Henry Holt, 1991), p. 250; Julie Nixon Eisenhower, *Pat Nixon: The Untold Story* (New York: Simon & Schuster, 1986), pp. 98–99.

54. Earl Mazo, *Richard Nixon: A Political and Personal Portrait* (New York: Harper and Brothers, 1959), p. 158.

55. Ibid., pp. 158–159; Gellman, *The Contender*, p. 75.

56. Eisenhower, *Pat Nixon: The Untold Story*, p. 99.

57. Earl Mazo, *Richard Nixon: A Political and Personal Portrait* (New York: Harper and Brothers, 1959), p. 159.

58. Nixon letter to Robert Matteson reprinted in Matteson, "Harold Stassen: His Career, the Man, and the 1957 London Arms Control Negotiations," letter dated April 30, 1993, p. 24.

59. Richard M. Nixon, *R.N.: The Memoirs of Richard Nixon* (New York: Grosset and Dunlap, 1978), p. 71.

60. Gellman, *The Contender*, p. 182.

61. Richard M. Nixon, *In the Arena: A Memoir of Victory, Defeat, and Renewal* (New York: Simon & Schuster, 1990), p. 198.

62. Ibid., p. 198.

63. Ezra Taft Benson, *Cross Fire: The Eight Years with Eisenhower* (Garden City, N.Y.: Doubleday, 1962), p. 5.

64. Mazo, *Richard Nixon*, p. 161.

65. William Costello, *The Facts About Nixon: An Unauthorized Biography* (New York: Viking Press, 1960), p. 76.

Chapter 20

1. *U.S. News and World Report*, 2 August 1956, p. 34.

2. Ibid.

3. Stewart Alsop, *Nixon and Rockefeller: A Double Portrait* (Garden City, N.Y.: Doubleday, 1960), p. 72.

4. Ibid.

5. Emmet John Hughes, *The Ordeal of Power: A Political Memoir of the Eisenhower Years* (New York: Atheneum, 1963), p. 173.

6. Harold Lavine, ed., *Smoke Filled Rooms: The Confidential Papers of Robert Humphreys* (Englewood Press, N.J.: Prentice Hall, 1970), p. x.

7. Horace Busby, *The Thirty-First of March: An Intimate Portrait of Lyndon Johnson's Final Days in Office* (New York: Farrar, Straus and Giroux, 2005), p. 133.

8. Ellis D. Slater and Ernestine Durr, *The Ike I Knew* (published by the Ellis D. Slater Trust, 1980), p. 122.

9. Ibid., p. 131.

10. Edward E. Martin, *Down Memory Lane*, p. 124

11. Elizabeth Bradley Heffelfinger, Minnesota Historical Society, 1979, p. 123.

12. "Professor Says Ike Tried to Dump Nixon," *San Francisco Chronicle*, 4 October 1979.

13. Israel Schlesinger, Jr., *History of American Presidential Elections 1789–1968, Volume VIII*, essay by Malcolm Moos, p. 3348.

14. James Reston, *New York Times*, 24 July 1956.

15. "Whatever Became of ... Harold Stassen?" *San Francisco Chronicle*, 22 October 1975.

16. James J. Kiepper, "For Stassen, GOP's Former 'Boy-Wonder,' It's No Lark," *The Knickerbocker News*, Albany, New York, p. 8B.

17. In an unpublished paper, "1955 — A Watershed Year in the History of Disarmament Policy," written in 1964–1965 for presentation at the National War College, Matteson said that as early as March 1955 — as Stassen was being appointed disarmament adviser — he was considering running for governor of Pennsylvania in 1958 as a way of re-establishing his political power, an idea Matteson found absurd for the Minnesotan. box 1, Robert Matteson Papers, MHS.

18. Robert Matteson to Harold E. Stassen, 9 July 1955, box 1, Robert Matteson Papers, MHS.

19. Alec Kirby interview with Robert Matteson, 30 May 1991. Two congressmen with whom Stassen worked extensively, Walter Judd and George MacKinnon, also noted Stassen's refusal to accept counsel when it concerned his career. Alec Kirby interview with Walter Judd, 3 August 1989; Alec Kirby interview with George MacKinnon, 19 March 1991.

20. Matteson, *The Eisenhower Years*, p. 111.

21. Harold E. Stassen, "Address to the National Young Republican Leadership Training School," 27 January 1956. Copy of address given to Alec Kirby by Harold E. Stassen.

22. Matteson, *The Eisenhower Years*, p. 106.

23. Ibid., pp. 108–109.

24. Adams, *Firsthand*, p. 229.

25. Undated memorandum by Harold E. Stassen, p. 2, box 34, Papers as President, Administrative Series, DDEL. The memorandum, written on Stassen's personal stationery, was probably written around July 26, 1956.

26. Matteson wrote: "Dewey and Nixon do not seem to be popular; Herter is not known; Warren doesn't seem to be interested; Knowland isn't on the Eisenhower side of the fence; and there don't seem to be any others."

27. Robert Matteson to Harold Stassen, 11 June 1956, box 2, Robert Matteson Papers, MHS.

28. Matteson, *The Eisenhower Years*, p. 112.

29. Robert Matteson, "Stassen's Dump Nixon Movement," p. 2, box 2, Robert Matteson Papers, MHS. This handwritten memorandum apparently was an early draft for use in Matteson's privately-published *The Eisenhower Years*.

30. "College GOP Group Supports Stassen," *Washington Post*, 8 July 1952, p. A2.

31. Stassen may indeed have been unaware of the "movement" (it fizzled out); no link between Stassen and the group has been uncovered. A recent attempt to contact Phelan was unsuccessful.

32. Richard Nixon, *RN: The Memoirs of Richard Nixon* (New York: Grosset and Dunlap, 1978), p. 174.

33. Matteson, "Stassen's Dump Nixon Movement," p. 2.

34. Undated Stassen memorandum, MHS, p. 6.

35. Stephen Ambrose's account (*Eisenhower the President*, p. 322) has Stassen arguing that Nixon would cost "four to six percent" of the electorate." Arthur Larson (*The President Nobody Knew*, p. 9) places the figure at four percent. Eisenhower gave no percentage in his memoirs (*Waging Peace*, p. 10). Stassen claimed that Nixon would cost "at least six percent" (undated Stassen memorandum, p. 2).

36. Undated Stassen memorandum, p. 5; Eisenhower, *Waging Peace*, p. 10; Harold Stassen to Dwight Eisenhower, 19 July 1956, box 34, Papers as President, Administrative Series, DDEL.

37. See Ambrose, *Eisenhower the President*, p. 323. Ambrose notes that Eisenhower was concerned about Nixon's effect on the ticket before July 20, but does not mention that the president had any idea what Stassen was up to; Charles Alexander says: "Eisenhower had enough political acumen to see that Nixon would again help his candidacy," *Holding the Line*, pp. 165–166; Lyon, *Portrait of the Hero*, p. 677; Parmet, *American Crusades*, p. 455.

38. Adams, *Firsthand*, pp. 238–240; Eisenhower, *Waging Peace*, p. 10; Nixon, *Memoirs*, p. 173.

39. Eisenhower, *Waging Peace*, p. 10.

40. Larson, *The President Nobody Knew*, pp. 8–9.

41. Lyon, *Portrait of the Hero*, p. 677.

42. Undated Stassen memorandum, MHS, p. 6.

43. "Text of the Stassen Statement and Transcript of News Parley," *New York Times*, 24 July 1956, p. 16.

44. Ambrose, *Eisenhower the President*, p. 323.

45. "A Persuasive Politician," *New York Times*, 24 July 1956, p. 16.

46. Harold E. Stassen to Dwight Eisenhower, 17 August 1956, box 34, Papers as President, Administrative Series, DDEL.

47. Robert Matteson memorandum "Stassen's Dump Nixon Movement"; "The Battle Stassen Started: A Blow-by-Blow Account," *U.S. News and World Report*, 3 August 1956, pp. 37 and 42.

48. Robert Matteson to Harold E. Stassen, 24 July 1956, box 2, Robert Matteson Papers, MHS.

49. Adams, *Firsthand*, pp. 240–241.

50. James Reston, "Herter to Nominate Nixon at the Request of Hall; Stassen to Continue Drive," *New York Times*, 25 July 1956, p. 1.

51. "The Vice Presidency," *New York Times*, 25 July 1956, p. 28.

52. James Reston, "Stassen Suggests Eisenhower State if He Is for Nixon," *New York Times*, 26 July 1956, p. 1.

53. Matteson memorandum, "Stassen's Dump Nixon Movement," MHS.

54. James Reston, "Stassen Holds Fire Pending a New Poll," *New York Times*, 27 July 1956, p. 1.

55. Nixon, *Memoirs*, p. 175.

56. Ambrose, *Eisenhower the President*, p. 335; Parmet, *American Crusades*, p. 457; Alexander, *Holding the Line*, p. 167.

57. Ambrose cites Parmet as his source; Parmet's source is unclear. Adams, in his version of the story, credits himself and Leonard Hall (*Firsthand*, p. 241).

58. "Stassen and Nixon Leave," *New York Times*, 18 August 1956, p. 10.

59. Harold E. Stassen to Dwight Eisenhower, 17 August 1956, box 34, Papers as President, Administrative Series, DDEL.

60. Harold E. Stassen to Dwight Eisenhower, 20 August 1956, box 34, Papers as President, Administrative Series, DDEL.

61. Matteson memorandum, "Stassen's Dump Nixon Movement," MHS.

62. Allen Drury, "Stassen Drops Presidential Aspirations," *New York Times*, 30 July 1956, p. 1.

63. Robert Matteson to Harold E. Stassen, 1 November 1957, box 3, Robert Matteson Papers, MHS.

64. Nixon, *Memoirs*, p. 167.

65. Drury, "Stassen Drops Presidential Aspirations," p. 1.

66. Robert Matteson to Harold E. Stassen, 15 November 1956, box 2, Robert Matteson Papers, MHS.

Chapter 21

1. Bulganin, chairman of the Council of Ministers, called for reduction of foreign forces in German, NATO and Warsaw Pact counties, partial acceptance of aerial inspection, another Summit Conference including India, and an immediate ban on testing, production, and use of nuclear weapons, as well as destruction of nuclear stockpiles and elimination of nuclear weapons. He also announced a successful nuclear weapons test.

2. Matteson, *The Eisenhower Years*, p. 122.

3. Harold E. Stassen to Dwight Eisenhower, 20 October 1956, box 34, Papers as President, Administrative Series, DDEL.

4. Henry Cabot Lodge to Dwight Eisenhower, 26 January 1956, box 24, Papers as President, Administrative Series, DDEL.

5. Matteson, *The Eisenhower Years*, p. 122–123; Ambrose, *Eisenhower the President*, p. 401.

6. James Reston, "Stassen Will Run in Pennsylvania," *New York Times*, 14 February 1957, p. 3.

7. Earl Mazo, "No Chance Is Seen for Stassen in Pa.," *Herald Tribune*, 15 February 1957. Copy of article found in box 2, Robert Matteson Papers, MHS.

8. "Dulles to Get Control of Stassen's Office," *Washington Post*, 24 February 1957, p. 1; "State Gets Quarters Ready for Stassen," *Washington Post*, 1 March 1957, p. 1.

9. "Downgrading Disarmament," *Washington Post*, 1 March 1957, p. 10.

10. Quoted in Matteson, *The Eisenhower Years*, p. 128.

11. "Memorandum on Disarmament Negotiations," *State Department Bulletin*, 5 November 1956, pp. 711–712.

12. Ambrose, *Eisenhower the President*, p. 347.

13. Divine, *Eisenhower and the Cold War*, p. 123; Divine, *Blowing on the Wind*, p. 143.

14. John Lewis Gaddis, "The Unexpected John Foster Dulles: Nuclear Weapons, Communism, and the Russians," in Immerman, *John Foster Dulles and the Cold War*, p. 51.

15. *Progress Report*, p. 18.

16. Department of State, *Disarmament*, p. 28.

17. Ibid., pp. 32–33.

18. Department of State, *Disarmament*, pp. 33–34; Matteson, *The Eisenhower Years*, p. 127.

19. Robert Matteson to Harold E. Stassen, 18 March 1957, box 2, Robert Matteson Papers, MHS.

20. Matteson, *The Eisenhower Years*, pp. 130–131.

21. Ibid., p. 131.

22. Ibid., p. 132.

23. Ibid., pp. 133–134.

24. Summary Minutes: Meeting of the President's Special Committee on Disarmament Problems, 1 May 1957, box 1, White House Office, Office of the Special Assistant for Disarmament, DDEL.

25. Divine, *Blowing on the Wind*, pp. 144–145; Eisenhower, *Waging Peace*, p. 472. Eisenhower's recollection of the meeting is odd in that he mentions all the aspects of Stassen's proposed "informal memorandum" except the most important — a test ban. The actual memorandum remains classified, but through an error, a copy of the memorandum — and the also-classified Soviet response — is quite accessible in the Robert Matteson Papers at the Minnesota Historical Society in St. Paul. The memorandum is obviously aimed at achieving a test ban in conjunction with international controls including aerial inspection.

26. Matteson, *The Eisenhower Years*, p. 136.

27. Harold E. Stassen, "Informal Memorandum of May 31, 1957," box 2, Robert Matteson Papers, MHS; Matteson, *The Eisenhower Years*, pp. 137–138.

28. Robert Matteson, "Memo for File," 5 June 1957, box 2, Robert Matteson Papers, MHS. See also Matteson, *The Eisenhower Years*, p. 137.

29. Matteson, *The Eisenhower Years*, p. 140.

30. Ibid., p. 138.

31. Eisenhower, *Waging Peace*, p. 473.

32. Matteson, *The Eisenhower Years*, p. 140; Larson, *The President Nobody Knew*, p. 77.

33. Matteson, *The Eisenhower Years*, p. 139.

34. Russell Baker, "President Favors Nuclear Test Ban on Certain Terms," *New York Times*, 20 June 1957, p. 1.

35. Divine, *Eisenhower and the Cold War*, p. 126.

36. Eisenhower, *Waging Peace*, pp. 473–474.

37. USSR Aide Memoire of June 7, p. 14, box 2, Robert Matteson Papers, MHS.

38. Stassen, "Informal Memorandum," p. 15.

39. Ambrose, *Eisenhower the President*, pp. 246–247.

40. In a curious encore test ban effort in early 1958, Dulles — who had changed his mind yet again on the desirability of a moratorium — argued for a ban against Strauss. At that time Science Advisor James Killian concluded that a relatively effective inspection system could be put into place. See Ambrose, *Eisenhower the President*, p. 452.

41. John Foster Dulles to Harold E. Stassen, 4 June 1957, box 35, Papers as President, Administrative Series, DDEL.

42. Matteson, *The Eisenhower Years*, p. 140.

43. V. Zorin to Harold E. Stassen, 16 June 1957, box 2, Robert Matteson Papers, MHS.

44. Quotation taken from a letter written by Dulles the following day "confirming our conversation." John Foster Dulles to Harold E. Stassen, 12 June 1957, box 35 Papers as President, Administrative Series, DDEL.

45. Matteson, *The Eisenhower Years*, p. 144.

46. "Transcript of President's News Conference on Varied Issues," *New York Times*, 20 June 1957, p. 18.

47. Matteson, *The Eisenhower Years*, p. 149; Divine, *Eisenhower and the Cold War*, p. 126.

Chapter 22

1. Robert Matteson to Harold E. Stassen, 14 July 1957, box 3, Robert Matteson Papers, MHS.

2. Robert Matteson to Harold E. Stassen, 1 November 1957, box 3, Robert Matteson Papers, MHS.

3. Harold E. Stassen to Dwight Eisenhower, 14 February 1958, box 35, Papers as President.

4. "Pretzels to Politics," *New York Times*, 22 May 1958, p. 20.

5. William Weart, "Career Not Over, Stassen Asserts," *New York Times*, 22 May 1958, p. 20.

Chapter 23

1. *Time*, 28 November 1958.

2. Mazo, *Richard Nixon*, pp. 185–186; *Time*, 28 November 1958.

3. Mazo, p. 187.

4. Ibid.

5. E. Frederic Morrow, *Black Man in the White House* (New York: Coward-McCann, 1963), p. 111.

6. Harrison Evans Salisbury, *A Journey for Our Times: A Memoir* (New York: Harper and Row, 1983), p. 84.

7. David Pietrusza, *1960: LBJ vs. JFK vs. Nixon: The Epic Campaign That Forged Three Presidencies* (New York: Union Square Press, 2008), p. 102.

8. Hugh Scott, *Come to the PARTY* (Englewood Cliffs, N.J.: Prentice-Hall, 1968), p. 104.

9. *Official Report of the Proceedings of the Twenty-seventh Republican National Convention*, p. 297.

10. "A Lively Agenda for the Baptists," San Francisco Chronicle, 18 May 1965, p. 6

11. Ibid.

12. *Candidates 1968 — A Publication of Congressional Quarterly Service*, p. 39.

13. "Goldwater Gains as GOP Choice," *San Francisco Chronicle*, 18 August 1963.

14. "Stassen Considering 1964 Race," *Associated Press*, 27 December 1963.

15. "Stassen Joins GOP Race for President," *The Evening Bulletin*, Philadelphia, Pennsylvania, 20 January 1964, p. 1.

16. Ibid.

17. Ibid.

18. James W. Davis, *Springboard to the White House* (New York: Crowell, 1967), p. 152.

19. Loudon Wainwright, "A Dignified Loser Drops One More," *Life*, p. 27.

20. Bob Condisne, "Hopeful Harold," *San Francisco Examiner*, 30 March 1964.

21. "Lodge Leading in California," *San Francisco Examiner*, 3 April 1964.

22. "Stassen Here on 'Last Stand,'" *San Francisco Examiner*, 4 April 1964.

23. Ibid.

24. "Stassen Is Optimistic," *San Francisco Chronicle*, 13 March 1964.

25. "Stassen's 4-in-1 Plan," *San Francisco Examiner*, 6 April 1964.

26. "Man of Five Faces," *San Francisco Examiner*, 9 April 1964.

27. Davis, *Springboard to the White House*, p. 153; "Stassen Renews Suit for Place on the Ballot," *San Francisco Chronicle*, undated article.

28. William Boquist, "Stassen's Evaluation of Race," *San Francisco Examiner*, 10 July 1964; files of John F. Rothman.

29. Arthur Hoppe, "The Candidate Who Was Not a Joke," *San Francisco Chronicle*, 21 July 1964, p. 35.

30. "Stassen Reappears with a Plan," *San Francisco Chronicle*, 15 April 1967, p. 7.

31. "Stassen First to Announce for President," *Los Angeles Times*, 15 November 1967, p. 10.

32. "Stassen GOP 'Peace Candidate,'" *United Press International*, 15 November 1967; "Here He Comes Again," *San Francisco Examiner*, 16 November 1967.

33. "Stassen Speaks of Deep Tragedy," *San Francisco Examiner*, 12 June 1968.

34. "Stassen's Regime Would Be Bi-partisan," *San Francisco Chronicle*, 13 June 1968.

35. Keith Power, "Stassen in San Francisco: A Man Who Looks Ahead" *San Francisco Chronicle*, 11 July 1968.

36. "The Quixote Candidate," *Time*, 5 July 1968.

37. *Official Report of the Proceedings of the Twenty-ninth Republican Convention, 1968*, pp. 340–341.

38. Ibid., p. 345.

39. "Baptists Will Give Stassen Peace Award," *Los Angeles Times*, 11 May 1972

40. Stewart Alsop, "STASSENIZATION," *Newsweek*, 3 January 1972, p. 13.

41. "Still on the Run," *Newsweek*, 3 November 1975, p. 12.

42. Ibid.

43. "Harold Stassen Is Thinking of Trying Again," *San Francisco Chronicle*, 22 May 1976.

44. "Newsmakers," *Newsweek*, 31 May 1976, pp. 42–43.

45. "Some Really New Faces for '76," *San Francisco Chronicle*, 6 June 1976, p. 4.

46. "Harold Stassen Says No Joking — He's in the Race," *Knight News Service*, 4 June 1976.

47. "Stassen Seeks Delegates," *San Francisco Chronicle*, 20 July 1976.

48. "Stassen's Convention Strategy," *San Francisco Chronicle*, 3 August 1976.

49. "A Choice Or a Muffled Echo?" *San Francisco Chronicle*, 8 August 1976.

50. "Stassen's Volunteers Still Give Out Buttons," *United Press International*, 16 August 1976.

51. "Harold Stassen Says He'll Run for the Senate," *San Francisco Chronicle*, 24 January 1978.

52. "Stassen 'Serious' About Running for President Again," *San Francisco Chronicle*, 10 November 1978, p. 13.

53. George Gallup, "The 12 'Unknown' G.O.P. Candidates," *San Francisco Chronicle*, 24 September 1979, p. 10.

54. "A Presidential Dozen in New Hampshire," *San Francisco Chronicle*, 28 December 1979, p. 7.

55. Harold E. Stassen to *United Press International*, 6 February 1980.

56. "A Last Hurrah, Maybe," *San Francisco Examiner*, 19 May 1984, p. A3.

57. David S. Broder, "Remember the Stassen Theorem," *Washington Post*, 13 June 1984. 58. "The Man Who ... Runs Again," *U.S. News and World Report*, 8 September 1986, p. 7.

59. "A Latter-Day Happy Warrior," *San Francisco Examiner*, 24 November 1986, p. A10.

60. "Stassen to Run Again," *San Francisco Examiner* 23 September 1987.

61. "Quotes of the Week," *U.S. News and World Report,* 5 October 1987, p. 11.

62. "Stassen Wants to Run with Dole," *San Francisco Examiner,* 9 July 1996.

63. "Stassen's Ready — Again," *Associated Press,* 29 May 1998.

64. Mickey Edwards, "Ross Perot, the New Harold Stassen," *San Francisco Examiner,* 8 August 1997.

Chapter 24

1. Amos J. Peaslee, ed., *Man Was Meant to Be Free* (New York: Doubleday, 1951), p. 159.

2. Wendell L. Willkie, *This Is Wendell Willkie* (New York: Dodd, Mead, 1940), pp. 218–219.

3. Ibid., p. 271.

4. Richard Norton Smith, *Thomas E. Dewey and His Times* (New York: Simon & Schuster, 1982), p. 583.

5. Barry M. Goldwater, *With No Apologies* (New York: William Morrow, 1979), p. 117.

6. F. Clifton White and William J. Gill, *Suite 3505: The Story of the Draft Goldwater Movement* (Ashland, O.H.: Ashbrook Press, 1967).

7. Arthur Larson, *A Republican Looks at His Party* (New York: Harper and Brothers, 1956), p. 197.

8. Barry Goldwater, *The Conscience of a Conservative* (Shepherdsville, K.Y.: Victor, 1960), p. 1.

Bibliography

Abels, Jules. *Out of the Jaws of Victory: The Astounding Election of 1948.* New York: Henry Holt, 1959.

Adams, Sherman. *First Hand Reports: The Story of the Eisenhower Administration.* New York: Harper, 1961.

Alexander, Charles. *Holding the Line: The Eisenhower Era, 1952–1961.* Bloomington: Indiana University Press, 1975.

Alsop, Stewart. *Nixon and Rockefeller: A Double Portrait.* New York: Doubleday, 1960.

Ambrose, Stephen E. *Eisenhower: The President.* New York: Simon & Schuster, 1984.

_____. *Nixon: The Education of a Politician, 1913–1962.* New York: Simon & Schuster, 1987.

Bain, Richard, and Judith Parris. *Convention Decisions and Voting Records, 2d ed.* Washington, D.C: Brookings Institution, 1973.

Barber, James David. *The Pulse of Politics.* New York: W.W. Norton, 1980.

Barnard, Ellsworth. *Wendell Willkie: Fighter for Freedom.* Marquette: Northern Michigan University Press, 1966.

Barnes, Joseph. *Willkie.* New York: Simon & Schuster, 1952.

Branyan, Robert. *The Eisenhower Administration, 1953–1961: A Documentary History,* Vol. 1. New York: Random House, 1971.

Brereton, Charles. *First in the Nation: New Hampshire and the Premier Presidential Primary.* Portsmouth, N.H.: Peter E. Randall, 1987.

Brownell, Herbert, and John P. Burke. *Advising Ike.* Lawrence: University Press of Kansas, 1993.

Chafe, William. *The Unfinished Journey.* New York: Oxford University Press, 1986.

Dallek, Robert. *Hail to the Chief: The Making and Unmaking of Presidents.* New York: Hyperion, 1996.

_____. *Harry S. Truman.* New York: Times Books, 2008.

_____. *An Unfinished Life: John F. Kennedy, 1917–1963.* Boston: Little, Brown, 2003.

David, Paul T. *Presidential Nominating Politics in 1952,* Vol. 2. Baltimore: Johns Hopkins University Press, 1954.

Dillon, Mary Earhart. *Wendell Wilkie.* New York: J.B. Lippincott, 1952.

Divine, Robert. *Eisenhower and the Cold War.* New York: Oxford University Press, 1981.

Eisenhower, Dwight D. *Mandate for Change.* Garden City, N.Y.: Doubleday, 1965.

_____. *Waging Peace.* Garden City, N.Y.: Doubleday, 1965.

Eisenhower, Julie Nixon. *Pat Nixon: The Untold Story.* New York: Simon & Schuster, 1986.

Elath, Eliahu. *Zionism at the U.N.* Philadelphia: Jewish Publication Society, 1976.

Ferrell, Robert H. *The Eisenhower Diaries.* New York: W.W. Norton, 1981.

_____, ed. *The Diary of James C. Hagerty: Eisenhower in Mid-Course, 1954–1955.* Bloomington: Indiana University Press, 1983.

Fried, Richard. *Nightmare in Red: The McCarthy Era in Perspective.* New York: Oxford University Press, 1990.

Frost, David. *The Presidential Debate, 1968.* New York: Stein and Day, 1968.

Gellman, Irwin F. *The Contender: Richard Nixon, The Congress Years, 1946–1952.* New York: Free Press, 1999.

Greenstein, Fred I. *The Hidden-Hand Presidency: Eisenhower as Leader.* Baltimore: Johns Hopkins University Press, 1982.

Gould, Lewis L. *Grand Old Party: A History of the Republicans.* New York: Random House, 2003.

Hamby, Alonzo. *Liberalism and Its Challengers.* New York: Oxford University Press, 1985.

Hughes, Emmet John. *The Ordeal of Power.* New York: Atheneum, 1963.

Immerman, Richard, ed. *John Foster Dulles and the Diplomacy of the Cold War.* Princeton: Princeton University Press, 1990.

Janeway, Michael. *The Fall of the House of Roosevelt.* New York: Columbia University Press, 2004.

Johnson, Donald Bruce. *The Republican Party and Wendell Willkie.* Urbana: University of Illinois Press, 1960.

Kabaservice, Geoffrey. *Rule and Ruin*. New York: Oxford University Press, 2012.

Karabell, Zachary. *The Last Campaign: How Harry Truman Won the 1948 Election*. New York: Alfred A. Knopf, 2000.

Kenneally, James J. *A Compassionate Conservative: A Political Biography of Joseph W. Martin, Speaker of the U.S. House of Representatives*. New York: Lexington Books, 2005.

Krock, Arthur. *Memoirs: Fifty Years on the Firing Line*. New York: Funk and Wagnalls, 1968.

Larson, Arthur. *Eisenhower: The President Nobody Knows*. New York: Charles Scribner's Sons, 1968.

_____. *A Republican Looks at His Party*. New York: Harper and Brothers, 1956.

Lyon, Peter. *Eisenhower: Portrait of the Hero*. Boston: Little, Brown, 1974.

Martin, Joseph W., and Robert J. Donovan. *My First Fifty Years in Politics*. New York: McGraw-Hill, 1960.

Matteson, Robert E. *Harold Stassen: His Career, the Man, and the 1957 London Arms Control Negotiations*. Inver Grove Heights, M.N.: Desk Top Ink, 1991.

_____. *A Search for Adventure and Service*, Vol. IV, *The Eisenhower Years: 1953–1961*. St. Paul: Privately published, 1985. Matteson's privately-published four-volume autobiography, *A Search for Adventure and Service*, is available at the Minnesota Historical Society.

Mayer, George H. *The Republican Party 1854–1964*. New York: Oxford University Press, 1964.

Mazo, Earl. *Richard Nixon: A Personal and Political Portrait*. New York: Harper and Brothers, 1959.

McCoy, Donald R. *Landon of Kansas*. Lincoln: University of Nebraska Press, 1966.

Montgomery, Gayle B., and James W. Johnson. *One Step from the White House: The Rise and Fall of Senator William F. Knowland*. Berkeley: University of California Press, 1998.

Morris, Roger. *Richard Milhous Nixon: The Rise of an American Politician*. New York: Henry Holt, 1990.

Neal, Steve. *Dark Horse: A Biography of Wendell Willkie*. Garden City, N.Y.: Doubleday, 1984.

Nixon, Richard M. *RN: The Memoirs of Richard Nixon*. New York: Grosset and Dunlap, 1978.

_____. *Six Crises*. New York: Doubleday, 1962.

Parmet, Herbert S. *Eisenhower and the American Crusades*. New York: Macmillan, 1972.

_____, and Marie B. Hecht. *Never Again: A President Runs for a Third Term*. New York: Macmillan, 1968.

Patterson, James T. *Mr. Republican: A Biography of Robert A. Taft*. Boston: Houghton Mifflin, 1972.

Peaslee, Amos J., ed. *Man Was Meant to Be Free: Selected Statements of Governor Harold E. Stassen*. New York: Doubleday, 1951.

Peters, Charles. *Five Days in Philadelphia: The Amazing "We Want Willkie!" Convention of 1940 and How It Freed FDR to Save the Free World*. New York: Public Affairs, 2005.

Pietrusza, David. *1948: Harry Truman's Improbable Victory and the Year That Transformed America*. New York: Union Square Press, 2011.

Rae, Nicol C. *The Decline and Fall of the Liberal Republicans*. New York: Oxford University Press, 1989.

Root, Oren. *Persons and Persuasions*. New York: W.W. Norton, 1974.

Rovere, Richard. *Senator Joe McCarthy*. New York: Harper Torchbooks, 1959.

Salisbury, Harrison E. *A Journey for Our Times: A Memoir*. New York: Carroll and Graf, 1984.

Schlesinger, Jr., Arthur M., ed. *The Coming to Power: Critical Presidential Elections in American History*. New York: Chelsea House in association with McGraw-Hill, 1971.

Schoenbaum, Eleanora W., ed. *Political Parties: The Eisenhower Years*. New York: Facts on File, 1980.

Scott, Hugh. *Come to the Party*. Englewood Cliffs, N.J.: Prentice-Hall, 1964.

Smith, Jean Edward. *FDR*. New York: Random House, 2007.

Smith, Richard Norton Smith. *Thomas E. Dewey and His Times*. New York: Simon & Schuster, 1982.

Southwick, Leslie H. *Presidential Also-Rans and Running Mates, 1788 through 1996*. Jefferson, N.C.: McFarland, 1998.

Stassen, Harold E. *United Nations: A Working Paper for Restructuring*. Minneapolis: Lerner, 1994.

_____. *Where I Stand*. New York: Doubleday, 1947.

_____, and Marshall Houts. *Eisenhower: Turning the World Toward Peace*. St. Paul: Merrill/Magnus, 1990.

Stuhler, Barbara. *Ten Men of Minnesota and American Foreign Policy, 1898–1968*. St. Paul, Minnesota, 1973.

Tompkins, C. David. *Senator Arthur H. Vandenberg: The Evolution of a Modern Republican*. East Lansing: Michigan State University Press, 1970.

Troy, Gil. *See How They Ran: The Changing Role of the Presidential Candidate*. Cambridge: Harvard University Press, 1996.

Wick, James L. *How NOT to Run for President*. New York: Vantage Press, 1952.

Willkie, Wendell L. *One World*. New York: Simon & Schuster, 1943.

Wormer, Michael D. *Election '84*. Washington, D.C.: Congressional Quarterly, 1984.

Worthen, James. *The Young Nixon and His Rivals*. Jefferson, N.C.: McFarland, 2010.

Index